SECURITY ANALYSIS AND PORTFOLIO MANAGEMENT

SECURITY ANALYSIS AND PORTFOLIO MANAGEMENT

K. NAGARAJAN
Assistant General Manager
The Tamilnadu Industrial Investment Corporation Limited
Coimbatore, Tamilnadu

G. JAYABAL
Professor
Department of Bank Management
School of Management
Alagappa University, Karaikudi, Tamilnadu

NEW AGE
MANAGEMENT

An Imprint of

NEW AGE INTERNATIONAL (P) LIMITED, PUBLISHERS

New Delhi • Bangalore • Chennai • Cochin • Guwahati • Hyderabad
Jalandhar • Kolkata • Lucknow • Mumbai • Ranchi
Visit us at **www.newagepublishers.com**

Published by New Age International (P) Ltd., Publishers
First Edition: 2011
Reprint: 2025

GLOBAL OFFICES

• **New Delhi** **NEW AGE INTERNATIONAL (P) LIMITED, PUBLISHERS**
7/30 A, Daryaganj, New Delhi-110002, (INDIA), **Tel.:** (011) 23253472, 23253771, **Mob.:** 9315905300
E-mail: contactus@newagepublishers.com • Visit us at www.newagepublishers.com

• **London** **NEW AGE INTERNATIONAL (UK) LTD.**
27 Old Gloucester Street, London, WC1N 3AX, UK
E-mail: info@newacademicscience.co.uk • Visit us at www.newacademicscience.co.uk

BRANCHES

• **Bangalore** 37/10, 8th Cross (Near Hanuman Temple), Azad Nagar, Chamarajpet, Bangalore-560 018
Tel.: (080) 26756823, **Mob.:** 9315905288, **E-mail: bangalore@newagepublishers.com**

• **Chennai** 26, Damodaran Street, T. Nagar, Chennai-600 017, **Tel.:** (044) 24353401, **Mob.:** 9315905309
E-mail: chennai@newagepublishers.com

• **Cochin** CC-39/1016, Carrier Station Road, Ernakulam South, Cochin-682 016
Tel.: (0484) 4051304, **Mob.:** 9315905289, **E-mail: cochin@newagepublishers.com**

• **Guwahati** Hemsen Complex, Mohd. Shah Road, Paltan Bazar, Near Starline Hotel
Guwahati-781 008, **Tel.:** (0361) 2513881, **Mob.:** 9315905296
E-mail: guwahati@newagepublishers.com

• **Hyderabad** 105, 1st Floor, Madhiray Kaveri Tower, 3-2-19, Azam Jahi Road, Near Kumar Theater
Nimboliadda Kachiguda, Hyderabad-500 027, **Tel.:** (040) 24652456, **Mob.:** 9315905326
E-mail: hyderabad@newagepublishers.com

• **Kolkata** RDB Chambers (Formerly Lotus Cinema) 106A, 1st Floor, S N Banerjee Road
Kolkata-700 014, **Tel.:** (033) 22273773, **Mob.:** 9315905319
E-mail: kolkata@newagepublishers.com

• **Mumbai** 142C, Victor House, Ground Floor, N.M. Joshi Marg, Lower Parel, Mumbai-400 013
Tel.: (022) 24927869, 24915415, **Mob.:** 9315905282, **E-mail: mumbai@newagepublishers.com**

• **New Delhi** 22, Golden House, Daryaganj, New Delhi-110 002, **Tel.:** (011) 23262368, 23262370
Mob.: 9315905300, **E-mail: sales@newagepublishers.com**

C-25-11-15201

Printed in India at Milan Enterprises., Delhi.
Typeset at In-house, Delhi.

NEW AGE INTERNATIONAL (P) LIMITED, PUBLISHERS
7/30 A, Daryaganj, New Delhi - 110002
Visit us at **www.newagepublishers.com**
(CIN: U74899DL1966PTC004618)

Preface

The economic development of any country depends, to a larger extent, on its ability to mobilise capital. Securities market aids in the mobilisation of capital towards investment in economic assets. While the primary market does the role of capital mobilisation, the secondary market complements the role of primary market by facilitating the trading of existing securities, thereby keeping the securities market active. An investor will be equipped to participate in the securities market if he/she gets himself/herself exposed to the fundamentals of stock valuation. Further, an investor also needs to understand how a portfolio of securities behaves, for him/her to be successful in building and maintaining an efficient portfolio of investments.

As far as students of finance are concerned, the subject 'Security Analysis and Portfolio Management' is the one that provides them with the skills required for effective management of investments. Keeping the difficulties faced by students in mind, the authors have made an attempt to give the students a simple and yet comprehensive coverage of the subject. The text has been so prepared that it is easily readable and understandable. No previous knowledge in the subject has been assumed and hence the book is expected to serve as an introductory course to students, making them understand the subject without any ambiguity.

The book is intended to serve as a textbook for undergraduate as well as postgraduate students of commerce and management. The book will also be of use to the students of professional courses like AICWA, ACA and CFA. Apart from students, investors who would like have some exposure to the field of security analysis and portfolio management will also find the book quite useful.

The authors strongly believe that the success of any textbook lies in its acceptance and appreciation by the readers and hence the authors have seen to it that readability is not affected at any stage throughout the text and the subject is presented in a very lucid style.

The authors earnestly look forward to suggestions from readers for improvement and presentation of the subject content.

K. Nagarajan
G. Jayabal

Contents

CHAPTER 1

Investment

1.1. INTRODUCTION

'Investment' and 'Risk' are the two words on which all the theories of investment and portfolio management hinges on. In order to understand the theories of investment and portfolio management, it is imperative that one should have a good knowledge of the two terms 'Investment' and 'Risk'.

1.2. INVESTMENT

A person spends his income on goods and services that he currently needs. He saves the excess of income over his current needs. From out of his savings he intends to purchase goods and services that he may require in the future. Such savings, that are not intended for current use results in investment. Thus, saving results in investment. Why does a person invest at all? Whatever may be the type of asset in which investment is made, the investor aims at achieving either some income on the money invested or some growth in the value of money invested or both. Thus, investment may be defined as deployment of funds made with an anticipation of earning some return. The return may be in the form of income, increase in value or both.

Hence, an essential attribute of investment is the expectation of return on the funds invested. But for the expectation of return on investment, the need for investment does not arise. The return on investment is however realised in the future. Since the future is always uncertain, the return on investment is also likely to be uncertain. In other words, there is a possibility that the return actually realized may be lower or higher than the return anticipated, i.e., the return on investment is variable in nature. The variability of return is called 'risk'. Thus, return and the risk associated with the return are the two factors associated with any investment.

1.3. FINANCIAL INVESTMENT AND ECONOMIC INVESTMENT

When a person invests his funds for the acquisition of some physical assets, say a building or equipment, such types of investments are called economic investments. Economic investment can be defined as the investment that contributes to the net additions to the capital stock of society. Capital stock refers to the goods and service that are used in the production of other goods and services. Hence, in short, it can be said that economic investments help create physical assets directly.

When a person invests his funds for the acquisition of some financial assets like shares, debentures, insurance policies, mutual fund units etc, such investments are known as financial investments. Financial investments also help in creating physical assets, but indirectly. Hence, economic investment and financial investment are inter-related. Increase in financial investment leads to increase in capital stock. When an investor invests in a financial asset, he indirectly invests in an underlying physical asset, since the financial investments are ultimately used in creation of physical assets.

1.4. INVESTMENT, SPECULATION AND GAMBLING

Both investment and speculation consists of deploying funds on an asset. However, there are certain differences between the two.

The element of risk involved in speculation is comparatively higher. Though any investment is not free from risk, an investor takes more care before investing his funds. He commits his funds to low/medium risk securities and anticipates moderate returns commensurate with risk. A speculator is prepared to take higher level of risks and hence he invests in high-risk securities in anticipation of higher returns.

An investor is more concerned with the income from the securities than with the capital appreciation. Though the investor does not completely ignore capital appreciation, he gives preference to certain regular stream of income. To an investor, capital appreciation is incidental and complementary. A speculator on the other hand is more interested in capital appreciation rather than in the income from the security. By virtue of this difference in their outlook, an investor invests his funds on securities that guarantees stable return while the speculator invests his funds on securities that offer hope for quick returns. Obviously, an investor commits his funds on securities for a longer period of time, while a speculator is engaged in frequent buying and selling of securities. By nature, investors are cautious and careful while speculators are daring and optimistic of earning higher returns.

Though investment and speculation are in a way related (the difference being only on the motives of the investor and the speculator with regard to the anticipated return), gambling is different from investment and speculation. Investment is a scientific and planned activity. Though speculation appears to be a hasty activity as compared to investment, still an element of analysis and planning underlies speculation activities also. A speculator analyses the market swiftly and looks for the ways to maximize his short term gains.

As against investment and speculation, gambling is unplanned. Gambling involves high risk. Though a speculator also takes high risk, he takes the risk in anticipation of a higher return. In gambling, though the risk involved is high, there is no certainly that the return will be high. Lottery is a typical example of gambling. A gambler enjoys the thrill and excitement in gambling and goes to the extent of taking more risks than what he can afford to take.

1.5. OBJECTIVES OF INVESTMENT

When a person earns more than what he spends, he is left with a surplus. When the money saved is kept in the form of cash, it will be readily available for use at any point of time. In other words, it will offer high level of liquidity to the owner. But, the other aspect is that money kept as cash remains stagnant and does not grow and does not offer any return. This is obviously because the money has not been put into any use. When the money saved is put into some form of use, it starts earning and the owner gets a return. Hence, a person who has surplus money with him is prone to invest the same in some assets with a view to earning some return. Is there any guarantee that the money invested in some asset will always give some return? No. It all depends on the type of investment made and the risk level associated with it. It is likely that when a person invests his savings in an asset that has a very high level of risk, he might even lose the money invested in part or full, leave alone earning any return on the investment made. Hence, from the investor's point of view, the investment should have less risk. At the same time, since there are different types of assets available for investment with different risk-return characteristics, the investor will opt to choose the asset that offers him higher return for the level of risk that the investor is prepared to take. The choice of the asset purely depends on the risk bearing capacity of the investor.

Consider a situation where the investor is totally risk averse. He might opt to invest his savings in Government securities that offer guaranteed rate of return. Though the return available may be less in such securities, the investment made will be almost risk-free. Another aspect that needs to be looked into while investing in risk-free securities is the effect of inflation. If a risk-free security offers a return of say, 8% per annum and if the rate of inflation is in the order of say, 10%, the effect of inflation will be more than offset the return earned on the investment and the real rate of return will only be negative. Government securities are practically risk-free and fall under the category of low risk investments. Debentures and preference shares of companies can be treated as medium risk investments while equity shares of companies are high risk investments. For any investor, the objectives of investment can be stated as under:

- Maximisation of return (for the given level of risk)
- Minimisation of risk (for the given level of return)
- Hedge against inflation

1.6. TYPES OF INVESTORS

Investors fall under the following two broad categories:

- Individual investors
- Institutional investors

Individual investors are individuals who invest their savings in financial assets. They are large in number. Each individual will have comparatively smaller amount of investible surplus. Majority of the individual investors lack the knowledge and skill required to carry out extensive analysis of the investment opportunities available in the market.

Institutional investors are institutions that mobilize money from individuals and other sources and invest the same in financial assets. Mutual funds, Insurance companies, Investment companies, Banks, Non-banking financial companies, Financial institutions etc., are some of the institutions that invest their surplus funds. The institutional investors have large investible resources as compared to individual investors. They engage professionals for managing their investment portfolio. The professionals carry out extensive analysis before investments are made and also continuously monitor the performance of the investments made and take corrective actions whenever required by altering the constitution of investments contained in the portfolio. In view of their systematic and scientific approach to investment, the institutional investors are better equipped to maximize their return and minimize their risk.

1.7. INVESTMENT AVENUES AND THEIR CHARACTERISTICS

There are many investment avenues available for investors. The investment avenues differ in their risk-return characteristics. The investment avenues with higher level of risk offer higher returns while the avenues with minimum level of risk offer lower returns. An investor has to choose the type of investment that suits his risk bearing capacity. The investor can opt for choosing a few investment avenues with different risk-return characteristics in such a way that the risk associated with the portfolio of investments suits his risk bearing capacity. Instead of choosing a single investment that suits the risk bearing capacity of the investor, choosing a portfolio of investments with different risk levels is helpful in maneuvering the risk involved. This is because, the investor can alter the combination of securities contained in his portfolio in such a way that the portfolio risk matches his risk bearing capacity at any point of time.

The major investment avenues available for investment can be broadly classified into two categories as below:

- Ownership securities
- Creditorship securities

Ownership Securities

Ownership securities are of two types, viz.,

- Equity shares
- Preference shares

Equity Shares

Equity shares are the source of permanent capital. The equity shareholders are the legal owners of the company. Being the owners of the company, equity shareholders bear the risk of ownership. They are entitled to dividends on their capital invested. However, dividends to equity shareholders are available only after interest obligations and dividends to preference shareholders are paid. Since, equity shareholders bear the risks associated with the ownership of the company, they anticipate handsome return on their investment, by way of attractive dividends and price appreciation of their shares.

Preference Shares

Preference shares bear a predetermined rate of dividend. They have priority of claim over equity shares in the matter of payment of dividend. They also have priority over equity shares on the assets of the company in the event of liquidation of the company.

Though dividend on preference shares is payable out of profits, if the company incurs loss in a particular year, the dividend not paid during that year is to be carried forward and is to be paid in subsequent year/years when the company earns profit.

Dividends on non-cumulative preference shares do not add up for future payment.

When the company earns profit, it has to pay arrears of dividends to preference shareholders before declaring any dividend on equity share. The dividend rate is fixed in the case of preference shares and the dividends paid on preference shares are not tax deductible.

Preference shares are of two types, viz., redeemable preference shares and irredeemable preference shares. While redeemable preference shares are redeemed after the stipulated period, irredeemable preference shares do not have any maturity date.

Creditorship Securities

While ownership securities represent the equity capital, creditorship securities represent the debt capital of company. Debentures and Bonds are the creditorship securities.

Debentures

Debentures are instruments for raising long term debt capital. The debenture holders are the creditors of the company. The company that has borrowed money by way of debentures has the obligation to repay interest and debt on specified dates.

Debentures are secured by a charge on the present and future immovable properties of the company. Interest on debentures is to be paid irrespective of the financial situation of the issuing firm since payment of interest to debenture holders is a statutory obligation. A company may also issue convertible debentures for mobilizing funds. Convertible debentures are those debentures that are convertible into equity shares at the option of the debenture holders.

The following are the advantages and disadvantages of debentures as a source of long term finance:

Advantages

- The cost of debentures is generally less than the cost of equity capital. This is because, investors consider debentures to be relatively less risky as compared to equity shares and hence they are prepared to accept a low/moderate return on their investment.
- The interest payments to debenture holders are tax deductible and this has an indirect effect of further reducing the cost of debentures to the debenture holders.
- Since, debenture holders do not have voting rights, there is no dilution of ownership.
- Even if the project earns extraordinary profit, the debenture holders are entitled to receive only interest at the stipulated rate, and this in turn improves the earnings on equity.

Disadvantages

- Debentures impose a legal obligation for the payment of interest and principal and in the event of the not being able to repay, there is a danger of the company being forced into liquidation.
- Projects that have fluctuating sales and earnings will find it difficult to meet the repayment obligation of debentures which are not related to the earnings pattern.

Bonds

A bond is more or less similar to a debenture and these two terms are frequently used interchangeably. In India, there is a tendency to reserve the term 'bond' to public debt securities issued by the Government and public sector undertakings.

1.8. AIM OF SECURITY ANALYSIS

The aim of security analysis is to identify under-priced and over-priced securities. A security that is under-priced is worthy of inclusion in the portfolio of securities. A security that is found over-priced does not deserve to be included in the portfolio. If a security that is considered over-priced is already in the portfolio, the better choice is to off-load the security from the portfolio and to invest the sale proceeds in under-priced securities.

In analysing as to whether a security is correctly priced or not, the risk vs return characteristics of the securities is studied. If a security is priced at a price that is commensurate with the risk involved in investing in that particular security, that security is considered as correctly priced. If a security is priced higher compared to the risk involved, it is over-priced i.e., for the same level of risk there may be other securities available at a lesser price. Similarly, if the security is priced lower compared to the risk involved, it is under-priced i.e., for the same level of risk, the securities available in the market may all be having a higher price.

However, it is not earlier to arrive at a conclusion as to whether a security is under-priced, over-priced or correctly-priced.

The analysis of securities, being the foundation for portfolio construction deserves more attention.

1.9. APPROACHES TO SECURITY ANALYSIS

There are two different approaches to security analysis, viz.,

- Fundamental analysis
- Technical analysis

Fundamental Analysis

Fundamental analysis is based on the logic that the price of a security depends upon the fundamental factors like the performance of the economy as a whole, the performance of a particular industry in the economy and the performance of the particular company in the industry.

Thus, in the fundamental analysis, first an analysis of the economy of the country is made. When the economy of the country is poised for growth, the different industrial sectors in the country are generally expected to perform well. While studying the economy, factors like the life cycle of the economy, the growth rate of the economy, the rate of inflation/deflation, the foreign exchange rates, interest rates, Government's budgets, developments in infrastructure, economic and political stability etc., are studied. When the overall economic conditions are favourable and encouraging, it will support the growth of industries.

Next to the analysis of the economy, comes the analysis of the industry. By industry we mean the different sectors of industries in an economy like cement industry, steel industry, textile industry, chemical industry, pharmaceutical industry, food processing industry etc. Though a growing economy will kinder growth of all industrial sectors, the growth rate of all the different industrial sectors will not be the same. One sector may be growing faster than another. One sector may have a greater potential for growth than another. It may also be likely that in spite of the economy growing well, a particular industrial sector may be dormant for valid reasons. Just as economy has a life cycle, industries also have their own life cycles. It should be studied whether the industry shows signs of growth in its life cycle before choosing a particular company in that industry for investment.

Next to the analysis of the industry comes the analysis of the company in that industry. The different companies that are engaged in the production of similar/allied products (i.e., the different companies belonging to a particular industry) may be performing differently. Their performance and scope for future growth may be different due to company specific factors like Earnings per share, Dividend pay-out ratio, the market share enjoyed by the company, the quality of management, the competitive strengths/ weaknesses of the company etc. Company analysis aims at studying such company-specific factors to arrive at a decision as to whether the securities of the company are worth investing in.

Technical Analysis

Technical analysis is based on the premise that future stock price can be predicted by studying the historical price movements of stock prices. Historical data on stock prices are recorded and are plotted in the form of a chart. The chart is scrutinised for repetitive patterns and the expected future movement of the chart is predicted. 'Buy' and 'sell' signals are taken from the charts in line with the anticipated price movement that is predicted from the chart. Technical analysts strongly believe that stock price movements are governed by supply and demand of stocks in the market which depend on numerous factors, both rational and irrational. Since, price movements that depend on rational factors can only be arrived at using the fundamental analysis, the effect of irrational factors can be predicted only through the price movements revealed by the charts. Hence, charts of stock prices contain in them the net effects of both rational and irrational factors. Technical analysis is the apt tool for predicting the future stock prices and for arriving at judiciously correct 'buy' and 'sell' decisions.

1.10. PORTFOLIO

Portfolio is a combination of securities held by an investor. In general, investors choose to invest in a portfolio of securities rather than investing in a single security. This is obviously due to the reason that prudent investors are averse to putting all the eggs in one basket. So, investors attempt to spread the risk by investing in different securities. The securities contained in a typical portfolio will consist of shares of different risk-return relationships and bonds of different nature and characteristics. Figure 1.1 gives the stages involved in a portfolio management.

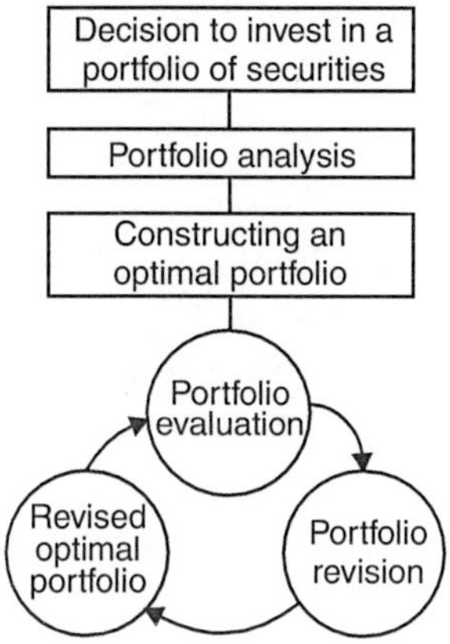

Fig. 1.1 Stages in portfolio management

1.10.1. Portfolio Analysis

A large number of portfolios can be formed by combining the securities that are considered worthwhile to invest. While security analysis identifies the securities that are worthwhile to invest, portfolio analysis consists of identifying all possible portfolios that can be formed by combining some or all of the worthwhile securities and studying their risk-return characteristics.

1.10.2. Portfolio Construction

While an investor can identify, with the help of security analysis, a set of worthwhile securities that suit his/her risk bearing capacity, deciding on the securities that can be included in the portfolio and the proportion of investment in each of the securities contained in the portfolio is not an easy task. This exercise should be done in such a way that the portfolio so constructed is an optimal portfolio for the investor. An optimal portfolio is one that offers the highest return at a given level of risk. The optimal portfolio for different investors will be different since it depends on the risk bearing capacity of the investor. Construction of an optimal portfolio can be done only through scientific analysis of the characteristic of the securities.

1.10.3. Portfolio Evaluation

A portfolio of securities once constructed can not be left alone. The performance of the portfolio is to be assessed over a selected period of time in terms of the risk and return. A quantitative assessment of the actual return realized and the risk borne by the portfolio over a period of time shall be assessed and compared with the objective based on which the portfolio was constructed. The actual performance of the portfolio, relative to its objective is studied. This will throw light on the defective/deficient areas, if any, that need to be attended in order to improve upon the portfolio performance.

1.10.4. Portfolio Revision

Portfolio evaluation will throw light on the things to be done to improve upon the performance of the portfolio. The required revision of the portfolio is to be done in order to ensure that the portfolio continues to remain as the optimal portfolio for the investor. Revision of portfolio is necessitated due to the following reasons:

- Security market being dynamic, many new securities enter the market continuously.
- The risk-return characteristic of some of the securities that were originally included in the portfolio might have got altered.

REVIEW QUESTIONS

1. Define the term 'Investment'.
2. Distinguish between Economic investment and Financial investment.
3. What are the objectives of investment?
4. Distinguish between individual investors and institutional investors.
5. What are the two types of ownership securities? Explain them in brief.
6. What are 'Debentures'? What are the advantages and disadvantages of having debentures as a source of long-term finance?
7. What is the objective of security analysis?
8. Briefly describe the two different approaches to security analysis.
9. What do you mean by 'Portfolio of securities'? What are the stages in Portfolio Management?
10. What is the need for portfolio revision?

2 CHAPTER

Risk

2.1. RISK IN INVESTMENT

As seen in Chapter 1, out of the three types of financial activities, viz., investment, speculation and gambling, it is investment that is more planned and hence is amenable for scientific analysis. Hence, the rest of the subject matter will be devoted to investment, setting aside speculation and gambling.

Every investment is characterised by risk and return. For a common man, the term 'risk' means a situation in which something unpleasant/ unexpected may happen. In other words, risk is a situation involving exposure to uncertainty. In the domain of investment, the term 'risk' has a definite financial meaning. As we are aware, an investor invests his funds in anticipation of a regular stream of income in the future. Since, future is always uncertain, however careful one may be in predicting the future and planning for it, there is bound to be difference between the expected return on investment and the return actually realised.

When an investor deploys his funds into some securities, he/she does so after analysing the expected returns. If the actual return obtained is the same as the expected return, such an investment could be considered to be risk-free i.e., an investment with no risk. For example, when an investor buys a Government security with a prefixed rate of return, the risk involved in such an investment is nil since the investor will realise the return that he expects i.e., there is no uncertainty over the return that will be available on the investment. On the other hand, when an investor who invested in a corporate security expecting a return of 20% on his investment realises only a return of 15%, such an investment is a risky investment. When the actual return is, say, 9% as against the expected return of 20%, the investment is obviously a more risky one. Thus, in financial terms, risk is defined as the potential for variability in returns. An investment whose return is fairly stable is considered to be a low-risk investment while an investment whose returns show wide variations is considered to be a risky investment. Higher the fluctuations between the expected and realised returns, more risky the investment is.

2.2. COMPONENTS OF RISK

For the purpose of better analysis and understanding, the total risk in an investment can be split into two types, viz.,

- Systematic risk
- Unsystematic risk

i.e.,

Total risk = Systematic risk + Unsystematic risk

2.2.1. Systematic Risk

The dictionary meaning of 'systematic' is "acting according to a fixed plan or system". Systematic risk is that risk that is caused by system-wide factors. Changes in economic conditions, changes in political system, changes in social system etc., are some factors that affect the entire community. These are called system-wide factors. For example, when the economy of a particular country moves into recession due to reasons specific to that country (may be due to war, failure of monsoon etc.,), profits earned by business establishments in that country will decline. Such decline in profits will be seen almost in all the business establishments in the country, i.e., the changes in economic conditions will affect almost all the companies that exist in that economy. Similarly, when the political set up of a country undergoes a change, all the companies will feel the change and the political change will have its effect on the performance of all the companies. Of course, the change in the political set up may be advantages to companies in certain sectors and may be disadvantages to companies in certain other sectors. Similarly, changes in social factors (for example, shift in consumer preferences) will tend to affect the performance of all companies that exist in the system.

Thus, the effect of such system-wide factors which are beyond the control of individual business establishments and which affect all the business establishments in the system is called systematic risk.

Systematic risk can be subdivided into the following three sub heads.

(*a*) Market risk

(*b*) Interest rate risk and

(*c*) Purchasing power risk

Market Risk

Market risk is a type of systematic risk that affects financial securities. The market risk is much greater in ownership securities (equity shares, preference shares) than in creditorship securities (bonds, debentures).

Market prices of shares do not remain constant. They fluctuate up and down over a period of time. When there is a general rise in the prices of all shares in the market, such a trend in share prices is referred to as bullish trend. When there is a general fall in the prices of all shares in the market, such a trend in share prices is referred to as bearish trend.

In general, the share markets alternates between the bullish trend and the bearish trend. The reasons for the fluctuations in share prices are many and varied. In general, when the economy is in an expansion phase, the prices of shares show a bullish trend and when the economy falls into recession, the prices of shares show a bearish trend. However, the expansion/recession phase of economy is a long-term phenomenon, often extending over longer time periods. Though the long-term fluctuations in share prices follow the phase of the economy, within the long-term price movements, the share prices show short-term fluctuations which are very pronounced. It often happens that the share prices changes considerably even when the earning powers of shares do not change significantly. Thus, the short term movements in share prices are found to be influenced more by mass psychology. Speculations play a major role in influencing the share prices in the short run. Expectations of speculators may be based on tangible factors like change in Government policy, change in consumer preference etc., or on intangible factors in the minds of the speculators. Though speculators act as the source for initiating share price movements, the movements in share prices even if not supported by rational reasons, influence the emotional stability of investors leading to a mass psychology in share price movements. Thus, the share market remains more or less volatile and in such a volatile market an investor cannot get the return he expects. The variation between the expected return and the actual return, which is due to the volatile nature of stock market, over which an individual investor has no control, is referred to as market risk.

Interest Rate Risk

Interest rate risk is a type of systematic risk that affects debentures and bonds. This risk arises due to fluctuations in the interest rate.

Bonds and debentures carry a fixed rate of interest (called 'coupon' rate). The rate of interest is printed on the bond/debenture certificate. Interest is calculated on the face value of the bond/debenture at the coupon rate. For example, if the coupon rate on a bond with face value of Rs. 100 is 9% p.a., the bondholder will receive annual interest of Rs. 9 till the maturity of the bond. The coupon rate is fixed and remains the same till the maturity of the bond/debenture in spite of fluctuations in interest rate in the market.

Coupon rate on bonds/debentures is normally fixed based on the interest rate prevailing at the time of issue of bonds/debentures. When the interest rate in the market changes, there arises a difference between the coupon rate and the market interest rate. This difference causes changes in the market value of bonds.

When the interest rate in the market falls below the coupon rate of a particular bond/debenture that particular bond/debenture attracts investors as it offers a higher return. This in turn, pushes the market value of the bond/debenture above its face value. Similarly, when the market interest rate raises above the coupon rate of bond/debenture, the bond/debenture will not attract investors and consequently the market value of the bond/debenture will fall below its face value.

Such variation in the market value (or market price) of bonds/debentures caused due to variations in interest rates in known as interest rate risk.

Changes in market interest rates are due to many macro level factors and the company that has issued bond/debenture has no control over those macro level factors. Hence, interest rate risk is a systematic risk.

Does the interest rate risk affect equity shares? Yes, it does affect share prices, but indirectly. Speculators who deal in shares often resort to margin treading, i.e., buying shares using borrowed funds and repaying the borrowed funds by disposing off the shares subsequently. When the market interest rates fall, the speculators will be more active in the stock market and the share prices may go up due to heavy buying activities and vice versa. Thus, interest rate risk also affects shares apart from bonds/debenture.

Purchasing Power Risk

This is a systematic risk caused by inflation. The effect of inflation prevails upon all securities in the market and the investors have no control over inflation. Hence, purchasing power risk is a systematic risk.

Purchasing power risk is that risk caused by variation in real returns from securities caused due to inflation.

Suppose an investor buys a debenture of face value Rs. 100, interest rate of 10% and maturity period of 1 year. The return on investment that the investor would receive after one year would be Rs. 10.00. Suppose during this period of one year there is a 6% inflation in the economy, it means that the purchasing power of Rs. 106 after one year would be equal to present purchasing power of Rs. 100. Though Rs. 100 invested would become Rs. 110 after one year, in real terms the return earned is not 10% but is below 10% due to reduction in purchasing power. Though the investor's return would have increased by 10%, his purchasing power would have increased only by 3.77%.

$$\text{Increase in purchasing power} = \frac{(100 \times 110)}{106} - 100 = 3.77\%$$

Thus, though the investors would receive a return of 10% on the investment, the return earned in real terms (i.e., in terms of increase in purchasing power) would be only 3.77%. The actual return and the real return would be same only in the event of nil inflation, during the period of investment. This however is a rarity and it depends on many economy-wide factors and is not within the control of individual investors.

It is obvious that fixed income securities are more affected by inflation than equity shares. Hence, purchasing power risk is more for bonds and debentures than for equity shares.

If the economy shows an inflationary trend, those who invest on fixed income securities will have to take into account the reduction in purchasing power and accordingly arrive at the expected rate of return that would compensate for the reduction in purchasing power and yield a net return that is acceptable. However, predicting the rate of inflation is not an easy task and hence purchasing power risk is very much present. It is a systematic risk since inflation in an economy is not in the hands of the individual investors and it affects all business establishments in the economy.

2.2.2. Unsystematic Risk

It is the opposite of systematic risk. We have seen that systematic risk is caused by 'system-wide' factors, which are beyond the control of individual investors and which affect all the business establishments in the system.

Unsystematic risk is caused by factors specific to the company issuing securities. In other words, unsystematic risk is caused by 'firm-specific' factors. Unsystematic risk is unique to companies and differs from one company to another.

The unsystematic risk, which is caused due to firm-specific factors, can be classified into two types.

Viz., (*a*) Business risk and (*b*) Financial risk.

Business Risk

Business risk is also called operating risk. Business risk is concerned with earnings before interest and tax (i.e., operating profit). Business risk arises due to the chances of variability in return caused by a firm's pattern of usage of funds. Every business establishment mobilises funds and uses funds for its business operations. The pattern of usage differs from one firm to another. For example, one company may have used a larger proportion of its funds on fixed assets while another company may have used only a smaller proportion of its funds on fixed assets and the balance on current assets.

A Company is exposed to business risk purely based on the pattern of usage of funds. Operating profit (i.e., profit before interest and tax) is sensitive to the pattern of usage of funds.

The pattern of usage of funds affects the operating cost of a company. Operating costs can be divided into fixed costs and variable costs. In general, a larger proportion of fixed cost is not advantageous.

Fixed costs are those costs that do not vary with the volume of output. For example, when a building is taken on lease for housing the production facilities, irrespective of the volume of production, the lessor will demand the same lease rent, i.e., the lease rent payable is fixed or constant and does not vary with the level of production.

A moment's reflection will make it clear that if the output level reduces the operating profit will get more than proportionately affected due to fixed costs.

The following illustration will make things clear:

Level of production	Company–A		Company–B	
1000 units	Fixed cost	Rs. 2.00 lakhs	Fixed cost	Rs. 0.50 lakhs
	Variable cost	Rs. 4.00 lakhs	Variable cost	Rs. 4.00 lakhs
	Total cost	Rs. 6.00 lakhs	Total cost	Rs. 4.50 lakhs
	Sales	Rs. 8.00 lakhs	Sales	Rs. 8.00 lakhs
	Operating profit	Rs. 2.00 lakhs	Operating profit	Rs. 3.50 lakhs
250 units	Fixed cost	Rs. 2.00 lakhs	Fixed cost	Rs. 0.50 lakhs
	Variable cost	Rs. 1.00 lakhs	Variable cost	Rs. 1.00 lakhs
	Total cost	Rs. 3.00 lakhs	Total cost	Rs. 1.50 lakhs
	Sales	Rs. 2.00 lakhs	Sales	Rs. 2.00 lakhs
	Operating loss	Rs. 1.00 lakhs	Operating profit	Rs. 0.50 lakhs

Note: *Operating profit/loss is that profit/loss that can be attributed purely to the operating efficiency of a business. Interest expenses and taxes are excluded for arriving at operating profit/loss i.e., the total cost consists of only operating costs.*

Suppose there are two companies A and B engaged in the same line of business activity and have the same installed capacity. Referring to the above table, though the sales revenue is the same for both the companies, when the output is 1000 units, company–B shows a higher operating profit. This is in view of the lesser fixed cost as compared to company–A. Fixed cost forms 33% of the total cost for company–A and 11 % of the total cost for company–B. A higher proportion of fixed cost in company–A suggests a higher business risk. Hence, for the same level of out put, the operating profit of company–A is less than that of company–B. When the output level comes down to 250 units from 1000 units, while company–B still manages to make an operating profit of Rs. 0.50 lakhs. Company–A, slips into an operating loss of Rs. 1.00 lakhs. This is because of the higher proportion of fixed cost, which remains constant, irrespective of the changes in output.

Thus, business risk can be said to be an unsystematic risk that arises on account of the way in which a firm has organised its fixed and variable costs. In order to reduce business risk, a firm should try to keep fixed costs to the minimum so that it can survive the threat of incurring operating loss when the business conditions turn unfavourable leading to reduction in the volume of business.

Financial Risk

All companies use both equity capital and debt capital. Just as the proportion of fixed cost to the total cost decides the business risk, the proportion of debt capital to the total capital decides the financial risk.

Debt capital is interest bearing, i.e., irrespective of the prospects of the business, interest on debt capital is to be paid. In other words, interest payable is "fixed" for a given amount of debt capital irrespective of the volume of business. Thus, debt capital in akin to 'fixed cost'. While the dividend payable on equity capital can be reduced/avoided depending on the operations of the business, interest on debt capital cannot be reduced or delayed. Thus, while debt capital is akin to fixed cost, equity capital is akin to variable cost. Obviously, a higher proportion of debt component indicates higher risk. Such risk, which arises due to debt component in the capital structure of a company, is called financial risk.

Consider the following illustration:

Company–A		Company–B	
Debt (@13%)	Rs. 10.00 lakhs	Debt (@10%)	Rs. 5.00 lakhs
Equity (15000 equity shares of Rs.100 face value each)	Rs. 15.00 lakhs	Equity (20000 equity Rs.100 face value each)	Rs. 20.00 lakhs
	Rs. 25.00 lakhs		Rs. 25.00 lakhs
Operating profit	Rs. 2.00 lakhs	Operating profit	Rs. 2.00 lakhs
Less: Interest	Rs. 1.30 lakhs	Less: Interest	Rs. 0.50 lakhs
Net profit before tax	Rs. 0.70 lakhs	Net profit before tax	Rs. 0.70 lakhs
Less: Tax @ 40%	Rs. 0.28 lakhs	Less: Tax @ 40%	Rs. 0.60 lakhs
Net profit after tax	Rs. 0.42 lakhs	Net profit after tax	Rs. 0.90 lakhs

Contd...

Earnings available to 15000 equity share-holders	Rs. 42,000.00	Earnings available to 20000 equity share-holders	Rs. 90,000.00
Earnings per share (EPS)	Rs. 2.80	Earnings per share (EPS)	Rs. 4.50

Companies A and B earn the same operating profit. However, their capital structure is different. While company–B that has a lesser proportion of debt capital offers an EPS of Rs. 4.50, company–A could offer an EPS of only Rs. 2.80.

Suppose the business conditions turn unfavorable and the operating profits come down to say, Rs. 1.25 lakhs, the position would be as under.

Company–A		**Company–B**	
Debt (@13%)	10.00 lakhs	Debt (@10%)	5.00 lakhs
Equity (15000 equity shares of Rs. 100 face value each)	20.00 lakhs	Equity (20000 equity shares of Rs. 100 face value each)	20.00 lakhs
	25.00 lakhs		25.00 lakhs
Operating profit	1.25 lakhs	Operating profit	1.25 lakhs
Less: Interest	1.30 lakhs	Less: Interest	0.50 lakhs
Net profit before tax	(0.05 lakhs)	Net profit before tax	0.75 lakhs
Less: Tax @ 40%	—	Less: Tax @ 40%	0.30 lakhs
Net profit after tax	(0.05 lakhs)	Net profit after tax	0.45 lakhs

While company–B still earns a Net profit after tax of Rs. 0.45 lakhs, Company–A runs into Net loss. Thus, though the operating profit remains the same for both the companies, the capital structure affects the earnings to the shareholder. This variably in the returns to the shareholders due to the presence of debt in the capital structure is called financial risk. Since, deciding upon the capital structure is within the purview of individual business organisations, financial risk is 'firm-specific' and hence is an unsystematic risk.

A firm that has debt in its capital structure is called a levered firm and a firm that has no debt in its capital structure is called an unlevered firm. A firm with a higher proportion of debt in its capital structure is said to have high leverage and the one with a lower proportion of debt in the capital structure is said to have low leverage. Sometimes the terms High Gearing and Low bearing are also used for the terms 'High leverage' and 'Low leverage' respectively.

Is leverage good or bad?

From the example shown above, we observed that both companies–A and B are levered firms (in view of debt capital in their capital structure). Out of the two, company–A is highly levered as compared to company–B as company– A has a higher proportion of debt capital than company–B. Out of these two levered firms, we find that company–A has a higher financial risk than company–B since the returns (i.e., net profit after tax which is available to the share holders) of company–A gets adversely affected by changes in the operating profit. Can it be generalised that a higher proportion of debt in the capital structure (i.e., higher leverage) is always prone to affect the net profit available to the shareholders? No. The adverse or favourable effect of debt capital depends upon the rate of interest payable on the debt capital and the rate of return that the company earns in terms of operating profit.

Let us again consider the same example.

Company–A		Company–B	
Debt (@13%)	10.00 lakhs	Debt (@10%)	5.00 lakhs
Equity	15.00 lakhs	Equity	20.00 lakhs
	25.00 lakhs		25.00 lakhs
Operating profit	2.00 lakhs	Operating profit	2.00 lakhs
% of operating profit on the total capital employed	8%	% of operating profit on the total capital employed	8%

Since the rate of return earned in terms of operating profit (viz. 8%) is less than the interest payable on the debt capital (viz. 13% and 10% respectively for company–A and B respectively) the presence of debt in the capital structure of both companies–A and B is not advantageous. As the rate of return in term of operating profit is less than the interest rate on debt capital, the EPS will get reduced. The EPS of company–B is Rs. 4.50. If there is no debt in the capital structure of company–B, for the same level of operating profit, the EPS would be Rs. 4.80 as under.

Debt	— Nil —
Equity	
(25000 equity shares of face value Rs. 100 each)	Rs. 25.00 lakhs
Operating profit	Rs. 2.00 lakhs
Less interest	— Nil —
Net profit before tax	Rs. 2.00 lakhs
Less tax @ 40%	Rs. 0.80 lakhs
Net profit after tax	Rs. 1.20 lakhs
i.e., Earning available to 2500 equity shareholders	Rs. 1.20 lakhs
EPS	Rs. 4.80

Thus, the presence of debt in the capital structure has led to reduction in EPS. This is due to the reason that the rate return earned in terms of operating profit is less than the interest rate on debt capital.

However, if debt capital is available at a cheaper rate of interest than the return earned by the business in terms of operating profit, the presence of debt capital will go to improve the EPS.

Suppose debt capital is available at the interest rate of, say 5% p.a. The position would be as under.

Company–A			Company–B		
Debt (@ 5%)	Rs.	10.00 lakhs	Debt (@ 5%)	Rs.	5.00 lakhs
Equity	Rs.	15.00 lakhs	Equity	Rs.	20.00 lakhs
(15000 equity shares of Rs.100/- face value each)			(20000 equity shares of Rs.100/- face value each)		
	Rs.	25.00 lakhs		Rs.	25.00 lakhs
Operating profit	Rs.	(*) 2.00 lakhs	Operating profit	Rs.(*)	2.00 lakhs
Less: Interest	Rs.	0.50 lakhs	Less: Interest	Rs.	0.25 lakhs
Net profit before tax	Rs.	1.50 lakhs	Net profit before tax	Rs.	1.75 lakhs
Less: Tax @ 40%	Rs.	0.60 lakhs	Less: Tax @ 40%	Rs.	0.70 lakhs
Net profit after tax	Rs.	0.90 lakhs	Net profit after tax	Rs.	1.05 lakhs
EPS (90,000/ 15,000)	Rs.	6.00	EPS (1,05,000/ 20,000)	Rs.	5.25

When company–B is considered as an unlevered firm, without any debt in its capital structure, the EPS is Rs. 4.80 while the EPS improves to Rs. 5.25 for company–B when it becomes a levered firm. This is because the interest rate payable on the debt capital is less than the rate of return earned by the company in terms of operating profit.

Thus, it can be inferred that the presence of debt in the capital structure of a firm is not always an undesirable factor. The presence of debt in the capital structure can also at times increase the EPS. The desirability or otherwise of debt in the capital structure depends upon the interest rate on debt vis-a-vis the rate of return that the company earns on the total capital employed in terms of the operating profit earned.

Irrespective of whether the interest rate on the debt is higher or lower than the rate of return in terms of operating profit, any change in the proportion of debt capital will lead to a change in the EPS. While the interest payable on the debt capital is fixed, the operating profit is not a fixed one as it depends upon the business operations. Hence, the rate of

(*) % of operating profit on the total capital employed : 8%

return measured in terms of the operating profit will also vary according to the change in the operating profit. If the business conditions turn unfavourable, the anticipated operating profit may not be generated and there is always an element of risk involved in employing debt capital.

Hence, whether leverage is good or bad can be answered only on the basis of the rate of interest on debt capital vis-a-vis the return earned by the business in terms of the operating profit. If the rate of return earned in terms of the operating profit is more than the interest rate on debt capital, leverage will have favourable effect. At the same time, when the rate of return earned in terms of the operating profit falls below the interest rate on the debt capital, leverage will have an unfavourable effect. Hence, a judicious decision needs to be taken in deciding upon the presence and quantum of debt capital in the capital structure.

2.3. MEASUREMENT OF RISK

Measurement of risk is central to investment management. Once the risk involved in investments is correctly assessed, the investor is in a better position to choose the securities of his choice for investing his funds. The entire gamut of investment management lies in providing or clear picture with regard to the risk-return characteristics of available investment avenues so that investors can choose those securities which suit their risk bearing capacity. The risk bearing capacity of investors vary. At the one end are those investors who shun risk of any kind and settle for risk-free investment in spite of the very low return such risk free investments may offer. At the other end are those investors who are prepared to invest in high-risk securities in anticipation of higher returns. Thus, measuring the correct level of risk associated with the different securities available for investment is crucial for making investment decisions.

2.3.1. Expected Return

The expected returns from investment on securities vary according to the type of the securities in which investment is made.

If an investor invests in Government guaranteed bonds with fixed rate of return, the expected return is equal to the coupon rate of return (i.e. the rate of return prescribed for that bond). If the coupon rate is 10%, the investor is sure to get 10% return on his investment, neither less nor more. Thus, the expected return is known before hand and the expected return is not likely to vary (i.e.,) the variability of return is nil. Since, 'risk' is measured in terms of variability in return, a security whose return is not likely to vary can be considered as a risk-free security. Thus, a fixed interest bond guaranteed by the Government can be considered as a risk-free security.

Consider the equity share of a company. The likely return from the equity share cannot be predicted in concrete terms as in the case of a fixed rate Government guaranteed bond. This is because of the fact that the returns from the equity shares is affected by many factors, both factors internal to the company and external to the company. Hence, we can say that the expected return from equity shares is variable. Since, the expected return from equity shares has an element of variability, such securities are risky securities and the level of risk depends upon the level of variability of returns.

2.3.2. Expected Return from an Equity Share

The return from an equity share consists of two components viz., dividend on the face value of the share and capital appreciation due to increase in the market price of the share.

Suppose a person buys the equity share of a company having a face value of Rs. 100 at a price of Rs. 120. Suppose he earns a dividend of Rs. 10.00 the next year and also disposes off the share at a price of Rs. 140 after one year, the return earned by the investor is as under.

Return earned by way of dividend	:	Rs. 10.00
Return earned by way of capital appreciation (140 – 120)	:	Rs. 20.00
Total return earned	:	Rs. 30.00
Initial investment	:	Rs.120.00
Rate of return earned:	: $\frac{30}{120} \times 100$:	25%

By the time the investor buys the share at a price of Rs. 120 he cannot be sure about the exact return that he may earn. He can only anticipate same dividend and some capital appreciation based on the nature of the security and stock market conditions.

Suppose he expects a dividend of Rs. 12 and a capital appreciation of Rs. 36 on his investment of Rs. 120, the expected return is Rs. 48 (on an investment of Rs. 120) which works out to an expected rate of return of 40%. However, accurately the investor may predict his expected return, there is bound to be some variation between the expected return and the actual return. This is because of the reason that the future is never certain. Both the actual dividend and the capital appreciation are likely to vary from the expected estimate. The question now arises as to how to measure the variability of the expected return.

Estimate of probability is made use of in measuring the variability of expected return. Since, the expected return on equity share is only an estimate that is likely to vary, the investor has to consider the probability of getting different possible returns. In other words, instead of estimating a single value for the expected return, the investor has to foresee different possible returns and the probability of getting these different returns.

The following table gives an example of the probability estimate of the expected return:

Possible return (r_i)	Probability of getting the return (p_i)
25%	0.10
30%	0.25
40%	0.30
50%	0.25
60%	0.10
	1.00

The task of assigning probabilities for different possible returns is however not an easy task for the investor; for this, the investor has to study the performance of the share in the past and has to project the performance into the future, duly incorporating the likely changes that he anticipates in the future. This requires great acumen and strenuous analysis is to be done with reasonable degree of accuracy. The rest of the work consists of arriving at certain statistical measures.

Once the different possible returns and their respective probability are arrived at, the data are then converted into two simple statistical measures, which will help in making investment decisions. There are two statistical means are,

(*a*) Expected return and

(*b*) Risk

Expected return

Expected return from an investment is the weighted average of all the possible returns the weights for the possible returns being their probability of occurrence.

Thus,

$$\bar{r} = \sum_{i=1}^{n} r_i \cdot p_i$$

where

$\bar{r}$ = expected return

$r_i = r_1, r_2, r_3, \ldots, r_n$ = different possible returns

and $p_i = p_1, p_2, p_3, \ldots, p_n$ = the probability of getting the different possible returns,

The following table gives an example for the calculation of the expected return on the basis of the possible returns and their respective probability of occurrence.

Possible returns (r_i)	Probability (p_i)	Expected return $\sum_{i=1}^{n} r_i \cdot p_i$
25%	0.10	2.50%
30%	0.25	7.50%
40%	0.30	12.00%
50%	0.25	12.50%
60%	0.10	6.00%
	$\sum = 1.00$	$\sum = 40.50\%$

The expected return on the basis of given data is 40.50%.

Risk

We have understood that risk arises due to variability of returns.

In the previous paragraph we have seen that the return from a particular security is expected to vary from 25% to 60% with varying degrees of probability resulting in an expected return of 40.50%.

The expected return of 40.50% can also be reached for a different pattern of variations in the possible return. For example if there is a possibility of getting 40% return with 50% probability and getting 41% return with 50% probability, the expected return is still 40.50%.

Possible returns (r_i)	Probability (p_i)	Expected return $\sum_{i=1}^{n} r_i \cdot p_i$
40%	0.50	20.00%
41%	0.50	20.50%
	$\sum = 1.00$	$\sum = 40.50\%$

However, this security shows lesser variations in the possible returns and hence is less risky. This makes it clear that apart from the expected return the risk associated with the expected return is also to be measured in order to '**describe**' the security in full.

The variability in realising the expected return is measured by way of a statistical measure called 'standard deviations'.

Let us consider the measurement of certain property, say the weight of students in a class (say, class – A). Obviously the weights of all the students in a class are not going to be the same. Each student will be having a different weight. Let there are 10 students. Let the weights (in kg) of these 10 students are as under. [For the sake of simplicity, whole number are assumed]

45, 44, 40, 45, 50, 35, 30, 42, 43, 46.

If we want to know the average weight of students in the class, we simply take the arithmetic mean of the available data.

Average weight of students of class–A (given by arithmetic mean)

$$= \frac{45+44+40+45+50+35+30+42+43+46}{10}$$

$$= \frac{420}{10} = 42 \text{ kg.}$$

Let there is another class (class–B) having 10 students with the following weights(in kg.):

56, 20, 25, 55, 57, 54, 24, 50, 53, 26.

Average height of students of class–B

$$= \frac{56+20+25+55+57+54+24+50+53+26}{10}$$

$$= \frac{420}{10} = 42 \text{ kg.}$$

Though the average weight of students of class A and class B are the same the arithmetical mean does not explain the differences between the weights of the individual students. We can observe that the variation in the weights of students of class–A is less compared to the variation in the weights of students of class–B. Thus, arithmetic mean alone does not give a true picture. Hence, another statistical measurement called 'standard deviation' is used to get an idea of the difference between the individual scores.

Before knowing about standard deviation another term 'mean deviation' is worth noting. Let us plot the individual scores of class–A and class–B in the form of graph. The graphs depict the deviation of the individual scores from the Arithmetic mean. (Refer Fig. 2.1)

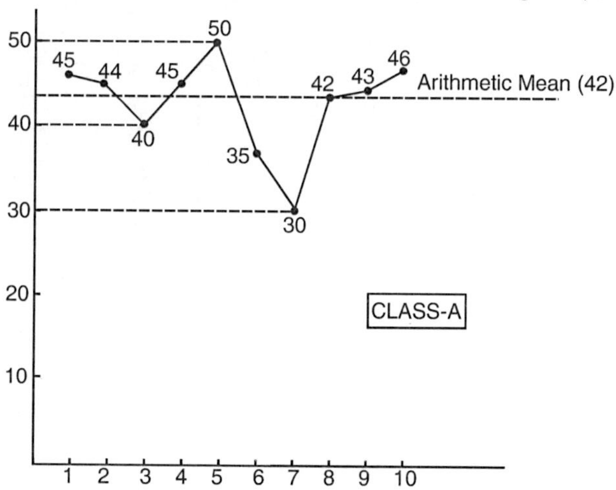

Fig. 2.1(*Contd...*)

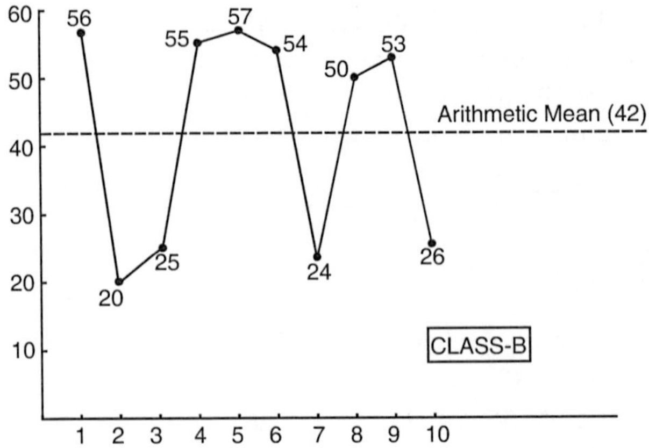

Fig. 2.1 Deviation of individual scores from arithmetic mean

Obviously the scores of class–B show high level of variations. In other words, we can say that the scores of class–B is widely dispersed from the Arithmetic mean than that of class–A. In both the classes we have scores above as well as below the Arithmetic mean of 42. We are interested in measuring the dispersion (or deviation) of the individual scores from the Arithmetic mean. Hence, we can ignore the (+) and (–) signs of the deviations and consider the absolute values of the deviations.

Class – A				Class – B			
Individual score (x)	Arithmetic mean ($\bar{x}$)	Deviation ($x - \bar{x}$) A – B	Absolute value of deviation	Individual score	Arithmetic mean	Deviation	Absolute value of deviation
45	42	3	3	56	42	14	14
44	42	2	2	20	42	–22	22
40	42	–2	2	25	42	–17	17
45	42	3	3	55	42	13	13
50	42	8	8	57	42	15	15
35	42	–7	7	54	42	12	12
30	42	–12	12	24	42	–18	18
42	42	0	0	50	42	8	8
43	42	1	1	53	42	11	11
46	42	4	4	26	42	–16	16
			$\sum = 42$				$\sum = 146$

$$\text{Mean Deviation} = \frac{42}{10} = 4.20; \qquad \text{Mean Deviation} = \frac{146}{10} = 14.60$$

The Mean Deviation of the scores of class–B is higher than that of class–A which shows that the individual scores of class–B deviate more from the

Arithmetic mean. When Mean Deviation is divided by the Arithmetic Mean, we get Coefficient of Mean Deviation.

$$\text{Coefficient of Mean Deviation for class–A} = \frac{4.2}{42} = 0.10$$

$$\text{Coefficient of Mean Deviation for class–B} = \frac{14.6}{42} = 0.348$$

A higher value of Coefficient of Mean Deviation indicates that the individual scores are widely dispersed from the Arithmetic Mean. Thus, Coefficient of Mean Deviation can be used as a relative measure of dispersion and can be used for comparing similar series of scores.

We have calculated the Mean Deviation by ignoring the algebraic signs of the deviations from the Arithmetic Mean. Another similar measure of dispersion that ignores the algebraic signs of the deviations from the Arithmetic Mean is the Standard Deviation. Unlike simply ignoring the algebraic signs as in the calculation of Mean Deviation, while calculating Standard Deviation the actual deviations are squared so that the algebraic signs get avoided.

Calculation of Standard Deviation

Class–A

Weight of students (in kg) (x) = 45, 44, 40, 45, 50, 35, 30, 42, 43, 46

Arithmetic Mean ($\overline{x}$) = 42

Deviation of individual scores from Arithmetic Mean ($x - \overline{x}$) = 3, 2, 2, 3, 8, –7, –12, 0, 1, 4

Square of deviation of individual scores from Arithmetic Mean $(x - \overline{x})^2$ = 9, 4, 4, 9, 64, 49, 144, 0, 1, 16

Sum of the squared deviation $\left\{\Sigma(x-\overline{x})^2\right\}$

$$= 9 + 4 + 4 + 9 + 64 + 49 + 144 + 0 + 1 + 16 = 300$$

Mean of the squared deviations (also called 'Variance')

$$= \frac{\Sigma(x-\overline{x})^2}{n}$$

$$= 300 \div 10$$

$$= 30$$

Standard Deviation (square root of the mean of squared deviations)

$$= \sqrt{\frac{\Sigma(x_A - \overline{x}_A)^2}{n}}$$

$$= \sqrt{30}$$

$$= 5.48$$

Thus, Standard Deviation is defined as the square root of the average of squares of deviations, when such deviations for the values of individual items in a series are obtained from the Arithmetic Mean.

Calculation of Standard Deviation

Class–B

Weight of students (in kg) (x) = 56, 20, 25, 55, 57, 54, 24, 50, 53, 26

Arithmetic mean ($\overline{x}$) = 42

Deviation of individual scores from arithmetic mean ($x - \overline{x}$) = 14, –22, –17, 13, 15, 12, –18, 8, 11, –16

$(x - \overline{x})^2$ = 196, 484, 289, 169, 225, 144, 324, 64, 121, 256

$$\Sigma(x - \overline{x})^2 = 2{,}272$$

$$\frac{\Sigma(x - \overline{x})^2}{n} = \frac{2{,}272}{10}$$

$$= 227.2$$

$$\sqrt{\frac{\Sigma(x - \overline{x})^2}{n}} = \sqrt{227.2}$$

$$= 47.67$$

Standard Deviation of scores of class–B is 47.67 as against that of class–A which is 5.48 which shows that the individual scores of class–B are highly dispersed.

When the standard deviation is divided by the Arithmetic Mean, we get coefficient of Standard Deviation.

$$\text{Coefficient of Standard Deviation for class–A} = \frac{5.48}{42} = 0.13$$

$$\text{Coefficient of Standard Deviation for class–B} = \frac{47.67}{42} = 1.135$$

Coefficient of Standard Deviation is used as a relative measure of dispersion for comparing similar series.

Of the two measures of dispersion (i.e., Mean Deviation and Standard Deviation) Standard Deviation is widely used as it is less affected by fluctuations of sampling.

***Illustration* 2.1:**

Past data for four years on two securities 'A' and 'B' show that the securities have yielded return on investment as under.

Year	Return from security 'A'	Return from security 'B'
1998–1999	15%	9%
1999–2000	5%	11%
2000–2001	18%	15%
2001–2002	7%	10%

Calculate the average return offered by the two securities and their relative riskiness.

Solution:

***Security* 'A'**

$$\text{Average return} = \frac{15+5+18+7}{4}$$

$$x_A = \frac{45}{4} = 11.25\%$$

***Security* 'B'**

$$\text{Average return} = \frac{9+11+15+10}{4}$$

$$x_B = \frac{45}{4} = 11.25\%$$

Both the securities yield the same average return.

The relative riskiness of the securities can be measured by the variations in the returns. This can be done by calculating their respective standard deviations.

Year	Security – A				Security – B			
	Return x_A	Ave. return $\bar{x}_A$	$(x_A - \bar{x}_A)$	$(x_A - \bar{x}_A)^2$	Return x_B	Ave. return $\bar{x}_B$	$(x_B - \bar{x}_B)$	$(x_B - \bar{x}_B)^2$
98–99	15	11.25	3.75	14.06	9	11.25	–2.25	5.06
99–00	5	11.25	–6.25	39.06	11	11.25	–0.25	0.06
00–01	18	11.25	6.75	45.56	15	11.25	3.75	14.06
01–02	7	11.25	–4.25	18.06	10	11.25	–1.25	1.56
	$\sum (x_A - \bar{x}_A)^2$		⇒	116.74	$\sum (x_B - \bar{x}_B)^2$		⇒	20.74

$$\text{Standard deviations of returns from} = \sqrt{\frac{\Sigma(x_A - \bar{x}_A)^2}{n}}$$

$$\text{Security A } (\sigma_A) = \sqrt{\frac{116.74}{4}}$$

$$= \sqrt{29.185}$$

$$= 5.40$$

Standard deviations of returns from

Security B (σ_B) $$= \sqrt{\frac{\Sigma(x_B - \bar{x}_B)^2}{n}}$$

$$= \sqrt{\frac{20.74}{4}}$$

$$= \sqrt{5.185}$$

$$= 2.28$$

Since, the Standard Deviations of returns from security–A is more than the standard deviations of returns from security–B, it indicates that security-A is a riskier than security–B.

Note: *In illustration 2.1., we have studied the past data of two securities and based on the past data we came to a conclusion as to which of the two securities is riskier, by comparing their Standard Deviations.*

Past data are no doubt an indication of the future. However, if we expect the future to be somewhat different and accordingly if we anticipate variations in future returns from securities, still the use of Standard Deviation comes handy, Illustrations 2.2 and 2.3 explain the use of Standard Deviations in assessing riskiness of securities with regard to anticipated future returns.

***Illustration* 2.2:**

The equity share of a particular company is currently yielding a return of 18% p.a. An assessment of the possibilities of the earning capacity of the share in future indicates the following:

Earning 18% return has a probability of 0.40

Earning 25% return has a probability of 0.10

Earning 22% return has a probability of 0.10

Earning 20% return has a probability of 0.10

Earning 16% return has a probability of 0.30

Calculate the expected return from the share.

Solution:

Possible returns (x_i)%	Probability $p(x_i)$	$x_i \cdot p(x_i)$
18	0.40	7.20
25	0.10	2.50
22	0.10	2.20
20	0.10	2.00
16	0.30	4.80
$\Sigma x_i \cdot p(x_i)$	⇒	18.70

Expected return from the share $[\Sigma\, x_i \cdot p(x_i)] = 18.70\%$

Note: *Based on the probability estimates, we have arrived at the expected return at 18.70%. Suppose we have another equity share that also gives an expected return of 18.70% but has different probabilities of possible returns. We should have a measure to compare these two securities in order to choose the one that is less riskier. This is done with the help of Standard Deviations of the possible returns.*

Standard Deviation of the possible returns of the share given in illustration 2.2 is calculated as under.

Probability $p(x_i)$	Possible return (%) (x_i)	Expected return $\bar{x}$	Deviation from expected return $(x_i - \bar{x})$	Square of deviation $(x_i - \bar{x})^2$	Product of probability and square of deviation $p(x_i) \cdot (x_i - \bar{x})^2$
0.40	18	18.70	–0.70	0.49	0.196
0.10	25		6.30	39.69	3.969
0.10	22		3.30	10.89	1.089
0.10	20		1.30	1.69	0.169
0.30	16		–2.70	7.29	2.187
				σ^2 ⇒	7.61

Variance (σ^2) = 7.61

Standard Deviation (σ) = $\sqrt{7.61}$ = 2.758

The Standard Deviation is 2.758%

We have defined Standard Deviation as the square root of the average of the "square of deviations". In this example we have not taken the average of square of deviations. This is because the different 'possible returns' have different probabilities. Hence, we have multiplied the square of deviations by the respective probability. If all the possible returns have the same probability, then taking the average value of the *return and multiplying by the probability will give the same result. For example, if 5 possible returns are having the same probabilities of occurrence each return will have a probability of **0.2**. Multiplying the square of deviations of each possible return with **0.2** and then adding up the same or dividing sum of the squared deviations with **5** will both give the same result.*

***Illustration* 2.3:**

The possible returns from two securities and their probabilities are as below.

Security–A		Security–B	
Possible return (x_i)	**Probability $p(x_i)$**	**Possible return (x_i)**	**Probability $p(x_i)$**
15%	0.50	12%	0.60
17%	0.20	20%	0.20
19%	0.10	22%	0.10
20%	0.20	34%	0.10

Estimate the expected return from the securities. Which of the two securities has lesser risk?

Solution:

***Security*–A**

(x_i)	$p(x_i)$	$x_i\,p(x_i)$	Expected return $\bar{x}$	$(x_i - \bar{x})$	$(x_i - \bar{x})^2$	$p(x_i)\cdot(x_i - \bar{x})^2$
15	0.50	7.50	16.80	–1.80	3.24	1.620
17	0.20	3.40		0.20	0.04	0.008
19	0.10	1.90		2.20	4.84	0.484
20	0.20	4.00		3.20	10.24	2.048
	$\sum \Rightarrow$	16.80			$\sigma^2 \Rightarrow$	4.160

Expected return = 16.80%

Variance of the expected return (σ^2) = 4.16

Standard deviations of the expected (σ) = $\sqrt{7.61}$

= 2.04

***Security*–B**

(x_i)	$p(x_i)$	$x_i\,p(x_i)$	Expected return $\bar{x}$	$(x_i - \bar{x})$	$(x_i - \bar{x})^2$	$p(x_i)\cdot(x_i - \bar{x})^2$
12	0.60	7.20	16.80	–4.80	23.04	13.824
20	0.20	4.00		3.20	10.24	2.048
22	0.10	2.20		5.20	27.04	2.704
34	0.10	3.40		17.20	295.84	29.584
	$\sum \Rightarrow$	16.80			$\sigma^2 \Rightarrow$	48.160

Expected return $= 16.80\%$

Variance of the expected return (σ^2) $= 48.16$

Standard deviations of the expected (σ) $= \sqrt{48.16}$

$= 6.94$

Though the expected return from the two securities is the same, the Standard Deviations of the return from security–B is higher than that of security–A. Hence security 'A' shows lesser risk.

2.4. COVARIANCE

Covariance is an absolute measure of the extent to which two sets of numbers move together i.e., move up or move down together. The measurement of movement is done from their means, i.e., the movements above/below their means is arrived at and compared.

If there are two sets of numbers, say set 'x' (x_1, x_2, x_3, ..., x_N) and set 'y' (y_1, y_2, y_3, ..., y_N) the covariance between the two sets is given by

$$\text{Cov}_{x,y} = \frac{(x-\bar{x})\cdot(y-\bar{y})}{N}$$

where $\bar{x}$ and $\bar{y}$ are the Arithmetic Means of the respective sets.

Positive Covariance

If both the numbers are consistently above or below their respective means at the same time, their products will be positive and the average will also be a positive value and the covariance between the two sets of numbers will be positive.

Negative Covariance

If the movements in the values of the numbers of the two sets are inconsistent, i.e., if 'x' value is below the arithmetic mean x while the y value is above the mean y and vice versa, their products will be negative and covariance will be negative.

***Illustration* 2.4:**

Find the covariance between the two sets of numbers given below.

x	2	4	5	8	10
y	3	7	8	15	24

Solution:

x	y	$(x - \bar{x})$	$(y - \bar{y})$	$(x - \bar{x})\cdot(y - \bar{y})$
2	3	–3.80	–8.40	31.92
4	7	–1.80	–4.40	7.92
5	8	–0.80	–3.40	2.72
8	15	2.20	3.60	7.92
10	24	4.20	12.60	52.92
				$\sum = 103.40$

$$\bar{x} = (2 + 4 + 5 + 8 + 10) \div 5 = 5.80$$

$$\bar{y} = (3 + 7 + 8 + 15 + 24) \div 5 = 11.40$$

$$\text{Cov}_{x,y} = \frac{103.40}{5} = 20.60$$

When the value of 'x' is above its mean '$\bar{x}$', the value of 'y' is also above its mean '$\bar{y}$' and vice versa. Hence, the covariance between the two sets of numbers is positive. A positive covariance between the returns offered by two securities indicates that their price movements are alike. In other words, their prices move either upwards or downwards together.

2.5. CORRELATION COEFFICIENT

Since covariance is an absolute measure of the relationship between two sets of numbers (i.e., variables), it can take values in the range of $-\infty$ to $+\infty$. In normal practice, the relationship between two sets of variables stated in relative terms for which the measure 'coefficient of correlation' is used.

The correlation coefficient between two sets of variables x and y is given by

$$\gamma_{xy} = \frac{\text{Cov}_{x,y}}{\sigma_x \cdot \sigma_y}$$

The coefficient of correlation is nothing but the covariance taken not as an absolute value, but taken relative to the standard deviations of the variables. The numerator of the term indicates how much x and y vary together. The denominator of the term indicates the combined individual variations of the two sets, measured by the product of their standard deviations. When the two series move 'completely' together (say, x = 2, 3, 4, 5, and 6 while y = 4, 6, 8, 10, 12) the covariance would be equal to $\sigma_x \cdot \sigma_y$ and hence the correlation coefficient will be equal to + 1.00. When the two series move exactly opposite to each other, the correlation coefficient will be equal to – 1.00.

Thus, as against covariance that can take values from $-\infty$ to $+\infty$, coefficient of correlation will take values only in the range of only –1.00 to

+ 1.00. As the coefficient of correlation is a normalized measure, it can be used for analysis in a better way.

Two variables are said to be correlated if the variables behave in such a way that changes in the value of one variable are associated with changes in the value of the other variable and hence it becomes possible to predict the value of one variable if the value of the other variable is known.

If the value of one variable increases with the increase in the value of another variable, the two variables are said to be possibility correlated i.e., their values move in the same direction. For example, if the "agricultural output" (one variable) increases with the increase in the "use of fertilizers" (another variable) there two variables are said to be possibility correlated.

If the value of one variable decreases with the increase in the value of another variable (or vice versa) the two variables are said to be negatively correlated i.e., their values move in the opposite directions. For example, if the "consumption level" of a product (one variable) decreases with the increase in 'price' (another variable) of that product, these two variables are said to be negatively correlated.

If the change in the value of one variable does not induce and change in the value of another variable, there two variables are not correlated. For example, changes in the "price of sugar" (one variable) may not have any effect on the "demand for wrist-watches". In such a case, these two variables are not correlated.

***Illustration* 2.5:**

Arrive at the coefficient of correlation for the problem given in illustration 2.4.

Solution:

x	y	$(x-\bar{x})$	$(y-\bar{y})$	$(x-\bar{x})^2$	$(y-\bar{y})^2$	$(x-\bar{x})\cdot(y-\bar{y})$
2	3	−3.80	−8.40	14.44	70.56	31.92
4	7	−1.80	−4.40	3.24	19.36	7.92
5	8	−0.80	−3.40	0.64	11.56	2.72
8	15	2.20	3.60	4.84	12.96	7.92
10	24	4.20	12.60	17.64	158.76	52.92
			$\sum\Rightarrow$	40.80	273.20	103.40

$$\text{Covariance } (\text{Cov}_{xy}) = 103.40/5$$

$$= 20.68$$

$$\sigma_x = \sqrt{\frac{\Sigma(x-\bar{x})^2}{N}}$$

$$= \sqrt{\frac{40.80}{5}}$$

$$= 2.587$$

$$\sigma_y = \sqrt{\frac{\Sigma(y-\overline{y})^2}{N}}$$

$$= \sqrt{\frac{273.2}{5}}$$

$$= 7.392$$

$$\gamma_{x,y} = \frac{\text{Cov}_{x,y}}{\sigma_x \cdot \sigma_y}$$

$$\gamma_{x,y} = \frac{20.68}{(2.857)\times(7.392)}$$

$$= 0.979$$

Note: *The coefficient of correlation can also be arrived at by using the following relationship*

$$\gamma_{x,y} = \frac{\Sigma(x-\overline{x})\cdot(y-\overline{y})}{\sqrt{\Sigma(x-\overline{x})^2\cdot\Sigma(y-\overline{y})^2}}$$

$$= \frac{103.40}{\sqrt{(40.80).(273.20)}}$$

$$= \frac{103.40}{105.577}$$

$$= 0.979.$$

This formula directly arrives at the value of correlation coefficient, without arriving at the Standard Deviations of the sets of values.

2.5.1. Positive and Negative Correlations

Coefficient of correlation between two variables 'x' and 'y' is given by the following formula.

Coefficient of correlation

$$\gamma_{x,y} = \frac{\Sigma(x-\overline{x})\cdot(y-\overline{y})}{\sqrt{\Sigma(x-\overline{x})^2\cdot\Sigma(y-\overline{y})^2}}$$

The above relationship for coefficient of correlation was devised by Karl Pearson and hence is also known as Karl Pearson's coefficient of correlation. It is also known by the term 'Product moment correlation.

The relationship between two variables can be measured in two forms. One is the measurement of the qualitative relationship between the two variables and the other is the quantitative relationship between the two variables.

For example, when the demand for the commodity comes down as its price increases the relationship "demand reduces as price increases" is a qualitative relationship. If we want to know as to what is the decrease in demand for a unit increase in price, we should know the qualitative relationship between the two variables. When the sign of the correlation coefficient is positive, it indicates that both the variables move in the same direction and when the sign of the correlation coefficient is negative, it indicates opposite movements of the variables. Thus, the sign of the correlation coefficient gives a qualitative measurement of the relationship. The magnitude of the correlation coefficient gives a quantitative assessment of the relationship. Correlation coefficient can take values from –1 to +1. If the value of the coefficient of correlation is positive, the relationship is direct, if the value is negative, the relationship is inverse.

Positive Correlation

Consider the following example:

$$y = 2.5x$$

where y = a dependent variable

and x = an independent variable

As the value of x increases the value of y also will increase. Thus, there is a positive correlation between x and y. Let the following are the set of values of x and y based on which, the relationship $y = 2x$ was derived.

x	y
1	2.50
2	5.00
3	7.50
4	10.00

What is the coefficient of correlation between x and y?

$$\gamma_{x,y} = \frac{\Sigma(x-\bar{x})\cdot(y-\bar{y})}{\sqrt{\Sigma(x-\bar{x})^2\cdot\Sigma(y-\bar{y})^2}}$$

$$\bar{x} = (1 + 2 + 3 + 4) \div 4 = 2.50$$

$$\bar{y} = (2.5 + 5 + 7.5 + 10) \div 4 = 6.25$$

x	y	$(x-\bar{x})$	$(y-\bar{y})$	$(x-\bar{x})^2$	$(y-\bar{y})^2$	$(x-\bar{x}).(y-\bar{y})$
1	2.5	−1.5	−3.75	2.25	14.0625	5.625
2	5	−0.5	−1.25	0.25	1.5625	0.625
3	7.5	0.5	1.25	0.25	1.5625	0.625
4	10	1.5	3.75	2.25	14.0625	5.625
			$\sum\Rightarrow$	5.00	31.25	12.50

$$\gamma_{x,y} = \frac{12.50}{\sqrt{(5.00)\cdot(31.25)}}$$

$$\gamma_{x,y} = \frac{12.50}{\sqrt{156.25}}$$

$$= \frac{12.50}{12.50} = 1$$

The coefficient correlation of 1.00 indicates that there is "*perfect positive correlation*" between the variables x and y.

If the coefficient of correlation is positive, but of value less than 1.00 it still indicates a positive correlation, but not a perfect positive correlation.

Consider the following set of values for x and y.

x	y
1	2.50
2	4.00
3	6.50
4	11.00

$\bar{x} = 2.5 \qquad \bar{y} = 6.00$

In the above set of values for x and y, as the value of x increases, the value of y also increases. Thus, there is a positive correlation between x and y. However, an increase in the value of x is not reflected by a proportionate increase in the value of 'y'. Hence, the value of coefficient of correlation for this set of values will be less than 1.00 indicating an imperfect positive correlation.

x	y	$(x-\bar{x})$	$(y-\bar{y})$	$(x-\bar{x})^2$	$(y-\bar{y})^2$	$(x-\bar{x})\cdot(y-\bar{y})$
1	2.5	−1.5	−3.5	2.25	12.25	5.25
2	4.0	−0.5	−2.0	0.25	4.00	1.00
3	6.5	0.5	0.5	0.25	0.25	0.25
4	10.0	1.5	5.0	2.25	25.00	7.50
			$\sum\Rightarrow$	5.00	41.50	14.00

$$\gamma_{x,y} = \frac{\Sigma(x-\overline{x})\cdot(y-\overline{y})}{\sqrt{\Sigma(x-\overline{x})^2\cdot\Sigma(y-\overline{y})^2}}$$

$$\gamma_{x,y} = \frac{14.00}{\sqrt{(5.00).(41.50)}}$$

$$\gamma_{x,y} = \frac{14.00}{\sqrt{207.50}}$$

$$= \frac{14.00}{14.4049}$$

$$= 0.97$$

*A Coefficient of correlation of **0.97** indicates a positive but imperfect correlation between x and y.*

The degree of imperfection in correlation between two variables is also reflected by the value of the coefficient of correlation. A coefficient of correlation of 0.97 arrived at in the previous example shows a lower degree of imperfection since the value of 0.97 is nearer to 1.00. A coefficient of correlation of, say 0.15 indicates a highly imperfect, but positive correlation.

Consider the following set of values for x and y:

x	y
1	10.00
2	2.50
3	39.00
4	4.50

$\overline{x} = 2.5 \qquad \overline{y} = 14$

x	y	$(x-\overline{x})$	$(y-\overline{y})$	$(x-\overline{x})^2$	$(y-\overline{y})^2$	$(x-\overline{x})\cdot(y-\overline{y})$
1	4	–1.5	–4.00	2.25	16.00	6.00
2	2.5	–0.5	–11.50	0.25	132.25	5.75
3	3.5	0.5	25.00	0.25	625.00	12.50
4	20.00	1.5	–9.50	2.25	90.25	–14.25
			$\Sigma \Rightarrow$	5.00	863.50	10.00

$$\gamma_{x,y} = \frac{\Sigma(x-\overline{x})\cdot(y-\overline{y})}{\sqrt{\Sigma(x-\overline{x})^2\cdot\Sigma(y-\overline{y})^2}}$$

$$\gamma_{x,y} = \frac{10.00}{\sqrt{(5.00)\cdot(863.50)}}$$

$$\gamma_{x,y} = \frac{10.00}{\sqrt{4317.5}}$$

$$= \frac{10.00}{65.71}$$

$$= 0.15$$

The coefficient of correlation of 0.15 indicates imperfect positive correlation. (In fact, it is a highly imperfect positive correlation since the value is $\gamma_{x,y}$ is very much below 1.00.)

A close observation of the set of values for x and y for which we have arrived at a coefficient of correlation of 0.15 indicates that the value of y changes erratically for different values of x though there is a positive correlation i.e., though for every increase in the value of x, there is in the value of y, the increase in the value of y for unit increase in the value of x is either in some proportion, nor follows any pattern but is erotic. Hence, the correlation between the two variables is 'imperfect' though the correlation is positive.

Negative Correlation

Consider the following example:

$$y = 2.5x$$

As the value of x increases the value of y will decrease. Thus there is a negative correlation between x and y.

Let the following are the set of values of x and y based on which the relationship

$y = -2.5x$ was derived.

x	y
1	– 2.50
2	– 5.00
3	– 7.50
4	– 10.00

$\bar{x}$ = (1 + 2 + 3 + 4) ÷ 4 = 2.5

$\bar{y}$ = (–2.50) + (–5.00) + (–7.50) + (–10.00) ÷ 4 = **–6.25**

x	y	$(x-\bar{x})$	$(y-\bar{y})$	$(x-\bar{x})^2$	$(y-\bar{y})^2$	$(x-\bar{x})\cdot(y-\bar{y})$
1	–2.50	–1.50	3.75	2.25	14.0625	–5.625
2	–5.00	–0.50	1.25	0.25	1.5625	–0.625
3	–7.50	0.50	–1.25	0.25	1.5625	–0.625
4	–10.00	1.50	–3.75	2.25	14.0625	–5.625
			$\Sigma \Rightarrow$	5.00	31.250	–12.50

$$\gamma_{x,y} = \frac{-12.50}{\sqrt{(5.00)\cdot(31.25)}}$$

$$\gamma_{x,y} = \frac{-12.50}{\sqrt{156.25}}$$

$$= \frac{-12.5}{12.5}$$

$$= -1$$

A correlation coefficient of – 1.00 indicates perfect negative correlation.

Similarly if for a set of values of variables x and y if the correlation coefficient lies between 0 and –1, it indicates imperfect negative correlation.

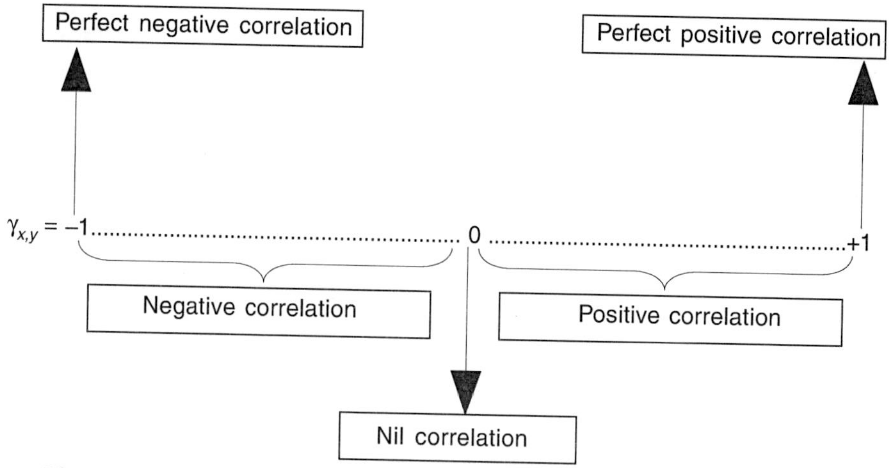

If $\gamma_{x,y} = 0$, it indicates that there exists no correlation between the variables x and y.

$\gamma_{x,y} = 0$ indicates that change in the value of one variable has no effect on the value of the other variable.

Nil Correlation

Consider the following example:

x	y
1	6
2	4
3	4
4	6

x	y	$(x-\bar{x})$	$(y-\bar{y})$	$(x-\bar{x})^2$	$(y-\bar{y})^2$	$(x-\bar{x})\cdot(y-\bar{y})$
1	6	–1.50	2	2.25	4	–3
2	4	–0.50	–2	0.25	4	1
3	4	0.50	–2	0.25	4	–1
4	6	1.50	2	2.25	4	3
			$\sum \Rightarrow$	5.00	16	0

$$\gamma_{x,y} = \frac{\Sigma(x-\overline{x})\cdot(y-\overline{y})}{\sqrt{\Sigma(x-\overline{x})^2\cdot\Sigma(y-\overline{y})^2}}$$

$$\gamma_{x,y} = \frac{0}{\sqrt{(5.00).(16)}}$$

$$\gamma_{x,y} = \frac{0}{\sqrt{80}}$$

$$= 0$$

A correlation coefficient of 'Zero' indicates that the variables x and y are not correlated.

Note: *Covariance and Correlation Coefficient are conceptually similar since both of them express the degree of co-movement between two variables.*

Figure 2.2 shows graphical representation of the correlation between two variables

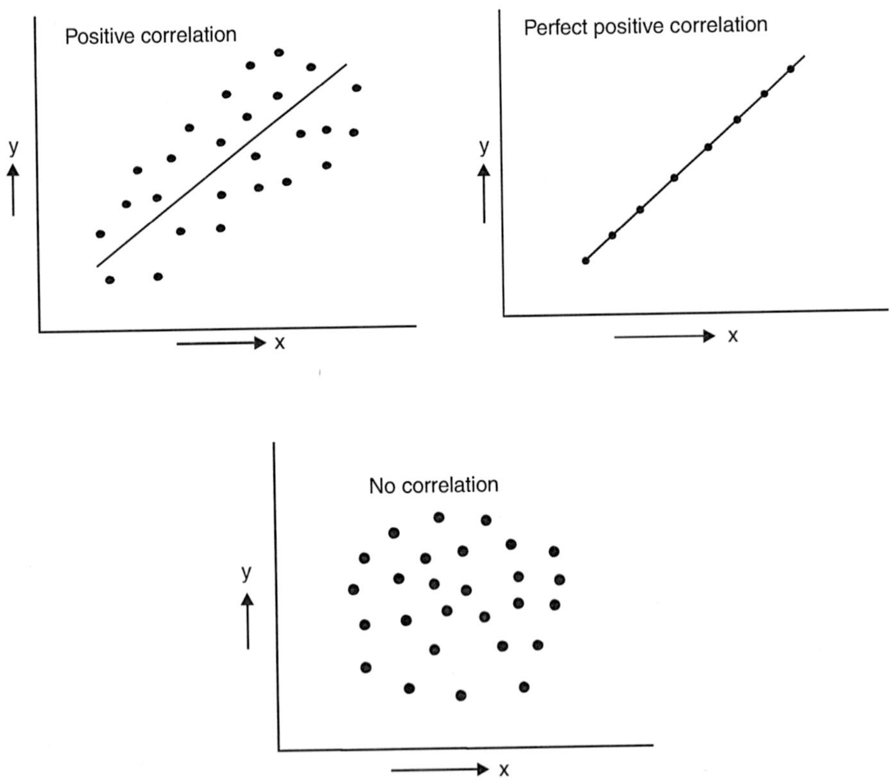

Fig. 2.2 (*Contd....*)

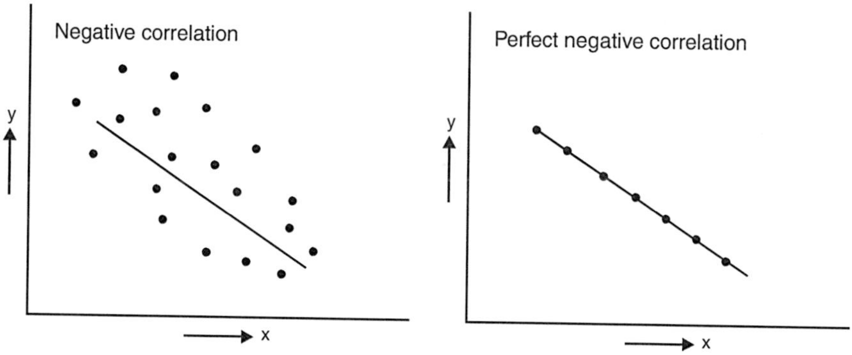

Fig. 2.2 Various types of correlation between two variables

2.6. MEASUREMENT OF SYSTEMATIC RISK

Refer to illustration 2.1. In this illustration we tried to identify the security that is more risky. We used standard deviation as a measure to identify the security that shows wider variation of returns. The returns offered by the securities based on the past data have been used and the variation in returns studied. In illustration 2.1 we observed that though the two securities–A and B offered the same average returns, the returns from security–A showed higher variations. Accordingly the standard deviation of returns from security–A is riskier of the two securities.

Let us recall the definition of 'risk'. It is a measure of the variability in returns. *The standard deviation of returns provides a measure of the total risk associated with a security.* We are aware that the total risk that is contained in a security consists of two components, viz. systematic risk and unsystematic risk. Systematic risk is the measure of variability in returns caused by changes in the economy. Changes in economic conditions bring forth changes in market returns. When the market return changes the returns from individual securities also changes. However, the changes or variations in returns of different securities will not be the same. For a particular change in the market return, the corresponding change in the returns of some securities may be more and that of some offer securities may be less.

The effect of changes in the economic conditions that leads to changes in market return is indicated by the stock market index. *Hence, stock market index in considered as the reference point for measuring systematic risk.* The systematic risk of a security is measured by relating the variability of return of that security with the variability in the stock market index. If relative to the variation in stock market index the returns from security shows higher variations that security is said to have a higher systematic risk and vice versa.

The systematic risk of a security is measurement by a statistical measure called Beta (β). For measuring Beta of a security the standard deviation of the returns of that particular security, the standard deviation of returns of the market (represented by the standard deviation of the stock market index) and the correlation coefficient between the returns of the security and the market return are made use of.

Beta is calculated using the following formula:

$$\beta_i = \frac{\text{Covariance of the security return with the market return}}{\text{Variance of the market return}}$$

For measuring the market return, market index is taken as the reference. Accordingly,

$$\beta_i = \frac{\text{Covariance of the security return with the market index}}{\text{Variance of the market index}}$$

$$\beta_i = \frac{\text{Cov}_{i,m}}{\sigma_m^2}$$

where $\text{Cov}_{i,m}$ = Covariance of the return of security 'i' with the market index 'm' and

and σ_m^2 = Variance of stock market index

Since, covariance between the return of an individual stock and the stock market index can also be written as the product of Correlation Coefficient and the standard deviations of the individual stock return and the market index,

[i.e., $\text{Cov}_{i,m} = \gamma_{i,m}\,\sigma_i\,\sigma_m$], we can write

$$\beta_i = \frac{\gamma_{i,m}\sigma_i\sigma_m}{\sigma_m^2}$$

where

β_i = beta of a security 'i'.

$\gamma_{i,m}$ = correlation coefficient between the return of the security 'i' and the stock market index.

σ_i = standard Deviation of returns of security 'i'.

σ_m = standard Deviation of stock market index.

σ_m^2 = variance of stock market index.

Since, Standard Deviation is the square root of variance, the above formula can also be stated as

$$\beta_i = \frac{\gamma_{i,m}\sigma_i}{\sigma_m}$$

Note on Standard Deviation, Variance, Covariance: *When there are 'n' data, while arriving at the Standard Deviation, (or Variance), the term 'n' comes in the denominator. Accordingly, the formula for Standard Deviation is given by,*

$$\sigma_x = \sqrt{\frac{\Sigma(x - \overline{x})^2}{n}}$$

Coming to the problem of arriving at the Standard Deviation or Variance of a security, we rely upon the past data on returns given by the security. From out of the available past data, we choose a few of the data and make use of them for arriving at the Standard Deviation/Variance. Since, we do not (and cannot) use all the available past data in arriving at the required statistical indicators, the value of Standard Deviation/Variance that is arrived at may not be exactly equal to the true value of Standard deviation/Variance. The Standard Deviation/Variance calculated by making use of a few data from among the available data is similar to calculating the Standard Deviation/Variance using a sample taken from a large population. Except for the rare cases where the sample Standard Deviation/Variance happens to be equal to the population Standard Deviation/Variance, the Standard Deviation/Variance calculated using the sample data will be closer to the actual Standard Deviation/Variance of the population. It will be slightly greater than the actual Standard Deviation/Variance of the population. Hence, to correct the error, the term '(n – 1)' is used in the denominator instead of 'n' in the formula for arriving at the Standard Deviation/Variance. Using the term '(n – 1)' in the formula gives an unbiased estimate of the Standard Deviation/Variance.

We know that the formula for arriving at the covariance between two variables 'A' and 'B' is given by the following relationship.

$$Cov_{A,B} = \frac{\Sigma(x_A - \overline{x}_A)\cdot(x_B - \overline{x}_B)}{n}$$

The term of 'n' in the denominator is to be replaced with '(n – 1)' when we want to find out the Covraiance between the returns offered by two variables. This is because we will be using only a sample data to arrive at an inference about the population. In other words, we will be using a few data showing the relationship between the returns offered by the two securities and will be attempting to establish the true relationship between the two variables.

In the formula that directly arrives at the value of Correlation coefficient the 'n' [or '(n – 1)'] in the numerator gets cancelled by the 'n' [or '(n – 1)'] in the denominator and hence the term 'n' or '(n – 1)' does not appear in the formula.

However, when we have only a few sets of data available and when there are no other sets of data in existence at all, the question of 'inference' does not arise. Whatever value calculated (of Standard Deviation, Variance, Covariance etc.,) will be the true value. Under such circumstances the term in the denominator will only be 'n' and not '(n – 1)'.

***Illustration* 2.6:**

The rate of return on a given stock and the return from the market portfolio for 10 periods are as given below.

Period	Return from stock (%)	Return from market portfolio (%)
1	12	10
2	11	9
3	10	7
4	13	12
5	13	11
6	12	11
7	11	8
8	10	7
9	10	9
10	9	8

Calculation β for the security.

Solution:

$$\beta \text{ for the security. } (\beta_s) = \frac{\gamma_{s,m}\sigma_s}{\sigma_m}$$

let r_s = return from the security

and r_m = return from the market

$$\bar{r}_s = \frac{\Sigma r_s}{n} = \frac{111}{10} = 11.10$$

$$\bar{r}_m = \frac{\Sigma r_m}{n} = \frac{92}{10} = 9.20$$

Period	r_s	r_m	$(r_s - \bar{r}_s)$	$(r_s - \bar{r}_s)^2$	$(r_m - \bar{r}_m)$	$(r_m - \bar{r}_m)^2$	$(r_s - \bar{r}_s)\cdot(r_m - \bar{r}_m)$
1	12	10	0.90	0.81	0.80	0.64	0.72
2	11	9	−0.10	0.01	−0.20	0.40	0.02
3	10	7	−1.10	1.21	−2.20	4.84	2.42
4	13	12	1.90	3.61	2.80	7.84	5.32
5	13	11	1.90	3.61	1.80	3.24	3.42
6	12	11	0.90	0.81	1.80	3.24	1.62
7	11	8	−0.10	0.01	−1.20	1.44	0.12
8	10	7	−1.10	1.21	−2.20	4.84	2.42
9	10	9	−1.10	1.21	−0.20	0.04	0.22
10	9	8	−2.10	4.41	−1.20	1.44	2.52
$\sum \Rightarrow$	111	92		16.90		27.96	18.80

Correlation coefficient between r_s and r_m is given by

$$\gamma_{s,m} = \frac{\Sigma(r_s - \bar{r}_s)\cdot(r_m - \bar{r}_m)}{\sqrt{\Sigma(r_s - \bar{r}_s)^2\cdot(r_m - \bar{r}_m)^2}}$$

$$\gamma_{s,m} = \frac{18.80}{\sqrt{16.90 \times 27.96}}$$

$$= \frac{18.80}{21.74}$$

$$= 0.86$$

Standard deviations of returns from security is given by (σ_s)

$$= \sqrt{\frac{\Sigma(r_s - \bar{r}_s)^2}{n-1}}$$

$$= \sqrt{\frac{16.9}{(10-1)}}$$

$$= 1.37$$

Standard deviations of returns from market portfolio is given by (σ_m)

$$= \sqrt{\frac{\Sigma(r_m - \bar{r}_m)^2}{n-1}}$$

$$= \sqrt{\frac{27.96}{(10-1)}}$$

$$= 1.76$$

$$\beta \text{ for the security } (\beta_s) = \frac{\gamma_{s,m}\sigma_s}{\sigma_m}$$

$$= \frac{0.86 \times 1.37}{1.76}$$

$$= 0.67$$

***Illustration* 2.7:**

Calculate the covariance of the returns from stock 'A' with the market return and the correlation coefficient between the stock and the market. Also find the 'Beta' value of stock 'A'.

Period	Return from Stock 'A' (%)	Return given by the market portfolio(%)	Period	Return from Stock 'A' (%)	Return given by the market portfolio(%)
1	12	15	6	8	9
2	11	13	7	3	5
3	13	17	8	7	9
4	9	11	9	5	6
5	10	14	10	6	7

Solution:

Covariance between the returns from stock 'A' and the market returns is given by,

$$\text{Cov}_{a,m} = \frac{\Sigma(r_a - \bar{r}_a)\cdot(r_m - \bar{r}_m)}{n-1}$$

Mean return from stock 'A'($\bar{r}_a$)= [12 + 11 + 13 + 9 + 10 +8 + 3 + 7 + 5 + 6]/10

= 8.40

Mean of Market return ($\bar{r}_m$) = [15 + 13 + 17 + 11 + 14 + 9 + 5 + 9 + 6 + 7]/10

= 10.60

Period	$(r_a - \bar{r}_a)$	$(r_m - \bar{r}_m)$	$(r_a - \bar{r}_a)\cdot(r_m - \bar{r}_m)$
1	3.60	4.40	15.84
2	2.60	2.40	6.24
3	4.60	6.40	29.44
4	0.40	0.40	0.16
5	1.40	3.40	4.76
6	(–)0.40	(–)1.60	0.64
7	(–)5.40	(–)5.60	30.24

Contd...

8	(–)1.40	(–)1.60	2.24
9	(–)3.40	(–)4.60	15.64
10	(–)2.40	(–)3.60	8.64
			$\sum$=113.84

Hence, Covariance = 113.84/(10 – 1)

= 12.649

The value of Beta of security 'A' is given by

$$\beta_a = \frac{\text{Cov}_{a,m}}{\sigma_m^2}$$

$$\sigma_m^2 = \frac{\Sigma(r_m - \bar{r}_m)^2}{(n-1)}$$

Period	$(r_m - \bar{r}_m)$	$(r_m - \bar{r}_m)^2$
1	4.40	19.36
2	2.40	5.76
3	6.40	40.96
4	0.40	0.16
5	3.40	11.56
6	(–)1.60	2.56
7	(–)5.60	31.36
8	(–)1.60	2.56
9	(–)4.60	21.16
10	(–)3.60	12.96
		$\sum$= 148.40

Hence, σ_m^2 = 148.40/(10 – 1)

= 16.489

β_a = 12.649/16.489

= 0.767

REVIEW QUESTIONS

1. What is systematic risk and what are its main components?
2. Define the term 'Unsystematic risk'.
3. How does interest rate risk affect the price of equity shares?
4. In order to reduce Business risk, a firm should attempt to keep its fixed costs to the minimum. Explain the statement with an example.
5. Explain how inflation affects the 'Purchasing power risk' associated with debentures.

6. Define the terms 'Covariance' and 'Correlation coefficient' and indicate the relationship between them.
7. What are the points to be considered in deciding upon the presence and quantum of debt capital in the capital structure of a firm?
8. The returns offered by two securities 'X' and 'Y' during five successive years are given below:

Return from security–X	Return from security–Y
16%	9%
13%	12%
17%	24%
19%	14%
15%	21%

Find out which of the two securities has a higher risk.

9. What do you mean by 'Perfect positive correlation' between two variables?
10. Define 'Beta' of a stock. Find the 'Beta' of stock –X from the data given below.

Period	Return from stock –X (%)	Return from stock Market (%)
1	13	15
2	14	15
3	12	17
4	13	16
5	15	18
6	16	19
7	18	20
8	17	18
9	15	17
10	14	16

3 CHAPTER Fundamental Analysis

3.1. INTRODUCTION

Investment in securities is made with the objective of earning some return on the investment. The return from a share consists of two components, viz., the periodical dividends offered on the share and the appreciation in the price of the share at the time of its disposal. Any investor is interested to know the likely dividend that he will be getting and the likely appreciation in the price of the share in future, before committing his/her investment on shares. Though there values cannot be predicted exactly, they can be estimated with a reasonable degree of accuracy. By estimating the likely dividends and the likely future price of a security, we try to assess the "intrinsic value" of that security. Fundamental analysis is all about estimating the 'intrinsic value' of a security. The word 'fundamental' is used because the analysis studies the fundamental factors that influence the intrinsic value of a security. The fundamental factors that influence the intrinsic value of a security are the performance of the company, the performance of the industry and the performance of the economy as a whole. Thus, fundamental analysis consists of three stages, viz.

(*a*) Economy analysis

(*b*) Industry analysis

(*c*) Company analysis.

Hence, we can define fundamental analysis of securities as that analysis that studies the fundamental factors relating to the economy, the industry and the company in order to arrive at the intrinsic value of the security. The fundamental analysis forbids buying or selling securities on the basis of rumours and guess work. If advises the investor to analyse the fundamental factors that decide the intrinsic value of securities. The three tier analysis is recommended since a company is not in isolation. A company belongs to an industry. Hence, apart from analyzing the company's fundamentals, the industry's fundamentals are also to be analysed. Suppose we want to assess the intrinsic value of shares of a company manufacturing automobile tyres. There are many companies engaged in the similar manufacturing activity and all such tyre manufacturing companies form an "industry". Hence, the fundamentals of the tyre industry as a whole are also to be analysed. This apart, the tyre industry is only one segment of the overall economy. Hence, the fundamentals of the economy affect the tyre industry also. For example, if there is a boom in the economy, just like many other industries that register a boom in their performance, the tyre industry will also register a growth. The reverse will be the case if the economy is going through recession. Thus, the three types of analysis, viz., economy analysis, industry analysis and company analysis are interrelated and all the three are to be carried out to arrive at a realistic value of a particular security. Figure 3.1 shows the stages of fundamental analysis.

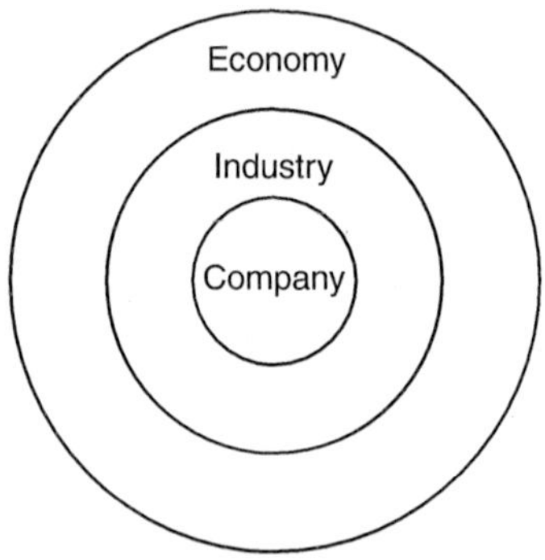

Fig. 3.1 Stages of fundamental analysis

3.2. INTRINSIC VALUE VERSUS MARKET VALUE

The intrinsic value of a security, as arrived at by fundamental analysis may or may not be equal to its market value. Fundamental analysis relies on intrinsic value and suggests that if the intrinsic value and the market value are different, the investor can take advantage of this and earn extra return. If the market price of a security is less than its intrinsic, the security is considered to be under-priced and hence the security can be purchased at the market price. Similarly, if the market price of a security is more than the intrinsic value, the security is considered to be over-priced and hence the security should be sold (if the investor holds the security in his portfolio) to reap extra benefits.

3.3. ECONOMY ANALYSIS

Economy analysis refers to the study of the economic factors. Economy analysis is of relevance since each company is a part of an industry which in turn is a part of the economy. If the economy is in boom, the performance of the companies will be good and if the economy is in recession, the performance of the companies will be generally poor. As a corollary to this statement, it can be said that when the performance of companies in the different sectors of the economy improves the economy as a whole will be in boom and when the performance of companies in the different sectors of the company falls down, the economy as a whole will fall into recession. The following are some of the major economic factors that influence the performance of the different sectors in the economy:

(*a*) Agriculture
(*b*) Population
(*c*) Interest rate
(*d*) Natural resources
(*e*) Government policies/Government spending, revenues
(*f*) Foreign trade, balance of payments and exchange rate
(*g*) Inflation
(*h*) National income
(*i*) Demographic factors
(*j*) Stability of government
(*k*) Level of savings
(*l*) Infrastructural facilities
(*m*) Research and development activities.

Agriculture

Agriculture and industry have strong forward and backward linkages. If the agricultural sector performs well, the agricultural income increases. This will lead to increase in the demand for industrial products and services and hence the industrial sector will register growth. Thus, the performance of companies engaged in the manufacture of industrial goods will improve. In spite of advancements in science and technology, agriculture still depends on monsoon, especially in an agrarian economy like India. Failure of monsoon means failure of agriculture which in turn means failure of industrial sector. Hence, if the monsoon is good, industrial climate is favourable and investors are attracted towards investment in shares of companies. This is more so in an agrarian economy. Similarly, when the performance of agricultural sector suffers due to the failure of monsoon, it is bound to have its effect on the industrial sector as well.

Population

The domestic demand for a product/service depends upon the size of the population of the country. When the population grows the demand for all goods and services grows. Further, high growth in population leads to the availability of cheaper labour which has a direct influence on the cost of production. Increase in population coupled with purchasing power increases the size of the market.

Interest Rate

When the interest rate that prevails in an economy is low, it makes cheaper credit available to companies operating in the economy. When the interest rate is high, cost of credit will also be high, which will affect the profitability of companies. Lower the rate of interest, lower the cost of credit. Lower the cost of credit, lower the cost of production of companies that have relied on debt capital to a smaller or greater extent. Lower the cost of production, higher the profitability of companies. Higher the profitably, higher the intrinsic value shares of the company, leading to increase in the price of shares of the company.

Interest rate in the organized financial sector, both short-term and long-term interest rates are to a larger extent determined by the monetary policy of the government. The interest rate in the unorganized sector, however, fluctuates purely on the basis of demand and supply of funds in the market. It is the interest rate prevailing in the organized financial sector that is more relevant since companies rely more on this sector for their credit requirements. A prudent investor will observe the current interest rates and the likely changes in the interest rates in the future on the basis of the Government's monetary policy.

Natural Resources

A country that is rich in natural resources has the inherent potential to prosper. Once the available natural resources are extracted and put into productive use, it will make the economy vibrant and the industrial activity will flourish. A country that possesses limited natural resources has to rely more upon value addition for making its economy prosper. In such a country, industries that offer value-addition to products alone will have good scope. Thus, the availability or otherwise of natural resources has a great bearing on the prospects of an economy.

Government Policies

Policies of government have great impact on the economic development of a country. For example, credit policy that accommodates the demands of the business community will favour the growth of business activities. A tax policy that offers liberal incentives for savings and investment will also favour the growth of business activities. Annual budgets of the Government point to the sectors where investments are planned. Long-term plans of the Government spell out the priority sectors for investment and this can provide investors with broad guidelines plan their investment. Annual budgets of the Government give details of the proposed Government spending and revenue generation. Since, the Government's spending is substantial, it will create a major demand in the economy. For example, if the Government proposes to spend heavily on building infrastructure like housing, highways, ports etc., the demand for construction materials like cement, steel etc., will increase.

Foreign Trade, Balance of Payments and Exchange Rate

The price of products that have export market and products that are imported from abroad are affected by the value of currency of the particular country against major currencies of the world. When the value of Indian rupee appreciates against major currencies of the world, Indian goods become costlier internationally. On the other hand, when the value of Indian rupee depreciates against major currencies, Indian goods become cheaper internationally and their competitive position improves. Thus, the demand for Indian goods that are exported varies based on the value of Indian currency vis-à-vis foreign currencies. Similarly, when the Indian currency appreciates against other major currencies, goods that are imported into India become cheaper and vice versa. Thus, the demand for foreign goods that are imported into India also gets affected on the basis of appreciation/depreciation of Indian currency. The appreciation/depreciation of the currency of a country against other major currencies of the world (in other words, the exchange rate of currency of a country with other currencies) are influenced by the Balance of trade, Balance of payment and foreign exchange reserve of a country. Balance of trade is the difference between the value of exports and the value of imports of a country. If the value of exports is more that the value of imports during a particular year, the balance of trade during that year is positive (also called 'favourable'). If the value of imports into a country during a particular year is more than the value of exports from the country, the balance of trade during that year is negative or unfavourable. Balance of trade deficit is the excess of imports over exports. While Balance of trade takes into account only visible exports and imports, Balance of payments takes into account both visible and invisible exports and imports. Balance of payment of country is a record of its monetary transactions for a year with the rest of the world. It includes,

(*a*) The value of visible import and export trade and

(*b*) Invisible exports and imports i.e., value of services rendered and received like transport charges, port duties, financial service charges, banking charges, insurance charges, interest on loans, expenses of tourist etc., and capital transactions like private and inter-government loan transactions, grants, export and import of shares and securities etc.

Thus, balance of payments deficit represents the net difference payable on account of all transactions in a year such as trade, service and capital transactions. Deficit in balance of payments account is unfavourable for a country and there arises a possibility that the currency of the country may depreciate in value. Foreign exchange reserve is the stock of foreign currency held by the domestic central bank. A country needs foreign exchange reserve to meet its commitments for the imports made from other countries and to service foreign debts. The deficit in the balance of payment account is to be met only from the foreign exchange reserve. Hence, continuous deficit in Balance of payment account will erode the foreign exchange reserve. Large foreign exchange reserve helps to increase the value of the home currency against major currencies of the world and also helps to stabilize the value of the home currency. A prudent investor will have to keep track of the changes in the exchange rate of his home currency with major currencies of the world. Likely future trends in the exchange rates can be predicted by analyzing the balance of trade, balance of payments and foreign exchange reserves.

Financial dailies publish the exchange rates of Indian rupee against major currencies of the world. An investor can have an idea about the stability or otherwise of Indian rupee against other currencies by keeping track of the daily exchange rates published.

Inflation

Inflation is a state of the economy in which the prices are raising and the value of money is falling. Inflation is not just high prices, but it is raising prices. It is a process and not a state of prices. If inflation prevails in an economy, it will have its impact on the performance of different industrial sectors. Hence, all companies whether in production, trading or service sector get affected by inflation. When the rate of inflation is high, it will have harmful efforts and will upset business plans. Profit margins in real terms will get reduced due to high rates of inflation. Inflation indicates the rise in the price of a basket of commodities on a point to point basis. It suggests that increase in the cost of living over a period of one year. For example, if a person bought the commodities in the basket on say, 1st March 2005 at Rs. 1000/- and if the same quantity of commodities in the basket costs say, Rs. 1060/- on 1st March 2006, the rate of inflation would be 6.00% (i.e., the price rise between 1st March 2005 and 1st March 2006 is 6.00%). Economists believe that a moderate inflation is good for a growing economy and provides incentive for growth. This is because of the reason that under moderate inflationary conditions, producers are able to increase their revenue; at the same time, if they increase their productivity and cut down their cost, it offers ample scope for increased profits.

Inflation is measured in terms of Wholesale Price Index (WPI) as well as in terms of Consumer Price Index (CPI). WPI is the most widely used price index in India. It is an indicator of the movement in wholesale prices of 435 commodities in all trade and transactions. It is available on a weekly basis with the shortest time lag of two weeks. It is widely used in business and industry circles and by the Government as an indicator of the rate of inflation in the economy. The base year for the WPI which is computed by the Ministry of Commerce and Industry is 1993–94. A revised WPI with a new base year is being worked out by the Government of India.

The consumer price index for industrial workers CPI (IW) is constructed in India on monthly basis, with a lag of one month. This index is constructed by the Ministry of Labour and is used as a measure of cost of living of the people of India. Dearness allowance given to the employees is based on CPI (IW). It measures the changes in retail prices of goods and services covering 260 items of consumption from 70 centers. The base year CPI (IW) is 1982. Updating the index with the base year 2001 is being worked out by the Government.

Reform process was initiated in India in the early 1990s with the primary objective of ensuring price stability. This had helped Indian economy to keep inflation under check. Domestic deregulation and tariff rationaliastion have resulted in greater competition and great cost-efficiency. The annual average inflation rate remained at a double digit figure of 10.60% between 1991–1992 and 1995–1996, which came down to 4.20% between 2001–02 and 2003–04.

An investor should analyse the prevailing rate of inflation in the economy in the past, its trend and its likely course of movement in the future.

The inflation rates based on WPI that prevailed in India in the recent past are given under:

Year	2002–03	2003–04	2004–05	2005–06	2006 07	2007–08	2008–09
Inflation Rate	3.40%	5.50%	6.50%	4.40%	5.40%	4.70%	8.37%

National Income

The total income of a country is called its National Income. National Income data of a country provides a summary statement of the economic activity of that country. Since, the present day economy is money economy. National Income of a country is expressed in monetary terms. Hence, National Income of a country can be defined as the money measures of the net aggregates of all good and services produced by the country during a specific period (usually during a year). National Income is measured in three ways, viz., by measuring the national product, national dividend or national expenditure.

Let us consider national product measure of National Income. National Product consists of all goods and services produced by a country and exchanged for money during a year. It excludes goods and services that are not paid for [such as hobbies, charitable work, services of housewives etc.] National product is expressed in two ways, viz., Gross National Product (GNP) and Net National Product (NNP).

GNP may be defined as the aggregate market value of all final goods and services produced in a country during a given year. The world 'gross' indicates that allowance for depreciation or replacement of capital assets is not given in arriving at the GNP. Further, in arriving at the GNP, only the market value of all final goods/services are accounted for and intermediate products/services are excluded to avoid double counting. GNP includes net exports [i.e. exports minus imports] and Net Factor Income earned from rest of the world. The Net Factor Income from the rest of the world consists of net compensation of employees, net income from properties and entrepreneurship in the form of interest, rent, dividend, profit etc. The word 'Net' stands for the receipts of current income by residents abroad reduced by disbursements of current income in India to non-residents. Thus, GNP represents the measure of economic output in an economic system.

When the Net Factor Income earned from rest of the world is excluded from GNP, the remaining measure is called Gross Domestic Product (GDP). Though GDP excludes net factor income earned from rest of the world, it includes net exports.

Another measure worth noting is the Net National Product (NNP). Machines used in production depreciate in value overtime. Some of them also become obsolete, needing replacement. If depreciation and obsolescence allowance are deducted from the GNP, we get NNP.

In its technical sense, National Income (NI) is obtained by deducting indirect taxes and adding subsidies from the NNP, measured at current market prices. Such a figure arrived at is also called NNP at factor cost. Indirect taxes (for example, Sales Tax) are added to the price of goods. Hence, if we want to know the original price, indirect taxes are to be deducted from the selling price. When a product is sold at a subsidized price, the subsidy portion is borne by the State. The original price will be the selling price plus subsidy. Hence, subsidy is to be added to the selling price to arrive at the original price.

A study of the National Income statistics of a country will give an idea about the economic health of the country. Higher the national income, higher the personal income of the people of the country; higher the personal income, higher the personal consumption expenditure and higher the personal savings. Hence, growth in National Income will stimulate further growth of the economy. If the level of the National Income is high and if it shows increasing trend, it indicates a strong economy and such an economy will offer scope for earning better returns on investment.

Demographic Factors

The term demography refers to the study of population and its characteristics. Study of population and its characteristics help the fundamental analyst in a big way. When the home country has a large population, there will be adequate demand for the goods and services produced. If the population of the home country is thin, then the country has to look for other countries of the world to market its products. The purchasing power of the population, number of males and females in a given population, age groups of the population, customs, tastes, preferences, literacy levels, geographic location etc., also decide to a large extent the types of goods and services that will be demanded by the community and the pattern of demand.

Stability of Government

Political stability is essential for the development of industry. The long-tem requirements of the industry can be adequately addressed only if the country has a stable political setup ensuring stable Government. If the political setup of a country is such that stability of the Government cannot be assured, it will erode investor, confidence in the Government and this will lead to stagnation in the growth of the economy.

Level of Savings

Capital is formed in an economy by way of savings and investment. Capital formation is a function of savings and investment. There must be adequate mechanism to channalise savings into investment. A high level of savings of the household sector, coupled with the assistance of an efficient mechanism, for channelising the savings into investment will accelerate the growth of the industry and the growth of the stock market.

Infrastructural Facilities

For the growth of industry and agriculture, the availability of adequate infrastructure is a prerequisite. Infrastructure consists of wide network of road, railways, airways, availability of electric power, water, communication network, efficient banking system, developed financial service sectors, presence of adequate financial intermediaries etc. The existence of strong infrastructure will aid in improving the efficiency of industrial sector as well as agricultural sector. Absence of adequate infrastructural facilities will act as a bottleneck for the growth of both industry and agriculture. Since, setting up of infrastructural facilities usually requires large investments, the Government has a major role to play in this regard. Hence, an investor, before committing his funds, should look into infrastructural facilities that are available, the Government's initiative and commitment to the development of infrastructural facilities, participation of private sector in the development of infrastructure etc., as these will have their impact on the performance of the economy.

Research and Development Activities

The technological advancement in the industries in an economy depends upon the level of technological advances that have taken place in the economy and the research and development activities that are taking place in the country. Since, Government is the largest investor in supporting research and development activities, investors should identify the sectors in which Government is giving thrust for research and development activities and choose industries in such sectors for investment.

3.3.1. Economic Forecasting

Analysis is the tracing of things to their source and so discovering the general principles underlying individual phenomena. It relates to what has already happened. Economic analysis makes a study on as to how the economy has performed. This is the first stage of study of the economy. But it should be noted that fundamental analysis is carried out not only for knowing as to how the economy has performed but also for predicting as to how the economy will perform in the future. This is because, fundamental analysis is done for ascertaining the scope for investment. Since, investment is a future oriented activity, apart from knowing the performance of the economy, the investor will be equally interested in knowing the expected level of performance of the economy and its various segments. Thus, economic forecasting is a major activity in the study of economy.

Since, National Income is an indicator of the economic health of a nation, economic forecasting is mainly aimed at forecasting the national income likely to be achieved and the various components of the National Income. Since, National Income measures the aggregate sum of all economic activities, it acts as an indicator of the economic health. An investor will be more interested in forecasting the income from the different sectors of the economy that make up the National Income. This is because, it will throw light on the sectors/segments of the economy that promise growth prospects and hence the investor can ascertain whether the expected growth prospects or otherwise of the different sectors of the economy have a bearing on the type of industries in which he is planning to invest.

Economic forecasting can be done for short-term periods, long-term periods or for intermediate term periods.

Forecasting done for periods up to 3 years are generally called short-term forecasting and when the period of forecast extends beyond 5 years, it is termed as long-term forecasting. Forecasting done for periods extending over 3 years and up to 5 years fall under the category of intermediate term forecasting.

I. Short Range Forecasting

The techniques used for short-term forecasting are as follows:

(*a*) Anticipatory surveys

(*b*) Barometric approach

(*c*) Econometric model building

(*d*) Opportunistic model building

(a) Anticipatory surveys

Government, public sector and private sector enterprises plan their activities ahead. They prepare their plan and convert them into financial terms in the form of budgets, which show their expected expenditure. Just as major institutions plan their budget, consumers also plan their budgets in advance. For example, when a person buys a new car for his family, the decision to go for buying a car might have been taken by him in advance sometime before he/she actually buys the car. Survey of intentions of major players in the economy as to their intentions about their likely spending will provide vital information for short-term economic forecasting.

The Government spells out its plans in the form of annual budgets. Since, Government's expenditure forms a sizable portion of the GNP, Government's plans must be considered first. Apart from the Government the other two segments are the producers and consumers. Hence, the survey should cover the producer's anticipated behaviour and the consumer's anticipated behaviour.

From the producer's angle, intention of the trade and industry regarding their planned activities in terms of investments in capital expenditure planned (like the investments in plant and machinery, investments in construction of building, infrastructure etc.) level of inventory proposed to be held etc., can be gathered. Industrial/business firms are queried about their anticipated investment during the next few years and their proposed sectors of investment. From the consumers angle, the consumer expectation surveys and these surveys can be conducted which cover the buying plans of individual consumers, their attitudes, their views on products/services that are available in the market vis-à-vis that are expected by them etc. From the survey results, an analyst can arrive at his own forecast of the future state of the economy and the growth prospects or otherwise of the different sectors of the economy.

Survey techniques have both positive and negative elements. They are helpful to identify psychological elements that are inherent in any most economic behaviour which cannot be correctly quantified. Further, likely changes in consumer tastes and preferences can be brought out only through survey of intentions. However, surveys suffer from the drawback that they cannot be exclusively relied upon since their results will be valid only when the intentions disclosed by the respondents are transformed into action. Thus, there can always be a gap between what was intended and what is done.

(b) Barometric approach

Barometric forecasting is also known as indicator forecasting. Barometer is an instrument that indicates the atmospheric pressure. By looking at the mercury level indicated by the barometer, the meteorologist forecasts the changes in the atmospheric pressure, changes in the weather condition etc.

Similarly, by observing certain economic indicators, we can infer the likely future trend of the economy. Hence, Barometric forecasting is known by the name 'indicator forecasting'. In this approach, different economic indicators are observed and studied and on the basis of the study, an inference about the likely performance of the economy in the future is arrived at. Over 125 years ago Andrew Carnegie is reported to have used the number of smoking industrial chimneys as the basis and forecasted the level of business activity and in turn forecasted the demand for steel. This is an example for indicator approach. The indictors used are 'time series data' on different economic variables.

The indicators can be categorized into three grouped viz.,

- Leading indicators
- Lagging indicators
- Coincidental indicators

Leading indicators

Leading indicators are those time series data that reach their peaks or troughs in advance of the peaks or troughs of the total economic activity. If we measure the total economic activity by, say GDP, the leading indictor will reach its peak before GDP reaches its peak. Similarly, the leading indicator will also reach its trough (By peak we mean a high value and by trough we mean a low value). Thus, the total economic activity will follow the leading indicator. For example, stock market index is a leading indicator of the economy. If the stock market anticipates a depression in the economic activity in the near future, stock prices fall down, bringing down the value of stock market index. Thus, stock market index, in a way, predicts the likely behaviour of the economy and thus, it acts as a leading indicator of the overall economy. Figure 3.2 gives a pictorial representation of Leader indicator.

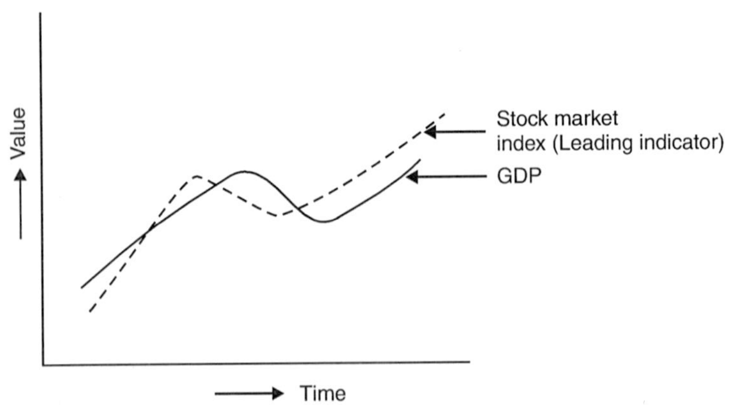

Fig. 3.2 Leading indicator

Lagging indicators

Lagging indicators are those time series data that reach their peaks or troughs after the economy has already reached its own peaks or troughs respectively. If we measure the total economic activity, by say GDP, the lagging indicator will reach its peak after the GDP has reached its peak. Similarly, the lagging indicator will also reach its trough after the GDP has already reached its trough. Thus, the lagging indicator will follow the total economic activity. For example, prime lending rate charged by the banks acts as a lagging indicator. When the overall economic activity declines, the demand for borrowing money from banks also decline leading to a reduction in the prime lending rate charged by the banks. Thus, prime lending rate depicts how the economy has already performed and it lags the overall economic activity. Figure 3.3 gives a pictorial representation of lagging indicator.

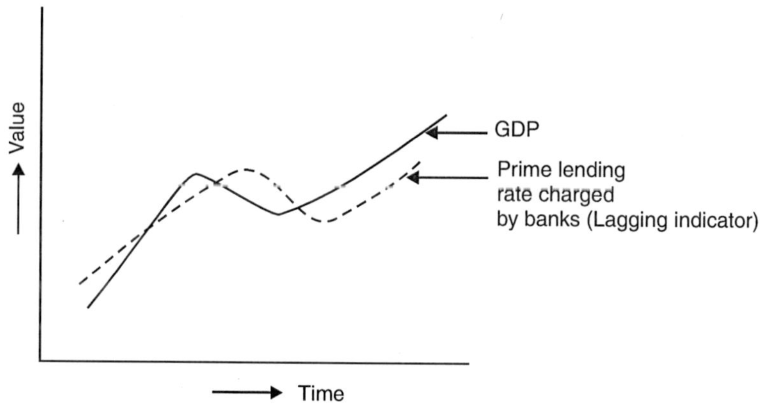

Fig. 3.3 Lagging indicator

Coincidental indicators

Coincidental indicators are those time series data that reach their peaks or troughs nearly at the same time as the economy. If we measure the total economic activity by GDP, the coincidental indicator will reach its peaks or troughs approximately at the same time when the GDP reaches its peaks or troughs. For example, index of total industrial production is a coincidental indicator. Coincidental indicator reflects the present state of economy. Figure 3.4 gives a pictorial representation of coincidental indicator.

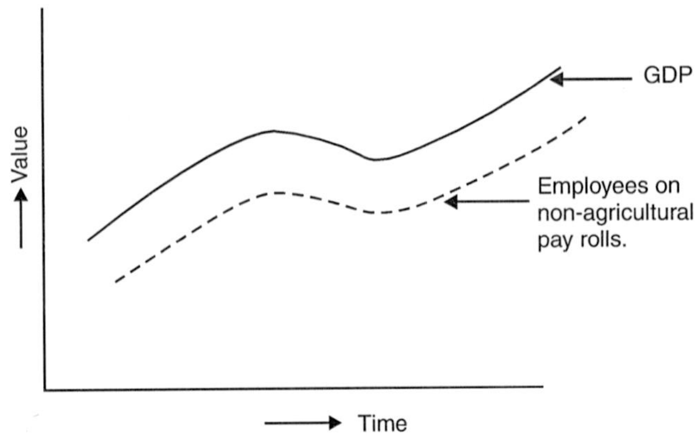

Fig. 3.4 Coincidental indicator

Of the three types of indictors, the leading indicators are more useful for economic forecasting since they help in predicting the trend of the economy. Of the other two indicators, the coincidental indicator gives an immediate confirmation of the economic prediction made using the leading indicator, while the lagging indicator gives a belated confirmation of the prediction.

The indicator approach has its advantage in the sense that it offers a quick and simple method to forecast the economy. Another advantage is that the prediction arrived at using leading indicators can be confirmed using coincidental and lagging indicators. However, the indicator approach also suffers from certain drawbacks. Some of the drawbacks of the indicator approach are as under.

(*a*) It aids in forecasting the direction of activity. However, it cannot precisely indicate the magnitude of the movement/change.

(*b*) There are many leading indicators identified. However, it cannot be taken for granted that all the leading indicators will behave alike. While some leading indicators give a strong signal, some may give a very weak signal and some other may even give opposite signals. When two leading indicators give conflicting signals, the forecasting based on any one of the signals is prone to have errors.

(*c*) The prediction of the economy based on leading indicators should be done by collecting the data on the leading indicators quickly and forecasting the economy without any delay. Delay in forecasting will defeat the very purpose of indicators.

The National Bureau of Economic Research (NBER), New York is a private non-profit research organization set up with the objective of ascertaining and presenting to the public important economic facts and their interpretation in a scientific and impartial manner. A shortlist of the economic indicators identified by the NBER is given below:

Leading indicators

- ⇨ Index of stock prices of 500 common stocks
- ⇨ New contracts and orders for plant and machinery
- ⇨ Number of new building permits issued
- ⇨ Money supply (M_2)
- ⇨ Average weekly hours of manufacturing workers engaged in production
- ⇨ Average weekly initial claims for state unemployment insurance
- ⇨ New orders for consumer goods and materials
- ⇨ Corporate profits after taxes
- ⇨ Changes in inventories on hand and on order.
- ⇨ Changes in prices of sensitive materials
- ⇨ Changes in credit level (both business and consumer borrowing)
- ⇨ Index of net business formation

Lagging indicators

- ⇨ Average duration of unemployment
- ⇨ Average prime lending rate charged by banks
- ⇨ Commercial and industrial loan outstanding
- ⇨ Ratio of manufacturing and trade inventories to sales
- ⇨ Labour cost per unit of manufacturing output
- ⇨ Ratio of consumer instalment credit to personal income
- ⇨ Business expenditure on plants and equipments

Coincidental indicators

- ⇨ Employees on non-agricultural payrolls
- ⇨ Personal income (less transfer payments)
- ⇨ Index of total industrial production
- ⇨ Manufacturing and trade sales
- ⇨ Sales of retail stores

Diffusion index

When the leading indicators give conflicting signals (which is not a rare case), there arises the need to summarize their net indication since relying on any one indicator may make the forecast wrong. To overcome this situation, the National Bureau of Economic Research had developed a method called the diffusion index.

The diffusion index is the percentage of members of a set of series that is moving upwards. Its value ranges from zero to hundred. When all the members of the series are moving upwards its value is hundred. When all the members of the series are moving downwards, its value is zero. Thus, the diffusion index indicates the extensiveness of an expansion or contraction. Considering all the leading indicators as a set, when the economy is expanding, most of the leading indicators will be moving upwards. Similarly when the economy is contracting, most of the leading indicators will be moving downwards. Changes in the value of diffusion index provide useful indication about the movement of the total economic activity. For example, let the economy is in an expansion phase. Since, most of the leading indicators are also expected to be moving upwards, the value of diffusion index may lie close to 100. Let the value of diffusion index stands at 95 for a few months. It indicates that during the past few months the economy has been expanding. If suddenly the value of the diffusion index begins to fall, it gives a warning signal that some of the leading indicators have reversed their upward trend and started falling down. Such an indication points out that shortly there is going to be a general decline in the overall economic activity.

(*c*) Econometric model building

Econometrics is a discipline for devising ways to represent abstract theoretical relationships arrived from the study of economics in terms of specific empirical relationships. Hence, econometric method of forecasting the economy combines economic theory with statistical and mathematical tools in order to help analyse economic relationships. It is a more precise technique of forecasting. The econometric models used for economic forecasting are usually complex in nature. This is because the inter-relationships between the different economic variables are complex. Economic variable can be grouped into two categories viz., dependent and independent variables. The relationships between the dependent and independent economic variables are arranged in the form of mathematical equations. The set of equations thus formed are then solved which gives a precise forecast of the economy.

In this method, the forecaster should have the acumen to identify the dependent and independent economic variables and to define correctly the interrelationships between these economic variables. The accuracy of forecast mainly depends on the accuracy of the assumptions made by the forecaster regarding the interrelationship among the economic variables. Moreover, the accuracy of forecasting also depends on the validity and quality of input data based on which the forecast is made.

Econometric models can be of two types, viz., (*a*) Single equation models and (*b*) Multiple equations models. In single equation models for economic forecasting, the relationships among the different economic variables are expressed in only one equation. For example, if the GDP of a country is a function of economic variables A, B, C and D a simple linear model expressing this relationship is written as follows:

$$\text{GDP} = a_0 + a_1 \cdot \text{A} + a_2 \cdot \text{B} + a_3 \cdot \text{C} + a_4 \cdot \text{D}$$

Forming the relationship among the economic variables (as shown above) is the first step. The next step is to estimate the parameters, i.e., the values of a_0, a_1, a_2, a_3, a_4,.... The most frequently used technique for estimating the value of the parameters is the Least Squares regression analysis with time-series data.

When the interrelationships between the economic variables used in the model are very complex, a single equation model may not be adequate to handle the problem. In such cases, a multiple equations model can be of use. Multiple equations model can be of use. Multiple equations model consists of two basic kinds of equations. They are definitional equations (or identities) and behavioural equations. The definitional equations express the relationship between the economic variables that are true by definition. The behavioural equation expresses how the variables in a system interact with one another.

Compared to other methods of forecasting, econometric models are expected to give more accurate results since they are based on formulation of relationships among the economic variables in a scientific way. Also econometric models are amenable for further improvement. A forecaster can compare the results obtained using the model with the actual results and can identify the ways to obtain more accurate results. Consequently, the forecaster can introduce the required modifications in the model and improve its reliability and acceptability. Unlike barometric methods that predict only the direction of change, econometric models give both the direction and the magnitude of expected changes.

The limitations of econometric models are that they are generally highly complex and they require vast volume of data to be collected and processed for arriving at the solution.

(*d*) Opportunistic model building

The word 'opportunistic' is not used with any wrong connotation. It only means that the forecaster takes advantage of all opportunities. He is expected to make use of all sources of information that are available before him and he is not expected to restrict himself to any particular technique or model for carrying out the analysis. Since, this method uses all sorts of information, the method is expected to perform better than other specific techniques of forecasting. However, the ability of the forecaster plays a vital role since the method is adhoc in nature and does not follow any particular technique. The accuracy of results obtained by this approach depends very much upon the intuition and judgment of the forecaster. This is a popularly used model and is also known as GNP Model Building or Sectorial Analysis. The basic assumption in DNP Model Building is that business activity is governed by demand. If the demand increases, total spending increases which gives rise to increase in business activity. Hence, the forecaster must hypothesize the total demand first. Based on the forecasted demand, the forecaster arrives at the total income during the forecast period. The forecaster forecasts the GNP for the forecast period by taking into account the prevailing economic conditions like the present level of GNP, the economic and fiscal policies of the Government, the prevailing interest rates, the existing tax structure, the rate of inflation etc. Next, the forecaster tries to build up another forecast of the GNP, this time by breaking up the GNP figure into its various components. He splits the GNP into its basic component like consumption expenditure, gross private domestic investment, purchase of goods and services by the Government and net exports. Based on the economic conditions, he forecast each component of the GNP for the forecast period and adds them up to arrive at the GNP forecast.

The forecaster then compares the two GNP forecasts and makes necessary adjustments to smooth out the difference and to make the two forecasts agree.

II. Long Range Forecasting

Anticipatory survey, barometric approach, econometric model building, opportunistic model building etc., are useful for forecasting for periods up to about 3 to 5 years. In the long run, these forecasts may not remain valid. Long range forecasting still remains an art and reliable techniques have not yet evolved. Long range forecasting deals with perceived forces that interact in complex ways. Changes in cultural trends, political trends, demographic trends etc., are studied and their effects on the economy are analysed for arriving at long range forecasts. Though no formal model exists for long range forecasting, the process of long range forecasting can be broken up into the following five phases.

Phase – I

Identifying the principal environmental forces, projecting, extrapolating the principal environmental factors one at a time, taking into account the potential breakthroughs and developments.

Phase – II

Analyzing the potentials for interaction among the principal environmental forces; studying the effect of interaction which may either reinforce or refard the trend originally projected; making adjustments in the forecasts taking into account the effect of interaction among the environmental forces.

Phase – III

Considering the effort of simultaneous environmental changes resulting from the adjusted trends on the business conditions.

Phase – IV

Appraising the social response to the anticipated changes in business environment.

Phase – V

Studying the possible relationships of social response to the evolving ecology and developing apparent states of future economic and business trends.

3.3.2. Sources of Information on Indian Economy

The sources of information on the economy that are relevant for economy analysis are given in Table 3.1.

Table 3.1 Sources of economic information

S. No.	Source	Published by	Contents
1.	Census of India	Registrar General & Census Commissioner, Govt. of India.	Demographic and economic characteristics of Indian Republic like population growth rate, male-female ratio, population density, rural-urban distribution, broad age groups, fertility and mortality rates etc.
2.	National sample survey reports	National sample survey organization	Maintenance of sampling frame, selection of samples and preparation of sample lists. Annual survey of industries, Socio-economic surveys, Follow-up surveys of economic census.
3.	Plan reports	Planning Commission, Govt. of India.	National plans, State plans, Financial targets, Actual outlays, Achievements, Human development reports, Reports on technology innovation and venture capital, On-going major projects, Plan statistics etc.
4.	Statistical abstract of the Indian Union	Central Statistical Organization	Estimates of National income, Industrial and agricultural statistics, Consumer price index, Wholesale price index, Environment statistics, Energy statistics, Social statistics, Gender statistics etc.
5.	India Year Book	Ministry of Information and Broadcasting	Data on economic affairs, agriculture, finance, environmental, energy, education, defence, scientific and technological developments, major events that took place during the year etc.
6.	Economic survey	Ministry of Finance	Data on public finance, Security markets, Monetary and banking, developpments, Wholesale and consumer prices, Food management, Industry, Agriculture, Infrastructure, Social sectors etc.
7.	Annual survey of industries	Central statistical organization	Industry related data

Contd...

8.	Annual bulletin of statistics of exports and imports	Ministry of Commerce	Commodity-wise and country-wise data on exports and imports.
9.	Techno economic surveys	National Council of Applied Economic Research	Techno economic surveys of various states
10.	Quarterly review of economy	National Council of Applied Economic Research	Performance and forecast on agriculture, industry, services, capital and money markets, public finance, external sectors etc.
11.	Industry potential surveys	IDBI	Potential survey on industries
12.	RBI Bulletin	RBI	Exchange rates, balance of payments, production indices etc.

3.4. INDUSTRY ANALYSIS

The term 'industry' refers to a group of firms producing similar or reasonably similar products. For example, textile industry includes spinning mills, weaving mills, dyeing units, textile processing units, garment manufacturing units etc. In an economy, there will be many industries. Textile, pharmaceutical, steel, automobile, chemical, food processing etc., are some of the major industries.

The prospects of a company depend on the fortunes of the industry to which the company belongs. Hence, an investor, before analyzing the company in which he is going to invest, has to analyse the industry to which the company belongs. If a particular industry has good scope for improved performance, a company belonging to that industry is also expected to perform well unless the company has some inherent weakness that may affect its performance. When a particular industry shows signs of growth, it offers a strong foundation for the different companies belonging to that industry to perform well. For example, let us assume that textile industry is found to have excellent growth prospects for the next ten years. This conclusion could have been arrived at only after studying and analyzing various factors that have a bearing on the performance of the textile industry. When the textile industry is expected to perform well for the next ten years, it reveals that the different firms/companies that are operating in the textile sector are also having goods scope for showing better performance for the next ten years.

In fundamental analysis, the analyst first studies the economy. He then studies the different industries (also called sectors) in the economy. After analyzing the industry, he then moves to the study of companies. Thus, he moves towards the company that has better prospects for improved performance by studying the economy first and the different industrial sectors in the economy next and then analyzing the companies that pertain to promising industrial sectors. If a particular industry show signs of stagnation or decline, the companies belonging to that industry can be safely avoided for investment. Though a few companies may perform well due to specific inherent strengths despite the concerned industry performing badly, the threat for their performance getting affected will very much prevail since the macro level factors will not be favourable for their sustained performance.

3.4.1. Components of Industry Analysis

Industry analysis can be performed by studying the factors affecting industries on the basis of the following three heads:

(*a*) Industry life cycle characteristics

(*b*) Analysis of industry characteristics

(*c*) Government's policies on industry.

(*a*) Industry life cycle characteristics

Every product is found to have a life cycle. Since, an industry is made up of firms producing same or similar category of products every industry also has a life cycle.

Industries have been found to go through the following four stages:

1. Pioneering stage
2. Rapid growth stage
3. Maturity and stabilization stage
4. Declining stage

The above four stages make a complete life cycle for an industry. (Refer Fig. 3.5)

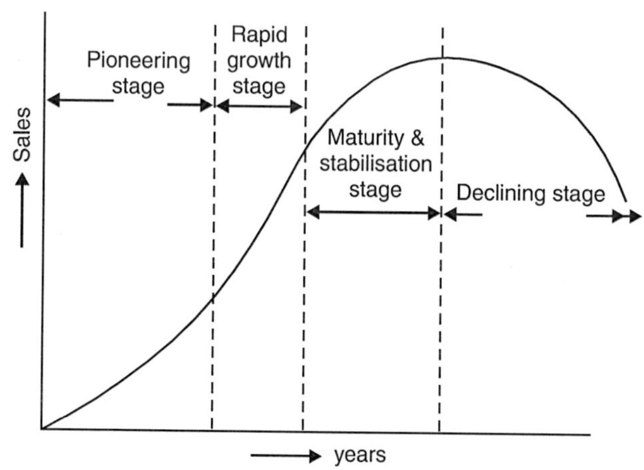

Fig. 3.5 The industry life cycle

1. ***Pioneering stage:*** This is the first stage in the life cycle. Let us assume that a new product is introduced in the market. The product might not have reached a state of perfection. Still, the product being new might be demanded by the consumers. Increasing demand will also offer attractive returns. Attracted by the high demand, many producers will enter the field which will bring about severe competition among producers. Non-price competition will be the characteristics of the pioneering stage, since the competitors will not be interested to bring the price down as they won't be prepared to sacrifice their profit. Non-price competition in the form of product differentiation will prevail and the competitors will try to make their products unique by building up a brand name for their product. As a large number of competitors will be attempting to capture a sizable market share for their product, firms that are weak will get eliminated from the market and only strong firms will survive the pioneering stage. Though a large number of firms would have entered the market, only a few of them will be successful in fighting the stiff competition and still survive. Since, a large number of firms that enter the field but that are not strong enough to withstand the competition will be eliminated, any investment made by investors in such weak firms will be lost forever. Moreover, in the pioneering stage, it will be also a difficult exercise to spot those firms that would stand competition and survive. Hence, when an industry is in its pioneering stage, investing in companies belonging to that industry will be loaded with higher risk element due to the probability of some of the companies getting sidelined and eventually going out of existence. Industries in their pioneering stage are also known as sunrise industries.
2. ***Rapid growth stage:*** When an industry is in its pioneering stage, there will be a lot of confusion and chaos and spotting of companies that would survive and emerge successful will be highly difficult. However, at the fag end of the pioneering stage the scene will become clear and those companies that have survived the pioneering stage will enter the next phase of rapid growth stage. In this stage, the companies will have rapid as well as stable growth rate, due to which they will earn increased profits and they will declare higher rates of dividend. The growth rate of the industry in rapid growth stage will be substantially more than the growth rate of the economy. Companies will offer to their customers technologically improved products at reduced prices. Since, all the companies that have emerged successful from the pioneering stage and entered the rapid growth stage will be growing at a faster rate and earning increased profits, investors will find it highly profitable to invest in companies pertaining to those industries that are in rapid growth stage.

3. ***Maturity and stabilization stage:*** We have seen that in rapid growth stage, the growth rate of the industry will be substantially more than the growth rate of the economy as a whole. After showing above average performance and earning above – average return in the rapid growth stage, the industry enters the next stage called maturity and stabilization stage. During this stage, the growth rate comes down and becomes more or less on par with the growth rate of the overall economy and the growth rate of the industry will begin to stagnate. In order to sustain the industry, new technological innovations will become a necessity. Investors who have already invested in industries that have since reached stabilization stage will have to closely observe the performance of the industry and take note of the events that are taking place that will have a bearing on the future performance of the industry.
4. ***Declining stage:*** When an industry has already been in stagnation stage for a few years, the demand for the products gets fulfilled and consumer preference starts changing. In tune with the changed performance of the consumers, new products enter the market and drive the products that are already in their stagnation stage for quite some time, out of the market. Also, new technological advancements bring new products to the market which will also induce consumers to change their habits/preferences. An investor should be watchful and locate the time at which an industry enters the declining stage. Once the industry has entered the declining stage, its fall is normally faster and continues till the industry reaches very low ebb. The industry will register a negative growth rate and profitability will drastically come down. Investors who have already made investments in industries that show signs of entering the declining stage should immediately liquidate their investment and come out of the industry without waiting further.

Industry life cycle has the following limitations:

The four phases which industries go through as explained above are based on the observation of the life cycle that different industries undergo. There can always be exceptions. For example, an industry that is in its stagnation stage may regain momentum and exhibit higher rate of growth if the industry has adapted to the changed circumstances and brought out the required product modifications. The duration of each phase and the rate of growth in each phase are highly variable and depend on the types of industries and also on the overall economic environment. Since, industry life cycle chart may not give distinct signals, it will be a difficult task for an investor to ascertain the phase in which a particular industry exists at the present point of time and the time at which it is likely to move to the next stage of life cycle.

However, continuous close observation and judicious interpretation can reveal the industry life cycle trend and characteristics. Despite the above limitations, a prudent investor can make use of the industry life cycle as under.

- Since, the performance of companies, to a larger extent depend on the performance of the industry concerned, a prudent investor will have to study the industry life cycle first before deciding upon the company in which he chooses to invest.
- When an industry is in its pioneering stage, an investor should be doubly cautious in choosing the companies for his investment. This stage of the life cycle which is marked by high growth rate as well as high mortality rate if more suited for speculators than for prudent investors.
- When an industry has moved into rapid growth stage, a prudent investor must act quickly and increase his investment in the industry in order to reap the benefits of rapid as well as stable growth. When an industry shows signs of stagnation, a prudent investor should avoid further financial commitments in that industry and should look for other avenues of investment that offers scope for better returns. He can even switch his investments from industries that are in stagnation stage to industries that are still in their growth stage.
- When an industry shows signs of decline, a prudent investor must act quickly and disinvest his holding in the industry in order to avoid heavy losses that may follow soon if the investments in the declining industrial sector are not withdrawn.

Figure 3.5 shows the industry life cycle which depicts sales achieved by the industry during the different stages in its life cycle on the *y*-axis and the number of years of the different stages on the *x*-axis.

(*b*) Analysis of industry characteristics

Under a given economic condition, on the basis of structural and operational features, one industry may perform better than another. Hence, apart from studying the industry life cycle, studying the characteristics of the different industries will throw light on the industrial sectors that promise growth and those sectors that are prone to decline/stagnation. The following are some of the key industry characteristics that need to be studied:

1. Demand supply gap
2. Competitive conditions in the industry
3. Growth rate of the industry
4. Performance of demand

5. Labour conditions/availability
6. Availability of raw materials
7. Cost structure and profitability
8. Research and development
9. Barriers to entry
10. Profit margins
11. Important technological changes on the anvil and their implications
12. Cyclical and defensive industries

1. ***Demand supply gap:*** The demand for a product depends on factors like consumer preference, affordability, availability of substitute products etc. Since, the factors that determine the demand for a product change gradually over a period of time, the change in demand for a product is also gradual. On the other hand, the supply of a product depends on the existing production capacity for the product and the rate at which additional production capacities are added. In view of this, the production capacity for producing a product does not vary smoothly, but will show irregular variations. Due to this, there is bound to be a gap between the demand and the supply. There can be shortage of production capacity in which case the demand will be more than the supply. There can also be a situation where the demand has come down, making the available production capacity excess in which case, the supply will be more than the demand. Thus, at different points of time an industry may possess either excess capacity or may experience under capacity. When there is excess supply(due to excess production capacity), the profitability of that industry will come down. But, when the supply is in short of demand (due to insufficient production capacity) it will improve the profitability of the industry. Thus, the prevailing demand-supply gap in an industry provides a good indicator of the scope for growth or the chances of decline of the industry.

2. ***Competitive conditions in the industry:*** The number of firms in an industry and the market share distribution of the different firms in the industry determine the nature of competition in the industry. If there are a large number of firms, each holding a fraction of the market share, the competition among the firms is likely to be a perfect competition. Under the condition of perfect competition, the price that firms offer for their products settle down at the equilibrium price, which is the price that is acceptable both to the buyers and sellers. Since, all the firms can price their products only at the equilibrium price, the profitability of all the firms, though very moderate, will be nearly equal. No one firm can earn abnormal profit.

   The opposite of perfect competition is monopoly. Monopoly refers to the absence of competition. This is an extreme situation of imperfect competition. It is a condition in which there is only a single firm producing the product and it has the power to fix the price and output of its product. There will be no substitute products available. It is a situation where there are strong entry barriers for new firms. Obviously, firms enjoying monopoly will reap greater profits due to the absence of competitors. An investor should foresee the chances for the removal of barriers for entry into the market. Removal of entry barriers will bring down the profit margin drastically. While perfect competition is on one extreme, monopoly is on the other extreme. A blend of monopoly and perfect competition is called monopolistic competition. It refers to a market situation in which there are many producers producing goods that are close substitutes to one another. However, there will be some form of product differentiation to identify the product with the firm that produces it. Thus, each firm will have some monopoly (due to differentiated product) and at the same time each firm has to compete in the market with other firms that produce fair substitutes. Thus, existence of many firms and product differentiation are the essential features of monopolistic competition. Producers of toothpaste is an example of monopolistic competition where there are many producers each having a brand distinguished by product differentiation.

The success of a firm in monopolistic competition depends on the firm's ability to grab a major portion of the market share by distinct and apt product differentiation and building a large group of loyal customers.

There is another form of competition called oligopoly. While there are many firms in monopolistic competition, there are only a few firms. The term oligopoly means competition among the few. In this type of competition, their will be a few big firms producing and competing in the market. As the number of firms is few, a reduction in the price by one firm will directly affect the fortunes of other competing firms and hence the rival firms will retaliate by reducing the price of their products, resulting in a price-war. As the firms are aware of the ultimate outcome of price-cutting, they will not resort to this. Hence, price rigidity will prevail. The price will be kept unchanged due to fear of retaliation. Instead of price cutting the firms will intensify sales through effective advertisement. In perfect oligopoly, the products will be of homogeneous nature with little scope for product differentiation. Cement industry, aluminium industry etc., are examples of perfect oligopoly.

3. ***Growth rate of the industry:*** The faster the growth of an industry, the better it is. Analyzing the past performance of the industry in terms of growth and profitability will throw light on the future prospects of the industry. The trend of growth in the immediate past will act as a pointer to the likely future performance of the industry. Centre for Monitoring Indian Economy (CMIE) publishes periodically, interalia, statistical data on industry-wise growth rate which will be of great use

for the analyst. CMIE has built a large and well integrated database on Indian economy. CMIE, interalia provides three kinds of services, viz.,

- Corporate Information on Magnetic Medium (CIMM)
- Economic Intelligence Service (EIS)
- Investments Intelligence Service (IIS)

CIMM is a computerized database on more than 3300 India's medium and large companies with a powerful easy-to-use querying, report generation and charting software. EIS documents contain information on all the major sectors of the economy including agriculture, industry and individual firms. Macro economic indicators like national income, public finance, balance of payments, prices and exchange rates are covered extensively. Further, historical, current and future trends of the economy, sectors and sub-sectors are provided along with expert analysis. EIS provides continuous and detailed updates on investment activity in the country. IIS service of the CMIE is very useful to corporate planners and investors in estimating future trend in supply and demand in industry and infrastructure sectors.

4. ***Performance of demand:*** In the present era of rapid technological advancements, if the technology used by a particular industry is already old and if fast technological advancements are taking place in that industry, the products might become absolute and outdated soon. Also, due to overall technological developments in the economy, technologically advanced substitute products may emerge in the market and existing products that face competition from such substitute products might vanish in the short run. It will not be advisable for prudent investors to invest in such industries that are fast undergoing changes/advancements.

5. ***Labour conditions and availability:*** The labour conditions prevailing in an industry and the type of labour required and its availability etc., should be studied. Industries that employ large number of labourers face the threat of labour unions, especially in a country like India. For example, Textile industry that employs huge volume of work force is known for its labour union activities. Workers frequently resort to strikes where labour unions are strong. The demands put forth by the labour unions may at time be unreasonable which may lead to even the closure of industrial units. Industries in which strong labour unions exist will also find it difficult to introduce automation in the production facilities as the labour unions will tend to oppose such moves for the fear of loss of jobs.

   Nature and type of labour force required and its availability is another aspect to be looked into. In a country like India, unskilled labour force is available in abundance, especially in the rural area. Due to the rapid growth of educational infrastructure during the past two decades or so, educated/skilled manpower is also available without much constraints. Another important factor is that labour is comparatively cheaper in India as compared to the developed countries. Hence, industries that need huge manpower will find Indian conditions advantageous as they can keep their production cost down due to lower labour component in their cost of production. Indian computer software industry is a standing example where well qualified labour is available in adequate number at a comparatively cheaper cost which makes Indian software industry enjoy competitive advantage.

6. ***Availability of raw material:*** The profitability of an industry, interlia, depends on the availability of raw materials at competitive costs. If the raw materials required for an industry are available indigenously and if there is no shortage of raw material availability, the concerned industry will be free from the threat of raw material shortage. If the indigenous availability of raw material is scarce and/or if the raw material is imported from abroad, such industries may face the threat of depending on the few indigenous raw material suppliers and/or imports from abroad. In the event of any eventuality of non availability/shortage of raw materials, it will affect the industry badly.

7. ***Cost structure and profitability:*** Every industry has its own cost structure. Cost structure refers to the proportion of fixed and variable costs. Certain industries (cement industries, steel industries etc. for example) require a larger proportion of fixed cost. When the proportion of fixed cost is higher, larger sales volumes are required to reach the Break Even Point. In such industries, profitability will improve steeply when the sales volume exceed the Break Even Point and profitability can be strengthened by improving the capacity utilization of the plant to its maximum possible limit. However, industries that have large fixed cost have longer gestation period. Moreover, when the demand for their product increases suddenly, the industry cannot immediately absorb the increased demand since it will take a longer time and will also require huge investments for creating additional production facilities to cater to the increased demand. On the other hand, in industries where the fixed cost forms only a smaller part of the total cost, the Break Even Point will be reached faster and additional production capacity, if warranted can be created within a short period of time and with a comparatively smaller investment. Thus, industries with lower proportion of fixed cost enjoy greater flexibility than industries that require a larger proportion of fixed cost.

8. ***Research and development:*** Research and development activities take place in all industries. However, the level of expenditure spent on R & D activities varies from one industry to another. R & D activities in general, aim at improving the products as well as production process in order to make products competitive. The percentage of expenditure

spent on R & D efforts acts as an indicator for the level of growth taking in the industry and this also acts as a leading indicator for the growth of the industry concerned.

9. ***Barriers to entry:*** Entry barriers for new firms will protect existing firms in the industry from competition. The entry barrier may be either due to Government's restrictions in allowing entry to new firms in the sector or due to inherent conditions that are specific to the industry that make entry of new firms difficult. For example, very huge capital investment required, non-availability of technical know-how etc. are some of the factors that may be inherent to a particular industry that will act as entry barriers to new comers in the field. An industry that does not possess any entry barrier is open to stiff competition and individual firms in the industry should be always on vigil to ensure that they do not lose their competitive position.

10. ***Profit margins:*** Average profit margins offered by industries differ. Over a period of time, some industries may be offering a higher return as compared to other industries. Higher profit margins over a period of time indicate growth of the concerned industrial sector while lower profit margins sustained for a longer period foretell stagnation/decline of the industry.

11. ***Important technological changes on anvil and their implication:*** Technology keeps improving. A technology that is current becomes outdated in the future. Whenever there is a quantum shift in the technological advancements, the industry undergoes considerable changes. Hence, an investor should look for the important technological changes that are about to take place in an industry and their impact.

12. ***Cyclical and defensive industries:*** The industries that follow a life cycle are called cyclical industries. There are some industries that do not have any life cycle at all. Such industries are called defensive industries (since they defend the forces that bring about industry life cycle and follow their own pattern of life).

Cyclical industries are those industries that are affected by the business cycle of the economy. It has been found that the economy experiences periods of expansion and contraction recurrently. Though the length and depth of the cycle of expansion and contraction varies the recurrence of expansion and contraction, one following the other is found to exist. This recurring pattern of growth and fall (or recovery and recession) of the economy is called the 'business cycle'. Cyclical industries perform more or less in tune with the business cycle.

Normally industries producing goods whose purchases can be deferred during a recession fall under the category of cyclical industries.

For example, industries producing capital goods (i.e., goods used by other firms to produce their own products) belong to cyclical industries.

This is because of the reason that at times of recession, manufacturing firms do not go for adding capital goods and they defer the purchase of capital goods. When the economy turns around and the business cycle switches over from contraction to expansion, capital goods industries perform well since the demand for capital goods will witness a spurt. Another example of cyclical industry is the industry producing durable goods (like TV, washing machine, automobile, household gadgets etc.) since their purchase can also be deferred at times of recession.

Unlike cyclical industries that have greater sensitivity to the business cycle, defensive industries show very little sensitivity to the business cycle. In other words they are not very much affected by the ups and downs of the economy. Hence, their growth is not cyclical in nature. Pharmaceutical firms, public utility industries etc., fall under the category of defensive industries. Even when the economy is in recession, these industries will perform consistently since the use of the products that they produce cannot be deferred by the consumers.

(c) Governments policies on industries

Government is a major player in the industrial development of a country. If the Government gives priority to the development of some chosen industries, the Government may come out with such policies that are favourable to the growth of that particular industry. The reason for the Government's encouragement to selected industries may be based on overall macro economic study of factors that are favourable to a country's growth. In India, for example man-power is available in plenty. Hence, the Government may encourage industries that employee larger man-power. If a country is rich in mineral resources, the Government of the country may encourage industries that are engaged in extraction/processing of the minerals. In short, the Government may support those industries in which the country enjoys a competitive advantage. Similarly, the Government may discourage certain industries based on certain valid reasons . Industries that pollute the environment heavily, industries that deplete the scarce natural resources of the country etc., may not be favoured by the Government. When the Government favours the growth of certain sectors of industries the Government may come out with policies favourble to the growth of such industries (like extending subsidies, extending credit on liberal terms, etc.). On the other hand, when the Government is not in favour of some other industries (due to macro level reasons) the Government may impose legal restrictions on its development. Therefore a prudent investor has to consider whether the Government is likely to support or restrict the growth of the industrial sector in which he proposes to invest.

The investor should also see whether the prices of products of a particular industry are regulated by the Government. The Government may regulate the prices of certain essential goods. For example, in India, sugar industry and pharmaceutical industry come under price regulation by the Government. When prices of products produced by a particular industry are regulated it will have its impact on the profitability and earning extra normal profit may not be likely.

3.4.2. Porter Model

Michael Porter identified the following five factors as the essential factors required for the sustenance of an industry. He puts forth that the profit potential of an industry depends on the combined strength of these five factors.

(*a*) Threat of new entrants

(*b*) Rivalry among the existing firms

(*c*) Pressure from substitute products

(*d*) Bargaining power of buyers

(*e*) Bargaining power of suppliers

These five factors act together and their combined effect determines the profit potential of the industry as a whole. (Refer Fig. 3.6)

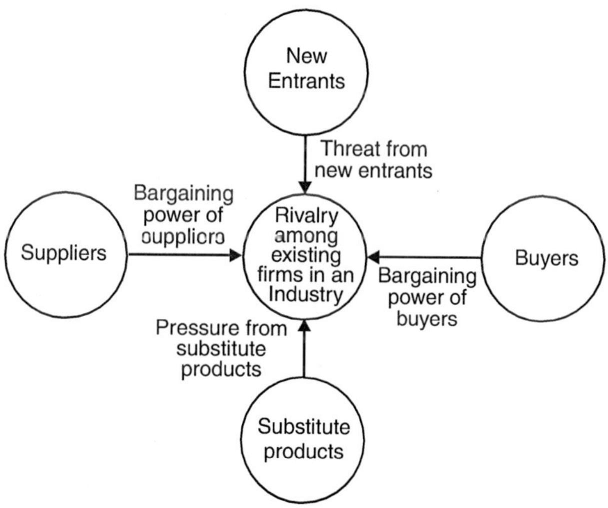

Fig. 3.6 Porter model

(*a*) Threat of new entrants

When an industry is such that there are strong entry barriers to new entrants, the existing players will find their survival safe. Some of the entry barriers are as below:

- The investment required to start a production unit may be substantial such that only very few can opt to enter.

- The Government's policy may sometimes prohibit new entrants (i.e., creation of additional production facilities) or the Government may impose restrictions for new players entering the fields.
- Existing firms in the industry might have established brand image and customer loyalty (in view of their long time existence in the market and due to product differentiation/improvement etc.) which new entrants may find difficult to overcome.
- For the consumers, switching costs (i.e., the cost required to switch over from the product of one manufacturer to another) may be high. Though quite often switching costs are one-time costs, they will still act as entry barriers to new entrants if the switching costs are higher.
- When there is no demand-supply gap new entrants may not find it worthwhile to invest. New entrants may at times venture into the business in spite of the fact that there is no demand-supply gap, with the hope of grabbing a slice of the market share from the existing players by adopting some strategy. However, their success is not guaranteed and it depends on many factors. Hence, in general, new entrants will hesitate to enter a field where the scope for their survival is not very promising.

(*b*) Rivalry among the existing firms

All firms in an industry always attempt to improve their competitive position. They do this in order to establish their position among the competitors. This may be done either by cost reduction followed by price reduction, quality improvement, offering better service terms etc. When a particular firm resorts to anyone or more or all of the techniques meant to consolidate its position of competitive advantage, other firms in the industry also react by resorting to price-cut, quality improvement, improvement of service conditions etc. This brings forth retaliatory action from all the firms existing in the industry, which will ultimately reduce their profitability. The following conditions favour the growth of rivalry among the existing firms:

- There are a large number of competitors in the industry, each trying to achieve competitive advantage over the others.
- There is excess capacity in the industry.
- The industry has strong exit barriers with the result the existing industries are under compulsion to remain in the field and at the same time achieve the desired level of performance. This leads to each firm attempting to grab a higher proportion of the market share.

(*c*) Pressure from substitute products

Substitute products, though different, perform the same function. For example, tea and coffee are substitute products. Consumers can easily switch over from one product to the other (i.e., to the substitute product) if the price difference is substantial. Hence, all firms in a particular industry face competition from those industries that produce substitute products. Substitute products pose greater threat when switching costs to the consumers are nil/minimum and when the price of substitute products come down considerably, making the price – performance trade-off offered by the substitute products attractive to consumers.

(*d*) Bargaining power of buyers

The buyers as a group act as a competitive force. When the buyers are in a stronger position, they start dictating terms. They may demand lower price, better quality products and superior service conditions. This will induce rivalry among the different firms in the industry and the rival firms will resort to price-cut, spend more towards improving service conditions, improve their R&D efforts etc., which may bring down their profitability. The bargaining power of buyers is more pronounced when the buyers are in the form of groups and the group purchases are relatively large as compared to the quantity purchased by individual consumers. Also, when the cost of switching over to other substitute or near-substitute products is low, the buyers will have greater bargaining power.

(*e*) Bargaining power of suppliers

When there are only a very few suppliers and if the suppliers are organized in the form of groups they can exert a competitive force in the industry by raising the price of their products, by lowering the quality of products for a given price etc. Bargaining power of suppliers increases when there are no substitute products available and when switching costs for the buyers are high in the event of availability of substitute products. When such conditions prevail, suppliers who are powerful can even affect the profitability of the buyer industry. Hence, under situations where suppliers (of raw materials) of a particular industry enjoy higher bargaining powers, those industries that depend on such supplier are forced to spend more on raw material leading to increased production cost.

3.5. COMPANY ANALYSIS

Company analysis is the last stage of fundamental analysis. The economy analysis offers the investor with broad idea about the prospects or otherwise for the growth of the economy as a whole. Industry analysis helps the investor to select the industry from among the many existing industrial sectors, that will offer comparatively better rewards than the other industrial sectors. Having chosen the industry/industries in which investment are to be made, the investor faces the problem as to which are the firm/firms that are to be chosen from among the many firms operating in the particular industrial sector.

In company analysis, the performance of a company is analyzed from three aspects, viz., (*a*) The management

(*b*) The company

(*c*) The financial statements

(*a*) The management

A bad company in the hands of a good management can turn out to be successful company, while a good company in the hands of a poor management can become a failure. Hence, the management of a company is a very important factor that should be considered in company analysis. In fact, this is the first factor to be studied in company analysis and if it turns out to be poor, further analysis can be safely given up as the company is not worth investing in. Both in India and across the world there are many examples of companies having flourished because of good management and also there are equal numbers of examples of companies having been doomed because of ineffective management.

As far as companies in India are concerned, there are still many companies that are family managed. Hence, management of companies in India can be grouped under the following two heads:

- Family management
- Professional management

Family managed companies are those that have a member of the controlling family as its chairman or the Chief Executive. The directors in the boards of such companies will also be persons belonging to the family members or their close relatives. A family managed company may have professional managers at the middle and lower levels in the organizational hierarchy. In spite of this, major decisions will be taken only by the family members. Since the family members will be more interested in their own welfare rather than in the welfare of the shareholders, some of the decisions that the company management takes may not be in the best interests of the shareholders. In this aspect, a family managed company is not considered suitable for investment by a prudent investor.

Professionally managed companies are those companies that are managed by its employees. The chief executive will be a professional manager. Often, he does not have any financial stake in the company. The chief executive of a professionally managed company is selected based on his qualification, experience and capabilities. In general, professionally managed companies produce better results than family managed companies. Professionally managed companies are able to show better performance since they are managed and run on professional lines without giving room for the whims and fancies and personal prejudices of a few, which is more prevalent in family managed companies.

The professionally managed companies on the other hand suffer from a different drawback. They are at times plagued with outdated corporate policies and infighting. This is because of the reasons that the managers often try to climb up the corporate ladder by fair or foul means. Such infighting will spoil team work and eventually the company will suffer. Such an eventuality of managers sacrificing their company's interests for their own personal gains cannot be possible in a family managed company. In a family managed company, the infighting among the organizational members is not possible since everything is controlled by the family members and they decide on the positions to be occupied by the different managerial personnel and the family members who are in control of the company make personnel decisions depending more on the loyalty of the organizational members than on other factors.

It can be said in general that professionally managed companies offer better choice for investment than family managed companies. However, there can also be family managed companies that are better managed and professionally managed companies that are poorly managed. Thus, there can be badly managed companies in both the categories. Hence, irrespective of whether a company is family managed or professionally managed, an investor should look for certain basic qualities of the management, some of them are as under.

- The integrity of the management should be beyond doubt. This can be known from how the management had behaved in the past. Whether the management of the company was genuine in its transactions or had manipulated things against the interests of the shareholders can be known by going through the past incidents and happenings.
- The management should have proved its competence. Continuous growth in profits, expansion/diversification done in the past, expansion/ diversification plans on the anvil, growth rate compared to similar companies in the industry etc., speak about the competence of the management. The competence of the management is put to test when the industry is not performing well. At times of recession in the economy, all the sectors of industries, in general, perform badly. It is during this phase that weekly managed companies are closed down. If the management is competent enough to steer the company ahead in difficult days, it is a proof that the management of the company has the required competence and that the company will do well under the management during normal times.
- The management should be proactive. In a world where changes are fast taking place in all spheres of business, unless the management anticipates the changes and acts accordingly, it will have to give up its position to the competitors. Analysis of the market share of the products of a company during the past will throw light on this aspect. The market share will act as indicator for the company's capacity to sustain which indirectly tells whether the management of the company has been proactive or not.

(*b*) The company

Before going into the financial indicators, a shrewd investor will study the company as such. Facts and figures about the financial performance of the company come next. What is required to be seen ahead of the financial performance is the status of the company and the general perception of the company by the peers and investors. Though there may be a few companies producing a particular product, among them, one or more companies will be the market leaders. They will set the trend for others to follow. For a company to remain a market leader, it must possess many favourable attributes. The management of the company must be innovative and proactive. It should have strong footings on all essential areas like raw materials procurement, production techniques, research and development, distribution network etc. At times when the market is sluggish, the share prices of companies in general, fall down. However, market leaders have the capacity to withstand the pressure of falling price and postpone the fall in the prices of their shares. In other words, market leaders are less affected by overall recessive trend in the market. This is because of their inherent strength. Those companies that do not possess this inner strength wither away during difficult times. Hence, an investor should see if the company that he/she going to choose is a market leader in its segment.

(*c*) The financial statements

The proof of the pudding is in the eating. The strengths and weakness of an enterprise are reflected by its financial statements. Financial statements reflect the financial health of an enterprise, just as a mirror reflects the face of a person (provided, of course, the accountant is impartial and projects a true image of the enterprise, without manipulating the facts and figures).

The two basic financial statements, of an enterprise are the profit and loss account and the balance sheet. Profit and loss account and balance sheet together are called final accounts. Financial statements of a company reflect the strength of the company. They help the investors to assess the financial health of the company and give indications as to their likely financial performance in the near future. Since, the analyst is primarily interested in foreseeing the likely future earnings of the company, financial statements will be of great use.

Profit and Loss Account

Profit and loss account is also called as Income statement. Income is the difference between earnings and expenses. Profit and loss account shows the income earned by the company, the cost incurred by the company in earning the income and the resulting profit earned by the company (or the resulting loss incurred by the company). Profit and loss account is prepared for one accounting year. Thus, the profit earned by the company as revealed by the profit and loss account is the profit earned during one accounting year.

Indian Companies Act does not specify any format for the preparation of profit and loss account. A specimen format of a profit and loss account is given below.

		Rupees
Net sales		********
Cost of goods sold:		
Stocks	****	
Wages and salaries	****	
Other manufacturing expenses	****	
		********
Gross profit		********
Operating expenses:		
Selling & Administrative expenses	****	
Depreciation	****	
		********
Operating profit		*********
Non operating surplus/deficit		*********
Profit before interest & tax (also called EBIT – earnings before interest & tax)		AAAAAAAAA
Less Interest:		
Interest on Term loan	*****	
Interest on debentures/bonds	*****	
		********
Profit before tax		********
Less Tax		********
Profit after tax		********
Less Dividends:		
Dividend on equity shares	*****	
Dividend on preference shares	*****	
		********
Retained earnings		*******

The profit after tax (PAT) divided by the number of shares gives the earnings per share (EPS). Investors are more interested in knowing the EPS of a company.

Balance Sheet

Balance Sheet is a statement of the financial position of an enterprise on a certain date. One portion of the balance sheet shows the various types of assets owned by the enterprise while the other side of the balance sheet shows the shareholders funds and liabilities owned by the enterprise. Table 3.2 shows the format for balance sheet prescribed by the Companies Act.

Table 3.2 Format of Balance Sheet as prescribed by Companies Act

Liabilities	Assets
Share capital	Fixed assets
Reserves and surplus	Investments
Secured loans	Current assets, loan & advances
Unsecured loans	Miscellaneous expenses & losses
Current liabilities & provisions	

Note : *The figures in the Balance Sheet are expressed in monetary terms. The total amount (in rupees) on the assets side will be equal to the total amount on the liabilities side i.e., the assets and liabilities balance each other. Hence, the name 'Balance Sheet'.*

Balance Sheet is a statement prepared to give a snap-shot picture of the financial position of a company. It indicates the financial position of a company on a particular date. The Balance Sheet is generally prepared on the last day of the accounting year, though it can also be prepared as on any date.

Liabilities

A company gets funds from two sources. The owners of the company contribute their share of funds. In addition, the company may get funds from some external agencies like banks, financial institutions, some other companies, individuals etc. The company has got the obligation to pay money back to the lenders. No doubt the company is under obligation to pay back the money that it has borrowed from external agencies like banks, financial institutions, other lenders etc. What about the money contributed by the owners of the company? Since a company is a separate legal entity, it is different from the owners. In fact, the owners also lend their money to the company when they contribute towards the share capital of the company. Though we mat not literally say that the company has borrowed from the owners, in effect the company is under obligation to repay the money that the owners have invested in the company. Liabilities are shown on the left side column of the Balance Sheet.

Liabilities can be broadly classified into two types, viz.,

(*a*) Long term liabilities

(*b*) Short term liabilities

Long Term Liabilities

Owners (shareholders are the owners of a company) invest their capital in a business with a view to earning profits over a period of time. They are not supposed to draw back their capital, at least within a short time. Hence, Share capital is obviously a long term liability of the company. The term 'long term' applies more specifically to borrowings for which repayments can be made after a period of more than one year. Secured loans, unsecured loans, bonds and debentures are some of the major long term liabilities.

Share Capital

This is the amount raised by a company by issuing equity/preference shares.

Reserves and Surplus

Reserves and surplus are the profits earned and retained in the company. The amount of profits after taxes not paid out as dividends is called retained earnings. The retained earnings can be of two types, viz., Revenue Reserves and Capital Reserves. Revenue reserves represent the accumulated retained earnings from the profits of normal business operations. These are again split into two types viz., General Reserve and Specific Reserve. Specific reserve is the reserve allocated for a specific purpose. For example, denture redemption reserve is a specific reserve.

Capital reserve represents the profits earned that are not related to the normal business operations. For example, profits earned by sale of fixed assets, gain on revaluation of asset, share premium received etc., are capital reserves. Capital reserves are not available for distribution as dividends to the shareholders.

'Surplus' represents the balance in the profit and loss account that has not been appropriated to any particular reserve account. ***Share capital along with reserves and surplus represents owner's equity and is termed as 'Net worth' of a company. (If the balance sheet contains miscellaneous expenses and losses' on the asset side, the same is to be deducted for arriving out the 'Net worth')***

Note: *Reserves and surplus represent undistributed profits. It does not mean that the undistributed profits are kept separately in the form of cash/bank balance which can be withdrawn at any time. Like share capital or loans the reserves and surplus also remains invested in the business. It remains invested in the different types of assets that the business owns and it can not be exactly traced out as to which are the assets in which* *the reserves and surplus are invested and how much. However, there is one exemption. If on the liabilities side of the balance sheet the word 'Reserve Fund' is found it means that a separate fund has been created out of reserves for some specific purpose. In such a case, the investment of the reserve fund will be specifically available on the assets side. For example, if a debenture redemption reserve appears on the liabilities side of the balance sheet, there will be an equivalent asset on the assets side of the balance sheet under the head 'investments' (for example, "7% deposit certificate").*

Secured Loans

Secured loan are borrowings of the company against which specific securities of the company have been provided. Loans from financial institutions, banks, debentures etc., fall under the category of secured loan. In general, a loan that is backed by an asset as a security is known as Secured loan. For example, when a company takes a loan from a bank/financial institution for the purchase of an equipment, the bank/ financial institution would have lent money on the strength of the equipment and would have created a charge over the equipment in its favour. In case the company fails to repay the loan, the bank/financial institution, by virtue of the charge created over the equipment in its favour, could take back the equipment from the company and realize its dues by selling the equipment. Such loans that are obtained by a company from banks/financial institutions by securing the assets purchased out of the borrowings in favour of the respective bank/financial institution are known as secured loans.

Unsecured Loans

Unsecured loans are borrowings of a company against which specific securities of the company have not been provided. Fixed deposits, loans and advances from promoters, intercorporate borrowings etc., fall under the category of unsecured loans. Unsecured creditors do not have charge over the assets of the company.

Debentures and Bonds

Debentures and bonds are issued by companies to raise long term loans and also for meeting working capital requirement. Debentures/bonds are issued against some securities, and the debentures/bonds will have a 'charge' over these securities. The charges created may be either a 'fixed charge' or a 'floating charge' or both. A 'fixed charge' is a charge created over some fixed assets of the company. A 'floating charge' is a charge on the undertaking in general. When debentures/bonds are secured either by fixed charge or by floating charge, they fall under the head of secured loans. At times they are also issued without any security back up. Such unsecured debentures/ bonds will be classified under unsecured loans.

Current Liabilities and Provisions

We know that liabilities are claims of outsiders against a business. Liability represents the amounts owed by a company to those who have lent money to the company. It also includes goods and services provided on credit to the company. The company is under obligation to pay in terms of money for the goods and services that it has received on credit. The liabilities that are to be paid by the company within one year of creation are classified as 'current liabilities'. Most of the current liabilities are incurred due to purchase of inventories on credit.

Current liabilities include the following:

- Advance payments received
- Amount due to suppliers of goods and services bought on credit
- Accrued expenses (accruals for wages, salaries, rentals, interest and other expenses). This head represents the services that have been received by the company but the payment for which has not fallen due.
- Loans that are payable within one year from the date of the balance sheet (Loans, both secured and unsecured which are long/medium term loans to start with, will, during the course of time, become current liability when they become payable within one year).

Provisions

When a company expects to incur some liability in future but is unable to determine the exact amount, the need for making provision arises. The company needs to estimate the likely amount and shows the same in the balance sheet. For example, 'Income tax payable' is one of the most common provisions that a company will be required to make in its balance sheet. Though payment of income tax is certain, the exact amount payable may not be known certainly at the time of preparation of the balance sheet. Under such circumstances, the income tax payable is estimated and shown on the liability side of the balance sheet. Apart from income tax, some of the other heads under which provisions are made in the balance sheet are as below:

- ⇨ Provision for bad debts
- ⇨ Provision for dividends
- ⇨ Provision for warranties
- ⇨ Provision for pension, gratuity etc.

Note: *Though we create a provision in case of liability, it is not the practice to create any provision for assets. Provisions made for liabilities are anticipated losses. We don't make any provision for anticipated gains and show the same on the assets side of the balance sheet. This is because of the principle of conservatism followed in preparing the financial statements.*

Contingent Liability

The word 'contingent' refers to an event that is likely to occur and not certain to occur. Its occurrence depends on the occurrence of some other events. For example, when a company is fighting a legal battle (against a supplier/customer/employee/statutory authorities), the company may become liable to pay some amount to the opponent party only when the legal case is adjudicated against the company, i.e., in favour of the opponent. But, till such time the case is decided by the court, it will not be known certainly as to whether the company will win or loose the case. Hence, contingent liabilities are not necessarily liabilities for the time being and they become liabilities only on the occurrence of a certain event. Till such time, it only remains as a 'likely liability' the probability of occurrence of which is not known. Hence, contingent liability is not shown in the balance sheet of a company. However, they are indicated separately in the form of 'notes' that are provided along with the balance sheet. This is done to make all those concerned know that there is a possibility of occurrence of such a liability in the future. Hence, while reading the balance sheet of a company, apart from reading the balance sheet proper, an investor (or any stake holder who wants to know the performance of the company) shall also read the 'notes forming part of the balance sheet', which are given along with the balance sheet.

Deferred Tax Liability

As per the Companies Act, depreciation has to be calculated at the rates specified in the Act taking into consideration the type of machinery, the number of shifts operated etc. This depreciation is the one that is shown in the balance sheet published by companies. Income tax Act provides for different slabs of depreciation and also allow excess depreciation (as compared to the depreciation allowed in the Companies Act) in certain cases as an incentives. For example, Income tax law provides for 80% depreciation for wind mills in the first year itself while Companies Act allows for 10% depreciation, if the life of the wind mill is considered as 10 years. Thus, there will be considerable savings in the income tax. If the depreciation as per the Companies Act had been charged for tax purposes also, excess tax would have been paid. The tax saved actually pertains to the future years. The tax saved over the normal tax on account of income tax laws is called 'Deferred tax liability'. Deferred tax liability is a part of PAT (Profit after tax). In order to give a correct picture to the stake holders, the Deferred tax liability which is contained in the PAT is separated from PAT and shown separately in the balance sheet. Every year, the savings in income tax due to the difference in income tax rates between the provisions of the Income tax Act and the Companies Act is taken away from the Deferred tax liability and shifted to 'Reserves' in the balance sheet. Since, the Deferred tax liability that appears in a balance sheet is a part of PAT and as it is not an outside liability, it is 'owned fund' of the company and has to be added to the net worth of the company. (Similar to Deferred tax liability, a balance sheet may also contain Deferred tax asset. For example, extra tax paid in a particular year that pertains to future years will be shown as Deferred tax asset. The Deferred tax liability and Deferred tax asset will get reduced every year to the extent it pertains to that particular year and will become part of the general reserve. At one stage they will get depleted completely).

Assets

Assets are made use of by the business to earn profit. Assets are the economic possessions of a company. It is the 'Assets' that generate profit for the business. Whenever profit is generated it has two effects on the balance sheet. The profit generated is reflected through an increase in the 'Assets side' of the balance sheet. In the first instance, the current assets will get increased. The debtors or the inventories or the cash/bank balance or any other head in the current assets will show an increase due to generation of profit, to start with. When the profit is huge enough it may also get reflected by an increase in investments, fixed assets etc. To match the increase on the 'Assets' side of the balance sheet, there will be an equal increase on the 'Liabilities' side of the balance sheet. The increase in the liabilities will be usually an increase in the 'Reserves and Surplus' head.

As and when profit generated by the business is distributed to the owners there will be reduction in the 'Reserves and Surplus' head. To the extent of reduction in the 'Reserves and Surplus' head, there will be an equal reduction on the Assets side of the balance sheet usually in the 'Cash and bank balances' head.

Fixed Assets

These are the assets like land, building, plant and machinery etc., that are used by the company for its operations. Fixed assets are characterized by the following two features:

(*a*) They are put into use by the company for a relatively larger period of time, for carrying out its production/business operations.

(*b*) They are not normally meant for resale. (They may, of course be sold when they have lost their economic life or when they are no longer required for the company/business).

Depreciation

Most of the fixed assets used in business have a limited life. They can not remain in the business forever without depletion in value. The time period upto which an asset can be used economically is called its economic life (also called useful life). After the economic life period, the asset will become uneconomical to use and will be incapable of being put into profitable use. Thus, as an asset is being used in a business, its value keeps on declining. The reduction in value of an asset with the passage of time could be due to wear and tear, obsolescence etc. A balance sheet should reflect the 'true value' of an asset. To account for the reduction in value of an asset with the passage of time, the asset is continuously depreciated and the depreciated value of the asset is shown in the balance sheet. Such reduction in value of an asset is called 'depreciation'. Depreciation can be calculated either by Written-down value method or by Straight line method. In Written-down value method, the percentage of depreciation is fixed and the value of the asset is reduced by that fixed percentage every year over its value in the previous year. This method assumes that the reduction in value of the asset will be higher in the initial years and will be progressively lesser during the later years. In the Straight line method, a fixed percentage of the original cost of the asset is depreciated every year till the asset's value becomes 'nil'. Thus, this is a fixed instalment method. This method assumes that the value of the asset gets depreciated uniformly throughout its economic life period.

Tangible and Intangible Assets

Tangible assets are those that can be seen, touched and felt. Fixed assets and current assets fall under this category. Intangible assets are those assets that have no physical presence. They cannot be seen, touched or felt. A balance sheet may contain intangible assets also apart from tangible assets. Examples of intangible assets are goodwill, copy right, trademark, patent etc. Though intangible assets have no physical existence, they add value to a business and enhance the earning capacity of business.

Net Worth and Tangible Net Worth

The term 'Net worth' refers to owned funds of a firm/company.

Net worth = (Assets – Borrowed funds)

If the assets consist of accumulated loss, the same should be deducted from the value of 'Assets' for arriving at the Net worth. For arriving at the Net worth, the Deferred Tax Liability should be treated as owned funds and not to be deducted as a liability.

An investor or a banker is more interested in knowing the Tangible Net worth of a company. For arriving at the tangible Net worth, the following intangible assets are to be excluded:

- Goodwill
- Preliminary expenses
- Pre-operative expenses
- Deferred tax asset
- Deferred revenue expenditure

(If a huge revenue expenditure is incurred in a particular year and if it is decided by the company to charge this expenditure in the Profit and Loss account during the next few years, the uncharged portion of the revenue expenditure appears as an asset in the balance sheet. For example, when a huge amount is spent on repair/reconditioning of plant and machinery, the uncharged portion of the expenditure will appear in the balance sheet as 'Deferred revenue expenditure').

⇨ Bad Debts to the extent not written off

⇨ Revaluation reserves

(If a company revalues its assets, the value of the assets will get stepped up to the level of present market value. An amount equal to the difference between the book value and the newly assessed present value will appear as 'Revaluation Reserve' in the liability side of the balance sheet).

Owner's Equity

It is also called Equity Net worth. It represents that part of the Net worth that belongs to the equity share holders. It can be arrived at by deducting preference share capital from the Net worth.

Investments

Investments are financial securities owned by the company. Investments may be of short term or long term in nature. For example, investments in equity shares of other companies are long term in nature. Investment in the equity shares of other companies is made either for the purpose of getting income or for having control over those companies. Short term investments can be in the form of short term fixed deposits, certificate of deposits issued by the banks etc.

Current Assets, Loans and Advances

The following items fall under this head:

- Cash balance
- Bank balance
- Inventories
- Debtors
- Prepaid expenses
- Loans given to employees
- Advances given to suppliers/contractors

Miscellaneous Expenses are Losses

Miscellaneous expenses are in reality prepaid expenses. A doubt may arise as to how miscellaneous expenses fall under the head of 'assets'.

Miscellaneous expenses represent preliminary and pre-operative expenses that have not been written off against revenue. Till such time they are written off against revenue they appear as assets of intangible nature in the balance sheet for the simple reasons that benefits out of this expenses will be available to the business during subsequent years also. Once written off, it will not appear as assets in the balance sheet (Note : Miscellaneous expenses is to be deducted from reserves and surplus while arriving at owned fund). Losses occurring on the assets side of the balance sheet may also be confusing. As per company law requirements, owner's equity cannot be reduced when the company incurs a loss. Hence, the share capital is left unaltered on the liabilities side of the balance sheet and the loss is shown on the assets side of the balance sheet.

3.5.1. Ratio Analysis

Financial statements of a company (viz., Profit and Loss account and Balance Sheet) are relied upon to study the past performance of the company and to arrive at a reasonably accurate estimate of the future performance. For analyzing the financial statements, Ratio Analysis is widely used. Ratio Analysis compares two items that are contained in a balance sheet or profit and loss account and arrives at an interpretation of the financial health of the company. Ratio Analysis is very widely used in company analysis.

(*a*) Liquidity ratios

Liquidity is very much essential for the short term survival of a company. A company can survive in the long run only if it has liquidity in the short run. Liquidity helps companies meet their financial commitments. Since, the integrity of a company is decided on the basis of the company's ability to meet financial commitments, liquidity ratios are given prime importance in company analysis.

If a company has earned net profit (of say, Rs. 25.00 lakhs), it does not necessarily mean that the company has got the capacity to pay dividend for an equivalent amount of Rs. 25.00 lakhs. The profit earned would have increased the total assets value by an equivalent amount. Only if the major portion of such increase is in the form of either cash or near-cash assets, then the company will be said to have the liquidity to pay dividend in cash. This shows that profit earned does not automatically improve liquidity. Liquidity can be studied by observing the cash and near-cash assets in the balance sheet. Since, profit does not automatically ensure liquidity, it is quite possible that we come across companies that have earned huge profits but still find it difficult to pay dividend, salaries to staff, dues/taxes to the Government etc. Hence, it is the 'cash profit' that is more relevant than the 'Accounting profit' to judge liquidity position.

The two liquidity ratios that are commonly used are (i) Current ratio and (ii) Quick ratio.

Current Ratio (CR)

It is the ratio of Current Assets to Current Liabilities

$$\text{Current Ratio (CR)} = \frac{\text{Current Assets}}{\text{Current Liabilities}}$$

A Current ratio of more than 1.00 : 1.00 indicates that some portion of the current assets are financed by long term funds. The larger the Current ratio, the larger the current assets that are funded by long term sources. Higher the Current Ratio, more the comfort level.

Net Working Capital (NWC) is another measure of judging the liquidity position.

NWC = Current Assets – Current Liabilities

NWC is an absolute figure in terms of Rupees while CR is a number without any unit. When NWC is positive CR will be more than 1.00. Current ratio is widely used as a measure of liquidity than Net Working Capital. A large Current ratio (say, CR > 2.00 : 1.00) indicates that the company is in a very comfortable position with regard to liquidity and there is a large scope for the company to expand. The Bench Mark Current Ratio is 1.33 : 1.00. Current Assets include cash and bank balances, sundry debtors, inventories, loans & advances and short term investments. Current Liabilities include secured and unsecured loans that are repayable within one year, current liabilities and provisions. In interpreting the Current Ratio, the composition of Current Asset should be given due consideration. For a given Current Ratio, when there is a higher proportion of cash and debtors, the liquidity of the firm will be comfortable; when a higher proportion of Current Assets is in the form of inventories the liquidity position will not be that good.

Quick Ratio (QR)

It is also called Acid Test Ratio.

$$\text{Quick Ratio} = \frac{\text{Quick Assets}}{\text{Current Liabilities}}$$

Quick assets are those current assets that are highly liquid. Inventories and prepaid expenses are excluded from current assets to arrive at quick assets.

Accordingly,

$$\text{Quick Ratio} = \frac{\text{Current Assets} - \text{Inventory} - \text{Prepaid Expenses}}{\text{Current Liabilities}}$$

A Quick ratio of 1.00 : 1.00 is considered to represent a satisfactory liquidity position.

Leverage Ratios

Leverage Ratios represent the nature of Capital Structure of a company. Leverage Ratios indicate the long term solvency of a company, i.e., the ability of the company to service long-term debts.

The following are some of the Leverage Ratios:

- Debt Equity Ratio
- Total Debt to Total Assets Ratio
- Proprietary Ratio
- Interest Coverage Ratio

While debt capital may be a comparatively cheaper source of finance, it is always a source of high risk. Since, debt capital bears interest which is payable irrespective of the business conditions, debt capital is always a riskier one. Leverage Ratios are used to assess the risk that a business firm is expected to undergo due to the use of debt capital in its capital structure. Even well managed companies might suffer unexpected losses leading to unhealthy financial position and might default in repayment of debt capital and interest on debt capital. Such a situation will be very difficult to overcome and the business firm might lose its credibility in the market.

$$\text{Debt Equity Ratio} = \frac{\text{Long Term Debt}}{\text{Owner's Equity}}$$

$$\text{Total Debt to Total Assets} = \frac{\text{Total Debts}}{\text{Total Assets}}$$

$$\text{Proprietary Ratio} = \frac{\text{Owner's Equity}}{\text{Total Assets}}$$

$$\text{Interest Coverage Ratio} = \frac{\text{Earnings Before Interest and Tax (EBIT)}}{\text{Interest on Long Term Debt}}$$

Profitability Ratios

Any business exists with the objective of earning profits. Hence, profitability ratios indicate how successful a company is in meeting its objective of profit maximization. The commonly used Profitability Ratios are given below:

$$\text{Gross Profit Margin Ratio} = \frac{\text{Gross Profit}^{*}}{\text{Net Sales}}$$

$$\text{Net Profit Margin Ratio} = \frac{\text{Net Profit}}{\text{Net Sales}}$$

* (Sales – Cost of goods sold)

$$\text{Return on Assets} = \frac{\text{Net Profit}}{\text{Total Assets}}$$

$$\text{Return on Capital Employed} = \frac{\text{Earnings Before Interest and Tax (EBIT)}}{\text{Total Capital Employed}}$$

$$\text{Return on Investment} = \frac{\text{Earnings after Tax}}{\text{Total Assets}}$$

$$\text{Return on Equity} = \frac{\text{Net Profit}}{\text{Shareholders' Equity}}$$

$$\text{Earnings Per Share (EPS)} = \frac{\text{Net Profit available to Equity Share-holders}}{\text{Number of Equity Shares}}$$

$$\text{Price Earnings Ratio [P/E Ratio]} = \frac{\text{Market Price per Share}}{\text{EPS}}$$

$$\text{Dividend Yield} = \frac{\text{Dividend per Share}}{\text{Market Price per Share}}$$

Activity Ratios

Activity Ratios measure the efficiency with which a business manages its assets. Some of the commonly used Activity Ratios are as below:

$$\text{Inventory Turnover} = \frac{\text{Sales}}{\text{Average Inventory}}$$

$$\text{Debtors Turnover} = \frac{\text{Sales}}{\text{Average Debtors}}$$

$$\text{Current Assets Turnover} = \frac{\text{Sales}}{\text{Current Assets}}$$

$$\text{Fixed Assets Turnover} = \frac{\text{Sales}}{\text{Fixed Assets}}$$

$$\text{Total Assets Turnover} = \frac{\text{Sales}}{\text{Total Assets}}$$

Ratios are arrived at from the financial statements. Hence, all ratios reveal the past performance of a company. An investor makes an analysis of the past performance of a company (through ratio analysis) in order to forecast its future performance. Investment decisions are made by investors on the basis of anticipated future performance. Banks/Financial institutions also make use of Ratio Analysis to study the past performance before arriving at a decision to lend long term/short term loans to companies.

3.5.2. Hints on Profit and Loss Account

The following aspects of Profit and Loss account deserve consideration.

Profit and loss accounts of successive years should show growth in sales turnover. If the growth rate in sales turnover of a company is below the growth rate of similar companies in the industry, it is not worth taking risk by investing in the shares of the company. Profits can be improved in two ways. The cost has to be reduced or the sales turnover has to be increased in order to register higher profits. Cost reduction may not be possible after a certain level. In a competitive scenario, the profit margins will follow a declining trend with more and more companies entering the market and with the introduction of latest production methods. Hence, growth in volume is the main area that a company should concentrate upon. If there is cost reduction along with growth in volume/turnover, it will improve the surplus further.

It may be noted that the gross sales will not always be a correct indicator of growth. This is because some units sold may attract sales tax and some excise duty. If one company comes under the purview of excise duty and another does not, their sales volume/growth cannot be straight away compared. Excise duty and sales tax collected by a company are to be paid back to the government. Hence, net sales (arrived at after deducting duties/taxes from the gross sales) will be a better indicator both for inter-company comparison and for studying the trend in sales over a few years.

Job order receipts are also to be considered as part of sales. Job order receipts should not be considered as 'other income' since apart from raw material, all other factors of production are included in the cost. Hence, if job order receipts are treated as 'other income' it will be difficult to assess the efficiency of operation of a company.

3.5.3. Hints on Balance Sheet

The size of a company is reflected by the balance sheet. The bigger the size of the company, the bigger the amount on the Assets/Liabilities side. The bigger the size of the company, the greater is the ability to handle difficult situations. Good will that a company enjoys also goes with the size of the company. Ability to mobilise funds improves with size. Hence, size gives extra edge to companies over competitors. Small sized companies also face the threat of being taken over by bigger companies.

When a company has one or more subsidiaries, the surpluses generated by the subsidiaries are to be studied. If a subsidiary is not performing well and simply remains as an asset without offering any return, or if the investment in the subsidiary has become bad, for arriving at the tangible net worth of a company, the assets of the subsidiary should be treated as intangible asset.

3.5.4. Discussion on P/E Ratio

$$\text{Price Earnings Ratio [P/E Ratio]} = \frac{\text{Market Price per Share}}{\text{EPS}}$$

P/E Ratio is the most popular ratio used by investors to assess the strength of a company. If P/E ratio is equal to, say 7.00, it indicates that the market price of the share is seven times its EPS. If the EPS remains constant, it will take seven years to recover the cost of buying the share. Hence, P/E Ratio is a reflection of the market's opinion of the earning capacity and future prospects of a company.

A high/very high P/E Ratio (say, in the order of 20 to 60) indicates that the investors foresee brighter prospects and higher future earnings by the company and the company enjoys the confidence of the investors. A low P/E ratio (say, in the range of 4 to 10) may look attractive for buying since the market price of share is low as compared to the EPS (say, 4 to 10 times the EPS). However, though such companies may be having moderate/ easonable current earnings, may pose very dim future prospects. Since, the future prospects do not appear to be attractive to the investors, they may not be prepared to pay a high market price due to which the P/E Ratio remains in a lower band. So, investors make use of P/E ratio along with the prospects of future earnings to come to a conclusion as to whether the P/E Ratio is low or high and accordingly arrive at their investment decisions.

***Illustration* 3.1:**

The face value of equity shares of M/s ABC Company Ltd., is Rs. 10 each. The EPS of the company during the past three years and the high and low market prices of shares of the company during the past three years are as below:

	Two years before last year	Year before last year	Last year
EPS	Rs. 6.00	Rs. 7.00	Rs. 9.00
Share Price (High)	Rs. 40.00	Rs. 50.00	Rs. 70.00
Share Price (Low)	Rs. 22.00	Rs. 24.00	Rs. 30.00

The equity share of the company is being currently sold in the secondary market at Rs. 40.00. There is not expected to be much variation in the future EPS of the company. Advise whether an investor can go for investing in the equity share of the company.

Solution:

$$\text{Price Earnings Ratio [P/E Ratio]} = \frac{\text{Market Price per Share}}{\text{EPS}}$$

	Two years before last year	Year before last year	Last year
Average Price Per Share	Rs. (40 + 22) / 2 = 31.00	Rs. (50 + 24) / 2 = 37.00	Rs.(70 + 30)/2 = 50.00
P/E Ratio (Average price / EPS)	31/6 = 5.20	37/7 = 5.30	50/9 = 5.50
Average P/E Ratio	(5.20 + 5.30 + 5.50) / 3 = 5.30		

Based on the past data, a P/E Ratio of 5.30 can be taken as the Bench Mark for the company's share. The EPS of the company in the last year is Rs. 9.00. Assuming the EPS to remain the same in future, the appropriate P/E Ratio for the company can be taken at 5.30.

i.e., $$\frac{\text{Market Price per Share}}{\text{EPS}} = 5.30$$

$$\frac{\text{Market Price per Share}}{9.00} = 5.30$$

$$\text{Market Price per share} = 9.00 \times 5.30$$

$$= 47.70$$

We have arrived at a Market price of Rs. 47.70 per share taking the average P/E Ratio into account and assuming that the EPS will remain at Rs. 9.00 in future. In any analysis with regard to investments, reasonable assumptions are always required to be made at various levels. Since the share is currently being sold at Rs. 40.00 in the secondary market, the investor can opt for buying the share of M/s ABC Company Ltd., at the prevailing market price of Rs. 40.00.

***Illustration* 3.2:**

M/s Highbeam Lamps Limited is a company engaged in the manufacture of electric bulbs. As on 31st March, the shareholders funds position of the company is as under:

4,55,000 Equity shares of face value Rs. 10 each : Rs. 45.50 lakhs

95,000 Preference shares of face value Rs. 10 each : Rs. 9.50 lakhs

Reserves : Rs. 60.00 lakhs

Preference dividend payable is 20% of the face value.

Profit after tax, before preference dividend : Rs. 58.00 lakhs

Market price of equity share as on 31st March : Rs. 114

Find the P/E Ratio.

Solution:

$$\text{Price Earnings Ratio [P/E Ratio]} = \frac{\text{Market Price per Share}}{\text{EPS}}$$

Preference dividend payable = 20%

= Rs. 2.00 per preference share

Total preference dividend payable = Rs. 95,000 × 2

= Rs. 1,90,000/-

Profit after tax & after preference Dividend = Rs. (58,00,000 – 1,90,000)

= Rs. 56,10,000/-

$$\text{EPS} = \frac{56,10,000}{4,55,000}$$

= 12.33

P/E Ratio = 114/12.33

= 9.25

3.5.5. Discussion on Intrinsic Value of Equity Shares

Intrinsic value of a share is the present value of all future amounts to be received by the owner of the share. When we say that intrinsic value is the present value of future amounts receivable, there arises a 'Discount Rate' at which the future incomes will be discounted to arrive at the present value. This 'Discount rate' depends on the investor's risk perception. The risk perceptions of investors differ. Two different investors may have different perceptions about the risk level of investments in the equity shares of a same company. It is due to this difference in perceptions that shares are getting traded in the secondary market. When an investor sells an equity share in the secondary market and another investor buys the same, it is because of the reason that the seller finds the price acceptable to him and at the same time the buyer also quite satisfied with the price. When a sale transaction takes place, both the seller and the buyer are in a win-win situation. When a seller prefers to sell, the buyer prefers to buy at that price. This is made possible mainly due to the difference in their risk perceptions.

Consider the following illustration.

***Illustration* 3.3:**

A company is expected to pay dividends of Rs. 2.00, Rs. 2.50 and Rs. 3.00 in the next three years. The face value of equity share is Rs. 10.00. It is estimated that the share can be sold at a price of Rs. 200.00 after three years from now. Investor Mr. Kumar wants to invest in the shares of the company with the idea of holding the shares for three years. He expects a return of 16% on his investments in the company's shares. Another investor Mr. Rajan also wants to invest in the shares of the company with the idea of holding it for a period of three years. He expects a return of 25% on his investment. Calculate the intrinsic value of the equity share of the company.

Solution:

There are two investors who are interested to invest in the equity shares of a particular company. Their risk perception of the company differs and this is evident from the difference in the returns expected by them on their investment. Mr. Rajan considers the investment in the company's shares more risky and hence expects a return of 25%. According to Mr. Kumar, investing in the company's share is not that risky (or at least not as risky as considered by Mr. Rajan). Hence, he finds himself comfortable with a return of 16% on his investment. As their risk perceptions differ (and hence the discount rate differs), the intrinsic value of the share will be different for the two investors. [If there are more numbers of investors opting to invest in the company's share, there will be more and more risk perception estimates and there will be many intrinsic values, each representing the estimate of a particular investor.

Intrinsic value according to Mr. Kumar

$$= \frac{2.00}{1.16} + \frac{2.50}{(1.16)^2} + \frac{(3.00 + 200.00)}{(1.16)^3}$$

$$= 133.63$$

Intrinsic value according to Mr. Rajan

$$= \frac{2.00}{1.25} + \frac{2.50}{(1.25)^2} + \frac{(3.00 + 200.00)}{(1.25)^3}$$

$$= 107.14$$

***Illustration* 3.4:**

The balance sheet of a company and the extract of Profit and Loss Account are given below.

Rs. in lakhs

Liabilities		Assets	
Equity Share Capital [36,65,000 shares at a face value of Rs. 10.00 each]	365.00	Fixed Assets	219.65
Reserves	640.15	Current Assets	1444.24
Loans	112.86		
Current Liability	545.88		
	1663.89		1663.89

Rs. in lakhs

Sales	9493.77
Cost of goods sold	8976.31
Profit before tax	517.46
Tax	232.86
Profit after tax	284.60
Appropriation of profit: Dividend : 93.78 Transfer to Reserves : 190.82	284.60

The equity share of the company is being traded in the market at a price of Rs. 29.00. Find the EPS, P/E ratio, Book value of equity share, Dividend pay out ratio, Dividend cover and Market-to-Book ratio.

Solution:

(*i*) $\text{EPS} = \dfrac{\text{Profit after Tax}}{\text{No. of Equity Shares}} = 28460000/3650000 = \text{Rs. } 7.80$

(*ii*) $\text{P/E Ratio} = 29.00/7.80 = 3.72$

(*iii*) $$\text{Book Value per Share} = \frac{\text{Shareholders' Funds}}{\text{No. of Equity Shares}}$$

$$= \frac{(\text{Total Assets} - \text{Liabilities})}{\text{No. of Equity Shares}}$$

$$= \frac{(1663.89 - 658.74)^{*}}{36,50,000}$$

$$= \text{Rs. } 27.54$$

(* This is nothing but the sum of Equity share capital and Reserves)

Note: *How is Book value useful? In companies that are in existence for a very long period, the gap between the Market value and the Book value of shares will be high. In such cases, the Book value will be of little value. In newly established companies, the Market value and the Book value of shares will be nearly equal. When the Market value of a share is very much greater than its Book value, it indicates two things, viz., (i) the assets are under-valued in the balance sheet and (ii) the investors have great confidence on the growth prospects of the company. When the Book value of the share is more than the Market value, it indicates that the company does not enjoy investor confidence.*

$$\text{Dividend Payout (DPO) Ratio} = \frac{\text{Dividend per Share (DPS)}}{\text{EPS}}$$

$$\text{DPS} = 93{,}78{,}000/36{,}50{,}000$$

$$= \text{Rs. } 2.57$$

$$\text{DPO Ratio} = \frac{2.57 \times 100}{7.80}$$

$$= 32.95\%$$

$$\text{Dividend Cover} = 1/(\text{DPO Ratio})$$

$$[\text{also} = \text{EPS/DPS}]$$

$$= 1/0.3295$$

$$= 3.03$$

Note: *A low Dividend Payout Ratio (or a high Dividend cover) suggests that the company may be aiming for expansion plans.*

$$\text{Market to Book Ratio} = \frac{\text{Market Value of Share}}{\text{Book Value of Share}}$$

$$= 29/27.54$$

$$= 1.05$$

Note: *When the Market to Book ratio is less than* ***1.00****, it indicates that investors have lost interest in the company. Investors do not anticipate that future profits will be sufficient to justify investment in the company's shares.*

3.5.6. Discussion on Bonus Shares

Investors invest in the equity shares of a company in anticipation of returns in the form of dividends and also in anticipation of capital appreciation. All the profit that a business firm earns is not distributed as dividends. Only a portion of the earnings is given out as dividend to the shareholders and the remaining is retained in the business. This retained surplus is also known as 'Retained earnings' or 'Reserves & Surplus' in the balance sheet of the company. Thus, the Reserves & Surplus is also the owned funds of the company. Over a period of time if a company continues to earn profits year after year, the 'Reserves & Surplus' will grow and will become quite large. When this accumulates to a substantial amount, the company may decide to transfer a portion of this amount from 'Reserves & Surplus' account to 'Share Capital' account. This is done by a mere book entry. This has the effect of reducing the 'Reserves & Surplus' amount in the balance sheet and increasing the 'Share Capital' account by the same amount. When the share capital is increased, the number of shares outstanding is also to be increased to the extent required. When this is done, the company is said to have made a bonus issue. It may be noted that the shareholders' wealth position does not improve as a result of bonus issue, since it is only a book entry.

When issue of bonus shares does not improve the wealthy position of the shareholders, why do companies resort to issuing bonus shares? There are a few reasons for this. They are,

- If bonus shares are not issued and if the retained earnings have grown too big, the market price of the company's share will shoot up and it may become so high that small investors may not be in a position to participate actively in the secondary market.
- The rate of dividend (as a percentage of the face value of equity share) will become too high and this may draw public criticism.
- When bonus shares are issued the number of floating stock increases and this improves tradability.

Some of the points to be noted with regard to bonus issues are as below:

Bonus issues are permitted to be made only out of free reserves. Reserves created by revaluation of fixed assets, debenture redemption reserve etc., are not permitted to be capitalized. The residual reserve after the proposed capitalization should be at least 40% of the increased paid up capital. Time limit between two bonus issues is minimum 36 months.

The share price before issue of bonus share and after issue of bonus share will vary widely due to the reason that the number of shares of the company before and after the bonus issue is different. The market price of equity share immediately before the bonus issue is called 'cum-bonus' price and the market price immediately after the bonus issue is called 'ex-bonus' price.

***Illustration* 3.5:**

The details of a company are as below:

Equity share capital (7,80,000 shares @ face value of Rs. 10): Rs. 78.00 lakhs

Reserves & Surplus

General Reserve : 114.50

Debenture Redemption Reserve : 10.50

125.00 lakhs

Market price of equity share of the company is Rs. 32. The company plans for a 3 : 5 Bonus issue (i.e., 3 additional shares will be issued for every 5 existing shares). Find the likely 'ex-bonus' price of share. Show that the wealth position of the shareholder remains the same before and after bonus issue.

Solution:

Equity share capital	: Rs. 78.00 lakhs
No. of equity shares before bonus issue (of face value Rs. 10 each)	: 7,80,000
No. of Bonus share that will be issued [7,80,000 × (3/5)]	: 4,68,000
Total No. of bonus share after bonus issue	: 12,48,000
Reserves & Surplus (after bonus issue):	
General reserve (114.50 – 46.80)	: Rs. 67.70 lakhs
Debenture redemption reserve	: Rs. 10.50 lakhs
	: Rs. 78.20 lakhs
Wealth position of shareholder before bonus issue :	
Equity share capital	: Rs. 78.00 lakhs
General reserve	: Rs. 114.50 lakhs
	: Rs. 192.50 lakhs
Wealth position of shareholder after bonus issue:	
Equity share capital (78.00 + 46.80)	: Rs. 124.80 lakhs
General reserve (114.50 – 46.80)	: Rs. 67.70 lakhs
	: Rs. 192.50 lakhs

Thus, the wealth position of the shareholder remains the same before and after bonus issue.

Since there is no change in the wealth position of shareholders,

Market price of 5 shares (before bonus issue) = Market price of 8 shares (after Bonus issue)

(5 × 32) = 8 × (ex-bonus price)

Ex-bonus price of equity share = (5 × 32)/8

= Rs. 20.00

Note: *The ex-bonus price as arrived at in the illustration above is Rs. 20 per share. Normally, the ex-bonus price is slightly more than what it should be as arrived at in the illustration given above. This is mainly due to the reason that companies usually pay the same rate of dividend on the expanded capital base.*

3.5.7. Discussion on Rights Issue

When an existing company wants to mobilize further equity capital, it should give reference to existing equity shareholders. The existing shareholders have the first right to subscribe to the issue in proportion to their existing share holdings. Only that portion of the issued share capital that is not subscribed by the existing shareholders can be offered to the public. The issue of share capital offered to the existing shareholders as their right to invest in the company is known as the 'Rights issue'. Public issue is an issue made by a company that is open to the public at a large and anybody can invest in the shares offered by the company.

The price of equity shares immediately before the Rights issue is known as cum-rights price and the price immediately after the Rights issue is known as ex-rights price. In case an existing investor is not interested to subscribe in the Rights issue, he can sell his 'rights' separately in the market and the buyer of the 'rights' can buy the share at the issue price.

***Illustration* 3.6:**

A company has 10,00,000 equity share outstanding. The market value of equity share is Rs. 45. The company wants to raise another Rs. 50,00,000 as equity capital and wants to go for Rights issue. The company proposes an issue price of Rs. 20 per share. What would be the ex-rights price of the share?

Solution:

No. of existing equity shares	: 10,00,000
Cum-rights price per share	: Rs. 45
Market Capitalisation (10,00,000 × 45)	: Rs. 4,50,00,000
No. of rights shares to be issued (50,00,000/20)	: 2,50,000
Rights ratio	: 2,50,000
	: 10,00,000
	: 1 : 4

[A Rights ratio of 1 : 4 means that an existing investor who holds 4 shares will get one 'rights'.]

Cum-rights price of share	: Rs. 45
No. of shares outstanding after the rights issue	: 10,00,000 + 2,50,000
	: 12,50,000

Ex-rights price is arrived at on the assumption that the additional capital raised is not going to affect the overall profit of the company significantly.

$$\text{Ex-rights price} = \frac{(4,50,00,000 + 50,00,000)}{(10,00,000 + 2,50,000)} = \text{Rs. } 40.00$$

Note: *The ex-rights price is expected to be Rs. 40. Since the rights are offered by the company to buy equity shares at Rs. 20 per share, an* *investor who is already holding equity shares of the company and who is not prepared to invest can as well sell the rights in the market which will fetch him any price near about Rs. 40 per share. Obviously, the rights will have market value only when the issue price is below the market price of the share.*

3.5.8. Stock Split and Reverse Split

When shares have high face value (or market value), trading gets restricted. Under such conditions the face value of share is reduced and the number of shares is increased proportionately, which is known as stock split. Since, stock split increases the number of shares, it improves tradability. In bonus issue, a part of the Reserves is capitalized (i.e., converted into equity shares). In stock split there is no conversion of reserves into equity shares. Reverse split is a case where a company increases the face value and accordingly reduces the number of shares. A share with a very low face value (or market value) gives a negative impression in the minds of the investors. Reverse split overcomes this impression.

REVIEW QUESTIONS

1. Define Fundamental Analysis. What are its three components?
2. Distinguish between intrinsic value and market value of an equity share.
3. Give a brief account of Economy Analysis.
4. What are the short-term forecasting techniques used in Economic forecasting? Explain them in brief.
5. Give five examples each for Leading indicators, Lagging indicators and Coincidental indicators.
6. Write short notes on the following:
    - Econometric Model Building
    - Opportunistic Model Building.
7. Enumerate the phases involved in Long range economic forecasting.
8. Explain industry life cycle analysis. What are its limitations?
9. Explain Porter Model of industry analysis.
10. Define P/E Ratio. What does a very high P/E ratio (say, a ratio of 60) Indicate?
11. What is 'Deferred tax liability'? Explain its implications in a Balance Sheet.
12. The difference between intrinsic value and market price of equity shares is due to the difference in risk perceptions of investors. Explain.
13. What are the reasons behind companies issuing Bonus shares to their share holders?

4 CHAPTER Share Valuation

4.1. INTRODUCTION

Each share of a company has an intrinsic value. By intrinsic value, we mean the inherent, genuine value of the share. How does the share of a company acquire inherent value? A share acquires inherent (or intrinsic) value by virtue of its ability to offer return to the investor. The returns available to an investor of shares are in the form of dividends and capital appreciation. Hence, the intrinsic value of a share depends upon the returns that a shareholder expects to receive from the share in future in the form of dividends and capital appreciation. A fundamental analyst arrives at the intrinsic value of a share by studying its capacity to offer returns. He then compares the intrinsic value of the share with its current market price. If the current market price of the share is less than its intrinsic value, he arrives at the decision to buy the share. If the current market price of the share is more than its intrinsic value, he arrives at the decision to sell the share (if he already owns it)

A share whose current market price is more than its intrinsic value is considered 'over-priced' and hence it is advised to be sold while a share whose current market price is less than its intrinsic value is considered 'under-priced' and hence it is advised to be purchased.

The fundamental analyst believes that the market price of share will reach its intrinsic value in due course. Thus, by buying an under-priced share, an investor stands to gain due to capital appreciation that is likely to take place by upward movement of the share price towards its intrinsic value. By selling an under-priced share an investor avoids the likelihood of incurring a loss due to capital erosion that is likely to take place by downward movement of the share price towards its intrinsic value.

Thus, to decide upon as to whether to buy or sell a share, an investor should have two data viz., the current market price of the share and its intrinsic value. While the current market prices of shares are available from the quotations of stock exchanges, their intrinsic values are estimated by the investor through the process of share valuation.

4.2. TIME VALUE OF MONEY

Money has a time value. A rupee received today and a rupee that will be received after one year are, obviously not equal in value. This is because of the simple fact that a rupee received today can be invested in some form of investments out of which it can earn some return. For example, if a rupee received today is invested in the savings account of a bank which gives a return of say, 7% p.a., after one year, the investment made of Rs. 1.00 would have earned an interest of Rs. 0.07. Since the amount is invested in a savings account, its safety is assured and hence the return of Rs. 0.07 after one year is also assured. From this angle, a rupee received today is equal to Rs. 1.07 received after one year.

Let us compare the value of a rupee received today and a rupee receivable after say, 5 years. If the interest rate offered by banks for savings account is 7% p.a., one rupee deposited in savings account will become Rs. 1.07 after one year. The accumulated amount of Rs. 1.07, if invested for one more year will earn 7% return on Rs. 1.07 and will accumulate to Rs. 1.1449 (1.07 × 1.07). Similarly, further reinvestment of the accumulated amount of Rs. 1.1449 for one more year will accumulate to Rs. 1.2250 and so on. After the end of 5 years, the accumulated amount will grow to Rs. 1.4025.

If an amount of 'P' is invested for a period of 'n' years at a rate of interest of r% p.a., the amount that will be available after a period of 'n' years is given by the following compound interest formula.

$$P_n = P(1 + r)^n$$

where P_n = future value of 'P' after 'n' years.

The above formula is based on the assumption that interest is payable only on yearly basis and hence interest is compounded on yearly basis.

Suppose a sum of Rs. 5,000 is invested in a bank for a period of 4 years at an interest of 8% p.a. The amount to be received after 4 years will be given by the compound interest formula.

$$\begin{aligned} P_n &= P(1 + r)^n \\ &= 5{,}000\ (1 + 0.08)^4 \\ &= 5{,}000\ (1.08)^4 \\ &= 6{,}802.00 \end{aligned}$$

Rs. 6,802 is the future value of the present sum of Rs. 5,000. The assumption is the compound interest formula given above is that interest is payable only once in a year and it is compounded annually. The same formula can be used for arriving at the present value of a sum to be received in the future.

$$P_n = P(1 + r)^n$$

If we want to know the amount to be deposited in a bank at an interest rate of 8% p.a. for a period of four years so that we can get Rs. 5,000 at the end of four years, the same formula can be made use of.

$$P_n = P(1 + r)^n$$

$$P = \frac{P_n}{(1+r)^n}$$

$$= \frac{5000}{(1+0.08)^4}$$

$$= \text{Rs. } 3{,}675$$

If we deposit Rs. 3,675 at 8% p.a. for a period of four years we will get Rs. 5,000, at the end of four years.

The reverse process that we have used above to calculate the present value of a sum to be received in the future is known as the ***process of discounting.***

4.3. SHARE VALUATION MODELS

By share valuation we mean arriving at the intrinsic value of shares. A share possesses intrinsic value because it offers returns to the shareholder in the form of dividends and capital appreciation.

The intrinsic value of a share is the present value of all future amounts to be received by the owner of the share. The present value of future amounts receivable is calculated by using an appropriate discount rate. Thus, for arriving at the intrinsic value of a share we need two data. First, the future receipts that are likely to come from the share and second, the appropriate discount rate. The future receipts consist of annual dividends and the sale proceeds of the share at the end of the holding period.

4.3.1. Discount Rate

The discount rate (i.e., the rate at which the future receipts are to be discounted to their present value) is the rate of return required by the investor on his investment in the share. This rate of return is arrived at taking into account the risk involved in the investment. Since, the discount rate depends on the level of risk associated with the share it will vary from shares of one company to another. Further, even for the shares of one particular company, the discount rate may vary from one investor to another based on the risk perception of the investor. Thus, when one investor may arrive at a particular intrinsic value for a share, another investor with a different risk perception may arrive at a different intrinsic value for the same share. This is one of the main factors that leads to selling and buying of shares in the secondary market.

***Illustration* 4.1:**

The ordinary equity share of a company is expected by investors to produce a dividend of Rs. 15 per share every year in perpetuity. The share has a market value of Rs. 125 and the market value has been remaining stable for quite some time. What is the expected return by the shareholders of the company?

Solution:

The market value of Rs. 125 represents the sum of expected future dividends discounted at an appropriate rate.

Accordingly,

$$125 = \frac{15}{(1+i)^1} + \frac{15}{(1+i)^2} + \frac{15}{(1+i)^3} + \ldots + \frac{15}{(1+i)^n}$$

$$= \frac{15}{i}$$

$$i = 15/125$$

$$= 0.12$$

$$= 12\%$$

Hence, the return expected by the shareholders is 12%.

***Note:** If an investor bought a share of the company for Rs. 125 and received dividend of Rs. 15 each year, it means that the investor would be getting a return of 12% per annum on his investment. (15/125 × 100 = 12, since the dividends are expected to be received perpetually).*

Let another investor expects a return of 15% per annum on this share. Since the market price of the share is Rs. 125, the dividend anticipated by him is Rs. 18.75 per share (15/100 × 125). Since the share is expected to offer a dividend of only Rs. 15, the investor will not be attracted to buy the share. Thus, an investor decides to buy an equity share only when the returns that the share is expected to offer matches the return that the investor expects from his investment.

4.3.2. Components of Discount Rate

The discount rate consists of two component, viz., risk-free interest rate and risk premium for the share concerned. An investor opts to invest in the shares of a company with a view to earning a return higher than the return offered by risk-free investments. Since, shares possess a higher risk than risk-free investments (like government guaranteed bonds), they offer a higher return and the excess return over and above the risk-free return is the risk premium. Risk premium is thus the additional return due to the element of risk associated with the investment. The higher the level of risk the higher the risk premium and accordingly the investor who opts to invest in a high risk share will expect a higher return. Though there are techniques available to assess the risk level of a share and the expected return from the share, such techniques are used only by a very few investors who are knowledgeable and make their investments in a systematic, planned way. Majority of the investors assess the level of risk associated with a particular share purely on a subjective basis/institution and accordingly estimate the risk premium required.

4.3.3. Dividend Discount Models

Based on the holding period and the dividend expected to be received, share valuation models can be grouped under the following two heads.

(*a*) Holding period models

- (*i*) One year holding period model
- (*ii*) Multiple year holding period model

(*b*) Dividend growth models

- (*i*) Constant growth model
- (*ii*) Multiple growth model

(*a*) Holding period models

(i) One year holding period model

Assumptions

- The investor purchases the share now.
- The investor intends to hold the share for a period of one year.
- The investor intends to dispose off the share at the end of one year.

The present value (or intrinsic value) of the share is given by the following relationship:

$$S_0 = \frac{D_1}{(1+k)^1} + \frac{S_1}{(1+k)^1}$$

where,

S_0 = present value of the share.

D_1 = dividend expected to be received at the end of first year.

S_1 = expected selling price of the share at the end of first year.

k = rate of return required by the investor. (also called 'capitalisation rate')

***Illustration* 4.2:**

An investor desires to purchase the equity share of a company from the secondary market. The investor prefers to hold share for one year and dispose off the share after one year. The investor expects to get a dividend of Rs. 5.00 per share next year and he is hopeful of selling the share in the secondary market at a price of Rs. 70 after one year. He expects a return of 20% on his investment, considering the level of risk associated with it. Calculate the present value of the share to the investor.

Solution:

Dividend expected after one year (D_1) = Rs. 5.00

Expected sales realisation after one year (S_1) = Rs. 70.00

Return required by the investor (k) = 20%

Hence, present value of the share for the investor (S_0) is given by the following relationship

$$S_0 = \frac{D_1}{(1+k)^1} + \frac{S_1}{(1+k)^1}$$

$$= \frac{5.00}{(1+0.20)^1} + \frac{70}{(1+0.20)^1}$$

$$= \frac{5.00}{(1+0.20)} + \frac{70}{(1+0.20)}$$

$$= 4.17 + 58.33$$

$$= \text{Rs. } 62.50$$

∴ Intrinsic value of the share for the investor = Rs. 62.50

Note : *If the share is available in the secondary market at a price of* ***Rs. 62.50*** *or less, the investor would opt to buy the share. If the share price in the secondary market is more than* ***Rs. 62.50****, the investor will not buy the share since it will offer a return that is below the expectation of the investor. The intrinsic value of* ***Rs. 62.50*** *is for the investor given in the problem who anticipates a return of 20%. If another investor is satisfied with a return of, say 18%, he will be prepared to buy the share even at a higher price. To be exact, his intrinsic value for the share, other things remaining the same, will be* ***Rs. 63.55*** *as under:*

$$S_0 = \frac{5.00}{1.18} + \frac{70}{1.18}$$

$$= 4.23 + 59.32$$

$$= \text{Rs. } 63.55$$

(ii) Multiple year holding period model

Assumptions

- The investor purchases the share now.
- The investor intends to hold the share for a certain number of years.
- The investor will dispose off the share at the end of the holding period.

If the investor wants to hold the share for a period of 'n' years, he will be receiving dividends every year and in the nth year, apart from the dividend he will also receive the sales realization due to disposal of the share. The present value of the share is the present value of future dividends and sales realization at the end of the holding period. This is arrived at by discounting the future income stream at an appropriate discount rate. The discount rate is nothing but the rate of return anticipated by the investor on his investment in the share.

Accordingly, the present value of the share as per multiple year holding period model is given by the following relationship

$$S_0 = \frac{D_1}{(1+k)^1} + \frac{D_2}{(1+k)^2} + \frac{D_3}{(1+k)^3} + \ldots + \frac{D_n + S_n}{(1+k)^n}$$

where

S_0 = present value of the share

$D_1, D_2, D_3, \ldots, D_n$ = annual dividend that will be received in the respective years.

S_n = expected sale price of the share at the end of the holding period

k = rate of return required for the investor

n = holding period (in years)

***Illustration* 4.3:**

An investor desires to purchase the equity share of a company from the secondary market. The investor prefers to hold the share for a period of four years and dispose off the share after four years. He expects to get a dividend of Rs. 6.00, Rs. 6.50, Rs. 7.50 and Rs. 9.00 per share in the next four years respectively. He is hopeful of selling the share in the secondary market at a price of Rs. 120 after the end of four years. He expects a return of 22% on his investment considering the level of risk associated with it. Calculate the present value of the share to the investor.

Solution:

$$S_0 = \frac{D_1}{(1+k)^1} + \frac{D_2}{(1+k)^2} + \frac{D_3}{(1+k)^3} + \ldots\ldots\ldots\ldots + \frac{D_n + S_n}{(1+k)^n}$$

$$= \frac{6.00}{(1+0.22)^1} + \frac{6.50}{(1+0.22)^2} + \frac{7.50}{(1+0.22)^3} + \frac{9.00+120}{(1+0.22)^4}$$

$= 4.92 + 4.38 + 4.13 + 58.23$

Present value of the share = Rs. 71.66

(*b*) Dividend growth models

The cash inflow from out of a stock consists of two components, viz., the dividends and the sale price of the stock (in the event of disposing off the stock in secondary market). The sale price is the expected price that the stock may fetch in the secondary market. The expected price itself is decided by the future dividends that the stock is likely to offer to its holder. Hence, the value of a stock can be taken to be the present value of dividend through infinity. Since dividends are assumed to be received for infinite period, the sale price of stock is not considered in arriving at its intrinsic value. Dividend growth models are based on this assumption that the intrinsic value of a stock is given by the present value of all future dividends.

(i) *Constant growth model*

Assumptions

- The investor buys and holds the share forever.
- The dividends from the share grow at a constant rate.
- The discount rate (used for arriving at the present value of the share) is greater than the dividend growth rate.

Let

D_0 = current dividend being offered by the share.

g = annual growth rate of dividend (which is constant every year).

D_1 = dividend expected to be received after one year.

D_2 = dividend expected to be received after two years.

D_3 = dividend expected to be received after three years.

...

...

D_n = dividend expected to be received after 'n' years.

Since, the dividend is assumed to grow at a constant rate every years.

$D_1 = D_0\,(1 + g)^1$

$D_2 = D_0\,(1 + g)^2$

$D_3 = D_0\,(1 + g)^3$

...

...

$D_n = D_0\,(1 + g)^n$

where 'g' is the annual growth rate of dividend.

As the share is assumed to be held indefinitely by the investor, the question of resale price of share does not arise. Hence, the present value of the share is the sum of present value of all future dividends.

$$S_0 = \frac{D_0(1+g)^1}{(1+k)^1} + \frac{D_0(1+g)^2}{(1+k)^2} + \frac{D_0(1+g)^3}{(1+k)^3} + \ldots + \frac{D_0(1+g)^n}{(1+k)^n}$$

When 'n' approaches infinity (since the investor is assumed to hold the share forever), the above formula can be simplified as

$$S_0 = \frac{D_0(1+g)}{(k-g)}$$

Since $D_1 = D_0(1 + g)$, the present value can also be written as

$$S_0 = \frac{D_1}{(k-g)}^{**}$$

The constant growth model was devised by Myron J. Gordan and hence is also known by his name as Gordon's Dividend model of share valuation. This model is one of the widely used models because of its simplicity. The only two data required for the model are the expected growth rate of dividend (g) and the rate of discount (k).

Limitations of Gordon Dividend Model

1. The use of this model is restricted to firms that have been growing and are expected to grow at a stable growth rate forever and are expected to offer dividends at the same rate of their earnings forever. In other words, the model can be used only if the dividend growth rate is expected to remain constant every year.

$$^{**}S_0 = \frac{D_1}{(1+k)^1} + \frac{D_2}{(1+k)^2} + \frac{D_3}{(1+k)^3} + \ldots$$

$$= \frac{D_1}{(1+k)^1} + \frac{D_1(1+g)}{(1+k)^2} + \frac{D_1(1+g)^2}{(1+k)^3} + \ldots \quad (i)$$

Multiplying both sides by $\frac{(1+k)}{(1+g)}$, we get

$$\frac{(1+k)}{(1+g)} S_0 = \frac{D_1}{(1+g)} + \frac{D_1}{(1+k)} + \frac{D_1(1+g)}{(1+k)^2} + \ldots \quad (ii)$$

Subtracting (*i*) from (*ii*), we get

$$\left(\frac{(1+k) \times S_0}{(1+g)}\right) - S_0 = \frac{D_1}{(1+g)}$$

$$S_0\left(\frac{(1+k)}{(1+g)} - 1\right) = \frac{D_1}{(1+g)}$$

$$S_0\left(\frac{(1+k-1-g)}{(1+g)}\right) = \frac{D_1}{(1+g)}$$

$$S_0\left(\frac{(k-g)}{(1+g)}\right) = \frac{D_1}{(1+g)}$$

$$\therefore \quad S_0 = \frac{D_1}{(k-g)}$$

2. If the dividend growth rate is more than the required rate of return, the model cannot be used since the value of the stock will become negative.
3. If the dividend growth rate is equal to the required rate of return, the model cannot be used since the value of the stock will become infinity.

***Illustration* 4.4:**

M/s. Good Tread Company Ltd. has declared a dividend of Rs. 4.50 per equity share for the current year. As a policy, the company has been enhancing its dividend by 12% every year. The company is expected to follow its dividend policy in the future also. An investor is interested to invest in the equity shares of the company as a long term investment. The investor expects a return of 18% on his investment considering the level of risk associated with the shares of the company. Estimate the intrinsic value of the share for the investor.

Solution:

Let us assume that the investor is going to hold the share for ever. Since the investor chooses the shares of M/s. Good Tread Company Ltd. as a long-term investment option, this assumption will be reasonably valid.

Hence, Gordon's share valuation model can be applied to arrive at the intrinsic value of the share.

Current year's dividend (D_0) = Rs. 4.50 per share

Return required for the investor (k) = 18% p.a.

Growth rate of dividend (g) = 12% p.a.

The intrinsic value of the share is given by,

$$S_0 = \frac{D_0(1+g)}{(k-g)}$$

$$= \frac{4.50\ (1 + 0.12)}{(0.18 - 0.12)}$$

= Rs. 84

The intrinsic value of the share = Rs. 84

Note: *The investor would buy the share from the secondary market if it is available at a price of Rs. 84 or less per share. If the price is more than Rs. 84 per share, the investor would not consider it as worth investing in. The intrinsic value of Rs. 84 per share is for the investor given in the problem. For another investor whose risk perception is different, the expected return from the investment in the company's shares will be* *different and consequently the intrinsic value of the share will also be different from Rs. 84 per share.*

***Illustration* 4.5:**

ABC Ltd. is a newly started company which has commenced its operations recently. The company is not expected to pay any dividend for the first two years. During the first two years the company is expected to make use of the earnings to meet its growth prospects. In the third year the company is expected to pay a dividend of Rs. 4.00 which is expected to grow at the rate of 10% in the subsequent years. The required rate of return is 16%. Find the value of the equity share.

Solution:

We have been asked to find the value of the equity share, which is nothing but the intrinsic value.

Since, the dividend is expected to grow at a constant rate, we can make use of the formula for constant growth model.

$$\text{Intrinsic Value } (S_0) = \frac{D_1}{(k-g)}$$

$$= \frac{4.00}{(0.16-0.10)}$$

$$= \text{Rs. } 66.67$$

Since, the company is not expected to pay dividends in the first two years, the intrinsic value arrived at as share is the value at the beginning of the third year (i.e., at the end of 2 years). Hence, the present intrinsic value can be arrived at by discounting the above value at 16% for 2 years.

P.V. factor for 2 years at 16% = 0.743

Hence, present intrinsic value of the share = 0.743 × 66.67

= Rs. 49.54

***Illustration* 4.6:**

ABC Co. Ltd. is paying dividend of Rs. 6.00 per share currently. The dividend that the company can pay in the subsequent years is expected to decline at the rate of 5% every year. The capitalization rate of the company is 18%. Calculate the intrinsic value of the company's equity share.

Solution:

The growth rate of dividend is expected to decline at a constant rate. In other words the growth rate is negative.

Intrinsic value of share

$$S_0 = \frac{D_0(1+g)}{(k-g)}$$

$$= \frac{6.00\,\{1 + (-0.05)\}}{\{0.18 - (-0.05)\}}$$

$$= \frac{6.00 \times 0.95}{(0.23)}$$

$$= \text{Rs. } 24.78$$

***Illustration* 4.7:**

ABC Company limited paid a dividend of Rs. 2.50 per equity share last year. The company is on a growth phase and the dividends are expected to grow at an annual rate of 8%. An investor who opts to invest in the equity shares of the company expects a return of 12% p.a. What is the intrinsic value of the equity share?

Solution:

Since, the company has paid a dividend of Rs. 2.50 last year and as the expected annual growth rate of dividend is 8%, the dividend expected at the end of the year (D_1) is equal to $D_0(1 + g)^1$ where D_0 is equal to Rs. 2.50.

Intrinsic value of share

$$S_0 = \frac{D_0(1+g)}{(k-g)}$$

$$= \frac{2.50\,(1 + 0.08)}{\{0.12 - (0.08)\}}$$

$$= \text{Rs. } 67.50$$

***Illustration* 4.8:**

The equity shares of Zenith Pharmaceuticals Limited are currently being sold in the secondary market at Rs. 90 per share. Market analysts predict a year end dividend of Rs. 5.20 per share and a constant dividend growth rate of 7% is also predicted in the subsequent years.

(*a*) If an investor buys the equity share at its prevailing price of Rs. 90, what is the rate of return expected by the investor?

(*b*) If another investor expects a return of 14% p.a. should he buy the share from the secondary market at its current price?

Solution:

(*a*) Intrinsic value

$$S_0 = \frac{D_1}{(k-g)}$$

$$90 = \frac{5.20}{(k - 0.07)}$$

$$90k - 6.30 = \text{Rs. } 5.20$$
$$k = 0.1278$$

∴ Rate of return expected by the investor = 12.78%

(b) For an investor who expects a return on investment of 14% p.a. the intrinsic value of the share is given by

$$S_0 = \frac{D_1}{(k - g)}$$
$$= \frac{5.20}{(0.14 - 0.07)}$$
$$= \text{Rs. } 74.29$$

Since, the prevailing price of the equity share in the secondary market is Rs. 90 as against the intrinsic value of Rs. 74.29 for the investor, the share is over-priced as far as the investor is concerned. Hence, he will not buy the share at its current price of Rs. 90 per share.

***Illustration* 4.9:**

ABC Company Ltd. has earnings per share of Rs. 15.20 last year. The company has paid 50% of its earnings as dividends. The company's earnings have grown at the rate of 6% per year in the last three years and the earnings are expected to grow at the same rate in the long run. The company has been following the policy of giving 50% of its earnings as dividends and is expected to continue the same policy. The rate of return required by an investor on the stock of the company is 12% p.a. Calculate the value of the stock using Gordon's Dividend model.

Solution:

Gordon's Dividend model takes into account only the dividend payable for arriving at the intrinsic value of the stock.

Earnings per share in the last year = Rs. 15.20

Dividend paid per share in the last year = Rs. 0.50 × (15.20)

= Rs. 7.60

Growth rate of earnings = 6%

Since, there is no change in the dividend pay-out ratio (which is given as 50%), the growth rate of dividend will also remain at 6%.

∴ Constant dividend growth rate (g) = 6%

Dividend expected to be received after one year (D_1) = D_0 (1 + g)

= 7.60 (1 + 0.06)

= Rs. 8.056

Rate of return expected (k) = 12%

∴ Intrinsic value of the stock

$$= \frac{D_1}{(k-g)}$$

$$= \left(\frac{8.056}{0.12-0.06}\right)$$

$$= \text{Rs. } 134.27$$

(ii) Multiple growth model

The shortcoming of the constant growth model is that it is far from reality. Though the constant growth model is simple for use, its assumption that the dividend from a share will grow at the constant rate every year indefinitely is rare to come by. The general tendency is that the growth in dividend may follow a constant rate for a few years after which the growth rate may change and the revised growth rate may continue for a few more years and so on. Thus, the infinite period in which dividends will be forthcoming can be divided into a few stages, each stage having a different but constant growth rate. (Refer Fig. 4.1)

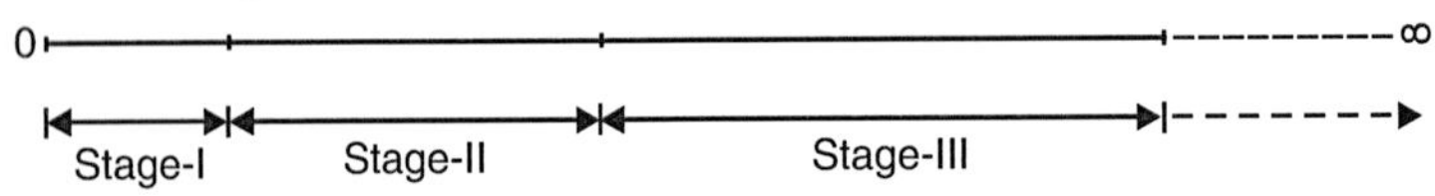

Fig. 4.1 Multiple growth model

The intrinsic value of a share on the basis of multiple growth model can be arrived at by knowing (or estimating) the growth rate for the different stages and discounting the stream of dividends to the present value at the rate required by the investor.

Two Stage Growth Model

This is multiple growth model which more or less resembles the actual growth pattern of dividends of majority of shares.

Assumptions

- The time period (in which the investor will be getting streams of dividends) is divisible into two different growth stages.
- During the initial growth stage (Stage-I) the growth rate of dividend is variable from year to year.
- During the latter growth stage (Stage-II) the dividend growth rate will remain constant from year to year. This stage will have indefinite time duration.

Thus, Stage-I (a stage of variable growth rate) will remain from period 1 to N years and Stage-II (a stage of constant growth rate) will remain from period (N + 1)th year to infinity. (Refer Fig. 4.2)

For arriving at the intrinsic value of a share using the two stage growth model, the investor should have the following estimated data:

(*a*) The number of years up to which the first stage will prevail i.e., '*N*' years

(*b*) The likely dividends from the share during the period of '*N*' years, viz.,

Dividend at the end of first year i.e., D_1

Dividend at the end of second year, i.e., D_2

...

...

Dividend at the end of *N*th year, i.e., D_N

(*c*) The constant growth rate of dividend in the second stage i.e., g

(*d*) The return required for the investor on his investment i.e., k

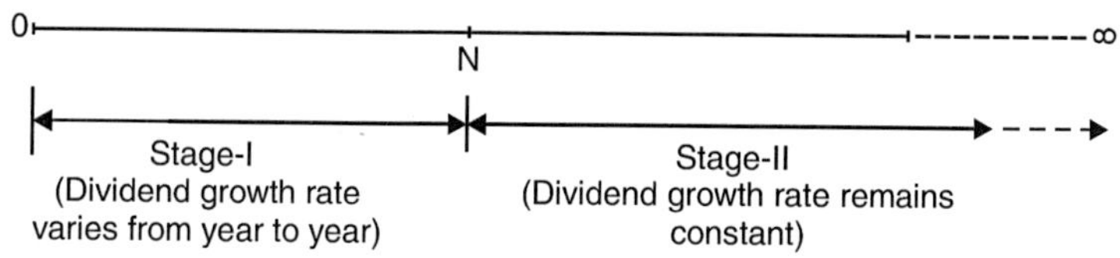

Fig. 4.2 Two stage growth model

The intrinsic value of the share is the sum of the present values (PV) of the dividend flows from the two stages.

P.V. of dividends from stage-I is given by

$$(\text{P.V.})_1 = \frac{D_1}{(1+k)^1} + \frac{D_2}{(1+k)^2} + \frac{D_3}{(1+k)^3} + \ldots + \frac{D_N}{(1+k)^N}$$

Stage-II (From period ($N+1$) to ∞) is a stage of constant growth rate. Using the present value formula for constant growth model, the value of the dividends from $(N+1)^{\text{th}}$ year to infinity as at the beginning of $(N+1)^{\text{th}}$ year is given by,

$$\frac{D_N(1+g)}{(k-g)}$$

The above is the discounted value of future dividends at the beginning of $(N+1)^{\text{th}}$ year (or at the end of Nth year). Its present value can be arrived at by discounting the above value at the rate of '*k*' for a period of '*N*' years.

$$(\text{P.V.})_{\text{II}} = \frac{D_N(1+g)}{(k-g)(1+k)^N}$$

Intrinsic Value = $(\text{P.V.})_{\text{I}} + (\text{P.V.})_{\text{II}}$

i.e., $$S_0 = \left\{\sum_{t=1}^{N}\left(\frac{D_t}{(1+k)^t}\right)\right\} + \left(\frac{D_N(1+g)}{(k-g)(1+k)^N}\right)$$

***Illustration* 4.10:**

A company has paid a dividend of Rs. 1.50 per share during the current year. The company is expected to pay a dividend of Rs. 2.00 per share during the next year. Analysts forecast a dividend of Rs. 3.00 and Rs. 3.50 per share during the subsequent two years. After three years, the company is expected to pay dividends that are expected to grow at the rate of 10% every year. The investor expects a return of 20% on his investment. Calculate the intrinsic value of the share.

Solution:

This is a two stage growth model. (Refer Fig. 4.3)

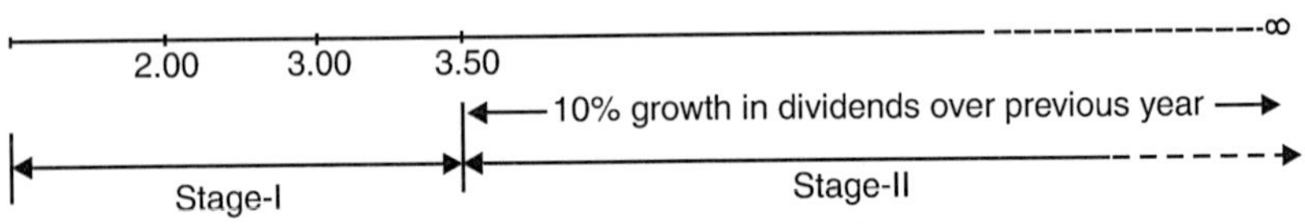

Fig. 4.3 Two stage growth model

I. Present value of stage growth model

$$= \frac{2.00}{(1+0.20)^1} + \frac{3.00}{(1+0.20)^2} + \frac{3.50}{(1+0.20)^3}$$

= Rs. 5.78

II. Present value of dividends from the fourth year to infinity

$$= \frac{D_1}{(k-g)}$$

$$= \frac{3.50(1+0.10)}{(0.20-0.10)}$$

$$= \frac{3.85}{0.10}$$

= Rs. 38.50

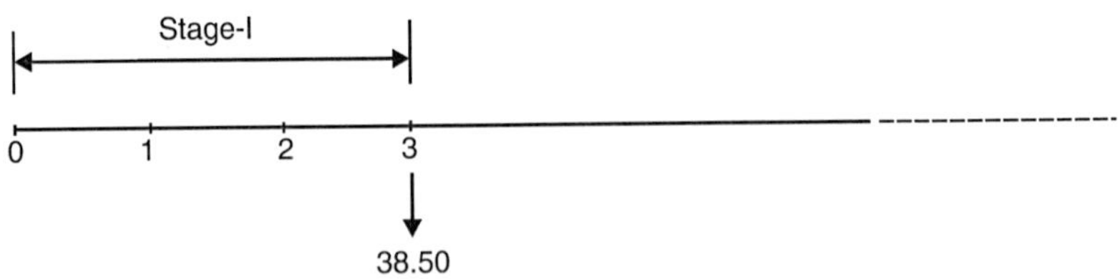

Fig. 4.4 Multiple growth model

Present value of Rs. 38.50 receivable after three years is arrived at as below (Refer Fig. 4.4):

$$= \frac{38.50}{(1+k)^3}$$

$$= \frac{38.50}{(1+0.20)^3}$$

$$= \frac{38.50}{1.728}$$

$$= \text{Rs. } 22.80$$

Intrinsic value of the share (S_0) = [Present value of dividends from Stage-I + Present value of dividends from Stage-II]

$$= 5.78 + 22.28$$

$$= \text{Rs. } 28.06$$

Note: *The intrinsic value of the share of* ***Rs. 28.06*** *arrived at is the intrinsic value for the investor who anticipates a return of 20% on his investment. The intrinsic value will differ for a different investor whose risk perception is different and who expects a return other than 20% (either above or below).*

***Illustration* 4.11:**

The equity shares of a company offer a current dividend of Rs. 4.00 per share. The rate of dividend is expected to grow at 6% for the first five years and at 8% per year thereafter. The rate of return required for an investor is 15%. Find the intrinsic value of the equity share.

Solution:

Current dividend D_0 = Rs. 4.00

D_1 = 1.06 (4.00)

= Rs. 4.24

D_2 = 1.06 (4.24)

= Rs. 4.49

D_3 = 1.06 (4.49)

= Rs. 4.76

D_4 = 1.06 (4.76)

= Rs. 5.05

D_5 = 1.06 (5.05)

= Rs. 5.35

The intrinsic value of share has two components viz., present value of dividends from Stage-I and present value of dividends from Stage-II.

The present value of dividends from Stage-II consists of present value of dividends from the sixth year to infinity.

Year	Dividend	Present value factor at 15%	Present value
1	4.24	0.870	3.6888
2	4.49	0.756	3.3944
3	4.76	0.658	3.1321
4	5.05	0.572	2.8886
5	5.35	0.497	2.6589
Present value of dividends from Stage-I			Rs.15.7628
	Say		Rs.15.76

Dividend for the sixth year (D_6) = $D_5(1 + g)$. Since the rate of growth of dividend from the sixth year onwards is 8% per annum, $g = 0.08$.

$\therefore \quad D_6 = 5.35\ (1 + 0.08)$

$= \text{Rs. } 5.79$

Present value of dividends from Stage-II on the beginning of Stage-II

$$= \frac{D_6}{k - g}$$

where $D_6 = 5.79$

$k = 0.15$

and $g = 0.08$

$$= \frac{5.79}{(0.15 - 0.08)}$$

$= \text{Rs. } 82.71$

The above value arrived at on the basics of dividends from the sixth year to infinity is the value as on the date of beginning of Stage-II i.e., after the end of 5 years. Hence, the present value can be arrived at by discounting it for a period of 5 years.

PV factor for 5 years at a discount rate of 15% = 0.497*

Present value of dividends from Stage-II $= 0.497 \times 82.71$

$= \text{Rs. } 41.11$

$\therefore$ Intrinsic value of share = (15.76 + 41.11) = Rs. 56.87

* $\left(\frac{1}{(1+0.15)^5} = 0.497\right)$

(iii) Zero growth model

Assumption

The dividend per share will remain constant every year, forever. The above assumption means that the dividend stream is a long term annuity. Symbolically it means,

$$D_1 = D_2 = D_3 = D_4 \dots = D_\infty = D$$

where

$D_1, D_2, D_3, \dots$, etc. are the expected dividends in the future years. As the dividends remain constant (i.e., $D_1 = D_2 = D_3 = D_4 \dots = D_\infty = D$), this model is also known as 'constant dividends' model.

The intrinsic value of the share as per zero growth model is given by

$$\text{Intrinsic value } (S_0) = \frac{D}{k}$$

where D = constant dividend expected to be available every year (per share)

and k = rate of return anticipated by the investor

Since, the dividends are assumed to be made available to the investor forever, sale price of the equity share does not appear in the formula.

***Illustration* 4.12:**

A company pays a dividend of Rs. 20 per equity share. The dividend is expected to remain the same. An investor requires a return of 16% for investments in the equity shares of the company. Calculate the value of the equity share.

Solution:

$$\text{Intrinsic value of the equity share } (S_0) = \frac{D}{k}$$

$$= \frac{20}{0.16}$$

$$= \text{Rs. } 125$$

(iv) H-model (Two stage dividend model)

The normal tendency of the growth rate of dividends of newly formed companies is that the dividends payable during the initial years will be higher than the dividends that can be paid after a few years. The dividend growth rate will stabilize at a particular level after some years. Till the dividend growth rate gets stabilized, there will be a gradual fall in growth rate (in other words there will be gradual decline in the dividend rate) till the growth rate gets stabilized. If these conditions are expected to prevail, the intrinsic value of the share can be arrived at using the H-model.

Assumptions of H-model

- Current above-normal growth rate is g_c.
- The dividend growth rate falls down gradually over a period of $2H$ years.
- After a period of $2H$ years, the dividend growth rate falls down to g_f.

The growth rate of g_f remains the same after $2H$ years for ever. (Refer Fig. 4.5)

***Note :** The suffix 'c' in g_c stands for 'current' and the suffix 'f' in g_f stands for 'future'.*

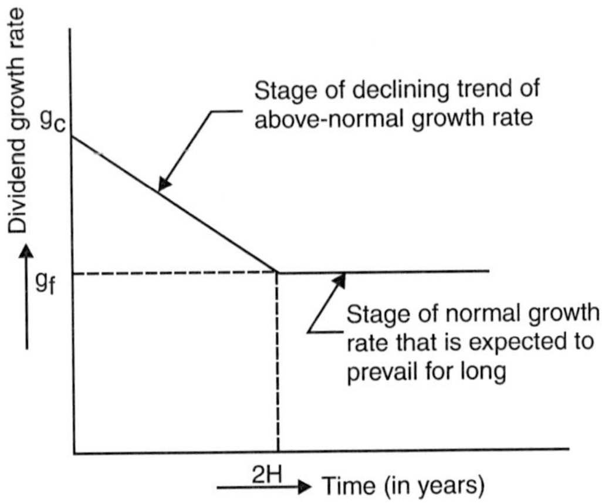

Fig. 4.5 H-model

Intrinsic value of share under the above conditions is given by the following relationship.

$$S_0 = \frac{D_0(1+\phi_f)}{k-g_f} + \frac{D_0 \cdot H(g_c - g_f)}{k-g_f}$$

Where, D_0 = current dividend per share

g_c = current growth rate of dividend

g_f = normal long run growth rate of dividend

***Note :** The derivation of the above formula is rather complex and is outside the scope of this book. While the first term of the equation represents the value of the share based on long-run growth rate, the second term represents the premium due to abnormal growth rate in the beginning.*

Illustration** **4.13:

The equity share of a company offers dividend of Rs. 4.00 at present. The present dividend growth rate is 40%. Analysts predict that the dividend growth rate will decline linearly over a period of 12 years after which it will stabilize at 15%. An investor requires a return of 18% for his investment in the equity share of the company. What is intrinsic value of the equity share?

Solution:

The dividend pattern resembles *H*-model

Current dividend (D_0) = Rs. 4.00

Current growth rate (g_c) = 40%

Period over which the dividend is expected to get stabilized ($2H$) = 12 years

$\therefore \quad H = 6$ years

Normal long-run growth rate (g_f) = 15%

Return expected by the investor (k) = 18%

$\therefore$ Intrinsic value of the equity share $(S_0) = \dfrac{D_0(1+g_f)}{k-g_f} + \dfrac{D_0 \cdot H(g_c - g_f)}{k-g_f}$

$$= \frac{4.00(1+0.15)}{0.18-0.15} + \frac{4.00 \times 6(0.40-0.15)}{0.18-0.15}$$

$$= 153.33 + 200$$

$$= \text{Rs. } 353.33$$

***Illustration* 4.14:**

ABC company Ltd. offers a dividend of Rs. 2.00 per share. The dividend is expected to grow at the rate of 18% per year for 5 years. Thereafter the dividend growth rate is expected to decline linearly over a period of 10 years and stabilize at 10%. An investor expects a return of 16%. What is the intrinsic value of the share of the company?

Solution:

Current dividend per share = Rs. 2.00

Expected dividend after 5 years = $2.00\ (1 + 0.18)^5$

= Rs. 4.58

The Dividend Pattern is shown in figure 4.6.

The dividend pattern can be considered to have two stages. Stage-I is a uniform growth stage for a period of 5 years and Stage-II resembles *H*-model

Applying the equation of H-model for Stage-II

$$S_0 = \frac{D_0(1+g_f)}{k-g_f} + \frac{D_0 \cdot H(g_c - g_f)}{k-g_f}$$

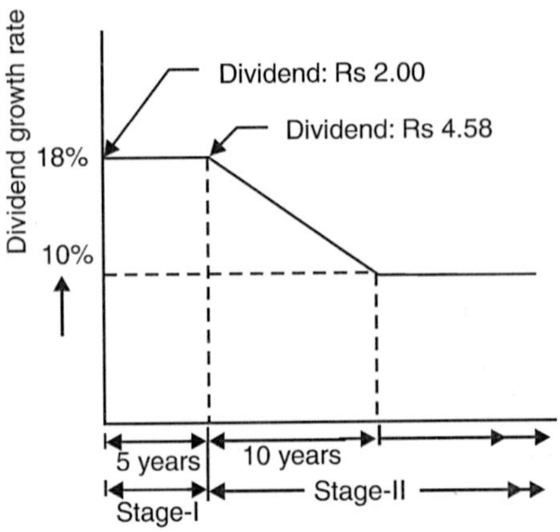

Fig. 4.6 Dividend pattern

In the above equation D_0 stands for the dividend after 5 years i.e., at the point of time from where the dividend rate is going to decline

Hence D_0 = Rs. 4.58

$g_c = 18\%$

$g_f = 10\%$

$2H = 10$ years i.e., $H = 5$

$k = 16\%$

$$\therefore \quad S_0 = \frac{4.58\,(1+0.10)}{0.16-0.10} + \frac{4.58 \times 5\,(0.18-0.10)}{0.16-0.10}$$

$$= 83.97 + 30.53$$

$$= \text{Rs. } 114.50$$

The intrinsic value arrived at as per H-model is the value at the beginning of the sixth year, i.e., after 5 years. The present value of Rs. 114.50 can be found out by discounting at the rate of 'k' i.e., at 16%.

$$\text{Present value of Rs. 114.50} = \frac{114.50}{(1+0.16)^5}$$

$$= \text{Rs. } 54.52 \qquad \text{(A)}$$

Present value of dividends receivable during the first five years

$$= \frac{2(1+0.18)}{(1+0.16)^1} + \frac{2(1+0.18)^2}{(1+0.16)^2} + \frac{2(1+0.18)^3}{(1+0.16)^3} + \frac{2(1+0.18)^4}{(1+0.16)^4} + \frac{2(1+0.18)^5}{(1+0.16)^5}$$

$$= 2.03 + 2.07 + 2.11 + 2.14 + 2.18$$

$$= \text{Rs. } 10.53 \qquad \text{(B)}$$

Intrinsic value of share = Present value of all future dividends

= A + B

= 54.52 + 10.53

= Rs. 65.05

***Illustration* 4.15:**

The earnings of ABC Company Ltd. grow at an above-average rate. The above average growth is expected to continue for 10 years. The dividend growth rate during these ten years is expected to be at the rate of 12% per annum. After 10 years, the dividend growth rate is expected to return to the average long-term growth rate of 8% p.a. The current dividend per share of the company is Rs. 4.00. the capitalisation rate of the company is 16%. Determine the intrinsic value of the equity share of the company.

Solution:

The intrinsic value consists of two components, viz., present value of dividends of the above-average growth stage lasting for 10 years and present value of dividends of the second stage of stable growth beginning from the eleventh year and extending for ever.

Capitalisation rate is the discount rate used for calculating the present value of a stream of cash flows.

End of year	Dividend expected (Rs.)	Present value factor	Present value of dividend (Rs.)
1	4.00	0.862	3.4480
2	4.48	0.743	3.3286
3	5.02	0.641	3.2178
4	5.62	0.552	3.1022
5	6.29	0.476	2.9940
6	7.05	0.410	2.8905
7	7.90	0.354	2.7966
8	8.84	0.309	2.7316
9	9.90	0.263	2.6037
10	11.09	0.227	2.5174
			29.6304
			Say Rs. 29.63

∴ Present value of dividends from Stage-I

[for a period of 10 years] = Rs. 29.63 (A)

The growth rate of dividend for Stage-II is 8% per annum and this rate of growth is expected to remain constant for all subsequent years.

Present value of dividends from Stage-II

$$= \frac{D_0(1+g)}{k-g}$$

$$= \frac{11.09(1+0.08)}{0.16-0.08}$$

= Rs. 149.72

Since, the second stage starts after 10 years from now, the above value of Rs. 149.72 is the discounted value of dividends of Stage-II at the beginning of Stage-II i.e., after 10 years from now. Hence, this value is to be again discounted to arrive at its present value.

∴ Present value of dividends from Stage-II

= 149.72 × [PV Factor for 10 years at 16%]

= 149.72 × 0.227

= Rs. 33.99 (B)

∴ Intrinsic value of equity share of the company

= (A) + (B)

= 29.63 + 33.99

= Rs. 63.62

***Illustration* 4.16:**

ABC Company Ltd., is a newly formed company. The company's gestation period is 2 years. After the gestation period of 2 years, the company is expected to retain all the earnings for 3 years to make use of them for funding its growth prospects. In the sixth year the company is expected to pay a dividend of Rs. 3.00 per equity share. The dividend is expected to grow at the rate of 10% p.a. in the subsequent years. The required rate of return is 16% p.a. Find the value of the equity share.

Solution:

In the initial 5 years the equity share is not going to offer any dividend. From the sixth year onwards the equity share is going to offer dividends that are expected to grow at a constant ratio of 10% every year.

Value of the equity share at the end of the fifth year (i.e., at the beginning of the sixth year) $= \frac{D_1}{(k-g)}$

$$= \frac{3.00}{0.16-0.10}$$

= Rs. 50.00

Intrinsic value of equity share

= Present value of Rs. 50.00, discounted at 16% p.a.

$= 50 \times$ (Present value factor)

$= 50 \times (0.476^*)$

= Rs. 23.80

***Illustration* 4.17:**

ABC Company Ltd. is engaged in the production of bulk chemicals. Due to depletion in mineral reserves and due to strong competitors with latest production technology entering the field, the company's earnings and dividends are declining at the rate of 6% every year. The company declared a dividend of Rs. 8.00 per equity share last year. An investor requires a return of 18% for investment in the Company's equity shares. Assess the current price of the equity share of the company.

Solution:

We have been asked to assess the current price of equity share. It can be assumed that the current share price is equal to its intrinsic value and accordingly we can assess the intrinsic value of the share.

There is constant decline in the dividend rate.

Hence, the constant growth rate formula can be used by adopting negative growth rate for '*g*'

$$\text{Intrinsic value } (S_0) = \frac{D_0(1+g)}{k-g}$$

D_0 = Rs. 8.00

$g = -6\%$

$k = 18\%$

$$S_0 = \frac{8.00(1-0.06)}{\{0.18-(-0.06)\}}$$

$$= \frac{7.52}{0.24}$$

= Rs. 31.33

Price of the equity share = Rs. 31.33

4.4. *P/E* RATIO

P/E ratio is the most popular financial ratio used by stock market investors. '*P*' stands for the price of the share and '*E*' stands for the earnings per share. It is also called *P/E* multiple or price-earnings multiple.

$$P/E \text{ ratio is defined as : } \frac{\text{Market price per share}}{\text{Earnings per share}}$$

* (0.476 = present value factor for 5 years at 16% p.a.)

Where,

Market price per share	= the prevailing price of share in the secondary market
and Earnings per share	= profit after tax less preference dividend divided by the number of outstanding equity shares.

4.5. COST OF EQUITY CAPITAL

If the shareholders of equity share expect a return of *r*% on their investment in equity shares, then the cost of equity capital can be taken as *r*%. The logic behind this is that the investors have implicitly indicated a return of *r*% on their investment, through the price of the equity shares set by the market. When investors expect a return of *r*% from the equity shares of a particular company, it is the going rate of return available elsewhere in the stock market for investments in equity shares of the same level of systematic risk. When investors expect a return of *r*%, it becomes mandatory for the company that it earns at least *r*% on the investments made/proposed to be made.

4.6. EARNINGS MODEL

The dividend discount model arrives at the intrinsic value of the share by calculating the present value of all future dividends. Suppose a company does not pay dividend despite earning profit. How to arrive at the value of the share? Though the company has not paid dividend, it does not mean that the company's equity shares will not have any value. The company might have retained the profits to plough back into its business with the intention of fostering faster growth. Similarly a company may retain part of its earnings for its future growth and may distribute only the remaining part of the earnings as dividend. Thus, arriving at the value of equity shares going purely by the dividends that a company is expected to offer may at times, not reflect the correct value.

The earnings models focus on the earning capacity of companies rather than on the dividends payable by them.

The following are the different approaches to arrive at the value of equity shares on the basis of earnings of the company.

(*i*) Gordon's model
(*ii*) Walter's model
(*iii*) Price Earnings Ratio model
(*iv*) Whitbeck Kisor model

(*i*) *Gordon's model*

Gordon's model is based on the following assumptions:

(*a*) The company has only equity financing.

(*b*) Investors consider future dividends and capital appreciation as risky proposition.

(c) Investors attach higher value to the shares of companies that offer dividend than to the share of companies that retain dividend. This is because of the reason that future capital gains are uncertain.

(d) The return on equity (ROE) is constant and the company's earnings are perpetual.

Note: *ROE is equal to the internal rate of return since the company is financed only by equity.*

(e) The capitalization rate for the company (k) remains constant.

(f) The dividend pay out ratio [or the retention ratio, which is [(1 – payout ratio)] once decided by the company will remain unaltered.

From Gordon's Dividend growth model we know

$$S_0 = \frac{D_1}{k - g}$$

Where S_0 = intrinsic value of share

$D_1 = D_0(1 + g)$ = Dividend available after one year

k = capitalisation rate

g = growth rate of dividend which is constant

Let E_1 = expected earnings per share after one year (i.e., estimated earnings per share)

ROE = return on equity

b = retention ratio

$D_1 = E_1 (1 - b)$

(i.e., Earnings per share times pay-out ratio)

Since, 'ROE' and 'b' are constant, the dividend growth rate 'g' will also be constant and is given by

$$g = \text{ROE} \times b$$

Let a company invests equity capital of Rs. 100.00 lakhs. Let the ROE is 15%. Total earnings of the company is Rs. 15.00 lakhs. Let there are 3 lakh equity shares. The earnings per equity share is Rs. 5.00. Let the retention ratio is 60%. Hence, 60% of the total earnings of Rs. 15.00 lakhs is reinvested, i.e., Rs. 9.00 lakhs will be reinvested out of the total earnings of Rs. 15.00 lakhs.

Original equity capital of Rs. 100.00 lakhs

Reinvestment (at a retention ratio of 60%) Rs. 9.00 lakhs

∴ The capital stock of the company increases by 9%. Since the company will have 9% more capital, the company will earn 9% more income and pays out 9% higher dividends.

∴ Growth rate of dividend = 9%

The growth rate of dividend 'g' is given by (ROE × b)

$$\begin{aligned} \text{ROE} &= 15\% \\ &= 0.15 \\ b &= 60\% \\ &= 0.60 \\ g &= 0.15 \times 0.60 \\ &= 0.90 \end{aligned}$$

As per Gordon's formula of Dividend Growth Model, the intrinsic value of share is given by,

$$S_0 = \frac{D_1}{k-g}$$

Since $D_1 = E_1(1 - b)$ and g = ROE × b, substituting the values of D_1 and g we get,

$$\text{Intrinsic value of share} = \frac{E_1(1-b)}{k-(\text{ROE} \times b)}$$

***Illustration* 4.18:**

The estimated earnings per share [EPS] of ABC Company Ltd. is Rs. 12.00, the retention ratio followed by the company is 40%. The return on equity is 14% and the capitalization rate is 15%. Calculate the value of equity share capital of the company.

Solution:

The value of equity share as per Gordon's model is given by,

$$S_0 = \frac{E_1(1-b)}{k-(\text{ROE} \times b)}$$

$$\begin{aligned} E_1 &= \text{Rs. } 12.00 \\ b &= 0.40 \\ k &= 0.15 \\ \text{ROE} &= 0.14 \end{aligned}$$

$$\therefore \quad S_0 = \frac{12(1-0.4)}{0.15-(0.14 \times 0.40)}$$

$$= \frac{7.20}{0.094}$$

$$= \text{Rs. } 76.60$$

***Illustration* 4.19:**

Gorden's model is based on the assumption that the ROE (Return on equity) and the retention ratio are constant. However, the earnings per share will keep growing since part of the earnings is reinvested in the business i.e., ploughed back in the business. For different retention ratios and for different ROE the value of equity share will change for a given rate of capitalization. The following illustration explains this aspect:

For the data given in illustration 4.18 find out the value of the equity share for the following combinations.

(*a*) Capitalisation rate = 15%

(*b*) Estimated earnings per share = Rs. 12.00

(*c*) ROE = 14%, 15% and 20%

(*d*) Dividend payout ratio = 0%, 40%, 60%, 80% and 100%

Solution:

The value of equity share for the different combinations of ROE and dividend payout ratio can be worked out using Gordon's formula.

$$S_0 = \frac{E_1(1-b)}{k-(\text{ROE}\times b)}$$

For different values of ROE and '*b*', the value of equity share arrived at are given below. In the problem *D*/*P* ratio (Dividend pay-out ratio) is given. Retention ratio '*b*' is equal to (1–*D*/*P* ratio).

D/P ratio	Retention Ratio 'b'	ROE = 8%	ROE = 14%	ROE = 15%	ROE = 20%
0.00	1.00	0.00	0.00	0.00	0.00
0.40	0.60	47.06	72.73	80.00	160.00
0.60	0.40	61.02	76.60	80.00	102.86
0.80	0.20	71.64	78.69	80.00	87.27

(The values inside the table indicate the share value for different combinations of retention ratio and ROE.)

Observations

If the company retains the entire earnings (i.e. if *D*/*P* ratio is zero), the investor is not prepared to offer any price for the shares of the company.

As long as the ROE is less than the capitalization rate, [for e.g. for ROE = 8% and ROE = 14%] as the retention ratio reduces, the share value increases. A company that earns a ROE which is less than the capitalization rate is called a 'declining company'.

A company that earns a ROE which is more than the capitalization rate is called a 'growth company'. For a growth company, as the retention ratio reduces, the share value also reduces.

For a company having ROE equal to the capitalization rate the share value is unaffected by the dividend policy. (In example given above, when

ROE = capitalization rate = 15%, the share value remain at Rs. 80 for different *D/P* ratios).

Since, the market price of an equity share is dependent on its intrinsic value, when a declining company does not distribute maximum dividend to its shareholders, the market price of its share will get adversely affected.

(ii) Walter's model

Walter's model and Gordon's model of share valuation are conceptually similar. According to Walter's model the market price of a share is decided by two factors, viz., the present value of all future dividends and the present value of all future retained earnings.

When a company retains a portion of its earnings, it will result in distribution of lesser dividends to the equity shareholders. But, the retained earnings are going to be only ploughed back, i.e., the company is going to use the retained earnings only for improving its own business. Hence, by retaining a portion of the earnings, though the current dividend will get reduced, the utilization of retained earnings for the business will bring certain benefits for the shareholders. Hence, Walter's model arrives at the value of equity share by taking into account the value of retained earnings also.

Market price of share = Present value of dividends + Present value of retained earnings

Assumptions of Walter's model

(*a*) The company has only equity financing.

(*b*) The company uses only retained earnings for its expansion activities.

(*c*) The return on equity (ROE) and the cost of capital '*k*' remain constant.

Note: *ROE is equal to the internal rate of return since the company is financed only by equity.*

(*d*) The earnings of the company are either distributed as dividend or reinvested in the company internally.

The relationship given by Walter for arriving at the market price of equity share is as below

$$\text{Price of equity share} = \frac{D}{k} + \frac{\left[\frac{\text{ROE}}{k}\right](E-D)}{k}$$

where, D = dividend per share paid by the company

ROE = return on equity

k = cost of equity share capital

E = earnings per share of the company

According to Walter's model, the dividend decision and investment decision of a company are mutually dependent.

Looking at the formula for the price of equity share, we can observe that for a given *D*, *E* and *k* the share price depends on the factor $\frac{\text{ROE}}{k}$

- If ROE > *k*, the company has to retain 100% of the earnings in order to maximize the market price of its shares.
- If ROE < *k*, the company has to give our all its earnings as dividend, i.e., its dividend pay out ratio should be 100% in order to maximize the market price of its shares.
- If ROE = *k* the dividend payout ratio is irrelevant. The share price is not likely to be affected through the *D/P* ratio may vary.

***Illustration* 4.20:**

The assets of company M/s ABC Limited are funded only by equity. The number of equity shares outstanding of the company is 80,000. The profit after taxes and preference dividends is Rs. 12,00,000. The dividend paid to equity shareholders is Rs. 5,00,000. Price Earnings ratio is 12. The rate of return on investment is 12%.

Ascertain whether the investor will be satisfied with the dividend policy of the company?

What should be the ideal dividend pay-out ratio according to Walter's model?

Solution:

Profit after taxes and preference dividends is available to equity shareholders

Earnings per share (EPS)

$$= \frac{\text{Equity earnings}}{\text{No. of equity shares}}$$

$$= \frac{12{,}00{,}000}{80{,}000}$$

$$= \text{Rs. } 15$$

$$\text{Dividend per share (DPS)} = \frac{\text{Dividend paid to equity shareholders}}{\text{Number of shares}}$$

$$= \frac{5{,}00{,}000}{80{,}000}$$

$$= \text{Rs. } 6.25$$

$$P/E \text{ ratio} = 12$$

$$\frac{\text{Price of share}}{\text{Earnings per share (EPS)}} = 12$$

$$\text{Price of share} = \text{EPS} \times 12$$
$$= 15 \times 12$$
$$= \text{Rs. } 180$$

$$\text{Dividend payout ratio} = \frac{\text{DPS}}{\text{EPS}} \times 100$$
$$= \frac{6.25}{15.00} \times 100$$
$$= 41.67\%$$

$$\text{Cost of capital } (k) = \text{Inverse of } P/E \text{ ratio}$$

$$\therefore \quad k = \frac{1}{12}$$
$$= 8.33\%$$

	ROE	k	Growth rate = (ROE x b)
A	8%	15%	For b = 60%, growth rate = 4.80% For b = 40%, growth rate = 3.20% For b = 20%, growth rate = 1.60%
B	14%	15%	For b = 60%, growth rate = 8.40% For b = 40%, growth rate = 5.60% For b = 20%, growth rate = 2.80%
C	15%	15%	For b = 60%, growth rate = 9.00% For b = 40%, growth rate = 6.00% For b = 20%, growth rate = 3.00%
D	20%	15%	For b = 60%, growth rate = 12.00% For b = 40%, growth rate = 8.00% For b = 20%, growth rate = 4.00%

Consider combinations (*A*) and (*B*) above. Since the capitalization rate is greater than the return on equity, it is a 'declining company'. For a declining company the value of share increases as the retention ratio decreases. In other words, as the pay-out ratio increases, the value of share increases.

Consider combination (*C*) above. Since the return on equity is greater than the capitalization rate, it is 'growth company'. For a growth company the value of share decreases as the retention ratio decreases. In other words, as the pay-out ratio increases the value of share decreases.

Return on investment = 12%

i.e., ROE = 12%

Since, ROE 12% is greater than k (8.33%) this is a growth company and the company can maximize the market price of its equity shares by retaining all the earnings i.e., by ploughing back all it profits. In other words, *D/P* ratio should be zero, i.e., the company should retain all its earnings and its retention ratio should be 100%.

As per Walter's formula

$$\text{Price of equity share} = \frac{D}{k} + \frac{\left[\frac{\text{ROE}}{k}\right](E-D)}{k}$$

Since dividend payout ratio = 0, dividend is zero.

$$\text{Price} = \frac{0}{k} + \frac{\left[\frac{0.12}{0.0833}\right](15-0)}{0.0833}$$

$$= 0 + 259.40$$

$$= \text{Rs. } 259.40$$

Since ROE is greater than k, the dividend payout ratio of 41.67% will not satisfy the investor. The prudent investor will be satisfied with zero dividend payout ratio, or 100% retention ratio.

The current price of the equity share is Rs. 180. When the retention ratio is made 100%, the share price of equity share will become Rs. 259.40.

***Illustration* 4.21:**

From the data given below ascertain whether the company is following an optimal dividend policy as per Walter's model. If not, ascertain the optimal *D/P* ratio and the maximum market price that the share can fetch.

Total earnings	: Rs. 24,00,000
Number of equity shares	: 2,00,000
Dividend paid	: Rs. 4,00,000
Price Earnings ratio	= 7
Return on Investment	= 13.50%

Solution:

Earnings per share (EPS)

$$= \frac{24,00,000}{2,00,000}$$

$$= \text{Rs. } 12$$

$$P/E \text{ ratio} = 7$$

$$\therefore \text{Cost of capital} = \frac{1}{\frac{P}{E}\text{ ratio}} = \frac{1}{7} = 0.1429$$

$$= \text{i.e., } 14.29\%$$

$$\text{Market price of equity share} = \frac{P}{E}\text{ ratio} \times \text{EPS}$$

$$= 7 \times 12$$

$$= \text{Rs. } 84$$

$$\text{Dividend per share } (D) = \frac{4,00,000}{2,00,000}$$

$$= \text{Rs. } 2$$

Since cost of capital (k) is more than the return on equity, the optimal D/P ratio is 100%.

$$D/P \text{ ratio of the company} = \frac{4,00,000}{24,00,000} = 0.17$$

Since the company pays out only about 17% of its earnings as dividend, it is not following an optimal dividend policy.

For maximizing the share price, D/P ratio should be 100%.

Price of equity share as per Walter's model

$$= \frac{D}{k} + \frac{\left[\frac{(\text{ROE})}{k}\right](E - D)}{k}$$

$$\text{To maximize share price, } D = \frac{24,00,000}{2,00,000}$$

$$\text{i.e., } D = \text{Rs. } 12$$

$$\text{i.e., Max. price} = \frac{12}{0.125} + \frac{\left[\frac{0.12}{0.125}\right](0)}{0.125}$$

[Since the entire earnings is to be given as dividend, $(E - D)$ is equal to zero.]

$$= \frac{12}{0.125}$$

$$= \text{Rs. } 96$$

∴ The maximum price that the the share can fetch Rs. 96.00 [when D/P ratio = 100%]

(iii) Price earnings ratio model (P/E ratio model)

It comes handy for investors to assess the value of shares in terms of an appropriate multiplier. The Price-Earnings Ratio (Popularly known as the P/E Ratio) is the most common multiplier uses by analysts and investors for share valuation. P/E Ratio is the ratio of the market price of a share to its earnings.

$$\text{P/E Ratio} = \frac{\text{Market price per share}}{\text{Earnings per share (EPS)}}$$

From an investor's point of view, the intrinsic value of a share is taken to be equal to the current earnings (or expected future earnings) per share times the P/E ratio that is considered appropriate for that share. For example, if the EPS of a share is Rs. 10 and if an investor considers a P/E ratio of say, 13 as appropriate for this share, then according to the investor the share has an intrinsic value of Rs. 130 (i.e., 10 × 13). The investor, after having arrived at the intrinsic value of a share using the appropriate P/E ratio, will compare the prevailing market price of the share and will arrive at a decision on whether to buy the share or not. Considering the example quoted above, if the P/E ratio of the share (arrived at by dividing the current market price by the EPS) is say, 9, it means that the investor will consider the share under-priced (since the investor considers a P/E ratio of 13 as appropriate, which when applied will give a higher share price) and the investor will opt to buy the share. The investor's higher estimate of P/E ratio may be based on the forecast of an increase in share price either due to anticipated hike in earnings or due to any other reasons.

(Please refer to chapter–3, paragraph 3.5.4 for further discussion on P/E ratio as a tool for share valuation).

(iv) Whitbeck-Kisor model

The success in correct valuation of shares on the basis of P/E ratio lies in correctly assessing the P/E ratio. The price that any investor would like to pay for a share is very much based on the future prospects of the company and the anticipated future earnings of the company. If the P/E ratio is calculated by using the current market price in the numerator and the EPS in the denominator, it will give a ratio that has its own flaw. This is because the numerator represents the 'present' price of the share whereas the denominator refers to the EPS that the company has already earned, i.e., it is a 'past' data. Hence, ideally the present market price of the share should be divided by the likely current earnings per share. But, arriving at the likely earnings will present certain difficulty. Hence, the use of statistical approach to arrive at the appropriate P/E ratio gained acceptance among investors. In statistical approach, the determinants of share price are considered and a relationship between the share price and its determinants is arrived at using multiple regression analysis. Earnings per share, earnings growth rate, dividend policy of the company, risk associated with the earnings etc., are some of the determinants considered for the analysis.

Many analysis have made studies in this direction and there are many models are available that relate the P/E ratio (an independent variable) to the determining variables (that are dependent variables). These relationships can be made use of to arrive at the P/E ratio that is considered appropriate for a given share. One of such attempts was done by Whitbeck. V. and Kisor. M., in the year 1963 who used data from Bank of New York as on 1962 for 135 stocks and arrived at the following relationship.

P/E ratio = 8.20 + 1.5 (Growth rate in earnings) + 6.70 (Dividend Payout ratio as a decimal) – 0.20 (Standard Deviation of earnings growth rate)

The above relationship can be make use of to estimate the appropriate P/E ratio which can be made use of in making investment decisions.

REVIEW QUESTIONS

1. 'The Fundamental Analyst believes that the market price of an equity share will reach its intrinsic value in due course'. Explain.
2. What is meant by Discount Rate and what are its components?
3. Explain 'Holding period model' of share valuation with an example.
4. What are the assumptions of 'Constant growth model' of share valuation Devised by Myron J. Gordan? What are its limitations?
5. Write short notes on the following:
   - Zero Growth Model of share valuation.
   - H-model of share valuation.
6. What is the conceptual difference between the Dividend Discount Model and Earnings Model of share valuation?
7. Explain Walter's Model of share valuation.
8. 'For a company having 'Return on Equity' equal to the Capitalisation rate, the share value is unaffected by the dividend policy' – Comment on the validity of the statement.
9. Explain the use of P/E Ratio in share valuation.
10. Give a brief account of Whitbeck-Kisor model of share valuation.

5 CHAPTER
Bond Valuation

5.1. INTRODUCTION

Bonds are fixed income securities. Just like bonds, debentures are also fixed income securities. Both bonds and debentures are debt securities. Though the two terms 'bonds' and 'debentures' are used interchangeably worldwide, in India, the debt securities issued by the Government and public sector undertakings are normally referred to as 'bonds', while debt securities issued by private sector joint stock companies are referred to as 'debentures'. Both bonds and debentures are similar in nature except for the issuing company. A bond/debenture is a legal document containing an acknowledgement of indebtedness by the issuing company. The bond/debenture will contain a promise to pay interest for a specified period and then to repay the principal at the end of the specified period, on a given date of maturity.

While shareholders are the owners of a company, debenture holders are the creditors of a company.

5.2. RETURN FROM BONDS

Returns from bonds are comparatively easier to determine as compared to the return from shares since the interest payable on bonds is fixed and known before hand.

Bond returns are expressed in the following five forms:

(*a*) Coupon rate

(*b*) Current yield

(*c*) Spot interest rate

(*d*) Yield to maturity

(*e*) Yield to call

5.2.1. Coupon Rate

This is the rate of interest fixed for the bond and printed on the bond certificate. Interest payable is calculated at the Coupon rate on the face value of the bond. If the face value of a bond is, say Rs. 1000 and if the coupon rate is fixed at, say 9% p.a., the annual interest payable by the company to the bond holder is Rs. 90 per bond.

5.2.2. Current Yield

Though the face value of a bond remains the same, the market price of the bond in the secondary market may be different. Suppose there is bond with a face value of Rs. 100 and a coupon rate of 12% p.a. If the interest rate prevailing in the market for securities of similar risk as the bond is, say 9% p.a. the bond will attract a higher price than its face value. Hence, in the secondary market the bond will have a market price which is higher than Rs. 100, thereby the bond will be selling at a premium. Similarly, a bond can also be selling at a discount in the secondary market (i.e., at a price below its face value) if the coupon rate of the bond is less than the prevailing market rate.

Current yield is the rate of return available from a bond on its current price in the secondary market.

Since the price of a bond in the secondary market cannot remain constant, the current yield will also be fluctuating depending on the bond price. Current yield only measures the annual rate of return accruing to an investor who purchases the bond from the secondary market.

***Illustration* 5.1:**

A bond has a face value of Rs. 1,000 and a coupon rate of 9% per annum. The bond is currently selling in the secondary market at a price of Rs. 800. Calculate the current yield.

Solution:

$$\text{Current yield} = \frac{\text{Annual interest payable on the bond}}{\text{Current price}} \times 100$$

Annual interest payable (calculated at coupon rate on the face value)

$$= \frac{9}{100} \times 1000$$

$$= \text{Rs. } 90$$

$$\text{Current yield} \quad = \frac{90}{800} \times 100$$

$$= 11.25\%$$

Note: *Since the bond is selling at a price below its face value, it is selling at a discount. When a bond is selling at a discount, the current yield will be more than the coupon rate and when a bond is selling at a premium, the current yield will be less than the coupon rate.*

5.2.3. Spot Interest Rate

Before understanding spot interest rate, a type of bond known as "Zero coupon bond" is to be understood.

Zero Coupon Bond

As the name indicates, this bond does not specify any coupon rate. Hence, such bonds do not pay annual interests. Such bonds are issued at a discount from their face value and the difference between the issue price and the face value represents the return offered by the bonds. For example, if a bond with a face value of Rs. 1,000 is issued at an offer price of Rs. 800 and has a maturity period of say, three years, an investor who purchases a bond at a price of Rs. 800 will receive Rs. 1,000 after three years. The difference of Rs. 200 between the face value and issue price represents the return offered by the bond. Zero coupon bonds are also known by the names 'deep discount bonds' or 'pure discount bonds'.

When a bond pays annual interest, the interest received is taxable. However in the case of zero coupon bonds interest payments are not available until maturity. Even at the time of maturity the return earned is not taxable as interest but is taxable only as capital gain.

Though zero coupon bonds do not offer annual returns in the form of interest payments, the return offered by a zero coupon bond can be calculated and expressed on an annualized basis. Spot Interest Rate is the annual rate of return on a bond that offers only one cash inflow to the investor. A zero coupon bond offers only one cash inflow to the investor on its maturity and hence the rate of return offered by a zero coupon bond calculated on an annualized basis is known as 'Spot Interest Rate'.

Mathematically, Spot Interest Rate of a zero coupon bond is the discount rate that equates the present value of the single cash inflow available to the investor on maturity of the bond to the price of the bond.

***Illustration* 5.2:**

A zero coupon bond of face value Rs. 1,000 is issued at a discounted price of Rs. 600. The bond has a maturity period of 5 years. Find the Spot Interest Rate of the bond.

Solution:

Let i% p.a. is the spot interest rate.

The face value of Rs. 1,000 will be received after a period of 5 years.

Amount receivable five years hence = Rs. 1,000

Amount receivable four years hence $= \text{Rs. } 1{,}000 \times \left(\frac{1}{1+i}\right)$

Amount receivable three years hence

$$= \text{Rs. } 1{,}000 \times \left(\frac{1}{1+i}\right)\left(\frac{1}{1+i}\right)$$

Amount receivable two years hence

$$= \text{Rs. } 1{,}000 \times \left(\frac{1}{1+i}\right)\left(\frac{1}{1+i}\right)\left(\frac{1}{1+i}\right)$$

Amount receivable one year hence

$$= \text{Rs. } 1{,}000 \times \left(\frac{1}{1+i}\right)\left(\frac{1}{1+i}\right)\left(\frac{1}{1+i}\right)\left(\frac{1}{1+i}\right)$$

$$\text{Present value} = \text{Rs. } 1{,}000 \times \left(\frac{1}{1+i}\right)\left(\frac{1}{1+i}\right)\left(\frac{1}{1+i}\right)\left(\frac{1}{1+i}\right)\left(\frac{1}{1+i}\right)$$

$$= 1{,}000 \times \left(\frac{1}{1+i}\right)^5$$

Thus, if the present value is Rs. $1{,}000 \times \left(\frac{1}{1+i}\right)^5$, at the end of 5 years a sum of Rs. 1,000 would be available.

Present value = discounted price of bond

$$600 = 1{,}000 \times \left(\frac{1}{1+i}\right)^5$$

$$\left(\frac{1}{1+i}\right)^5 = \frac{600}{1{,}000}$$

$$\left(\frac{1}{1+i}\right) = \sqrt[5]{0.60}$$, which gives i(i.e., spot rate) = 0.1076 i.e., 10.76%

Note: *From the above example, the following relationship is available between present value of zero coupon bond, face value of zero coupon bond, spot interest rate and maturity period.*

$$\text{Present value} = \text{Face value} \left(\frac{1}{1+i}\right)^n$$

$$= \frac{\text{Face value}}{(1+i)^n}$$

where n = maturity period of bond in years

and i = spot interest rate

***Illustration* 5.3:**

A company proposes to issue 10 years zero coupon bonds of face value of Rs. 1,000 each. The company expects an annualized return of 9%. What is the discounted price at which the bond is to be issued?

Solution:

$$\text{Present value} = \text{Face value}\left(\frac{1}{1+i}\right)^n$$

$$= 1{,}000\left(\frac{1}{1+0.09}\right)^{10}$$

$$= 1{,}000\ \frac{1}{(1+0.09)^{10}}$$

$$= 1{,}000 \times (0.91743)^{10}$$

$$= 1{,}000 \times (0.4224)$$

$$= \quad 422.4 \text{ say Rs. } 425$$

The company can issue the 10 year zero coupon bond of face value Rs. 1000 at a discounted price of Rs. 425.

5.2.4. Yield to Maturity (YTM)

Yield to maturity (YTM) is the most commonly used measured for calculation the return on bonds. Yield to maturity (YTM) is nothing but the internal rate of return earned from a bond, holding the bond till its maturity.

When a bond is held till maturity, the bond holders receive annual returns (i.e., interest payments) and also receive the face value of the bond on its maturity.

The Yield to maturity (YTM) is calculated by equating the cost of bond to the present value of cash inflows from the bond held till maturity. Hence Yield to maturity (YTM) is the discount rate that makes the cost of bond equal to the present value of cash inflows from the bond held till maturity.

$$\text{Cost of bond} = \sum_{t=1}^{n}\frac{\text{Annual Interest receivable}}{(1+i)^t} + \frac{\text{Terminal value of bond}}{(1+i)^n}$$

where

i = yield to maturity

t = time period

n = no. of years to maturity

***Illustration* 5.4:**

A bond of face value Rs. 1,000, with a coupon rate of 8% p.a. and present value of Rs. 700 has a maturity period of 5 years. Calculate the Yield to maturity (YTM) on the bond.

Solution:

Cost of bond =

$$\sum_{t=1}^{n}\frac{\text{Annual interest receivable}}{(1+i)^t}+\left(\frac{\text{Terminal value of bond}}{(1+i)^n}\right)$$

Annual interest available @ the coupon rate of 8% = Rs. 80
(on the face value of Rs. 1,000)

Cost of the bond = Present value viz., Rs. 700

$$700=\left(\frac{80}{(1+i)^1}+\frac{80}{(1+i)^2}+\frac{80}{(1+i)^3}+\frac{80}{(1+i)^4}+\frac{80}{(1+i)^5}\right)+\left(\frac{1,000}{(1+i)^5}\right)$$

$$=80\left(\frac{1}{(1+i)^1}+\frac{1}{(1+i)^2}+\frac{1}{(1+i)^3}+\frac{1}{(1+i)^4}+\frac{1}{(1+i)^5}\right)+\left(\frac{1,000}{(1+i)^5}\right)$$

The value of Yield to maturity (YTM) can be arrived at only any trial and error method by assuming a certain value for Yield to maturity (YTM) are reworking with a different value until the value on the RHS matches with the value on the LHS of the equation.

Let us assume a Yield to maturity (YTM) of, say 9.50%.

$$700=80\left(\frac{1}{(1+0.095)^1}+\frac{1}{(1+0.095)^2}+\frac{1}{(1+0.095)^3}+\frac{1}{(1+0.095)^4}+\frac{1}{(1+0.095)^5}\right)+\left(\frac{1,000}{(1+0.095)^5}\right)$$

$$=80\ (0.9132+0.8340+0.7616+0.6956+0.6352)+\left(\frac{1,000}{1.574238}\right)$$

$$=307.17+635.23$$

$$=942.40$$

Since the LHS and RHS are not equal, we will have to go for further trail assuming another value for Yield to maturity (YTM).

Let as assume a Yield to maturity (YTM) of say 10%.

$$700=80\left(\frac{1}{(1+0.1)^1}+\frac{1}{(1+0.1)^2}+\frac{1}{(1+0.1)^3}+\frac{1}{(1+0.1)^4}+\frac{1}{(1+0.1)^5}\right)+\left(\frac{1,000}{(1+0.1)^5}\right)$$

$$=80\ (0.8696+0.7561+0.6575+0.5717+0.4972)+\left(\frac{1,000}{2.011357}\right)$$

$$=268.17+497.20$$

$$=765.37$$

Still the LHS and RHS values do not match.

Let as assume a Yield to maturity (YTM) of say 17%.

$$700 = 80\left(\frac{1}{(1+0.17)^1}+\frac{1}{(1+0.17)^2}+\frac{1}{(1+0.17)^3}+\frac{1}{(1+0.17)^4}+\frac{1}{(1+0.17)^5}\right)+\left(\frac{1{,}000}{(1+0.17)^5}\right)$$

$$= 80\ (0.8547 + 0.7305 + 0.6244 + 0.5336 + 0.4561) + \left(\frac{1{,}000}{2.1924}\right)$$

$$= 255.94 + 456.10$$

$$= 712.04$$

The value of RHS is more than the value of LHS.

Let as assume a Yield to maturity (YTM) of say 18%.

$$700 = 80\left(\frac{1}{(1+0.18)^1}+\frac{1}{(1+0.18)^2}+\frac{1}{(1+0.18)^3}+\frac{1}{(1+0.18)^4}+\frac{1}{(1+0.18)^5}\right)+\left(\frac{1{,}000}{(1+0.18)^5}\right)$$

$$= 80\ (0.8474 + 0.7182 + 0.6086 + 0.5158 + 0.4371) + \left(\frac{1{,}000}{2.2878}\right)$$

$$= 250.17 + 437.10$$

$$= 687.27$$

The value of RHS is now less than the value of LHS.

The Yield to maturity (YTM) lies in between 17% and 18% which can be arrived at by interpolating between 17% and 18%.

$$\text{Yield to maturity (YTM)} = 17\% + \left(\frac{(18-17)}{(712.04-687.27)}\right)\times(712.04-700)$$

$$\text{Yield to maturity (YTM)} = 17\% + \left(\frac{1}{247.70}\right)\times 12.04$$

$$= 17\% + 0.05\%$$

$$= 17.05\%$$

The yield to maturity = 17.05%

Note: *The yield to maturity is higher than the coupon rate since the present value of bond is less than the face value. Suppose a company issues a bond with a face value of say, Rs.* ***1,000*** *at a coupon rate of say, 12%*

and if the bond is issued at par (i.e. if the issue price is equal to the face value) then, the yield to maturity will be equal to the coupon rate itself. Let us verify this assuming a maturity period of 5 years.

$$1{,}000 = 120\left(\frac{1}{(1+0.12)^1}+\frac{1}{(1+0.12)^2}+\frac{1}{(1+0.12)^3}+\frac{1}{(1+0.12)^4}+\frac{1}{(1+0.12)^5}\right) + \left(\frac{1{,}000}{(1+0.12)^5}\right)$$

$$1{,}000 = 120(0.8929 + 0.7972 + 0.7118 + 0.6355 + 0.5674) + \left(\frac{1{,}000}{1.7623}\right)$$

$$= 432.58 + 567.40$$

$$= 999.98$$

The values of RHS and LHS of the expression are equal (but for the minor difference due to rounding off error) which shows that the Yield to maturity (YTM) is equal to the coupon rate when the cost of the bond is equal to its face value.

Shortcut method for arriving at yield to maturity (YTM)

As seen from the above illustration, the calculations for arriving at Yield to maturity (YTM) are tedious and time consuming. An approximate value of Yield to maturity (YTM) can be arrived at using the following formula:

$$\text{Yield to maturity (YTM)} = \frac{\text{Average annual return}}{\text{Average investment}}$$

Average annual return

$$= \text{Annual interest} + \left(\begin{matrix}\text{Maturity value of} \\ \text{bond at the end} \\ \text{of holding period}\end{matrix} - \begin{matrix}\text{Current} \\ \text{market} \\ \text{price of} \\ \text{bond}\end{matrix}\right) \div n$$

where n = holding period till maturity

When the bond is held till maturity, the bond holder can redeem it from the company that issued the bond at its face value. Hence, we can substitute Face value for Maturity value of the bond at the end of the holding period.

$$\text{i.e.,} = \text{Annual interest} + \left(\begin{matrix}\text{Face value} \\ \text{of bond}\end{matrix} - \begin{matrix}\text{Current market} \\ \text{price of bond}\end{matrix}\right) \div n$$

$$\text{Average investment} = \left(\begin{matrix}\text{Face value} \\ \text{of bond}\end{matrix} + \begin{matrix}\text{Current market} \\ \text{price of bond}\end{matrix}\right) \div 2$$

$$\text{Yield to maturity (YTM)} = \frac{I + (\text{FV} - C)/n}{(\text{FV} + C)/2}$$

where I = annual interest

FV = face value of bond

C = current price of bond (i.e., current market price)

n = bond period

Note: *The above formula is applicable when the bond is selling at a discount, i.e., when the current market price is less than the face value (or par value) of the bond.*

If the bond is selling at a premium, i.e., if the current market price of the bond is more than its face value, the formula for Yield to maturity (YTM) is as under.

$$\text{Yield to maturity (YTM)} = \frac{I - (C - \text{FV})/n}{(C + \text{FV})/2}$$

***Illustration* 5.5:**

Arrive at the Yield to maturity (YTM) by shortcut method for the problem given in illustration 5.4.

Solution:

Annual interest @ 8% on face value of Rs. 1,000 = Rs. 80 (I)

Face value = Rs. 1,000 (FV)

Current price = Rs. 700 (C)

Bond period = 5 years (n)

Since the bond is selling at a discount,

$$\text{Yield to maturity (YTM)} = \frac{I + (\text{FV} - C)/n}{(\text{FV} + C)/2}$$

$$= \frac{80 + (1{,}000 - 700)/5}{(1{,}000 + 700)/2}$$

$$= \frac{80 + 60}{850}$$

$$= 0.1647$$

Approximate value of Yield to maturity (YTM) = 16.47%

***Illustration* 5.6:**

A bond with a coupon rate of 8%, par value of Rs. 1,000 and maturity period of 5 years is selling at a price of Rs. 1,100.

Arrive at the Yield to maturity (YTM).

Solution:

Annual interest (@8% on face value of Rs. 1,000) = Rs. 80 (I)

Face value = Rs. 1,000 (FV)

Current price = Rs. 1,100 (C)

Bond period = 5 years (n)

Since the bond is selling at a premium,

$$\text{YTM} = \frac{I-(C-\text{FV})/n}{(\text{FV}+C)/2}$$

$$= \frac{80-(1{,}100-1{,}000)/5}{(1{,}000+1{,}100)/2}$$

$$= \frac{80-20}{1050}$$

$$= 0.0571$$

Approximate value of Yield to maturity (YTM) = 5.71%

5.2.5. Yield to Call (YTC)

Some bonds are issued with an option to redeem the bonds even before their maturity period. The option is available either to the bond holder or to the bond issuer. Whenever such a provision for redeeming bonds prior to their maturity is available, the redemption is allowed at a specified period prior to maturity and at a specified price. The price specified is called the call price.

Yield to call is calculated assuming that the bond is redeemed on the call date at the specified call price. Hence, yield to call is the discount rate that makes the present values of cash inflows to call (i.e., the annual interests till the call date and the specified call price of the bond at which it is redeemed) equal to the cost of the bond.

When the option to redeem a bond prior to its maturity period is available to the investor, he can exercise his option and redeem the bond on the call date if the 'Yield to call' is higher than the Yield to maturity (YTM). If the yield to call is less than the Yield to maturity (YTM), it is advisable that the bond holder holds the bond till its maturity. 'Yield to call' can be calculated on similar lines as Yield to maturity (YTM) is calculated, viz., by assuming different values for the Yield to call (YTC), checking if the present value of cash inflows reduced at the assumed rate equals the cost of the bond and interpolating between the two assumed rates for Yield to call (YTC) that are above and below the correct value of Yield to call (YTC). Alternately the short cut method that gives a near approximate value can also be used.

5.3. BOND PRICES

Any investment derives its value on the strength of the cash inflows that the investment is expected to generate to the investor. A bond is expected to offer periodical returns (in the form of interest payments) till maturity.

At maturity the bond is expected to fetch its face value (also called par value) to the investor. Thus, the cash inflow from a bond occurs over a period of time in the future. The price of a bond is the present value of future stream of cash inflows reduced at an interest rate equal to the current market rate for investments of similar risk. Hence, the price of a bond will change if the current interest rate on comparable securities changes, though the future cash inflows expected to be offered by the bond remain the same.

***Illustration* 5.7:**

A bond with a face value of Rs. 1,000 maturity period of 10 years and coupon rate of 10% was issued 4 years ago. The current interest rate prevailing in the market for securities of similar nature is 12% p.a. Determine the price of the bond.

Solution:

Maturity period of bond = 10 years

Balance maturity period available = 6 years

Hence, the bond will offer interest income for 6 years and at the end of the sixth year, will offer the redeemed value of the bond, which is equal to its face value. The bond price can be determined by arriving at the present value of future stream of cash inflows reduced at the prevailing interest rate of 12% p.a.

$$\text{Bond price} = \left(\frac{100}{(1+0.12)^1} + \frac{100}{(1+0.12)^2} + \frac{100}{(1+0.12)^3} + \frac{100}{(1+0.12)^4} + \frac{100}{(1+0.12)^5} + \frac{100}{(1+0.12)^6}\right)^* + \frac{1,000}{(1+0.12)^6}$$

$$= (89.29 + 79.72 + 71.18 + 63.55 + 56.74 + 50.66) + \frac{1,000}{1.9738}$$

$$= 411.14 + 506.64$$

$$= \text{Rs. } 917.78$$

---

* $\left(\frac{100}{(1+0.12)^1} + \frac{100}{(1+0.12)^2} + \frac{100}{(1+0.12)^3} + \frac{100}{(1+0.12)^4} + \frac{100}{(1+0.12)^5} + \frac{100}{(1+0.12)^6}\right)$

$$= \sum_{t=1}^{6} \frac{100}{(1+0.12)^t}$$

$$= 100 \times \sum_{t=1}^{6} \frac{1}{(1+0.12)^t}$$

= 100 × (PV factor for 6 year annuity at 12%)

Referring to present value factor table for annuity,

= 100 × (4.1114)

= 411.14

5.4. PRICE OF PERPETUAL BOND

The price of a perpetual bond (i.e., a bond that offers return in the form of periodical interest payment perpetually) is the discounted sum of the infinite series.

$$\text{Price} = \frac{\text{Annual interest payment}}{\text{Current interest rate for similar security}}$$

Illustration **5.8:**

A perpetual bond of par value Rs. 1,000 has a coupon rate of 8%. Determine the price of the bond. Assume a current interest rate of 10%.

Solution:

Annual interest payments @ the rate of 8% = Rs. 80

$$\text{Price of the bond} = \frac{80}{0.10}$$

= Rs. 800

5.5. BOND PRICING PRINCIPLES

The principles by which bond prices are fixed were stated by Burton G. Malkiel in the form of five principles. These principles are commonly known as Bond pricing theorems.

The five principles of pricing bonds are as under.

1. If the market interest rate is different from the coupon rate of bond, the bond price in the market will be different from the face value of the bond. [When a bond is issued, the coupon rate on the bond is normally kept equal to the prevailing market interest rate. While the coupon rate, once fixed, will remain unchanged, the market interest rate may keep changing. When the market interest rate falls down, the bond that has a higher coupon rate than the market rate would be offering higher return than the market return for similar securities. Under such circumstances, the bond price will raise above its face value. Similarly when the market interest rate is higher than the coupon rate of bond, the price will come down below its face value.]
2. For a given change in the level of market interest rate, the bond price varies in direct proportion to the period for maturity. [In other words, bonds with longer period of maturity suffer greater variation in price as compared to bonds with shorter period of maturity. Suppose there are two bonds of same coupon rate but with different maturity period issued on the same date. When the market interest rate falls down below the coupon rate, the bond prices will increase. The prices of bonds with higher maturity period will show a higher increase than bonds with lower maturity period. Similarly when the market interest rate increases above the coupon rate, the bond prices will come down.

The prices of bonds with higher maturity period will experience a higher fall in bond price than the bonds with lower maturity period.]

3. The lesser the period remaining until maturity, the higher the sensitivity of the bond to changes in the market interest rate. [In other words, the price of a bond with a lesser period to maturity will be more sensitive to changes in market rates than the price of a similar bond with a higher period to maturity.]
4. For any given maturity period, the price changes of bonds resulting from an equal absolute change in market interest rate are not symmetrical since a decrease in the market interest rate raises bond prices more than a corresponding increase in the market interest rate lowers the bond prices. [Suppose the current price of a bond is Rs. 1,000. Suppose the market interest rate falls by, say 1%. Due to the fall in the market interest rate of 1% let as assume that the bond price increases by, say Rs. 100. If the market interest increases by 1% , the reduction in the bond price will not be Rs. 100 but will be less than Rs. 100.]
5. Bond price volatility is related to the coupon rate. The higher the coupon rate of a bond, the smaller the percentage change in bond price for any given change in the market interest rate.

5.6. RISKS ASSOCIATED WITH BONDS

Bonds are obviously less risky than equity shares. This is because the returns offered by bonds are fixed and are known before hand. Hence, the problem of variability of return which is the major characteristic of equity share is not present with bonds. However, bonds cannot be considered as entirely risk free. The following are the two types of risks associated with bonds.

- Default risk
- Interest rate risk

5.6.1. Default Risk

Default risk arises when the company defaults on the periodical interest payments or on the repayment of principal on maturity. When the performance of a company suffers set back, the company may not be in a position to meet the interest/principal obligations. Suppose a company becomes bankrupt. The bond holders of the company may lose their investment either in part or full. Even if at all they receive their money back, it will be only after a long delay. Thus, the delay in realizing the interest/principal or the possibility of losing interest/principal due to poor financial performance of the company implies that bonds have default risk. Even if a company pays its bond holders both interest on bonds and the principal amount, but with a delay, such delays will go to reduce the return from the bonds in terms of present value and this also implies that bonds have default risk.

To offer safeguard against default risk, the mechanism of credit rating the debt securities is being widely followed. Credit rating agencies offer rating to bonds/debentures after carrying out both quantitative and qualitative analysis of the bonds/debentures being rated. While quantitative analysis refers to the analyzing the financial performance of the company issuing bonds/debentures, the qualitative analysis refers to studying factors like boom/recession of the economy, Government policies and changes if any anticipated in Government policies, the phase of life cycle of the industry, vulnerability to technological obsolescence likely growth/decline in market share etc. Credit rating gives a measure of default risk.

5.6.2. Interest Rate Risk

Changes in the market interest rates have the effect of changing the price of bonds. The risk of the price of bonds getting reduced due to the increase in the market interest rate is called interest rate risk. When the market interest rate increases and become more than the coupon rate of bond, the price of bond will get reduced below its face value. Hence, if the investor decides to dispose off the bond prior to its maturity period, his returns will get affected due to the reduced price (below the face value) at which he could dispose off the bond. When the market interest rate is more than the coupon rate and if the investor decides to hold the bond till maturity, he can reinvest the annual interest payments received at a higher rate (i.e., at the market rate) than the coupon rate. Thus, as far as the reinvestment of interest from the bond is concerned, the investor gets additional return than what he envisaged. However, if the market interest rate falls below the coupon rate, the investor can reinvest the annual interest receipts only at a lesser interest rate (i.e., at the market rate) than the coupon rate. Thus, the investor under such circumstances would get lesser return that what he envisaged.

From the above discussion, are can infer that the interest rate risk can be split up into two components, viz.,

- Price risk
- Reinvestment risk

Price risk

When the market interest rate increases above the coupon rate, the bond price will reduce. If an investor decides to dispose off the bond prior to its maturity period, he will incur a loss due to reduced price of the bond. Though he would have gained by way of additional returns on reinvestment of interest payments received, if the loss due to reduction in bond price is more than the additional return earned by way of reinvestment of interest receipts, the investor will suffer a net loss. This is referred to as price risk.

Reinvestment risk

When the market interest rate falls below the coupon rate, though the bond price will increase beyond its face value, the investor could reinvest the interest receipts only at a rate lower than the coupon rate and thus will suffer a loss due to reduced return on reinvestment. If the investor decides to dispose off the bond prior to its maturity period and if the loss due to reduction in return on reinvestment of interest receipts is more than the additional return earned due to selling the bond at a higher price than the face value, the investor will suffer a net loss. This is referred to as reinvestment risk.

5.7. DURATION

Those who invest in bonds are exposed to interest rate risk. Interest rate risk can be explained as under.

"When the market interest rates rise, the investors in bonds gain on reinvestments of periodical interest receipts. However, the investors suffer loss on liquidation of bonds. When the market interest rates fall, the investors in bonds suffer loss on reinvestments of periodical interest receipts while they gain on liquidation of bonds.

Thus, the two components of interest rate risk (viz., price risk and reinvestment risk) affect the investor differently. For every bond, there is a holding period for which the effects of price of bond and loss/gain on reinvestment exactly balance each other. When a bond is held till this holding period, what is gained by way of additional returns due to reinvestment of interest receipts is lost on liquidation of the bond due to reduction in bond price; similarly what is lost by way of reduction of returns due to reinvestment of interest receipts is gained on liquidation of the bond. Thus, when a bond is held till this holding period, the bond does not suffer from interest rate risks. This is because the effect of price risk is offset by the effect of reinvestment risk. The holding period of bond for which there is no interest rate risk is known as the "duration" of the bond. When a bond is held till its duration, the bond holder is relieved of interest rate risk. Any change in the market interest rate during the period will not have any effect on the returns available to the bond holders.

Thus, 'duration' of a bond can be defined as the time period at which the price risk and the reinvestment risk of the bond are equal in magnitude but opposite in direction.

The following illustration containing a series of workings explains the concept of bond duration.

***Illustration* 5.9:**

A 5 year bond with a face value of Rs. 100 has a coupon rate of 10%. What is the terminal value that will be available to an investor in this bond, if the market interest rate is 12%.

Solution:

	At the end of I year	At the end of II year	At the end of III year	At the end of IV year	At the end of V year
Cash flow to the bond holder	10.00	10.00	10.00	10.00	10.00 100.00 (redeemed value of bond)
					110.00

Since the yearly interest receipts of the Rs. 10 will be invested at the market interest rate of 12%, the terminal value can be arrived at by charging interest at 12% on the periodical interest receipts.

Terminal value

$= 10\ (1 + 0.12)^4 + 10\ (1 + 0.12)^3 + 10\ (1 + 0.12)^2 + 10\ (1 + 0.12) + 110.00$

$= 15.735 + 14.049 + 12.544 + 11.20 + 110.00$

= **Rs. 163.53**

***Illustration* 5.10:**

Calculate the terminal value of the bond given in Illustration 5.9 if the market interest rate drops to 8% immediately after the bond holder buys the bond.

Solution:

Since the market interest rate is 8%, the bond holder can reinvest his yearly interest receipts only at an interest rate of 8%.

	At the end of I year	At the end of II year	At the end of III year	At the end of IV year	At the end of V year
Cash flow to the bond holder	10.00	10.00	10.00	10.00	10.00 100.00
					110.00

Terminal value

$= 10\ (1 + 0.08)^4 + 10\ (1 + 0.08)^3 + 10\ (1 + 0.08)^2 + 10\ (1 + 0.08) + 110.00$

$= 13.605 + 12.597 + 11.664 + 10.80 + 110.00$

= **Rs. 158.67**

***Illustration* 5.11:**

Calculate the terminal value of the bond given in illustration 5.9 if the market interest rate rises to 15% immediately after the bond holder buys the bond.

Solution:

	At the end of I year	At the end of II year	At the end of III year	At the end of IV year	At the end of V year
Cash flow to the bond holder	10.00	10.00	10.00	10.00	10.00 100.00
					110.00

$$\text{Terminal value} = 10\ (1 + 0.15)^4 + 10\ (1 + 0.15)^3 + 10\ (1 + 0.15)^2 + 10\ (1 + 0.15) + 110.00$$

$$= 17.490 + 15.209 + 13.225 + 11.50 + 110.00$$

$$= \textbf{Rs. 167.42}$$

Observation

From illustrations 5.9, 5.10 and 5.11 we can understand that when the bond is held till maturity, the terminal value to the bond holder changes as the market interest rate changes. While the market interest rate falls down, the terminal value also falls down and vice versa.

***Illustration* 5.12:**

For the bond described in illustration 5.9,

(A) If the bond holder can hold the bond only for a period of 2 years, calculate the terminal value after the holding period of 2 years. Assume the market interest rate at 12%. Also calculate the terminal values for market interest rates of 8% and 15% respectively.

(B) If the bond holder can hold the bond only for a period of 3 years, calculate the terminal value after the holding period of 3 years. Assume the market interest rate at 12%. Also calculate the terminal values for market interest rates of 8% and 15% respectively.

(C) If the bond holder can hold the bond only for a period of 4 years, calculate the terminal value after the holding period of 4 years. Assume the market interest rate at 12%. Also calculate the terminal values for market interest rates of 8% and 15% respectively.

Solution:

(A) - I

Maturity period : 5 years

Holding period : 2 years

Market interest rate : 12%

When the holding period is 2 years, the investor would be selling his bond at the end of two years. The sale price at the end of two years will be equal to the present value of the bond at the end of 2 years (i.e., at the beginning of the third year)

	At the end of III year	At the end of IV Year	At the end of V year
Cash flow to the bond holder	10.00	10.00	10.00 100.00
			110.00

$$\left.\begin{array}{l}\text{Present value of cash}\\\text{flow at the beginning}\\\text{of the third year}\end{array}\right\} = \frac{10.00}{(1+0.12)} + \frac{10.00}{(1+0.12)^2} + \frac{110.00}{(1+0.12)^3}$$

$$= 8.929 + 7.972 + 78.296$$

$$= \text{Rs. } 95.20$$

After the holding period of two years the investor will be able to sell the bond at a price of Rs. 95.20.

	At the end of I year	At the end of II year
Cash flow	10.00	10.00 95.20
		105.20

$$\text{Terminal value at the end of the second year} = 10(1 + 0.12) + 105.20$$

$$= 11.20 + 105.20$$

$$= \textbf{Rs. 116.40}$$

(A) - II

Maturity period : 5 years

Holding period : 2 years

Market interest rate : 8%

	At the end of III year	At the end of IV year	At the end of V year
Cash flow to the bond holder	10.00	10.00	10.00 100.00
			110.00

$$\left.\begin{array}{l}\text{Present value of cash}\\\text{flow at the beginning}\\\text{of the third year}\end{array}\right\} = \frac{10.00}{(1+0.08)} + \frac{10.00}{(1+0.08)^2} + \frac{110.00}{(1+0.08)^3}$$

$$= 9.259 + 8.573 + 87.321$$

$$= \text{Rs. } 105.15$$

After the holding period of 2 years the investor will be able to sell the bond at a price of Rs. 105.15.

	At the end of I year	At the end of II year
Cash flow	10.00	10.00 105.15
		115.15

Terminal value at the end of the second year

$$= 10\ (1 + 0.08) + 115.15$$
$$= 10.80 + 115.15$$
$$= \textbf{Rs. 125.95}$$

(A) - III

Maturity period : 5 years
Holding period : 2 years and
Market interest rate : 15%

	At the end of III year	At the end of IV year	At the end of V year
Cash flow to the bond holder	10.00	10.00	10.00 100.00
			110.00

$$\left.\begin{array}{l}\text{Present value of cash}\\ \text{flow at the beginning}\\ \text{of the third year}\end{array}\right\} = \frac{10.00}{(1+0.15)} + \frac{10.00}{(1+0.15)^2} + \frac{110.00}{(1+0.15)^3}$$

$$= 8.696 + 7.561 + 72.327$$
$$= \text{Rs. } 88.58$$

	At the end of I year	At the end of II year
Cash flow	10.00	10.00 88.58
		98.58

Terminal value at the end of the second year $= 10\ (1 + 0.15) + 98.58$

$$= 11.50 + 98.58$$
$$= \textbf{Rs. 110.08}$$

(B) - I

Maturity period : 5 years
Holding period : 3 years and
Market interest rate : 12%

When the holding period is 3 years, the investor would be selling his bond at the end of three years. The sale price at the end of three years will be equal to the present value of bond at the end of three years. (i.e., at the beginning of the fourth year)

	At the end of IV year	At the end of V year
Cash flow	10.00	10.00 100.00
		110.00

$$\left.\begin{array}{l}\text{Present value of cash}\\\text{flow at the beginning}\\\text{of the fourth year}\end{array}\right\} = \frac{10.00}{(1+0.12)} + \frac{110.00}{(1+0.12)^2}$$

$$= 8.929 + 87.691$$
$$= \text{Rs. } 96.62$$

After the holding period of three years, the investor will be able to sell the bond at a price of Rs. 96.62.

	At the end of I year	At the end of II year	At the end of III year
Cash flow	10.00	10.00	10.00 96.62
			106.62

$$\left.\begin{array}{l}\text{Terminal value of cash}\\\text{flow at the end of the}\\\text{third year}\end{array}\right\} = 10\ (1 + 0.12)^2 + 10\ (1 + 0.12) + 106.62$$

$$= 12.544 + 11.20 + 106.62$$
$$= \textbf{Rs. 130.37}$$

(B) – II

Maturity period : 5 years
Holding period : 3 years and
Market interest rate : 8%

	At the end of IV year	At the end of V year
Cash flow	10.00	10.00 100.00
		110.00

$$\left.\begin{array}{l}\text{Present value of cash}\\\text{flow at the beginning}\\\text{of the fourth year}\end{array}\right\} = \frac{10.00}{(1+0.08)} + \frac{110.00}{(1+0.08)^2}$$

$$= 9.259 + 94.307$$
$$= \text{Rs. } 103.57$$

	At the end of I year	At the end of II year	At the end of III year
Cash flow	10.00	10.00	10.00 103.57
			113.57

$$\left.\begin{array}{l}\text{Terminal value of cash flow at}\\\text{the end of the third year}\end{array}\right\} = 10(1+0.08)^2 + 10(1+0.08) + 113.57$$

$$= 11.664 + 10.80 + 113.57$$
$$= \textbf{Rs. 136.03}$$

(B) – III

Maturity period : 5 years
Holding period : 3 years and
Market interest rate : 15%

	At the end of IV year	At the end of V year
Cash flow	10.00	10.00 100.00
		110.00

$$\left.\begin{array}{l}\text{Present value of cash}\\\text{flow at the beginning}\\\text{of the third year}\end{array}\right\} = \frac{10.00}{(1+0.15)} + \frac{10.00}{(1+0.15)^2}$$

$$= 8.696 + 83.176$$
$$= \text{Rs. } 91.87$$

	At the end of I year	At the end of II year	At the end of III year
Cash flow to the bond holder	10.00	10.00	10.00 91.87
			101.87

$$\left.\begin{array}{l}\text{Terminal value of cash flow at}\\\text{the end of the third year}\end{array}\right\} = 10(1+0.15)^2 + 10(1+0.15) + 101.87$$

$$= 13.225 + 11.50 + 101.87$$
$$= \textbf{Rs. 126.60}$$

(C) - I

Maturity period : 5 years
Holding period : 4 years and
Market interest rate : 12%

When the holding period is 4 years, the investor would be selling his bond at the end of four years. The sale price at the end of four years will be equal to the present value of bond at the end of four years (i.e., at the beginning of the fifth year)

	At the end of V year
Cash flow	10.00 100.00
	110.00

$$\left.\begin{array}{l}\text{Present value of cash}\\ \text{flow at the beginning}\\ \text{of the fifth year}\end{array}\right\} = \frac{110.00}{(1+0.12)}$$

$$= \text{Rs. } 98.21$$

	At the end of I year	**At the end of II year**	**At the end of III year**	**At the end of IV year**
Cash flow	10.00	10.00	10.00	10.00 98.21
				108.21

$$\left.\begin{array}{l}\text{Terminal value of cash}\\ \text{flow at the end of the}\\ \text{fourth year}\end{array}\right\} = 10(1+0.12)^3 + 10(1+0.12)^2 + 10(1+0.12) + 108.21$$

$$= 14.049 + 12.544 + 11.20 + 108.21$$

$$= \textbf{Rs. 146.00}$$

(C) – II

Maturity period : 5 years

Holding period : 4 years and

Market interest rate : 8%

	At the end of V year
Cash flow	10.00 100.00
	110.00

$$\left.\begin{array}{l}\text{Present value of cash}\\ \text{flow at the beginning}\\ \text{of the fifth year}\end{array}\right\} = \frac{110.00}{(1+0.08)}$$

$$= \text{Rs. } 101.85$$

	At the end of I year	At the end of II year	At the end of III year	At the end of IV year
Cash flow	10.00	10.00	10.00	10.00 101.85
				111.85

Terminal value of cash flow at the end of the fourth year $= 10(1+0.08)^3 + 10(1+0.08)^2 + 10(1+0.08) + 111.85$

$= 12.597 + 11.664 + 10.80 + 111.85$

$=$ **Rs. 146.91**

(C) – III

Maturity period : 5 years

Holding period : 4 years and

Market interest rate : 15%

	At the end of V year
Cash flow	10.00 100.00
	110.00

Present value of cash flow at the beginning of the fifth year $= \dfrac{110.00}{(1+0.15)}$

$=$ Rs. 95.65

	At the end of I year	At the end of II year	At the end of III year	At the end of IV year
Cash flow	10.00	10.00	10.00	10.00 95.65
				105.65

Terminal value of cash flow at the end of the fourth year $= 10(1+0.15)^3 + 10(1+0.15)^2 + 10(1+0.15) + 105.65$

$= 15.209 + 13.225 + 11.50 + 105.65$

$=$ **Rs. 145.58**

Discussion on the Terminal value of bonds vis-à-vis the holding period

The results of illustration 5.10, 5.11 and 5.12 are tabulated below

Terminal value of cash flow at the end of the holding period (Rs.)				
Market interest rate	Holding period 5 years (i.e., till maturity)	Holding period 2 years	Holding period 3 years	Holding period 4 years
12%	163.53	116.30	130.37	146.00
8%	158.67	125.95	136.03	146.91
15%	167.42	110.08	126.60	145.58

The following are the observations that can be made from the results indicated in the above table:

(*a*) When the investor holds the bond till its maturity period of 5 years the terminal value that would accrue to the investor is Rs. 163.53 when the market interest rate is 12%. The investor suffers a loss if the market interest rate falls down while the investor gains if the market interest rate rises.

(*b*) When the investor holds the bond for a period of 2 years which is less than its maturity period of 5 years, the investor suffers a loss when the market interest rate increases while the investor gains when the market interest rate falls down. This change of fortune to the investor based on the change in market interest rate is opposite to the change of fortune to the investor when he holds the bond till its maturity.

(*c*) When the investor holds the bond for a period of 3 years, which is also less than the maturity period of 5 years, the investor suffers a loss when the market interest rate increases while the investor gains when the market interest rate falls down. (This situation is similar to the situation when the investor holds the bond for two years.)

(*d*) When the holding period is 4 years, the results give a different picture. The investor does not either gain or loss due to the changes in the market interest rates (ignoring the minor differences in the terminal values for different market interest rates). This leads to an important conclusion that the bond when retained up to a certain period, overcomes the risk of interest rate changes in the market. The period of time, up to which when a bond is held by an investor, makes the investor overcome the interest rate risk is called 'duration' of the bond.

(*e*) Every bond has a duration and when the bond is held by the investor till its 'duration' and then disposed off immediately after its 'duration' the investor will not be affected by interest rate risk. When a bond is liquidated either prior to its 'duration' or is held till its maturity, the bond bears interest rate risk. The holding period at which the interest rate risk of a bond disappears either due to the gain out of reinvestment getting exactly compensated by the loss on sale of the bond or due to the loss on reinvestment getting exactly compensated by the gain out of sale of the bond is called 'duration' of the bond.

Note: *In the illustration given above, we have found that when the bond is held for a period of 4 years, the terminal value available to the investor at market interest rates of 12%, 8% and 15% remain nearly the same. The terminal value at different interest rates can be exactly equal if the holding period is slightly over 4 years. However, since interest on the bond is paid on yearly basis, for all practical purposes the duration can be taken as 4 years.*

Let us check up whether this is valid at a different market interest rate, say at a market interest rate of 20%.

Maturity period : 5 years
Holding period : 4 years and
Market interest rate : 20%

	At the end of V year
Cash flow	10.00 100.00
	110.00

$$\left.\begin{array}{l}\text{Present value of cash}\\ \text{flow at the beginning}\\ \text{of the fifth year}\end{array}\right\} = \frac{110.00}{(1+0.20)}$$

$$= \text{Rs. } 91.67$$

	At the end of I year	At the end of II year	At the end of III year	At the end of IV year
Cash flow	10.00	10.00	10.00	10.00 91.67
				101.67

$$\left.\begin{array}{l}\text{Terminal value of}\\ \text{cash flow at the end of}\\ \text{the fourth year}\end{array}\right\} = 10(1+0.20)^3 + 10(1+0.20)^2 + 10(1+0.20) + 101.67$$

$$= 17.28 + 14.40 + 12.00 + 101.67$$

$$= \textbf{Rs. 145.35}$$

The terminal value of Rs. 145.35 at market interest rate of 20% indicates that there is no significant difference in terminal values at different market interest rates. The terminal values are Rs. 146.00, Rs. 146.91, Rs. 145.88 and Rs. 145.35 at market interest rates of 12%, 8%, 15% and 20% respectively. When the exact duration of bond is arrived at, then the terminal value of bonds at different interest rates will all be the same.

Formula for arriving at duration of bond

A bond that has a duration equal to the investor's investment horizon is said to immunize the investor against changes in interest rates in the market. When a bond is held till its duration, any change in bond value due to change in Yield to Maturity (YTM) is exactly balanced by the change in income and change in bond price. In other words, the investor is freed of interest rate risk. When the market interest rises above the coupon rate of bond, there is gain on reinvestments and loss on liquidation. Conversely, when the interest rate falls below the coupon rate of bond, there is loss on reinvestments and gain on liquidation. Thus, for every bond there is a holding period for which the effects of gain/loss on reinvestment and loss/gain on liquidation cancel out each other. What is lost on reinvestment is exactly gained on liquidation and vice versa. This holding period for which the interest rate risk ceases to exist is known as the duration of the bond.

For arriving at the duration of bond, it is not necessary to make trial & error calculations as done in illustration 5.12. Instead, Frederick R. Macaulay had developed a formula.

Macaulay defined duration as 'the weighted average of time periods to maturity. According to Macaulay's formula, Duration (D) is given by the following relationship.

$$D = \frac{\sum_{t=1}^{n} \frac{(t).(C_t)}{(1+i)^t}}{\sum_{t=1}^{n} \frac{(C_t)}{(1+i)^t}}$$

where

t = time period of each cash flow.

C_t = interest and/or principal payment that occurs in period 't'.

i = market interest rate.

n = maturity period of bond.

The numerator of the formula is the present value of all cash inflows weighted according to the length of time to receipt. The denominator is the price of the bond determined by the present value model.

***Illustration* 5.13:**

A 5 year bond with a face value of Rs. 100 has a coupon rate of 10%. The market interest rate is 12%. The bond is redeemable at par after 5 years. Calculate the duration of the bond.

Solution:

Annual interest receipts (at the rate of 10%)	=	Rs. 10.00
Maturity period of bond (n)	=	5 years
Market interest rate (i)	=	12%

$$\text{Therefore Duration } (D) = \frac{\sum_{t=1}^{n} \frac{(t).(C_t)}{(1+i)^t}}{\sum_{t=1}^{n} \frac{(C_t)}{(1+i)^t}}$$

t	C_t	$\frac{C_t}{(1+i)^t}$	$\frac{(t).(C_t)}{(1+i)^t}$
1	10.00	9.091	9.091
2	10.00	8.264	16.528
3	10.00	7.513	22.539
4	10.00	6.830	27.320
5	110.00	68.299	341.495
		Σ = 99.997	Σ = 416.973

$$\text{Duration} = \frac{416.973}{99.997}$$
$$= 4.17 \text{ years}$$

Note: *The duration of the bond was arrived at 4 years in illustration 5.12 by trail and error method. This is only the approximate value of duration since we have not made any trail in between holding period of 4 years and 5 years. Since, the terminal values of bond at market interest rates of 12%, 8% and 15% for a holding period of 4 years showed only minor variations and as interest on the bond is payable annually, for all practical purposes, the duration can be taken as 4 years. This is because 4 years is only the approximate value of duration.. For the exact value of 4.17 years, the terminal value will be the same for any market interest rate.*

5.7.1. Characteristics of "Duration"

From the formula for the duration of bonds, the following characteristics of duration can be inferred:

(*a*) Other factors remaining the same, the higher the market interest rate, the lower the duration.

(*b*) Other factors remaining the same, the longer the maturity period of a bond, the higher the duration.

(*c*) Other factors remaining the same, the larger the coupon rate, the shorter the duration.

(*d*) When a bond has coupons (i.e., when it offers periodical interest payments at coupon rate) the duration of the bond will always be less than its maturity period since duration gives weight to the periodical payments in increasing order of the period.

(*e*) Duration of a zero coupon bond is equal to the bond's term to maturity.

(*f*) If the duration of a bond is significantly different from the desired holding period of an investor, the investor will consider the bond risky.

Hence, under such circumstances, the investor would invest in the bond only if the bond offers a higher YTM.

***Illustration* 5.14:**

A new bond is issued by a company with a maturity period of 5 years and a coupon rate of 12%. The face value of the bond is Rs. 100 and the bond is redeemable at par after its maturity period of 5 years. The market interest rate is 12%. Prove that the duration of the bond is less than its period to maturity.

Solution:

Since, the bond is newly issued, its coupon rate is equal to the market interest rate (viz., 12%). As the coupon rate and the market interest rate are equal and as the bond is redeemable at par, the price of the bond will be equal to its face value (i.e., Rs. 100.00).

Annual interest receipts (at the rate of 12%) = Rs. 12.00

Period to maturity (n) = 5 years

Market interest rate (i) = 12%

$$D = \frac{\sum_{t=1}^{n} \frac{(t)\cdot(C_t)}{(1+i)^t}}{\sum_{t=1}^{n} \frac{(C_t)}{(1+i)^t}}$$

t	C_t	$\frac{C_t}{(1+i)^t}$	$\frac{(t)\cdot(C_t)}{(1+i)^t}$
1	12.00	10.714	10.714
2	12.00	9.566	19.132
3	12.00	8.541	25.623
4	12.00	7.626	30.504
5	112.00	63.552	317.769
		$\Sigma = 99.999$	$\Sigma = 403.733$

$$\text{Duration} = \frac{403.733}{99.999}$$

$$= 4.03733 \text{ say } 4.04 \text{ years}$$

Thus, it is proved that the duration of the bond is less than its period to maturity.

5.7.2. Duration of Zero Coupon Bonds

For zero coupon bonds, the duration is equal to the Term to Maturity. This is because the payment to the bond holder is made only at maturity and hence there is only one cash flow and this cash flow is at maturity.

5.8. BOND PORTFOLIO

The duration of a portfolio of bonds is equal to the weighted average of the duration of the individual bonds contained in the portfolio.

Every investor may have a desired holding period for the portfolio of bonds. The desired holding period depends on the investor's funds requirement at a future date. Since market interest rates change, the realized YTM for a bond may be either greater or less than the YTM envisaged while investing in the bond. If the investor wants the portfolio of bonds that he holds to give the desired yield, one way to achieve this is to immunize the portfolio. Immunization of a bond portfolio takes place when the desired holding period of the portfolio equals the portfolio duration. For example, if the investor's desired holding period is, say, 5 years, the investor should look at bonds with duration of at or about 5 years. The investor should look at the duration and not the maturity period. The bond portfolio should be constructed in such a way that the duration of the portfolio (which is the weighted average of the durations of the individual bonds contained in then portfolio) matches with the desired holding period.

REVIEW QUESTIONS

1. Define Coupon rate of a bond.
2. Define Zero coupon bond. What is the spot interest rate of a zero coupon bond?
3. Define YTM of a bond. Derive a short-cut formula for arriving at the YTM.
4. Enumerate the five principles of bond pricing.
5. Explain the two types of risks associated with bonds.
6. What are the components of Interest rate risk? Explain them in brief.
7. Define 'Duration' of a bond. A 5 year bond with a face value of Rs. 100 has a coupon rate of 8.50%. The market interest rate is 11.75%. The bond is redeemable at par after 5 years. Calculate the duration of the bond.
8. What are the characteristics of 'Duration'?
9. What is the 'Duration' of a zero coupon bond?
10. What do you mean by immunization of a bond portfolio and how can this be achieved?

6 CHAPTER Technical Analysis

6.1. INTRODUCTION

In carrying out fundamental analysis of a security, the analyst attempts to determine the intrinsic value of the security (i.e., the true worth of the security). He decides to buy/hold/sell the security based on its intrinsic value. If the intrinsic value of a security is more than the current market price of the security, we would buy the security. If the intrinsic value of a security is less than the current market price of the security, he would sell the security. If the intrinsic value of a security matches with its current market price, he would hold the security till such time he could decide on selling/buying the security. The analyst arrives at the intrinsic value of a security by studying the current earnings from the security and also by analysing its future earning capacity based on long term judgements. A fundamental analysist believes that the price of a security would approach its intrinsic value in the future. Obviously, any assessment that is based on long term judgements may give a result that is different from short term reality. Most investors are not prepared to wait to reap the long term benefits that the fundamental analysis predicts. Hence, in the short run, the market prices of securities deviate considerably from the intrinsic value. Fundamental analysis fails to justify such short term fluctuations in the price of securities. This is because the security price movements are based more on psychological factors than on economical factors. Technical analysis comes to the help of investors where fundamental analysis proves inadequate.

6.2. TECHNICAL ANALYSIS

Those who rely on technical analysis (let us call them 'technicians' in future) contend that it is not necessary to study the economic fundamentals in order to know as to where the price of a security is moving. They believe that the past price movements indicate the future price movements.

Technicians are not against fundamental analysis. They put forth their arguments as under in support of Technical analysis, which forms the basic principles of Technical analysis.

(a) The market prices of securities are determined by the forces of demand and supply operating in the market.

(b) These demand and supply forces are under the influence of both fundamental factors as well as psychological factors.

(c) While the fundamental factors can be analysed and quantified, the psychological factors cannot be quantified.

(d) Since the security price movements are affected both by quantifiable factors (fundamental factors) and by non-quantifiable factors (psychological factors) fundamental analysis is inadequate to predict the future price of securities.

(e) The combined effect of fundamental factors and technical factors is reflected in the price movements of securities.

(f) In view of the above, merely by examining the past price movements of securities, the future prices can be predicted since the past price movements contain all the relevant factors that affect the price.

The analysis comprising of techniques that make use of historical security price data to forecast the future price of securities is called Technical analysis.

6.3. LOGIC BEHIND TECHNICAL ANALYSIS

The market prices of securities are determined by the forces of demand and supply operating in the market. All analysts, whether fundamental analysts or technical analysts or hybrid analysts will agree with this view. There can be no difference of opinion on this. However, technical analysts believe that new information do not cause an instantaneous change in the demand-supply relationship. Though they believe that the market is efficient enough to adjust the demand-supply relationship on the basis of new information, the technical analysts are of the opinion that the adjustment takes place *"over a period of time"* and not instantaneously. Since there are different types of investors in any market, all of them do not receive new information at the same point of time. Insiders may receive information immediately. Well-informed professionals may receive information some time after the insiders have received the same. Average investors will receive information further belatedly. Since every investor decides to buy or sell securities on the basis of new information and as new information reach the different types of investors at different points of time, the buying/selling of securities in the market on the basis of new information takes place over a period of time. The security price starts its movement from an equilibrium price level (either upward or downward) on the basis of new information and reaches a new equilibrium price level by the time the new information has reached all the investors and all the investors have acted on the basis of the new information (Refer Fig. 6.1).

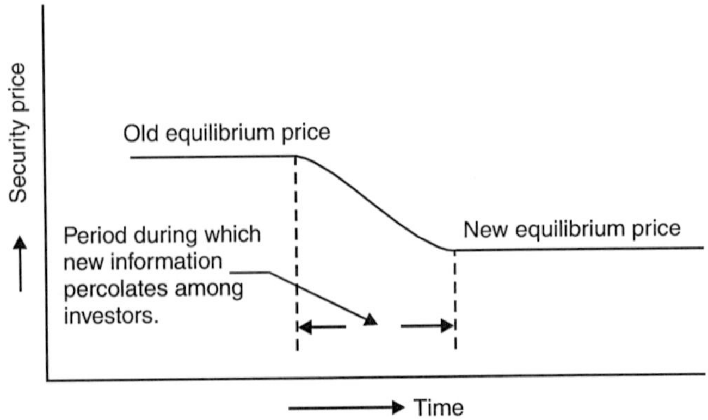

Fig. 6.1 Price adjustment on the basis of new information

Technicians are keen to detect the beginning of price movement from one equilibrium level to another equilibrium level. This is because, once the beginning of a price movement is discerned, the prudent investor can earn above-average return by selling/buying securities immediately after the price movement has started. Hence, technical analysis is devoted to deriving a system that allows the investor to detect the price movement of security from one equilibrium level to another equilibrium level. It may be noted here, that the technician is interested only in knowing the start of a price-movement and he is least interested in knowing as to why the price movement has started.

6.4. TYPES OF CHARTS USED IN TECHNICAL ANALYSIS

Technicians use the following four types of charts for depicting the price movements of securities:

(*a*) Line chart
(*b*) Bar chart
(*c*) Point and figure chart
(*d*) Japanese Candle Stick chart

(*a*) Line chart

The line chart has 'time' on the x-axis and 'price' on the y-axis. The closing price of security for each time period is plotted as a point and these points are joined to for the line chart. Figure 6.2 is a line chart for the following data:

Period	Price (Rupees)
1	100
2	150
3	200
4	150
5	150
6	200

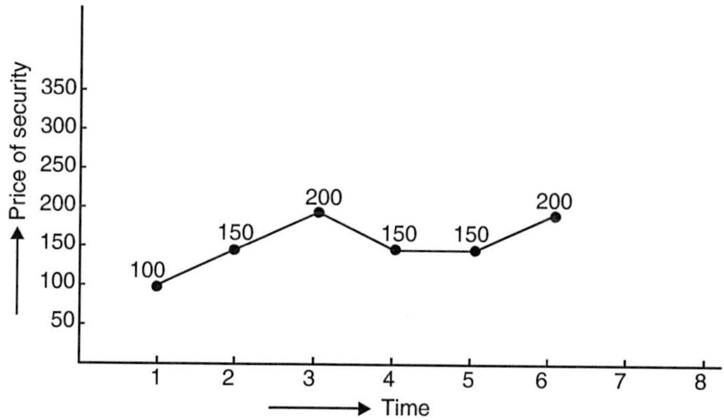

Fig. 6.2 Line chart depicting price movement of security

The time period taken for recording the security prices may be a day, a week or a month.

(*b*) Bar chart

Similar to Line chart, Bar chart also has 'time' on the *x*-axis and 'price' on the *y*-axis. The time period taken for recording the security prices may be a day, a week or a month. Against each time period on the x-axis, a vertical line (bar) is drawn representing the lowest to the highest price. The lower most point on the bar represents the lowest price and the top most point on the bar represents the highest price. A small horizontal line is drawn across the bar. This horizontal line represents the closing price at the end of the time period.

Figure 6.3 is a bar chart for the following data:

Period	Lowest price	Highest price	Closing price for the period
1	50	150	100
2	100	200	150
3	150	250	200
4	75	225	150
5	125	175	150
6	175	225	200

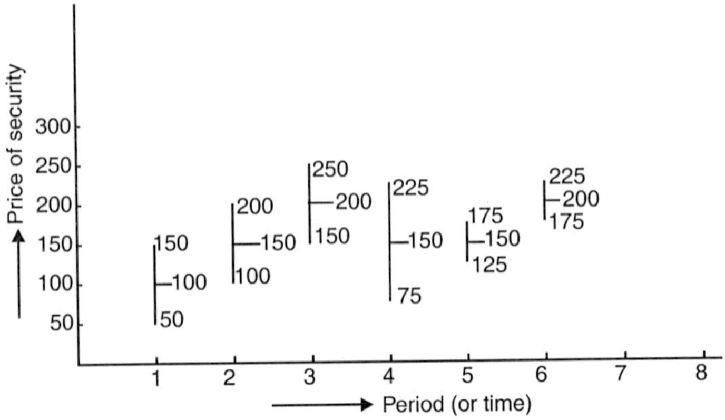

Fig. 6.3 Bar chart depicting price movement of security

(c) Point and figure chart

While line chart and bar chart are concerned with depicting the movement of price of security with respect to time, point and figure chart ignores time element totally. Another feature of point and figure chart is that it ignores 'small' changes in stock prices. Further, the stock price movement in the reverse direction is noted in the chart only if the stock price reverses its direction of movement to an extent equal to or more than a predetermined value. For constructing a point and figure chart, two parameters are to be decided upon. First, the box size and second the reversal criterion. Fixing of box sizes aids in ignoring small changes in stock prices. Defining the reversal criterion aids in correctly predicting the reversing trend in stock prices and ignoring trivial changes of stock prices in the reverse direction.

The following illustration will help to understand the mode of construction of point and figure chart.

Let us plot a point and figure chart for the following data:

Period	Price
1	200
2	201
3	203
4	204
5	205
6	204
7	203
8	205
9	202
10	200

11	199
12	198
13	195
14	196
15	197
16	196
17	197
18	196
19	195
20	196
21	197
22	198
23	204
24	205
25	205
26	206
27	202
28	203
29	205
30	200
31	201
32	202
33	203
34	205
35	206
36	207
37	207
38	208
39	209
40	210

Let us assume a box size of 1 and a reversal criterion of 3 boxes.

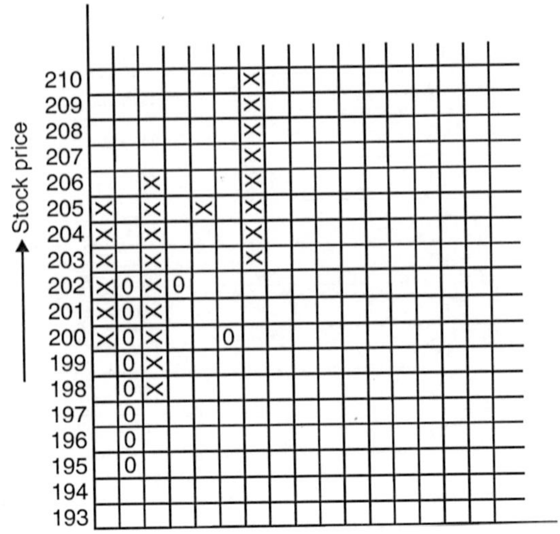

Fig. 6.4(a) Point and figure chart

The price at period – 1 is 200. (Refer Fig. 6.4(a))

This is marked in the point and figure chart by putting a 'X' mark in the box in the first column, against the stock price 200.

The stock price of 201 in period – 2 is marked in the chart by placing a 'X' mark in the box in the first column, against the stock price 201.

The stock price of 203 in period – 3 is marked in the chart by placing a 'X' mark in the box in the first column, against the stock price of 203.

Since, the stock price has risen from 201 to 203, the box against the price of 202 is also marked by placing a 'X' mark.

Similarly the increase in the price levels of 204 & 205 are marked in the chart by placing 'X' marks in the box in the first column, against the stock price of 204 & 205 respectively.

So far, the price has been on an increasing trend. The trend now reverses.

In period – 6 the stock price has fallen from 205 to 204. However, this is not recorded in the chart. This is because, the fall in stock price is only to the extent of one box (i.e., 205 – 204 = 1) whereas the reversal criterion has been assumed as 3 boxes.

In period – 7 the stock price has further fallen to 203. This is also not recorded in the chart since the fall in stock price from the moment the fall has started is only 2 boxes (205 – 203) as against the reversal criterion of 3 boxes.

In period – 8 the stock price has risen to 205. Since, we have ignored the fall in prices in periods 6 & 7, we virtually stand at the price of 205. The stock price of 205 at period – 8 does not need to be recorded in the graph since the price of 205 has already been recorded in the first column.

In period – 9 the stock price falls down to 202. The number of boxes by which the stock price has fallen is 3 (205 – 202) which matches the reversal criterion. Hence, the fall in stock price to 202 is to be recorded on the graph. Since the trend has reversed, the price of 202 is marked in the next column against the price 202 by placing a zero '0' mark in the box.

In period – 10, the stock price has fallen to 200, which means that the downward trend continues. Hence, this is marked with '0' against the price 200 in column–2. Since, the price has fallen from 202 to 200, the intervening box corresponding to the price 201 is also marked with '0'.

In periods–11, 12 & 13 there is continuous drop in stock price from 199 to 195. Hence, all the blocks starting from the block corresponding to the price 199 to the price 195 are marked with '0'.

In period – 14 there is a reversal of trend. The price has reversed its downward movement and has gone upto 196. However, this reversal is not registered in the chart since the rise in share price has occurred only to the extent of one point (i.e., one box) as against the reversal criterion of 3 boxes.

Similarly, the rise in price during in period – 15 is also not registered in the chart as the quantum of rise is below the reversal criterion.

The fall in the price to 196 in period–16, the rise in the price to 197 in period – 17, the fall in the price to 196 in period – 18 and the fall in the price to 195 in period – 19 are not registered in the chart for the same reason mentioned above.

Since, the prices in periods 14 to 19 are ignored, we are at price 195 which corresponds to period – 13. From period 19 onwards there is a gradual rise in the price. In period 22, the price has moved upto 198, there by recording increase to the extent of 3 boxes. Hence, this points to reversal of trend.

To mark the price of 198 in period – 22 a 'X' mark is made in the box corresponding to the price level of 198 in the third column.

After period – 22, there is continuous rise in the price till the period – 26. Hence all the boxes from the price level 198 to the price level 206 are recorded in the chart by marking 'X' in the respective boxes.

In period – 27 there is a fall in trend and the price has fallen to 202 from 206 registering a fall of 4 which is more than the reversal criterion. Hence, the fall in stock price of 202 is recorded by marking '0' in the fourth column.

In period – 28, there is a reversal of trend. The price increases from 202 to 203. However, since the quantum of increase is less than the reversal criterion, the increase is ignored.

In period – 29, the price further increases to 205. The increase from 202 to 205 extends to 3 boxes (205 – 202 = 3) which is equal to the reversal criterion of 3 boxes. Hence, the reversal of trend is marked in the chart by placing a 'X' mark in the next column against the price level of 205.

In period – 30, the price falls to 200, registering a fall of 5 boxes (205 – 200 = 5) which is more than the reversal criterion of 3 boxes. Hence the reversal of trend is marked in the chart by placing a '0' mark in the next column against the price level of 200.

The increase in the price for the periods 31 and 32 are ignored as the increase is below the reversal criterion.

In period – 33 the price has increased to 203, registering an increase of 3 boxes (203 – 200). Since the reversal of trend in equal to the reversal criterion of 3 boxes the trend reversal is marked in the chart by placing a 'X' mark in the next column against the price level of 203.

From period 34 onwards till period 40, there is a continuous increase in the price which are marked in the chart by placing a 'X' mark from price level 205 to 210.

Point and figure chart using the actual values of prices

For the illustration discussed before, if we draw the point and figure chart using the actual values of prices instead of using 'X' and '0' signs, the chart will look like as under (Refer Fig. 6.4(b))

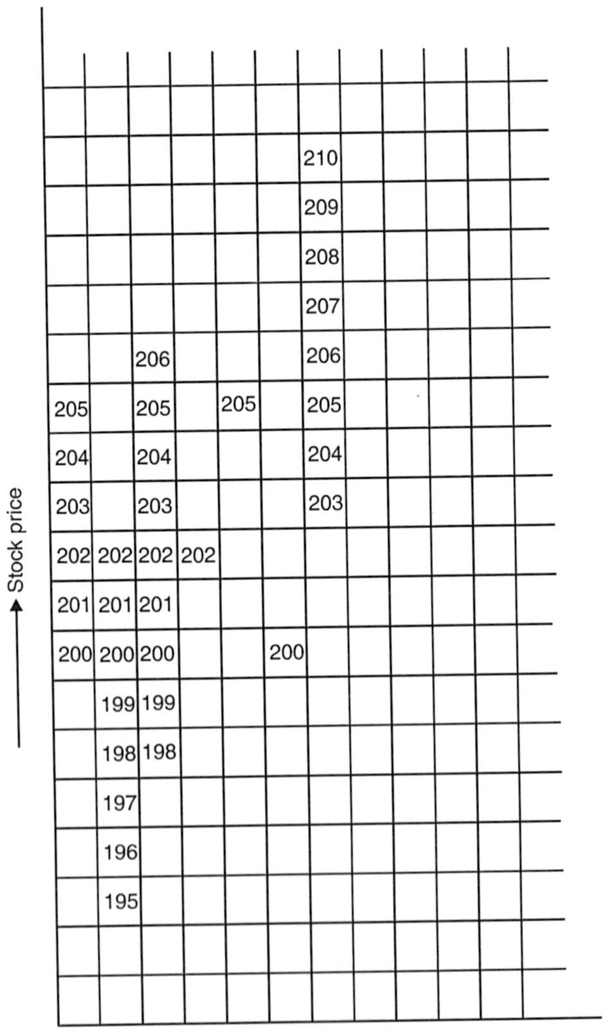

Fig. 6.4(b) Point and figure chart (using actual values of stock prices)

Since the technician is keen to notice any real trend reversal in the price of securities, the actual prices are not required and hence more often the use of 'X' and '0' marks is resorted to.

Interpretation of point and figure chart

The main drawback of Point and Figure chart is that since the time period at which changes in stock prices take place are not marked in the chart, it provides no information about the period(s) of time at which changes in the stock prices take place. However, Point and Figure charts help in identifying reversal of trend in stock prices.

The 'X' mark in the chart indicates that the prices are moving up and the '0' mark in the chart indicates that the prices are moving down.

The technicians look for "Congestion areas" in the point and figure chart. A congestion area is a horizontal band of X's and 0's. A congestion area is created by a series of reversals around a given price level. (Refer Fig. 6.5)

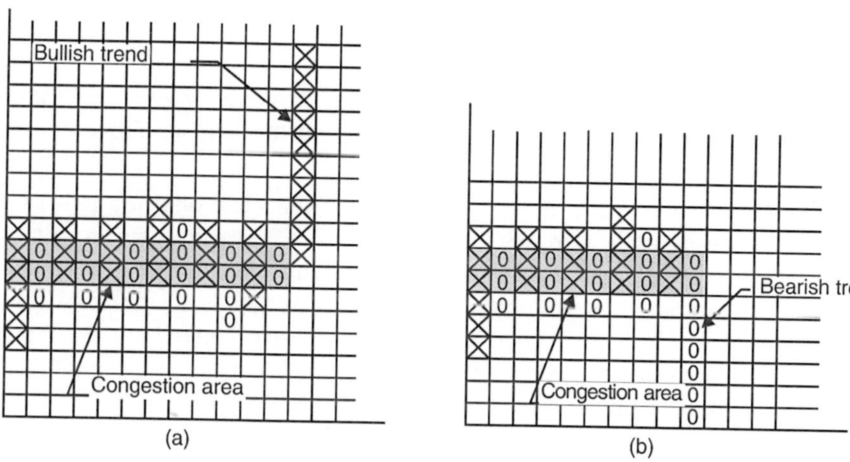

Fig. 6.5 Point and figure chart with congestion area

A congestion area in the chart indicates that the supply and demand are nearly equal.

When the column of X's rises above the top of the congestion area, a 'break-out' is said to have occurred. Such a penetration of X's column above the top of the congestion area signals a bullish tread. The penetration of 0's column at the bottom of the congestion area signals a bearish tread.

(*d*) Japanese candle stick chart

In a candle stick chart, every day price movement is marked using a candle stick pattern. The opening price and the closing price of the day are represented by a rectangle.

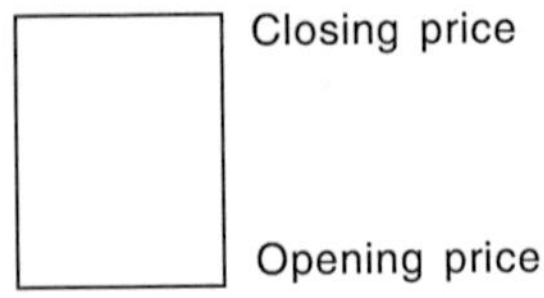

The highest and the lowest price of the day are marked at the top and at the bottom of the rectangle respectively and are joined by a vertical bar.

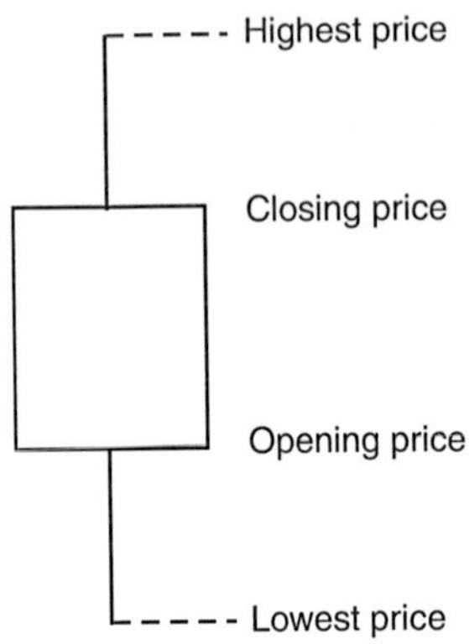

The rectangle along with the vertical bar joining the highest and the lowest price looks like a candle stick. Thus, each day's price movements are represented by a candle stick.

When the closing price of the day is higher than the opening price of the day, the candle stick is represented by a white rectangle and is called a white candle stick. A white candle stick indicates that the price movement is bullish. When the closing price of a day is lower than the opening price of the day, the candle stick is represented by a black rectangle and is called a black candle stick. A black candle stick indicates that the price movement is bearish.

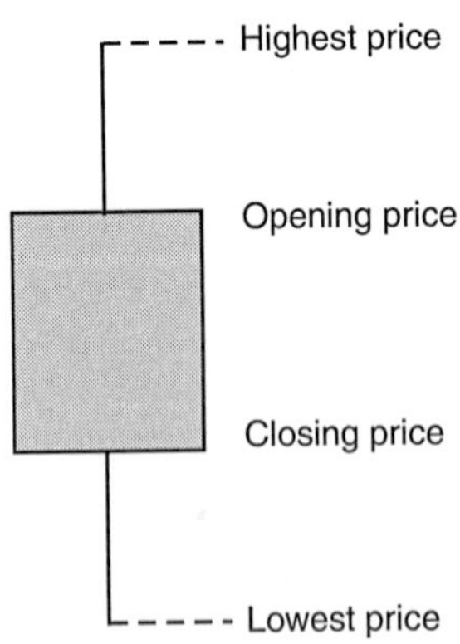

When the opening and the closing price happens to be the same, the price movements of the day are marked on a single vertical bar and such a candle stick is called Doji Candle stick.

Figure 6.6 Depicts a Candle stick chart.

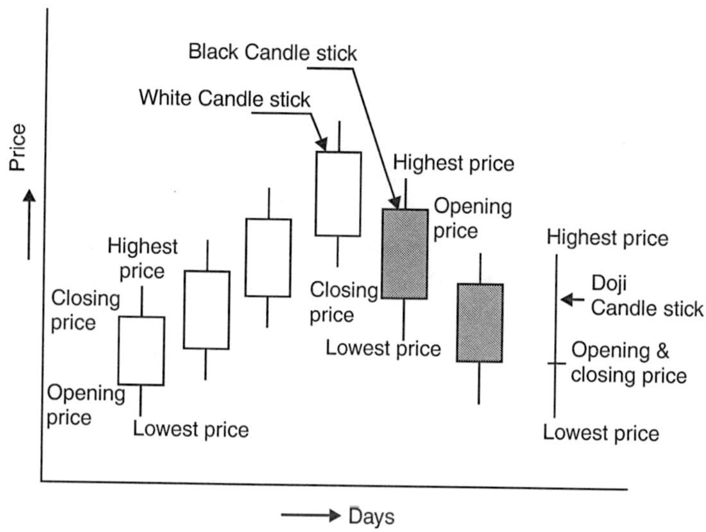

Fig. 6.6 Candle stick chart

6.5. DOW THEORY

Charles H DOW was the editor of the wall street journal in the U.S.A. He was a pioneer in technical analysis and the series of editorials that he wrote in the wall street journal during the years 1900–1902 constituted the foundation for much of the latter studies in technical analysis. The writings of Charles H DOW are better known among technicians as 'DOW Theory'.

According to Dow Theory the prices of securities in the stock market do not move at random, but more in cyclical pattern influenced by three distinct cyclical trends. DOW observed that the price of most stocks move in accordance with the movement of the market. When the market goes up, the price of most stocks also go up and vice versa. Hence, before attempting to predict the price movement of a particular security, the behaviour of the market as a whole is to be studied and understood. Dow theorized that the trend of overall stock prices could be determined by studying the price movements of a selected group of stocks. To understand the behaviour of the market,

DOW constructed two indices calling them as Industrial Average and Rail Average. The industrial average is known by the name DOW-Jones Industrial Average (DJIA)*.

The DJIA is a price-weighted average of 30 large, well-known industrial stocks that are generally the leaders in their industry and are listed on the New York Stock Exchange. By the time the index was built by Charles H. DOW there were 15 stocks included in the index which was later expanded to 30.

The Rail Average was built with 12 rail road stocks. The Rail Average was intended to serve as a representative index for transportation stocks. With the evolution of joint stock companies of other modes of transportation, the Rail Average was latter modified as the Transportation Average incorporating addition of stocks of transportation companies of other modes than Rail road mode and the index later came to be known as DOW-Jones Transportation Average (DJTA).

Postulates of Dow Theory

(*a*) All kinds of available market information have their influence in the stocks contained in the averages and hence the averages reflect the market.

(*b*) The averages exhibit three types of trends, viz., the primary trend, the secondary reactions and the minor movements.

(*c*) All the three trends occur simultaneously.

Note: *Though DOW observed three trends (or movements) he relied only on the primary and the secondary movements and ignored the minor movements and considered them insignificant and of no analytical value.*

Primary Trend

The primary trend is the long term trend that takes the entire market either up or down. The primary trend, being one of long term nature, will have average period of at least 18 months.

Secondary Trend (or Secondary Reaction)

The secondary trend occurs simultaneously with the primary trend. The secondary trend is called 'Secondary reaction' as this trend acts as a restraining force on the primary trend. The secondary trends usually last from several weeks to a few months. The secondary reactions trend to correct deviations from the general boundary of the primary trend.

---

* Charles DOW was the founder of DOW Jones And Co. and the index was known by the name of the company.

Minor Movements

The minor movements are the day-to-day fluctuations in the market and are not of analytical significance.

Figures 6.7(a) and 6.7(b) show primary and secondary trends.

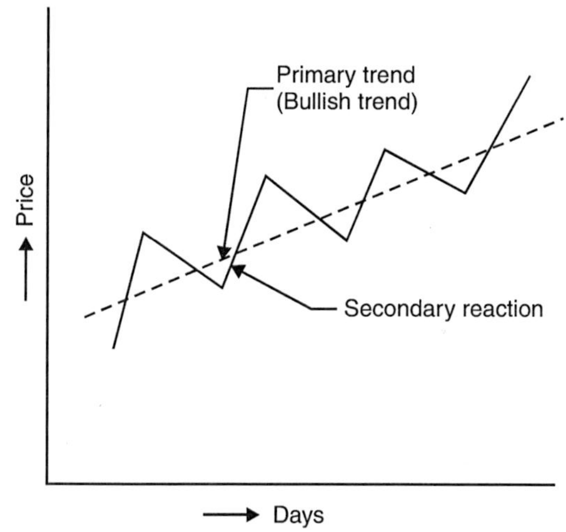

Fig. 6.7(a) Primary and secondary trends (Bullish)

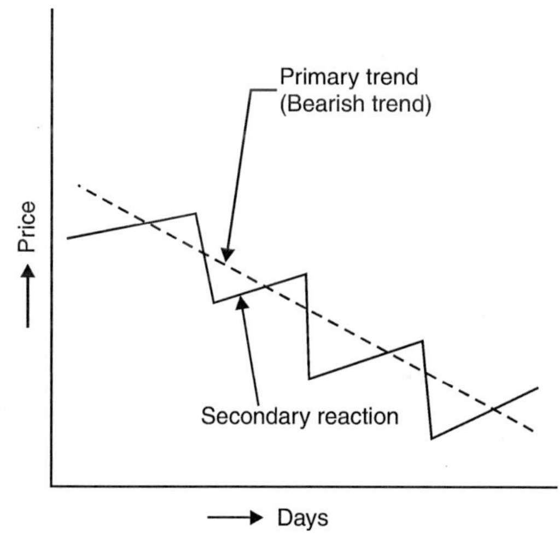

Fig. 6.7(b) Primary and secondary trends (Bearish)

Phases of Primary Trend

Of the three movements in the market price of shares, the primary trend is considered to be the most important as it depicts the long term prospects. DOW proposed that the primary trend has three phases in it.

Bullish Trend

The three phases of Bullish Primary trend are shown in Fig. 6.8(a).

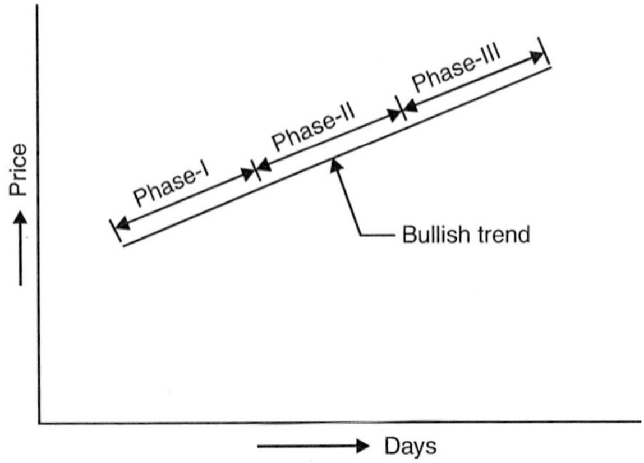

Fig. 6.8(a) Primary trend (Bullish)

The three phases of bullish trend are as under.

Phase-I

Far-sighted and knowledgeable investors who forecast promising returns from the market start investing in stocks.

Phase-II

When the forecast made by the knowledgeable investors prove good, the same is reflected in the form of good earnings by the joint-stock companies. On the arrival of information about better return on stock market investments, more of prudent investors are attracted and their investment in the stock market supports the continuance of the primary trend.

Phase-III

Widespread knowledge on the superior returns offered by stock market investments attracts average investors. At this phase there will be a lot of speculation in the market and the investment in stock market securities further increases, thus carrying the primary trend for a further period.

Bearish Trend

Just as the bullish trend has three phases, the bearish trend also was of three phases. The three phases of the bearish primary trend are shown in Fig. 6.8(b).

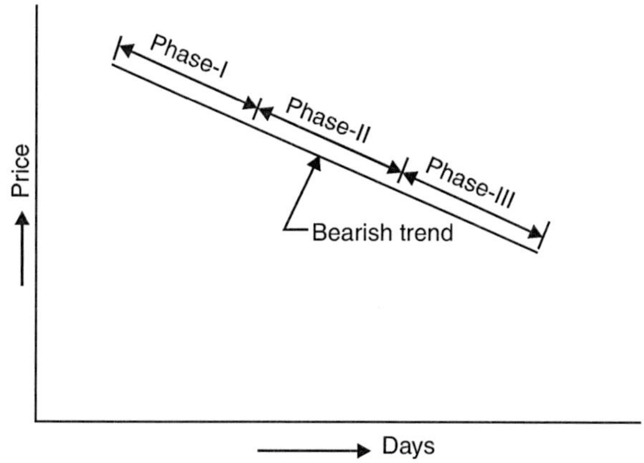

Fig. 6.8(b) Primary trend (Bearish)

Phase-I

Towards the end of the third phase of bullish trend, the far-sighted, knowledgeable investors realise that the peak is over and that the higher levels of returns offered by securities may not be sustained. Hence, they start selling their securities. This initiates the bearish trend.

Phase-II

When the forecast made by the knowledgeable investors prove good, the same is reflected by the poor earning of joint stock companies. As they start reporting lower profits and declaring lower dividends, more and more investors join in disinvesting their stock holdings and this supports the continuance of the bearish trend.

Phase-III

Due to increased selling pressure, the prices fall still further and investors resort to distress selling. This causes the bearish trend to continue still further till such time the prices reach their lowest level in the cycle.

Note: *The primary trend lines for Bullish trend and Bearish trend have been shown as straight lines in Fig. 6.8(a) and in Fig. 6.8(b) for the sake of simplicity. If the actual price movements are plotted the chart will resemble a stepped ladder moving upwards from the left to the right for bullish trend and a stepped ladder moving downwards from the left to the right for bearish trend as shown in Fig. 6.9.*

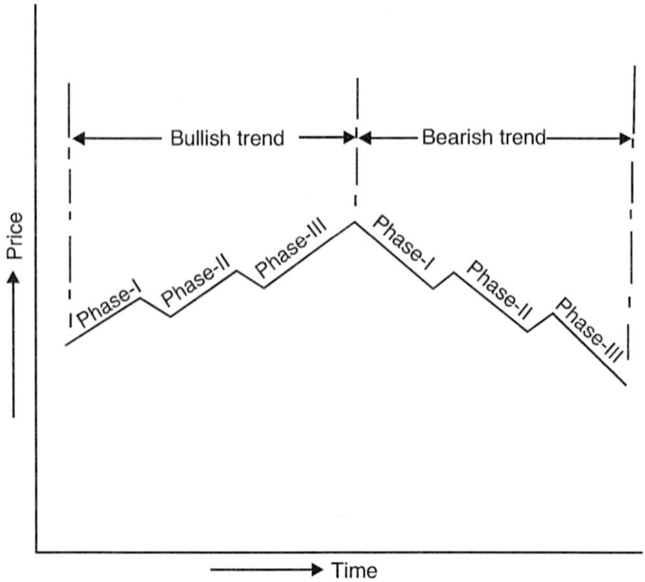

Fig. 6.9 Primary trend (Bullish and Bearish)

Interpretation of Primary Trends

- Primary trend is bullish if the high point of each rally is higher than the high point of the preceding rally and the low point of each decline is higher than the low point of the preceding decline.
- Primary trend is bearish if the high point of each decline is lower than the high point of the preceding decline and the low point of each rally is lower than the low point of the preceding rally. Refer Fig. 6.10 (a) to 6.10(d) that show the trends that are/are not bullish and bearish. Figure 6.10(e) shows a combination of bullish and bearish trends.

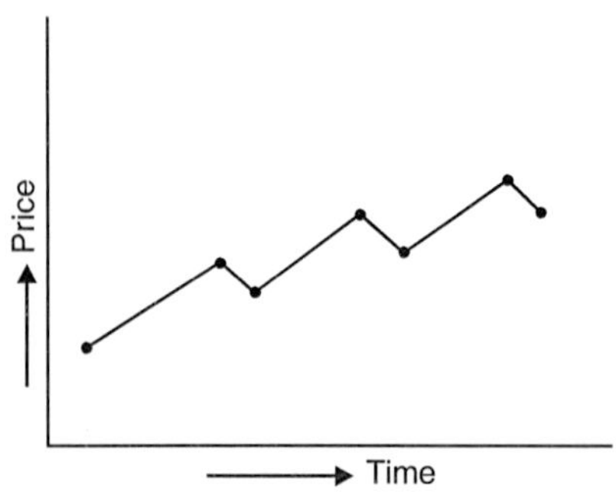

Fig. 6.10(a) Bullish trend

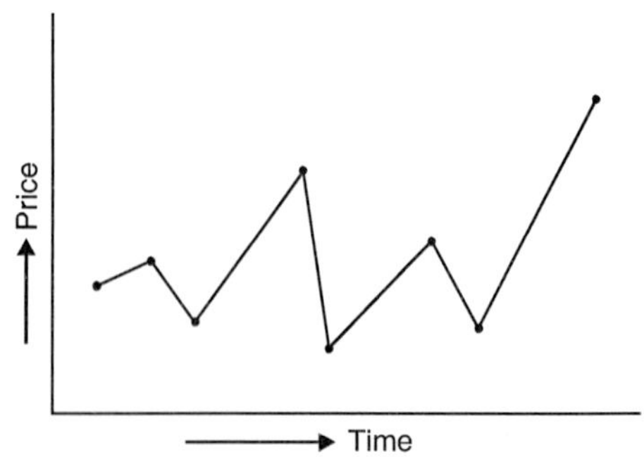

Fig. 6.10(b) Not a Bullish trend

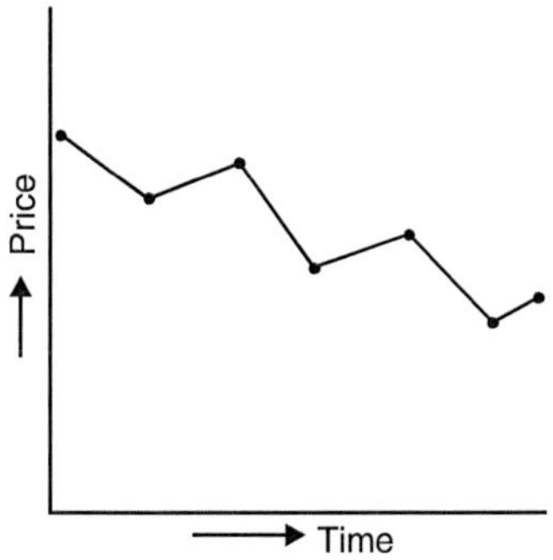

Fig. 6.10(c) Bearish trend

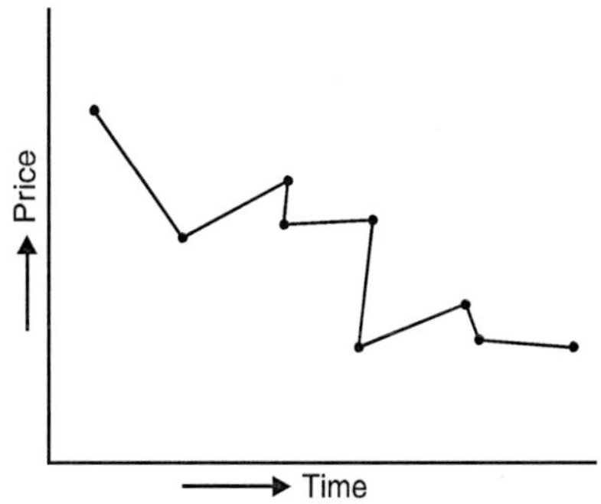

Fig. 6.10(d) Not a Bearish trend

Figure 6.10(e) shows an uptrend in stock price. When the successive price bottoms are higher than the previous bottoms, the price is said to be in uptrend. [Similarly, when the successive price tops are lower than the previous tops, the price is said to be in down trend as shown in Fig. 6.10(f)]. After a line denoting the uptrend is drawn by joining successive bottoms, if subsequent bottoms reach at or near this trend line, the uptrend is confirmed. The price levels corresponding to the intervening tops are of no relevance as far as establishment and confirmation of uptrend is concerned.

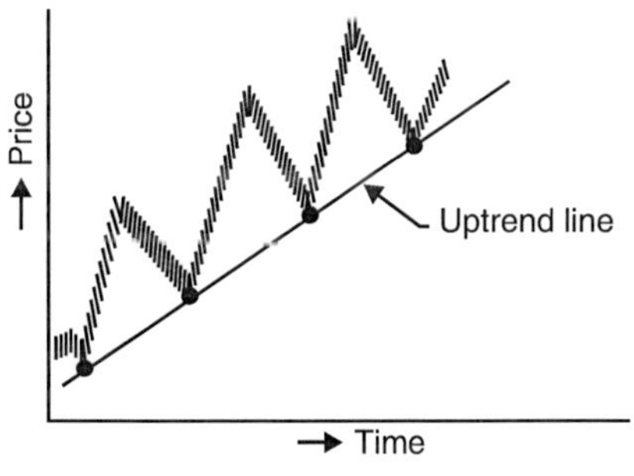

Fig. 6.10(e) Uptrend

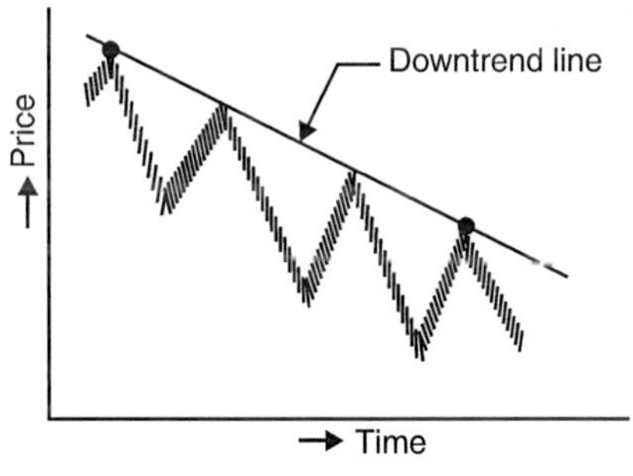

Fig. 6.10(f) Downtrend

When a price bottom breaks through the uptrend line and extends below the uptrend line by 5% of the stock price at the point of crossing, the breakthrough is confirmed. Let the stock price at the point of crossing the uptrend line is Rs. 100. If the fall in price continues by another Rs. 5 (i.e., 5% of 100) and reaches a price level of Rs. 95, the price breakthrough is considered to have set in and reversal of the uptrend is established. This gives a 'sell' signal since the price is expected to fall down.

The uptrend line may not always be a neat straight line connecting all the bottoms. At times, a few bottoms may lie above or below the uptrend line also [Refer Fig. 6.10(g)].

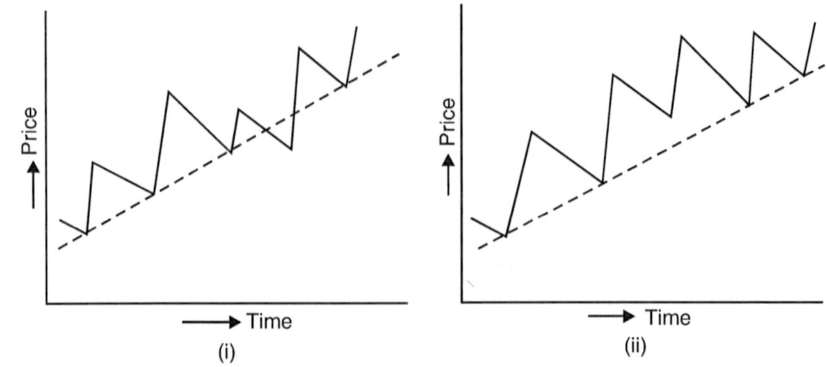

Fig. 6.10(g) Uptrend

When successive price bottoms do not lie above their previous bottoms, uptrend is not confirmed. Such a trend will be called a Doubtful trend. Refer Fig. 6.10(h) that depicts a Doubtful trend.

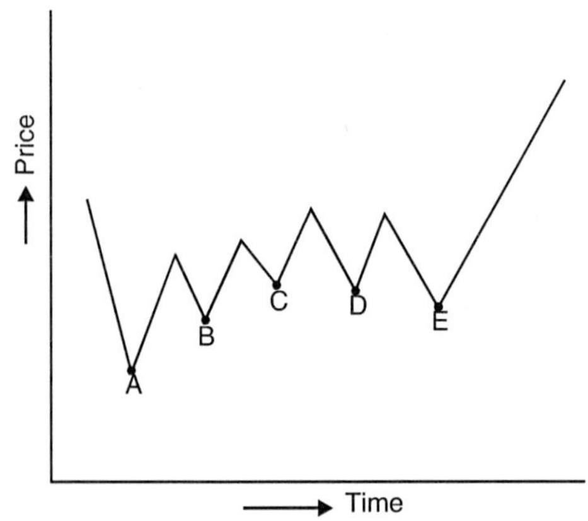

Fig. 6.10(h) Doubtful trend

Referring to Fig. 6.10(h), the bottom 'B' is above its previous bottom 'A'. The bottom 'C' is above its previous bottom 'B'. However, bottoms 'D' and 'E' are below the bottom 'C'. Even though the price rises steeply after point 'E' we cannot immediately come to the conclusion that there is uptrend beyond point 'E'.

During an uptrend, stagnation for a short period can be ignored provided the price keeps its uptrend after the stagnation. (Refer Fig. 6.10(i)).

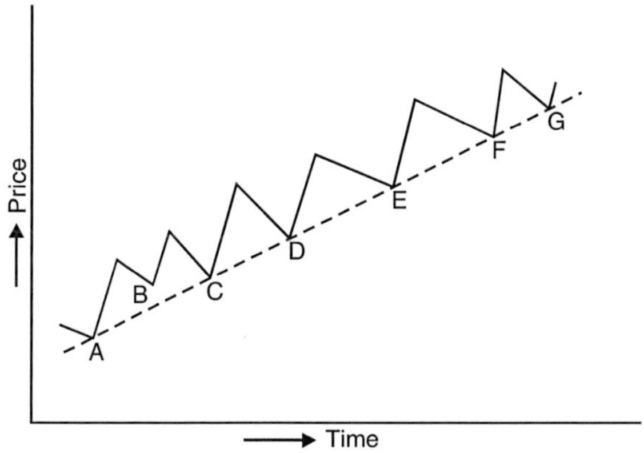

Fig. 6.10(i) Uptrend

Though bottoms 'B' and 'C' almost remain at the same level, the uptrend is confirmed since successive bottoms (D, E, F and G) are higher than their respective previous bottoms.

An uptrend is confirmed only if the general price trend shows a continuous increase. The price trend cannot be decided upon if there are continuous fluctuations despite the presence of a few intermittent hikes in the price (Refer Fig. 6.10(j)).

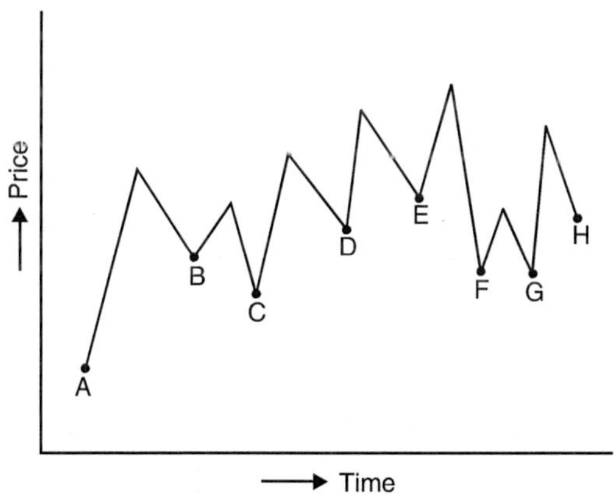

Fig. 6.10(j) Unclear (or Undefined) trend

Referring to Fig. 6.10(j), we find that between points 'A' & 'B', 'C' & 'D', 'D' & 'E' and 'G' & 'H' the price attempts to register an uptrend. But, between 'B' & 'C' and 'E' & 'F' there is a downtrend in price. The price is stagnant at points 'F' and 'G'. Hence, the price movement does not give any conclusive evidence about the price trend and the trend indicated is only an unclear (or undefined) price trend.

6.5.1. Prediction of Market Trend using Dow Theory

We have seen earlier the two market averages, viz., the DOW-Jones Industrial Average (DJIA) and the DOW-Jones Transportation Average (DJTA). According to Dow Theory, if both the averages are rising, it indicates a bull market and if both the averages are falling it indicates a bear market; if one average is rising while the other is falling, the market is uncertain.

The buy and sell signals that can be observed using Dow Theory is illustrated below. Refer to Fig. 6.11 which depicts both DJIA and DJTA.

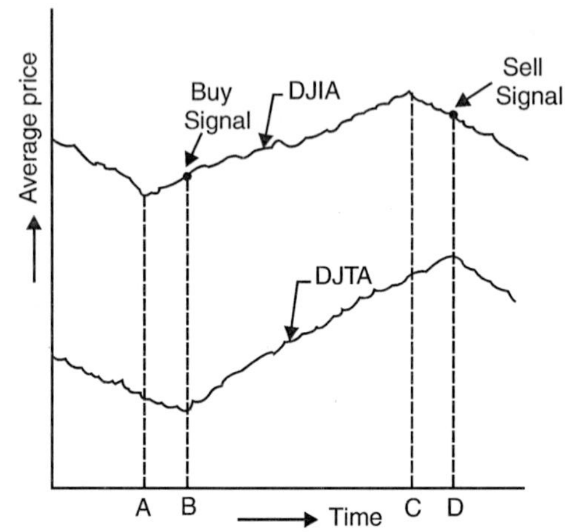

Fig. 6.11 Indication of buy/sell signal using DJIA and DJTA

A trend, whether bearish or bullish is considered to remain the same until a reversal of trend is indicated by both the averages (DJIA and DJTA).

Referring to Fig. 6.11, to start with both the DJIA and DJTA have been falling. First the DJIA has started rising while the DJTA still continues to fall. Hence, a reversal of trend is not indicated at the point A. At point of time B, the DJTA also starts increasing. Hence, this confirms the reversal of general market trend and a 'Buy' signal is indicated.

Later, it is found that both the averages have been rising. At the point of time 'C' DJIA has started falling while DJTA still continues rising. Hence, the reversal of market trend is not confirmed at point 'C'. A little later, DJIA also starts falling at the point of time 'D'. This confirms a definite reversal of trend from bullish to bearish mode. Hence, at the point of time 'D' where both the averages have started falling, a 'sell' signal is indicated.

6.6. SUPPORT LEVEL AND RESISTANCE LEVEL

While plotting the price movement of an individual security or while plotting the movement of an index, the price/index which, when on a rising trend, reaches a peak and then comes down. This peak is known as the resistance level. The word 'resistance' is used because after reaching this point the price index shows resistance to increase further and starts to fall down.

When the price/index is on a falling trend, it reaches a low and then rebounds. This lowest value reached is known as the support level. It is called 'Support level' because the price/index is supported at this level and further fall is not allowed to take place.

The price is normally expected to move between the resistance level and the support level (Refer Fig. 6.12).

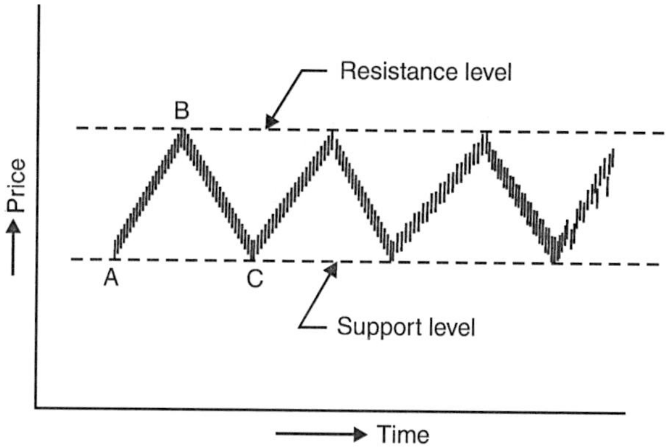

Fig. 6.12 Price movement between resistance and support levels

The existence of resistance and support levels can be explained as under. When the price is on the rising trend, the demand-supply gap gradually gets filled up and the demand-supply relationship reaches a balance at the resistance level. Once the resistance level is reached, the price trend reverses either because there will be more sellers (attracted by the higher prices) or there are few buyers (because the demand-supply relationship has nearly reached equilibrium) or both these factors may prevail.

Immediately after the price starts falling down from the resistance level, there will be few buyers. As the price keeps falling down, more number of buyers opt to buy the security and the demand increases. Finally, the demand-supply relationship again settles down to equilibrium at the support level.

Referring to Fig. 6.12, when the price moves from A to B, the demand-supply gap gradually gets reduced. The demand-supply gap reaches a balance at point 'B'. Attracted by the high price prevailing at point 'B' more and more investors start selling, thereby increasing the supply of stocks which again brings a higher demand-supply gap. The demand-supply gap again gradually gets reduced and reaches a balance at point 'C'.

The concept of resistance and support levels is used in the various chart patterns that are used in technical analysis.

When the price trend deviates away from the resistance level or support level it indicates a departure from the stable conditions and points to the fact that the market has either started acting more in favour of the security (represented by the price trend line breaking the resistance level and moving upwards) or started acting more against the security (represented by the price trend line breaking the support level and moving downwards).

6.7. CHART PATTERNS AND THEIR INTERPRETATION

When bar/line charts are drawn for the price movements of a security or a market index for several days, the chart reveals certain patterns. The technician is always in search of standard patterns from which he can interpret the price behaviour of the security/index in the near future. In the literature of Technical analysis a large number of standard patterns have been documented which provide clues as to how the price is going to move. Let us see some of the common chart patterns.

6.7.1. Channel

If the price of a security continues its movement in one direction for a long period of time, it forms the pattern of 'channel'. In a channel, the support and resistance levels run parallel to each other.

Channel is formed both during bullish and bearish trends and also at times when the market is more or less stable (Refer Fig. 6.13).

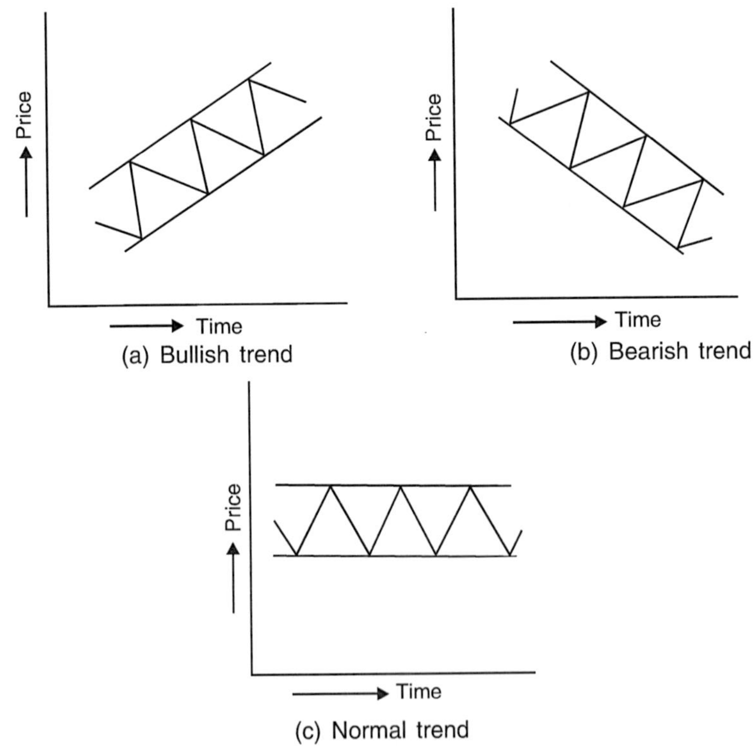

Fig. 6.13 Channel pattern

When the channel is horizontal it shows stability of price with only minor variations between the resistance and support levels. When the channel is sloping, the direction of the slope indicates the direction of movement of the price. An upward sloping channel indicates a bullish trend while a downward sloping channel indicates a bearish trend.

Sloping channels (whether upward sloping or downward sloping) indicate that the changes in the resistance and support levels are identical and constant over time.

As long as prices move within the channel boundaries, it proves that the market sentiments remain the same. When the market sentiments change, the price breaks through the channel boundaries. Figure 6.14(a) indicates a situation when the market sentiments change from bullish to bearish trend.

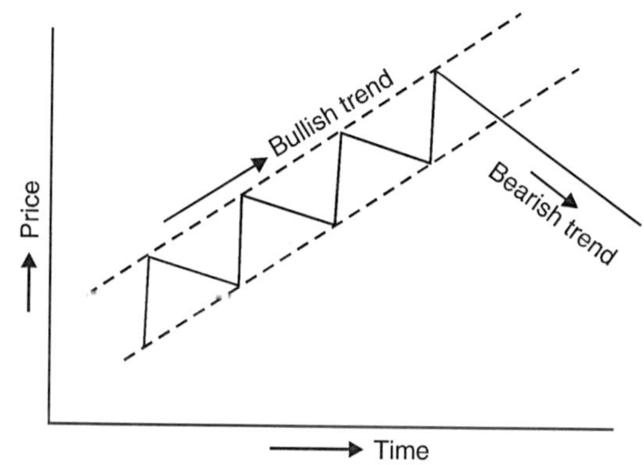

Fig. 6.14(a) Change of market sentiment (from bullish to bearish)

The price break out from a channel can also take place in such a way that the market sentiments change from bearish to bullish [Refer Fig. 6.14(b)].

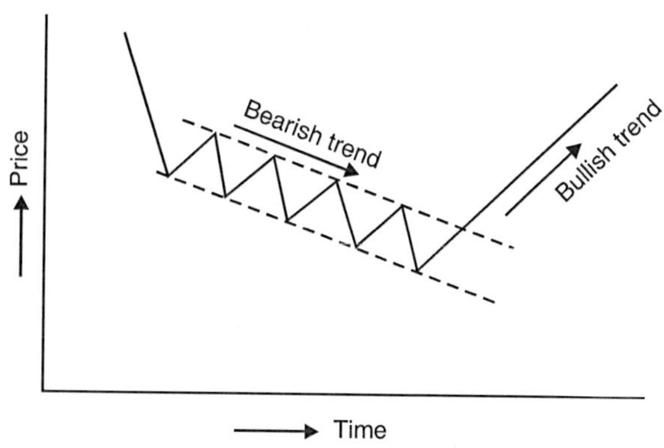

Fig. 6.14(b) Change of market sentiment (from bearish to bullish)

When a horizontal channel is formed, the price moves between the support and resistance levels (which run parallel to each other) and after some time the price breaks through. When the price breaks out in the same direction in which it was moving prior to the formation of the channel pattern, the channel behaves like a pattern indicating continuation (or confirmation) of the price trend [Refer Fig. 6.14(c)].

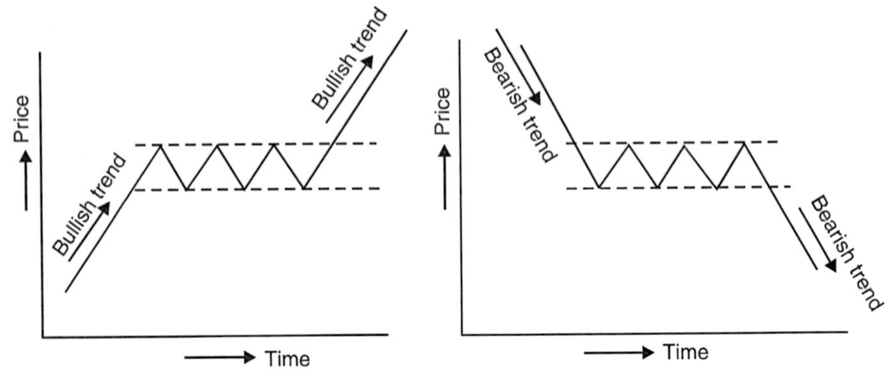

(i) Confirmation of Bullish trend (ii) Confirmation of Bearish trend

Fig. 6.14(c) Channel pattern showing continuation of price trends

When the price breaks out in the direction opposite to which it was moving prior to the formation of the channel pattern, the channel behaves like a reversal pattern indicating reversal of price trend. [Refer Fig. 6.14(d)]

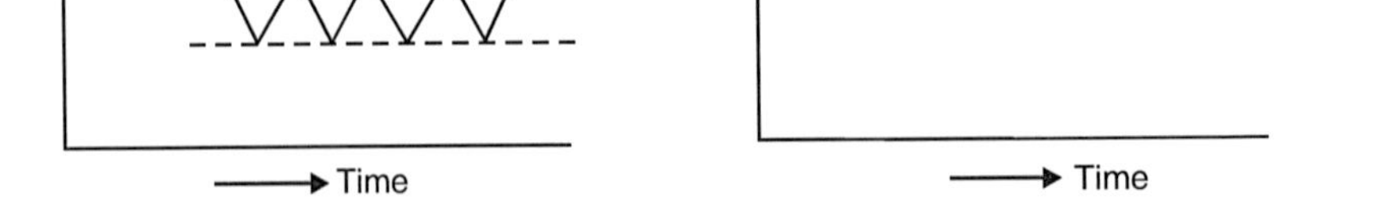

(i) Reversal of Bearish trend (ii) Reversal of Bullish trend

Fig. 6.14(d) Channel patterns showing reversal of price trends

6.7.2. Continuation Patterns

These are those patterns that offer a brief spell of breathing time to the sharp rise or fall of price. After the completion of the patterns, the price will tend to move along the original trend. During the period of formation of continuation pattern, the market verifies the past trend, gets convinced that the price trend is in order and then the price proceeds in the same direction as it was proceeding prior to the formation of the continuation pattern. These patterns reassure the general trend of the price. Such continuation patterns occur both during bullish and bearish trends. A bullish trend will continue its bullish march after the completion of the pattern. Similarly, a bearish trend will continue its course after completion of the pattern.

If the rising trend exhibits a series of continuation patterns, it indicates that the market has accepted that the rise in price is justified and sustainable. Hence, under such conditions, there won't be any reversal of trend from bullish to bearish. Similarly, if the falling trend exhibits a series of continuation patterns it also indicates that the market has accepted that the fall in price is justified and sustainable. Hence, there won't be any immediate reversal of price trend from bearish to bullish. The volume of transactions will be less during the period of formation of continuation patterns and the volume will increase sharply once the price crosses the barrier.

The following are some of the continuation patterns:

- Wedge
- Triangle
- Flag
- Pennant

Wedge

A wedge pattern is formed when the changes in the resistance and support levels are not constant over time, though the direction of the changes is the same. Figure 6.15 indicates the formation of a wedge where in though both the resistance level and the support levels are falling down, the rate of fall of the resistance level is faster than the rate of fall of the support level.

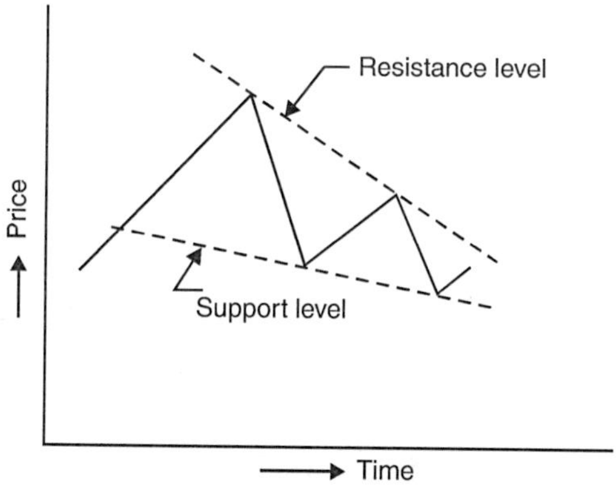

Fig. 6.15 Wedge pattern

A wedge is formed either during the course of a rising trend or during the course of a falling trend. The wedge formed during the course of a rising trend will have the shape of a falling wedge while the wedge formed during the course of a falling trend will have the shape of a rising wedge. A falling wedge represents a temporary interruption of a rising trend and a rising wedge represents a temporary interruption of a falling trend. Figure 6.16 shows the formation of falling and rising wedges.

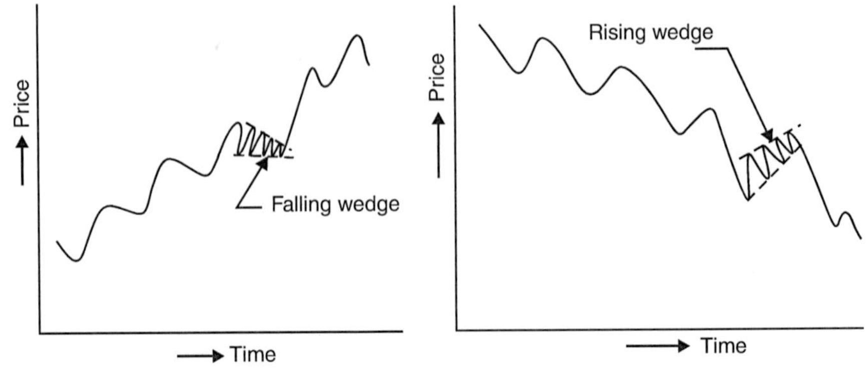

(a) Falling wedge (b) Rising wedge

Fig. 6.16 Wedge patterns

As against a channel formation in which the slopes of the support line and the resistance line are the same, a wedge is formed when the slopes of the support line and the resistance line are different.

Triangle

The wedge is formed after the arrival of some information about the scrip in the market. The commencement of wedge formation means that the market has started to react on the basis of information received. However, to start with, there used to be greater uncertainty about the validity as well as the influence of the information on the performance of the company. As the time progresses, the information received and its impact are better assimilated by the market and the uncertainty gradually gets reduced. This is reflected in the formatting triangle from wedge. Finally, when the uncertainty is resolved, the resistance and support boundaries intersect. Refer Figs. 6.17 and 6.18 which show the formation of a triangle pattern from a wedge pattern.

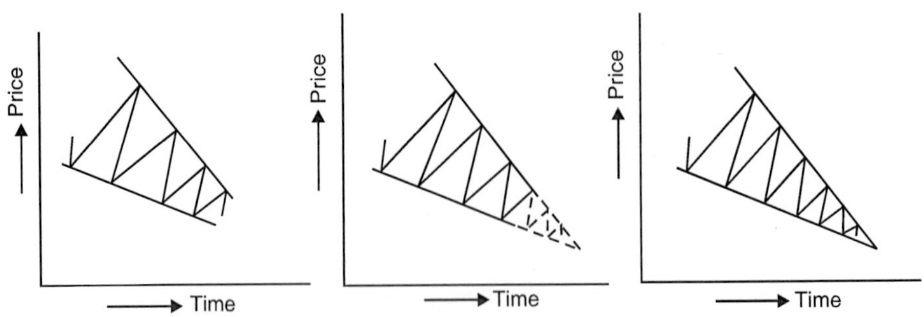

Fig. 6.17 Formation of triangle pattern

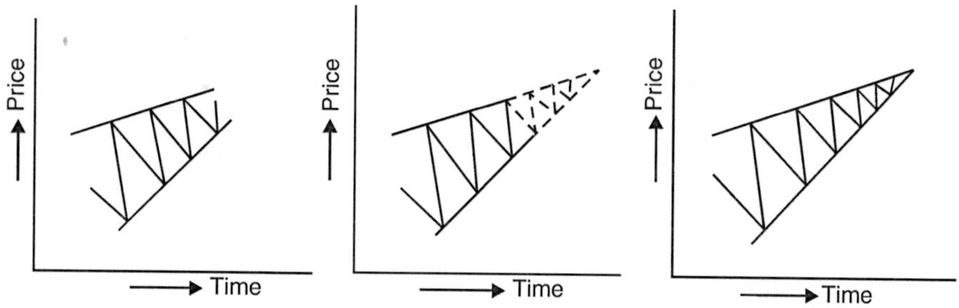

Fig. 6.18 Formation of triangle pattern

A breakout from the triangle (either passing over the resistance boundary or the support boundary) gives a strong indication of the direction of future price movement. This is because, during the period in which the price moves within the boundaries of the triangle, the market uncertainty is resolved and the market arrives at a consensus about the future price movement of the security. Hence, a breakout from the triangle gives a strong signal about the future price movement. [Refer Figs. 6.19(a) and 6.19(b)]. Evidently, a 'Triangle' pattern gives a stronger signal than a wedge about the future price movement.

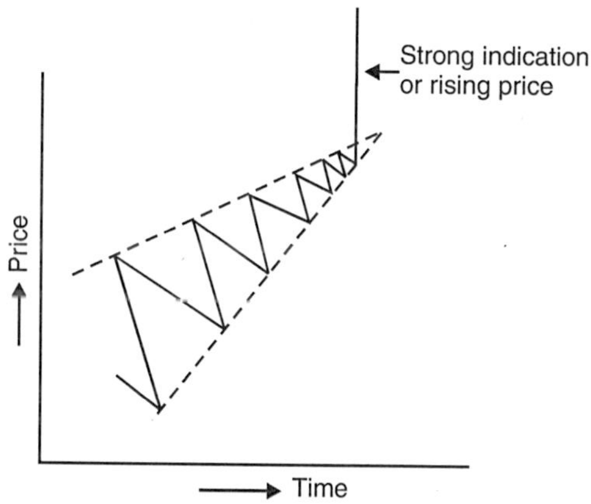

Fig. 6.19(a) Rising trend confirmed by triangle pattern

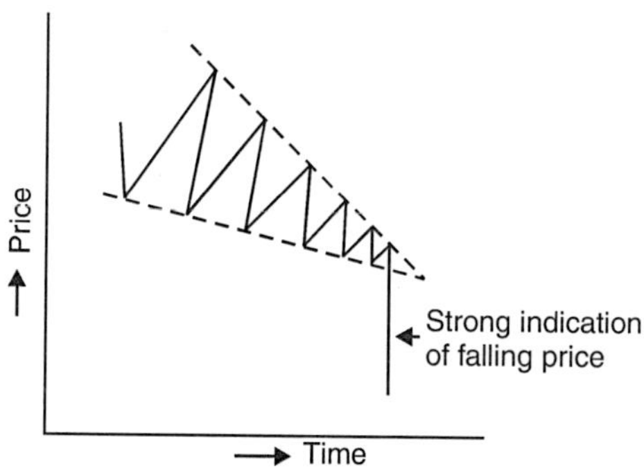

Fig. 6.19(b) Falling trend confirmed by triangle pattern

Flag

The flag pattern usually occurs after a significant rise or fall in the market price of stocks. The steep upward price movement is called the 'flag pole'. The flag pole is often nearly vertical. The flag pole is followed by a consolidation pattern that can last for a few weeks. This consolidation period creates a flag formation which may be in the form of a rectangle or parallelogram. When a parallelogram is formed, the two parallel trend lines tend to slope against the prevailing trend. The flag formation mostly acts as a continuation pattern and hence after the resting period, the price continues in the same direction in which it was moving before [Refer Fig. 6.20(a)].

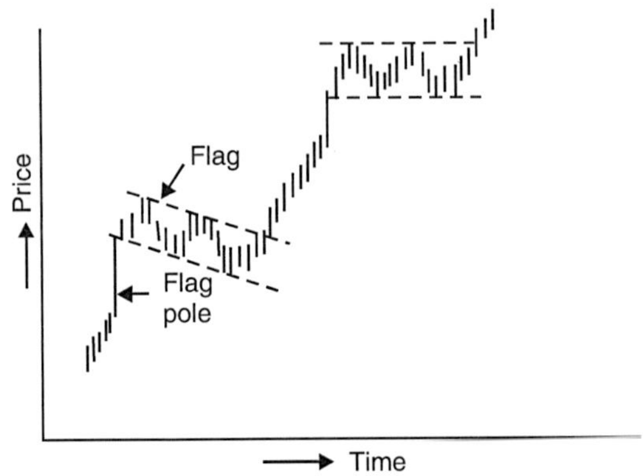

Fig. 6.20(a) Flag formation during Bullish trend

Very rarely the price trend reverses after a flag formation [Refer Fig. 6.20(b)].

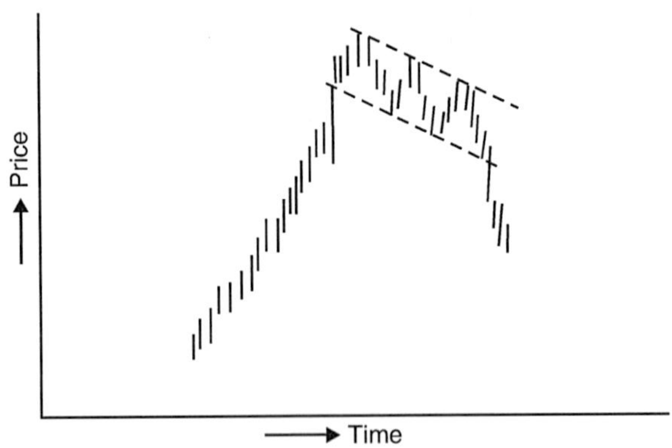

Fig. 6.20(b) Flag formation showing reversal of trend (a rare phenomenon)

The price fluctuation during the course of flag formation indicates that the market goes through process of verification of the worth of the security based on some news/information received. When the market reaches a consensus about the price of the security, the price breaks the flag's boundary. A breakout from the flag's boundary indicates that the market has decided upon the intrinsic price of the security and hence the direction of breakout gives a definite direction of the price movement.

If rising trend exhibits a series of flags, it is an indication that the market has verified whether the rise in price is justified and sustainable. Similarly, if a falling trend exhibits a series of flags, it is an indication that the market has verified whether the fall in price is justified. Hence, a rising trend containing a series of flags may not come down sharply as the market is convinced about the rising prices. Similarly, a falling trend containing a series of flags may not reverse into a rising mode as the market is convinced about the falling prices.

Pennant

A pennant formation resembles a symmetrical triangle. The resistance level falls down while the support level moves upwards leading to the formation of a pennant. A pennant is formed midway between either a bullish trend or a bearish trend. A pennant formation, most of the time indicates continuation of the same trend whether bullish or bearish. Figure 6.21(a) shows a pennant formation in which the price breaks the barrier in the same direction as the original price trend which means that the pattern confirms continuation of the price trend.

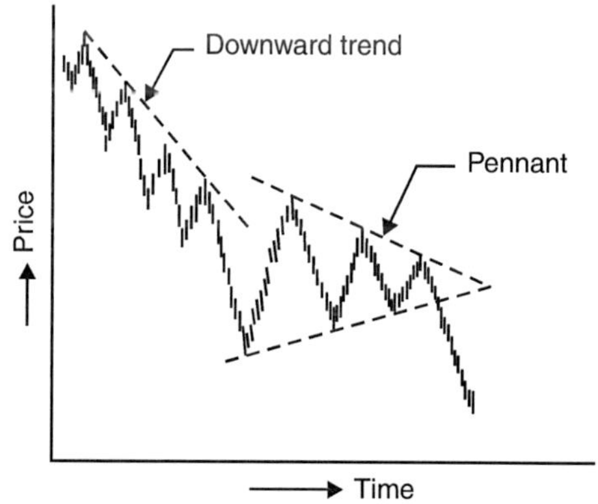

Fig. 6.21(a) Pennant formation (showing continuation of trend)

In Fig. 6.21(a), a downward price trend is confirmed by the Pennant formation in which the price breaks the support line which is the lower price barrier and falls further downwards.

It also happens (though very rarely) that the price trend reverses after a pennant formation [Refer Fig. 6.21(b)].

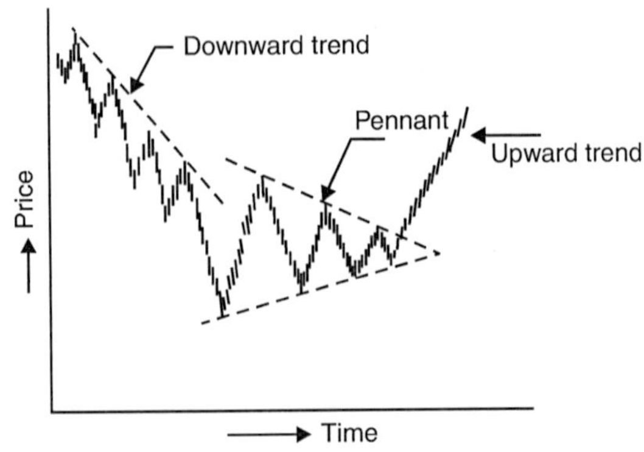

Fig. 6.21(b) Pennant formation (showing reversal of trend)

6.7.3. Interpretation of Continuation Patterns

If the rising trend exhibits a series of continuation patterns one after the other, it indicates that the market has verified whether the rise in price is justified and sustainable. Hence, more number of continuation patterns along a rising trend justifies the rising trend and confirms that the rising trend will continue for some more time. Similarly, if the falling trend exhibits a series of continuation patterns one after the other, it indicates that the market has verified whether the fall in price is justified and sustainable. Hence, more number of continuation patterns along a falling trend justifies the falling trend and confirms that the falling trend will continue for some more time.

The volume of transactions will be less during the period of continuation patterns. This is because the market verifies the acceptability of the trend during this period. Once the price crosses the barrier and moves past the pattern, the volume will increase sharply since the market is convinced about the continuance of the price trend.

6.7.4. Reversal Patterns

These patterns indicate reversal of price trends. The price of a security that exhibits a bullish trend, after a period of time, will eventually reverse its direction and enter a bearish trend. Similarly, a bearish trend, after a period of time, will enter a bullish trend. Reversal patterns are formed at the point of time where the price trend changes from bullish to bearish mode and vice versa.

The following are the common reversal patterns:

- Head and shoulders
- Inverse head and shoulders
- Double top formation

- Triple top formation
- Double bottom formation
- Triple bottom formation

Head and Shoulders

This pattern occurs after a long period of upward trend in price movement. After the completion of the pattern, the price reverses its direction of movement and starts falling down.

The pattern shows a large hump in the middle with two smaller humps on its both sides. The two small humps resemble the shoulders of human form and the large hump at the centre resembles the head. Hence, the pattern is known by the name 'Head and Shoulders' (Refer Fig. 6.22).

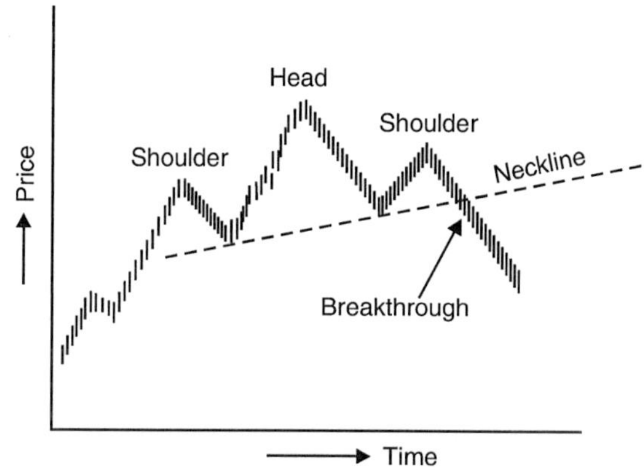

Fig. 6.22 Head and shoulders pattern

The humps are generated due to buying pressures. At the peak of each hump, selling pressure develops which leads to decline in prices. After the price decline from the peak of the hump is repeated three times, a clear lack of demand for the security is established which leads to the fall in the price level. Hence, after the third hump, the price trend reverses from upward movement to downward movement. The line joining the bottom of the two shoulders is called the neckline. While the price level starts falling from the peak of the third hump (i.e., right shoulder), the crucial point is reached when the price level touches the neckline. When the price level goes below the neckline, the reversal of general price trend is confirmed and the general price trend changes from bullish to bearish mode. The neckline may either be horizontal or sloping in the direction of the price trend that prevailed prior to the formation of the Head and Shoulders pattern. At times, after penetration of the neckline, the price might again return back to the neckline in its last effort to continue the uptrend that existed prior to the formation of the pattern. If the price is unable to rise above the neckline, it will fall down rapidly confirming the reversal of trend from bullish to bearish [Refer Fig. 6.23].

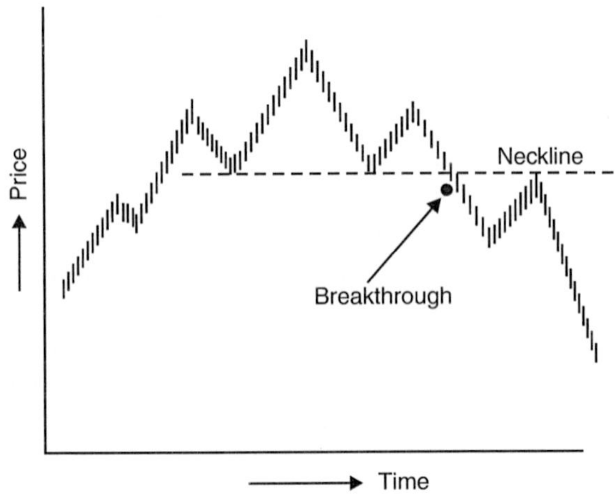

Fig. 6.23 Head and shoulders pattern

Inverse Head and Shoulders

This pattern occurs after a long period of downward trend in price movement. After the completion of the pattern, the price reverses its direction and starts rising up.

The pattern shows a large inverted hump (head) in the middle with two smaller inverted humps (shoulders) on its both sides. Similar to Head and shoulders pattern, in Inverse Head and shoulders pattern also a definite price reversal is indicated. Once the price increase in the third hump crosses the neckline, the reversal of the general price trend is confirmed and the general price trend changes from bearish to bullish mode (Refer Fig. 6.24).

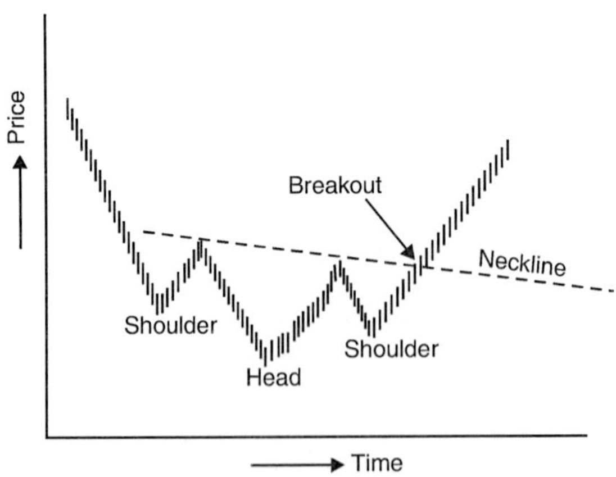

Fig. 6.24 Inverse head and shoulders pattern

Double Top Formation

When the price of a stock reaches a peak, falls down and then rises again to reach the same/almost the same level of peak reached earlier, a double top formation is said to have occurred. After reaching the second peak, the price starts falling down. Once the decline from the second peak goes 5% below the price at the valley floor between the two peaks, the price is expected to fall further downwards and the fall is expected to exist for long durations. The price level at the two peaks can be the same or there can be a slight difference between the two price levels. The important point to be noted is the price level at the lowest point in the valley floor between the two peaks. When the decline from the second peak penetrates the price level at the lowest point in the valley floor, a 'sell' signal becomes due. When the price further falls down by 5% below the lowest point in the valley floor, a 'sell' signal is indicated because the price is only expected fall further steeply. Figure 6.25(a) shows 'Double top' pattern.

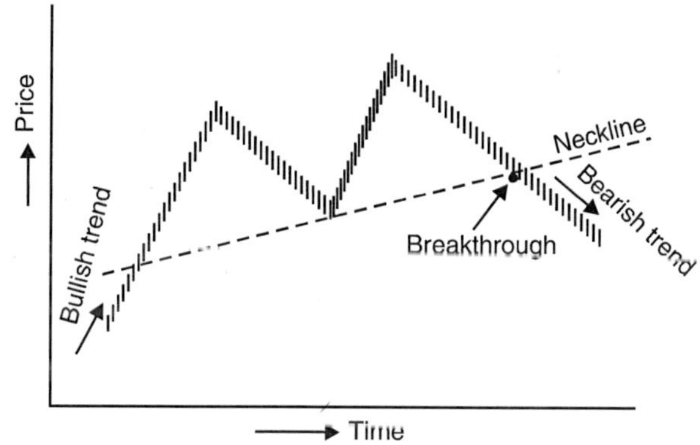

Fig. 6.25(a) Double top pattern

Investors have good memories. When the price reaches the first peak, not all of those holding the concerned stock will offer the stock with them for sale. After the price declines from the first peak, those investors who are still holding the stocks and who did not sell their stocks at the peak price realize that they should have sold their stocks when the price was at the peak. When the price reaches the second peak, bouncing back from the valley, the holders of the stock feel that they have got another chance to sell their stocks at an attractive price. At this stage, many of the stock holders offer their stocks for sale which leads to decline of the price trend, since by this time the supply would have exceeded the demand.

Triple Top Formation

Triple top formation is a close associate of the Double top formation. When the price declines from the second peak, some buyers who had known the earlier two peaks reached by the stock start buying heavily (in anticipation of another peak), thus increasing the price level of the stock. When the price reaches a third peak, the holders of the stock visualize that it is their last chance to sell at peak prices and start selling. When too many sellers enter the fray, the price starts falling from the third peak. The Triple top pattern is confirmed when the decline from the third peak penetrates the bottom of the lowest valley between the three peaks [Refer Fig. 6.25(b)].

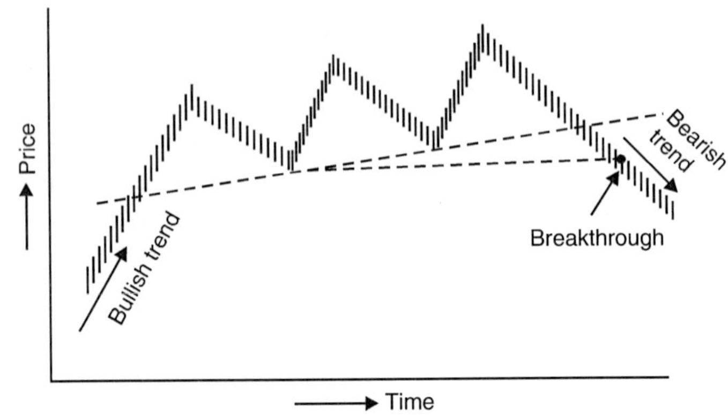

Fig. 6.25(b) Triple top pattern

Double Bottom and Triple Bottom Formations

Just as a 'Double top' is a reversal pattern from bullish to bearish trend, 'Double bottom' is a reversal pattern from bearish to bullish trend. Similarly, 'Triple bottom' is also a reversal pattern from bearish to bullish trend. Refer Figs. 6.26(a) and 6.26(b) for 'Double bottom' and 'Triple bottom' patterns.

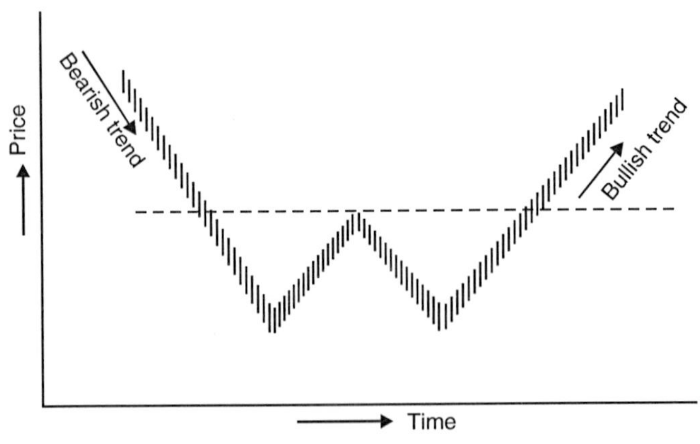

Fig. 6.26(a) Double bottom pattern

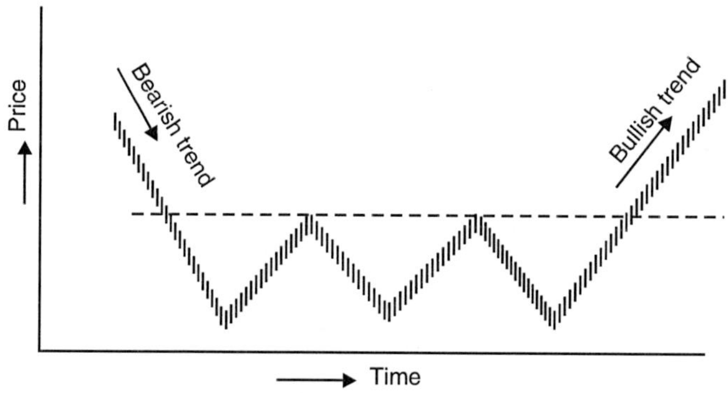

Fig. 6.26(b) Triple bottom pattern

6.8. INTERPRETATION OF TREND LINES

A trend line is the line joining a series of ascending bottoms in a rising market or a series of descending tops in a falling market (Refer Fig. 6.27).

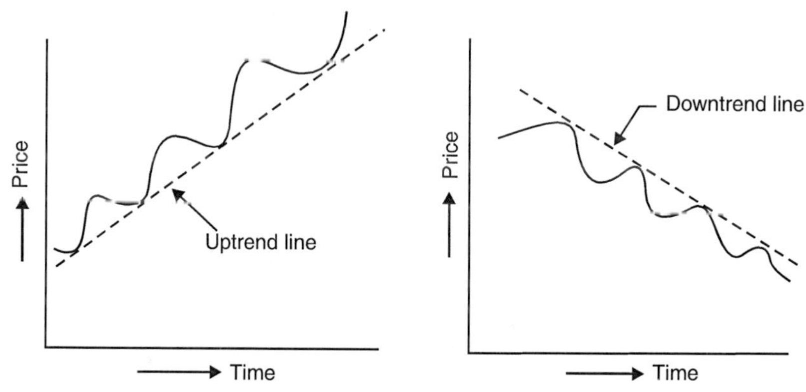

Fig. 6.27 Trend lines

When two trend lines cross each other, it indicates either continuation or reversal of price trend.

When a trend line cuts the preceding trend line at the beginning of the preceding trend line, it indicates continuation of trend at a reduced phase. Referring to Fig. 6.28(a), extending the trend line – CD backwards meets the preceding trend line – AB at point 'P'. The point of intersection 'P' lies at the beginning stage of trend line – AB. This indicates that the upward price trend is likely to continue, but at a reduced phase.

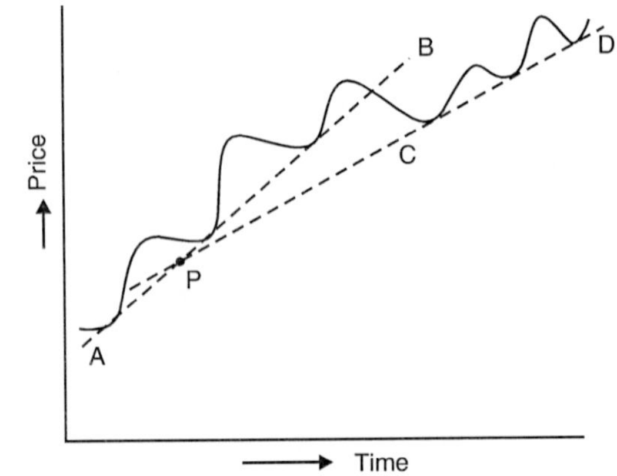

Fig. 6.28(a) Penetration of trend lines (Continuation of trend)

When a trend line cuts the preceding trend line at the end of the preceding trend line, it indicates reversal of price trend. Referring to Fig. 6.28(b), the trend line – CD, when extended backwards cuts the extension of the preceding trend line – AB at point 'P'. The point of intersection 'P' lies at the end of the trend line – AB, in fact after the end and at the extension of trend line –AB. This indicates reversal of price trend from bullish to bearish. Figure 6.28(c) shows trend line – CD intersecting trend line – AB at point 'P'. The point of intersection 'P' lies at the end of the trend line – AB. Hence, this indicates reversal of price trend from bearish to bullish.

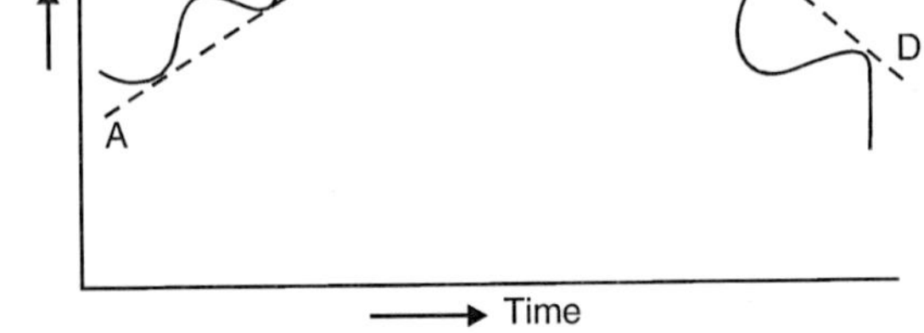

Fig. 6.28(b) Penetration of trend lines (Reversal of upward trend)

It may be noted that a very sharp trend is difficult to be maintained and the trend will get broken easily, either as a reduced phase of continuation of the original trend or as a trend reversal. Penetration of an upward trend line by its succeeding trend line (which is the current trend line) signals a 'sell' position. This is revealed in Fig. 6.28(b). Similarly, penetration of a downward trend line by its succeeding trend line (which is the current trend line) signals a 'buy' position. This is revealed in Fig. 6.28(c).

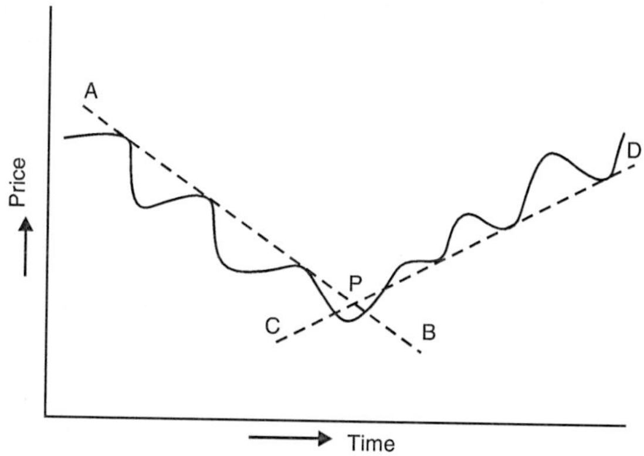

Fig. 6.28(c) Penetration of trend lines (Reversal of downward trend)

6.9. GAP

A gap is the difference between the opening price of a scrip on a trading day and its closing price on the previous trading day. If the gap is wider it indicates continuation of the current trend. When the market is bullish, the opening price on a day is considerably higher than the closing price on the previous day, thus producing a larger gap. Similarly, when the market is bearish the opening price on a day is considerably lower than the closing price on the previous day, and this produces a larger gap.

If we represent the price movements of a scrip on consecutive days using a bar chart, the diagram will be as under (Refer Fig. 6.29).

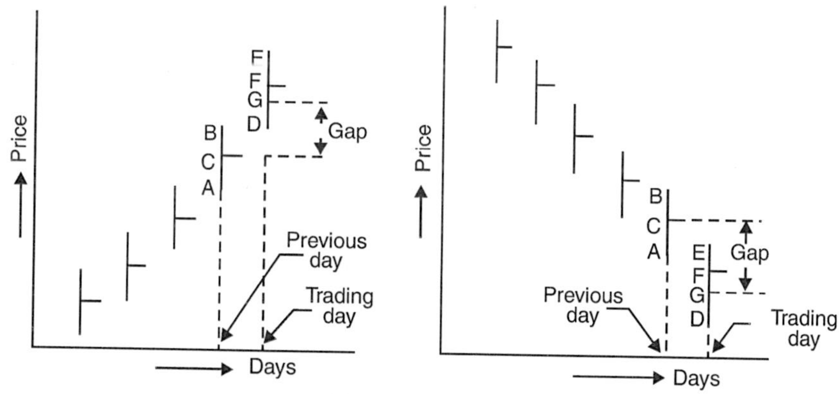

Fig. 6.29 Gap

A – Minimum price on the previous day
B – Maximum price on the previous day
C – Closing price on the previous day
D – Minimum price on the trading day
E – Maximum price on the trading day
F – Closing price on the trading day
G – Opening price on the trading day

It may be noted that the opening price on a trading day may not be equal to the lowest price on that particular day. Even in a rising market, the minimum price on a day may be below the opening price.

Gaps are produced due to the following reasons:

- Due to unexpected news/rumours
- Due to the occurrence of some surprise events
- Due to oversold/overbought position requiring an immediate correction

6.10. MATHEMATICAL INDICATORS

Apart from studying the price patterns, technicians also make use of some simple statistical analysis of the past data; certain rules have been developed based on the statistical analysis of data. Since share prices do not move in straight lines, it is difficult to predict the future trend purely based on the price patterns. The use of mathematical indicators along with price patterns helps to do a more accurate analysis and to arrive at a more realistic prediction. The following are some of the mathematical indicators.

- Moving Averages (MV)
  - ⇨ Simple Moving Average
  - ⇨ Exponential Moving Average
- Oscillators
  - ⇨ Rate of Change (ROC)
  - ⇨ Relative Strength Index (RSI)
  - ⇨ Moving Average Convergence Divergence (MACD)

Moving Averages

The movement of stock prices is not uniform. They don't move on straight lines, but exhibit wide variations and fluctuations. The movement is even haphazard at times. Moving average technique attempts to tone down the fluctuations in stock prices and converts the price trend into a smoother curve, reducing distortions to the minimum.

There are two types of moving averages.

They are,

(*a*) Simple moving average

and (*b*) Exponential moving average.

Simple Moving Average (SMA)

This is the widely used moving average. As we know, average of a set of data is the sum of the data divided by the number of data. Moving average is calculated by first calculating the average for a set of data and then calculating the average for the second set of data and so on. The second set is arrived at by including a new data and by deleting the first data from the previous set. The process is repeated till all the data are covered. Thus, a set of averages is calculated for a specified number of data in each set.

The calculation of simple moving average is illustrated below.

***Illustration* 6.1:**

The closing price of a script for a continuous period of 20 days is given below. Calculate the 5 day moving average for the given data.

Day	1	2	3	4	5	6	7	8	9	10
Closing price (Rs.)	90	95	94	96	100	98	96	95	97	100

Day	11	12	13	14	15	16	17	18	19	20
Closing price (Rs.)	102	100	99	98	96	94	90	95	98	100

Solution:

Day	Closing price (Rs.)	Total price of 5 days	Five day moving average (3 ÷ 5)
(1)	(2)	(3)	(4)
1	90	--	--
2	95	--	--
3	94	--	--
4	96	--	--
5	100	475	95.00
6	98	483	96.60
7	96	484	96.80
8	95	485	97.00
9	97	486	97.20
10	100	486	97.20
11	102	490	98.00

Contd...

12	100	494	98.80
13	99	498	99.60
14	98	499	99.80
15	96	495	99.00
16	94	487	97.40
17	90	477	95.40
18	95	473	94.60
19	98	473	94.60
20	100	475	95.00

The sum of first five day's closing price (i.e., 90 + 95 + 94 + 96 + 100) is arrived at and entered against the fifth day, in column-3. This comes to 475. The next five days total price is arrived at by adding 98 to the previous total of 475 and deleting the first data of 90 from this. This gives a total of 483 which is entered in column-3 against the sixth day. The next five days total price is arrived at by adding 96 to the previous total of 483 and deleting the second data of 95 from this. This gives a total of 484 which is entered in column-3 against the seventh day. The process is repeated till the last data of 100 is included in the set.

The last column, viz., five day moving average is obtained by dividing each of the figures in column-3 by 5.

Exponential Moving Average (EMA)

EMA assigns weights to the data before calculating the average. While assigning weights, the highest weight is assigned to the latest price. It assigns a weight of $1/n$ to each of the 'n' prices used for computing the average, with the highest weight being assigned to the latest price. If we are going to calculate 5 days EMA, the data on the fifth day of the set is assigned a weight of 1/1 i.e. 1. The data on the first day of the set is assigned with a weight of 1/5 i.e. 0.2.

Though the EMA can be calculated using the above relationship of weights for the individual scores, the following simplified formula can be used which will reduce the extent of calculations involved.

EMA = Previous EMA + (Current closing price – Previous EMA) $\times f$

Where

$$f = \frac{2}{n+1}$$

Where n = number of days for which EMA is calculated.

The above formula is useful for calculating EMA for the second period onwards. Since, the term 'Previous EMA' is included in the formula, it can not be applied for arriving at the EMA for the first data. To overcome this problem, the value of the first data itself is taken as the EMA for that period (i.e., the closing price of the first day itself is taken as the EMA for day – 1).

***Illustration* 6.2:**

For the data given in illustration 6.1 calculate the 5 day EMA.

Solution:

Day	Closing price (Rs.)	EMA
(1)	(2)	(3)
1	90	90.00
2	95	91.67
3	94	92.45
4	96	93.63
5	100	95.75
6	98	96.50
7	96	96.33
8	95	95.89
9	97	96.26
10	100	97.51
11	102	99.00
12	100	99.33
13	99	99.22
14	98	98.81
15	96	97.87
16	94	96.58
17	90	94.39
18	95	94.59
19	98	95.73
20	100	97.15

The EMA for day – 1 is assumed to be equal to the closing price on day – 1. i.e., Rs. 90.

The EMA for the subsequent days are calculated using the formula.

EMA = Previous EMA + (Current closing price – Previous EMA) × f

$$f = \frac{2}{n+1}$$

Since 5 day EMA is required to be calculated, $n = 5$

$$f = \frac{2}{5+1} = 0.333$$

EMA (for day – 2) = 90 + (95 – 90) × 0.333
= 91.67

EMA (for day – 3) = 91.67 + (94 – 91.67) × 0.333
= 92.45

EMA (for day – 4) = 92.45 + (96 – 92.45) × 0.333
= 93.63

.... and so on.

The EMA for all the other days have been calculated and entered in the table.

Use of Moving Average

The moving average curve, when used along with the price curve, aids in interpreting the price trend. The following rules will be of use for arriving at inferences about the price trend.

- When the price curve cuts the moving average curve from below, it is expected that the prices would go up. Hence, this gives a 'buy' signal.
- When the price curve cuts the moving average curve from above, it is expected that the prices would go down. Hence, this gives a 'sell' signal.

Normally 'buying' or 'selling' of securities is not done immediately after signals are available by the intersection of price curve and moving average curve. A cushion is used before taking buy/sell decisions by introducing a filter. If $x\%$ filter is used, it implies that a share could be bought only after the price of that share increases by $x\%$ after the 'buy' signal is made available. Similarly, when a 'sell' signal is available, shares will be sold only after the share prices have fallen $x\%$ below the price at which the 'sell' signal was available (Refer Fig. 6.30).

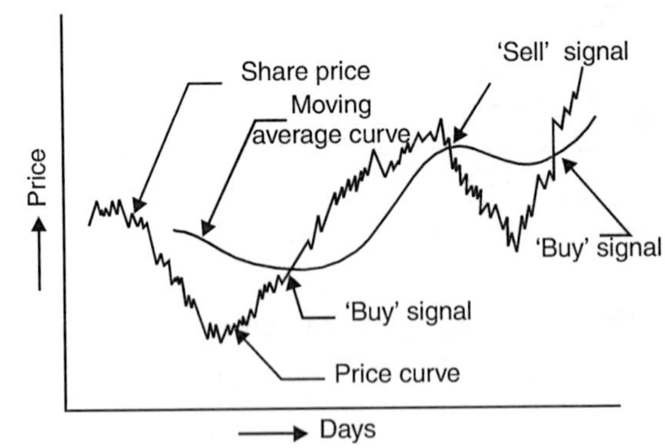

Fig. 6.30 Price curve and moving average curve

Time Span for Moving Average

Moving average can be calculated for any period, starting from a few days to several months or even several years. The choice of time span for calculating moving average is to be done carefully. There is no simple and straight rule available to fix the time span. It depends upon the nature of the price trend. When too long a time span is chosen it may not reflect the movement of prices exactly. When too low a time span is chosen it will catch up every minor movement in the stock price cycle, but will not be of use for identifying the top and bottom of the overall price cycle of the stock.

The time span that is found suitable for one market over a specific period of time may not be suitable for another market or even for the same market at a different period of time. The time span to be chosen for the moving average depends upon the type of market trend proposed to be identified/predicted. For identifying/predicting short term market trends, 10-day, 15-day or 30-day moving averages can be used. For identifying/predicting intermediate term market trends, 1-month, 6-month or 9-month moving averages can be used. For identifying/predicting long term market trends, 12-month, 18-month or 24-month moving averages can be used.

As the time span is increased, the moving average will become more and more smoother. If the time span chosen is too small, the moving average will catch all minor movements. If the time span is kept too long, the moving average may not even recognize the primary trend as it will smooth out all fluctuations. There is no one perfect time span. It depends on the objective of the investor.

Use of Multiple Moving Average

Some times instead of using only one moving average, dual moving averages (with different time spans) are also used. The 'buy' or 'sell' signal given by one moving average curve is not immediately acted upon. The 'buy' or 'sell' transaction is put through only if identical buy/sell signals are given by the several set of dual moving averages. Apart from the above, the following rules are also of use for making buy/sell decisions using multiple moving averages.

- When a shorter-term moving average curve crosses a longer-term moving average curve from below and both the moving average curves are moving in the upward direction, a 'buy' signal is indicated.
- When a shorter-term moving average curve crosses a longer-term moving average curve from above and both the moving averages are moving in the downward direction, a 'sell' signal is indicated.

Figure 6.31 shows 12-day and 48-day exponential moving average curves. The time periods that offer buy/sell signals are indicated.

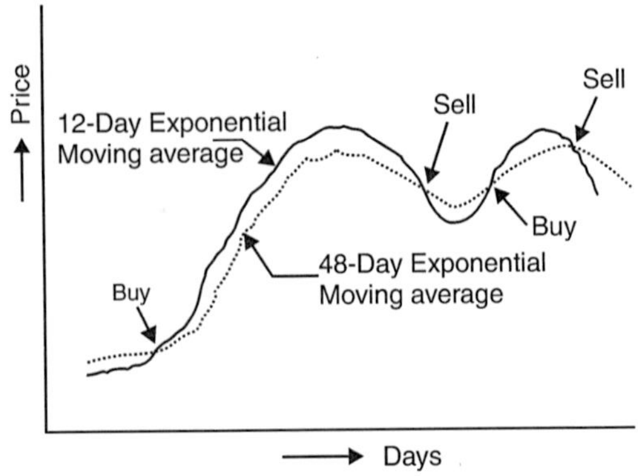

Fig. 6.31 Dual moving averages for predicting buy/sell signals

Rate of Change (ROC)

The price chart depicts simply the movement of price with time. Rate of Change (ROC) chart depicts the acceleration/retardation of price movements. Just as moving average is calculated for a specified number of days, Rate of change is also calculated for a specified number of days. Suppose we want to calculate 10-day ROC, each day's price is divided by the price that prevailed 10-days ago and from this price ratio, 1 is subtracted to arrive at 10-day ROC for the respective day's price.

$$\text{ROC} = \frac{\text{Current price}}{(\text{Price prevailed `}n\text{' period ago})} - 1$$

The following formula for ROC is also in vogue

$$\text{ROC} = \frac{\text{Current price}}{(\text{Price prevailed `}n\text{' period ago})} \times 100$$

[The above formula gives the ROC as a percentage]

Let us understand the concept and use of ROC chart with an example, by calculating the 10 day ROC for the data given below.

Day	1	2	3	4	5	6	7	8	9	10
Closing price (Rs.)	50	55	60	65	60	64	62	60	58	64

Day	11	12	13	14	15	16	17	18	19	20
Closing price (Rs.)	68	72	70	72	68	64	60	54	50	52

Day	21	22	23	24	25
Closing price (Rs.)	64	72	74	78	82

Let us use the formula

$$\text{ROC} = \frac{\text{Current price}}{\text{(Price prevailed '}n\text{' period ago)}} - 1$$

Days	Closing price	Closing price 10 days ago	Price ratio 2 ÷ 3	ROC = Price ratio –1
(1)	(2)	(3)	(4)	(5)
1	50	–	–	–
2	55	–	–	–
3	60	–	–	–
4	65	–	–	–
5	60	–	–	–
6	64	–	–	–
7	62	–	–	–
8	60	–	–	–
9	58	–	–	–
10	64	–	–	–
11	68	50	1.36	0.36
12	72	55	1.31	0.31
13	70	60	1.17	0.17
14	72	65	1.11	0.11
15	68	60	1.13	0.13
16	64	64	1.00	0.00
17	60	62	0.97	– 0.03
18	54	60	0.90	– 0.10
19	50	58	0.86	– 0.14
20	52	64	0.81	– 0.19
21	64	68	0.94	– 0.06
22	72	72	1.00	0.00
23	74	70	1.06	0.06
24	78	68	1.15	0.15
25	82	64	1.28	0.28

The ROC values have been plotted in Fig. 6.32.

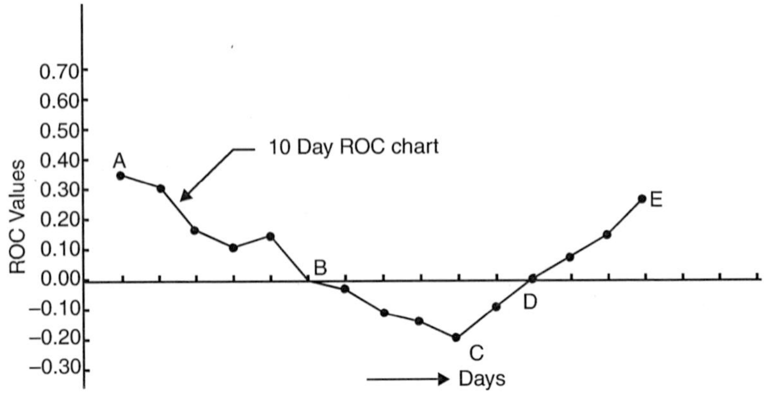

Fig. 6.32 ROC chart

The ROC values may be positive, negative or zero. As seen from figure 6.32 ROC values travel above and below the zero line. When ROC value is zero, it indicates that the price remains stagnant. Interpretation of the 10 day ROC chart shown in Fig. 6.32 is as under.

From point – A to point – B:

The ROC indicator is above the central line (zero line) and is falling. Hence, the price is above the price level 10 days ago, but the price is falling.

From point – B to point – C:

The ROC indicator is below the central line (zero line) and is falling. Hence, the price is below the price level 10 days ago and the price is also falling.

From point – C to point – D:

The ROC indicator is below the central line and is rising. Hence, the price is below the price level 10 days ago and the price is rising.

From point – D to point – E:

The ROC indicator is above the central line and is rising. Hence, the price is above the price level 10 days ago and the price is also rising.

In general, a rising ROC indicator implies increasing momentum in the price level and a falling ROC indicator implies reducing momentum.

The zero line serves as a reference line for identifying buying and selling opportunities. When the ROC line crosses the zero line from below, buying opportunity is signaled (point – D in Fig. 6.32). When the ROC line crosses the zero line from above, selling opportunity is signaled (point – B in Fig. 6.32).

Relative Strength Index (RSI)

Relative strength index (RSI) is a momentum indicator developed by Wells Wilder. Being a momentum indicator, it offers signals for buying and selling.

RSI for a share is calculated using the following formula.

$$\text{RSI} = 100 - [100/(1 + \text{RS})]$$

Where

$$\text{RS} = \frac{\text{Average gain per day}}{\text{Average loss per day}}$$

The average gain and average loss can be calculated for any time span. Wilder recommended a 14 day period for calculating RS.

A 14 day RSI for a given share is calculated as under:

- Take the 15 days closing price of the stock.
- Calculate the gain/loss every day, starting from day – 2. The gain/loss is calculated by comparing the closing price of the day with the closing price of the previous day.
- Sum up the gains during the 14 days which gives the total gains in 14 days. Divide this sum by 14 to get the average gain per day.
- Sum up the losses during the 14 days which gives the total losses in 14 days. Divide this sum by 14 to get the average loss per day.
- Calculate the RSI using the formula, RSI = 100 – [100/(1 + RS)]
- RSI values can lie in the range of 0 to 100.

The following example explains the method of calculating RSI.

Calculation of 14 Day RSI

The table below gives the gain/loss over the previous day

Day	Closing price	Gain	Loss
1	142	--	--
2	144	2	--
3	148	4	--
4	152	4	--
5	155	3	--
6	153	--	2
7	150	--	3
8	148	--	2

Contd...

9	144	--	4
10	142	--	2
11	140	--	2
12	142	2	--
13	144	2	--
14	146	2	--
15	149	3	--
	$\Sigma =$	22	15

$$\text{Average gain} = \frac{22}{14} = 1.57$$

$$\text{Average loss} = \frac{15}{14} = 1.07$$

$$\text{RS} = \frac{1.57}{1.07} = 1.47$$

$$\begin{aligned}\text{RSI} &= 100 - [100/(1 + \text{RS})] \\ &= 100 - [100/(1 + 1.47)] \\ &= 100 - [100/2.47] \\ &= 100 - 40.49 \\ &= 59.51\end{aligned}$$

The RSI calculated above is the RSI for the fifteenth day. The RSI for the subsequent days can be calculated on similar lines by taking the closing prices of 14 previous days.

The RSI can take values in the range of 0 to 100. Let the RSI calculated for subsequent days are as under.

Day	16	17	18	19	20	21	22
RSI	60.22	65.75	70.11	76.12	81.25	80.00	74.14

Day	23	24	25	26	27	28
RSI	70.19	66.95	62.45	50.55	44.85	40.22

Day	29	30	31	32	33	34	35
RSI	35.75	29.45	25.15	20.12	24.15	31.12	35.65

Interpretation of Buy/Sell Signals from RSI

The values of RSI given in the table are plotted in Fig. 6.33. Wilder recommended over-bought and over-sold lines to be drawn at 70 & 30 levels of RSI respectively. Using there boundaries, buy/sell signals can be obtained from the RSI chart.

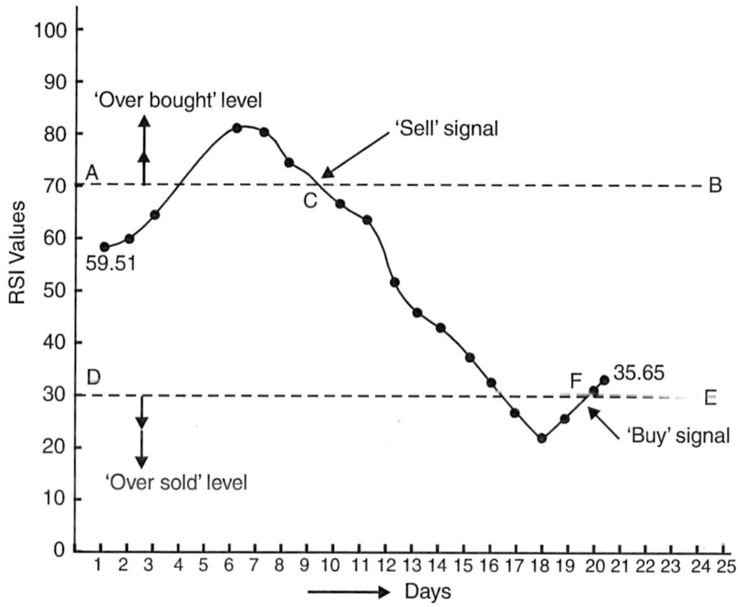

Fig. 6.33 RSI chart

Referring to Fig. 6.33, levels above the line – AB are 'over-bought' levels. At point – C, the RSI line crosses the over bought boundary from above. This indicates a "sell" signal.

Levels below the line – DE are 'over-sold' levels. At point – F the RSI line crosses the over-sold boundary from below. This indicates a 'buy' signal.

Moving Average Convergence and Divergence (MACD)

While discussing about moving averages, we have already seen the use of dual moving averages in finding out buy/sell signals. MACD chart is drawn in an oscillator format (i.e., the curve will be oscillating above and below zero line).

For drawing MACD curve, first a short term and a long term exponential moving average is calculated. A 12 day exponential moving average is commonly used as the short term moving average while a 48 day exponential moving average is commonly used as the long term moving average.

The difference between the short term and long term exponential moving average represents MACD.

$$\text{MACD} = \frac{\text{(short term exponential}}{\text{moving average)}} - \frac{\text{(long term exponential}}{\text{moving average)}}$$

MACD is calculated from the two sets of exponential moving averages (short term and long term). The resulting curve will be in oscillator format. The MACD curve will oscillate across the zero line. When the MACD curve crosses the zero line from below, a 'buy' signal is indicated and when it crosses the zero line from above, a 'sell' signal is indicated. Figure 6.34 shows a 12-day exponential moving average curve and a 48-day exponential moving average curve. The figure also shows the corresponding MACD curve.

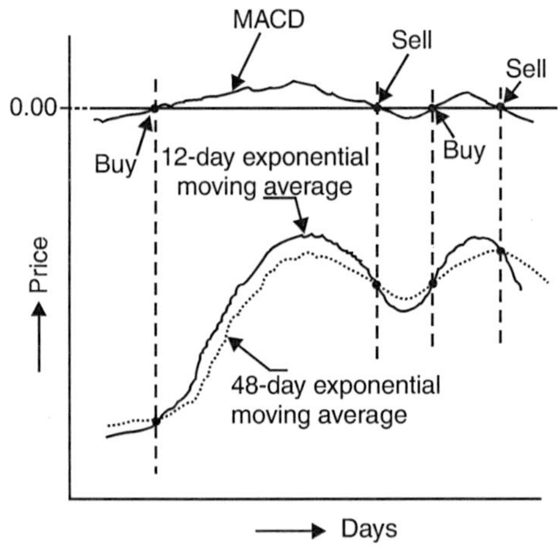

Fig. 6.34 MACD chart

6.11. MARKET INDICATORS

Indicators that help to study the trend of the market as a whole are called market indicators. For example, the BSE index is a market indicator. Technical analysis makes use of certain market indicators to study the overall behaviour of the market. The following are some of the market indicators used in technical analysis:

- Breadth of the market
- New Highs and New Lows cumulative indicator
- Short selling

- Odd lot trading
- Mutual fund activity

Breadth of the Market

In general, out of the total stocks available, a few stocks may be moving ahead, a few may be moving down and a majority of the remaining stocks may not be making any progress. The majority stocks that remain without any significant movement do not contribute to the price movement of the market index. It is the number of shares that advanced and the number of shares that declined during a particular period that decides the price trend in that period.

The phrase 'Breadth of the market' refers to the comparison of advances and declines in the price of stocks. The most common method of measuring the breadth of the market is to calculate the daily net difference between the number of stocks listed in a stock exchange that advance and the number of stocks that decline. The net difference is added to the next day's net difference and so on and thus a cumulative index is formed. This cumulative index refers to the breadth of the market. The index is thus plotted in the form of a line graph and is compared with the stock exchange price index.

Let us see an example.

Day	No. of stocks that advanced	No. of stocks that declined	Breadth (cumulative advances less cumulative declines)
Monday	1050	420	+ 630
Tuesday	600	740	+ 490
Wednesday	550	950	+ 90
Thursday	700	825	– 35
Friday	650	480	+ 135

The breadth is compared with the stock market index such as BSE. It is found that the breadth and the stock market index normally move together. Refer Fig. 6.35 which shows how the trend of stock market index and Breadth move over a period of time.

Figure 6.35 shows that the Breadth and the stock market index move in unison. Normally, the market index will follow the Breadth. When they diverge, it indicates an important signal. At this point, the likely direction of the market is indicated by the advance – decline line (i.e., Breadth line). The stock market index and the Breadth index are expected to move in unison. The divergence cannot last for long since the stock market index cannot move contrary to the market as a whole, which is represented by the Breadth index. If at all there is divergence between the two, the longer the period of divergence, the greater the expected reversal.

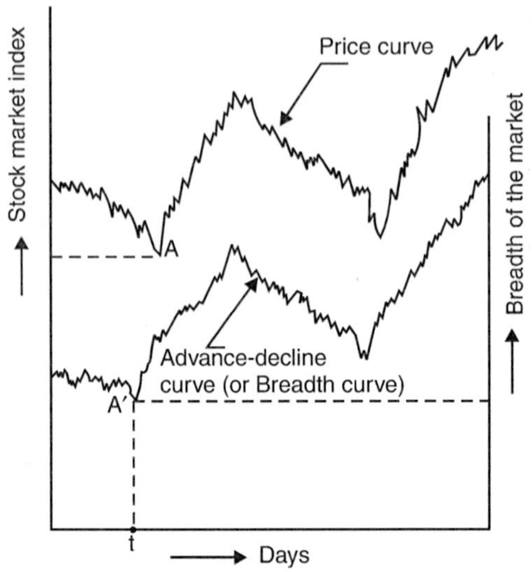

Fig. 6.35 Breadth of market

In a bearish market, let us assume that the market index reaches a new low at a particular point of time. Let there is divergence between the market index and the Breadth index and that the Breadth index has already started rising. What is the signal available? Yes. You guessed it. Since, it is the advance-decline line that points to the truer direction of the market, market would rise sharply. Similarly, when the market index line is reaching a new high while the Breadth index has already begun to fall, a reversal of the market trend is expected and the market prices are expected to register sharp fall. Thus, the Breadth index acts as a leading indicator of the Price trend.

Referring to Fig. 6.35, the market price has reached a low at point – A. But, even before the price has reached a low, the Breadth index has already started rising after reaching a low at point – A'. This gives an indication that at time period '*t*', though the price is falling, it is expected to start rising shortly. Hence, at period '*t*', a 'buy' signal is indicated in view of the anticipated price rise in the immediate future.

As indicated by the Breadth, the stock index has started rising after point – A.

***Illustration* 6.3:**

For the data given below, plot the Breadth index line and the Price index line; give your inference.

Day	No. of stocks that advanced	No. of stocks that declined	Difference (Advance – Decline)	Cumulative advances less cumulative declines (Breadth)	Price Index
1	350	300	50	50	2,000
2	400	325	75	125	2,500
3	450	350	100	225	3,000
4	325	400	(–)75	150	3,300
5	300	350	(–)50	100	2,700

Solution:

The Breadth index curve and the Price index curve for the given data are plotted in Fig. 6.36.

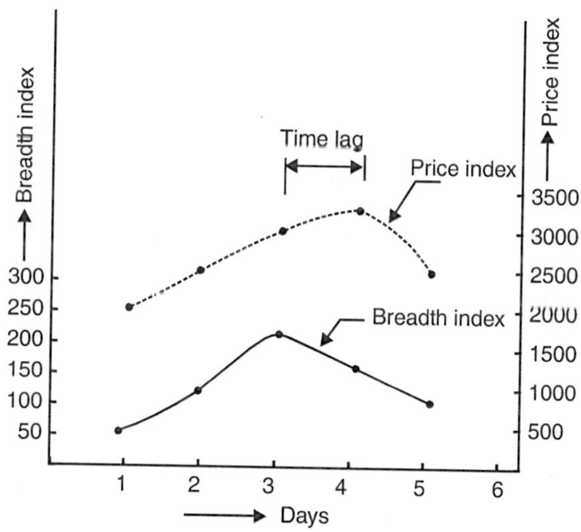

Fig. 6.36 Breadth index and price index

Inference

The Breadth index has started falling after Day–3. The Price index continues its upward trend from Day–1 to Day–4. Though from Day–3 to Day–4, the Price index has moved ahead, in view of the fall of Breadth index on Day–4, a reversal of Price index is on the anvil. On Day–4, the investor is offered a 'sell' signal since the Price index is expected to fall, following the BREADTH INDEX. The 'sell' signal offered by the Breadth index on Day–4 is proved right on Day–5 when the price index has also fallen.

New Highs and New Lows Cumulative Indicator

Similar to the Breadth index, the New Highs and New Lows Cumulative Indicator is also an index to measure whether the market is booming or declining. It is a long term market momentum indicator.

New Highs represent the number of stocks that have reached new highs during the latest 52-week period. New Lows represent the number of stocks that have reached new lows during the latest 52-week period.

The difference between the New Highs and new Lows exposes the market trend. The cumulative total of the difference between New Highs and New Lows is used as the long term indicator of the market movement. Similar to the Breadth index, the New Highs and New Lows cumulative indicator is also a leading indicator of stock price movement.

Consider the following example.

Day	Number of stocks that have attained New High in the latest 52-week period	Number of stocks that have attained New Low in the latest 52-week period	Cumulative number of stocks that have reached New High less Cumulative number of stocks that have reached New Low in the latest 52-week period.
1	2100	840	(+) 1260
2	1200	1480	(+) 980
3	1100	1900	(+) 180
4	1400	1650	(–) 70
5	1300	960	(+) 270
6	2000	1000	(+)1270

The New Highs and New Lows Cumulative index (or indicator) is plotted in Fig. 6.37.

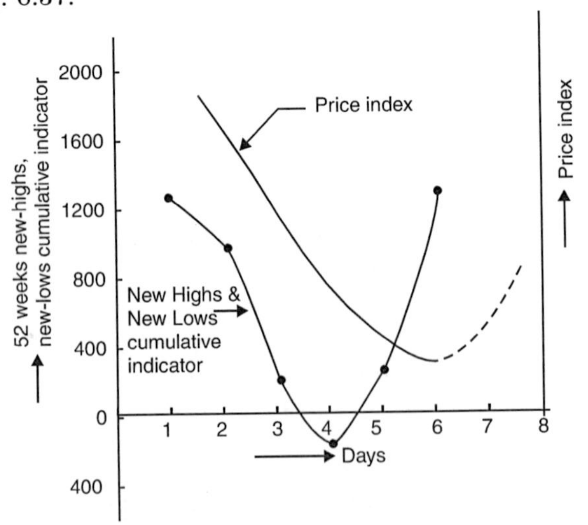

Fig. 6.37 Movement of price index vis-à-vis new highs & new lows cumulative indicator

Note: *Suppose we are on Day–6. The dotted line indicates the likely trend of the Price Index.*

After Day–4, the indicator reverses its trend. The price index of the market continues its downward trend till Day – 6. Since, the New Highs & New Lows Cumulative Indicator has already started rising from Day–4, it gives the indication that the market Price Index is sure to rise up. The likely trend of the Price Index based on an interpretation of the movement of the New Highs & New Lows Cumulative Indicator is shown in figure 6.37 in dotted line. Thus, the new Highs & New Lows Cumulative Index acts as a leading indicator of long term market trend.

Short Selling

Short selling refers to selling of shares not owned by the sellers. A seller short sells shares as he hopes that the stock prices will fall further. Short selling is a speculative operation undertaken under the belief that the price of shares will fall. The seller resorts to short selling with the hope to buy the shares at a later date when the prices have fallen down. Thus, the seller hopes to make a profit out of the transaction. On the face of it this appears that a higher level of short selling points to a bearish market trend, while a smaller short selling points to a bearish trend. Short selling is also referred to as 'short interest'.

$$\begin{array}{c}\text{Short interest ratio (SIR)}\\ \text{(or Short Interest Indicator)}\end{array} = \frac{\begin{array}{c}\text{[Total Number of shares sold short}\\ \text{during a particular period]}\end{array}}{\text{Average Trading volume during the period}}$$

When a particular stock is sold short in large numbers, SIR for that stock can act as an indicator for a future price rise since all the short sellers will have to scramble to close out their positions, thereby creating a greater demand for the stock which in turn will push its price higher. Technicians consider that a higher level of short-selling will prompt a bullish trend because those who sold their stocks short have to buy them again to cover their positions. This would lead to heavy buying pressures and will lead to a bullish trend. Short selling has significance on the individual stocks and also on the market as a whole.

Odd Lot Index

Small investors, who cannot afford to buy the normal trading lot of 100 shares, buy smaller number of shares than the trading lot. These shares whose number is less than the trading lot are called 'odd-lots' and the buyers and sellers of odd-lot shares are called odd-lotters.

Like all prudent investors, odd-lotters also participate in share market transactions. Like other investors, odd-lotters buy stocks when the market retreats and sell stocks when the market advances. However, according to technicians, the odd-lotters, though behave like any other investors during normal time, behave differently at crucial times. Technicians believe that the odd-lotters do the wrong thing at times of critical turns in the market conditions. The odd behaviour of the odd-lotters, it is believed, is due to the fact that they lack correct knowledge about the market. An odd-lot index can be constructed by dividing the odd-lot purchases by odd-lot sales.

$$\text{i.e.,} \quad \text{odd lot index} = \frac{\text{(odd-lot purchase)}}{\text{(odd-lot sales)}}$$

An increase in the odd-lot index means relatively more buying while a decrease in the odd-lot index indicates relatively more selling.

When a bullish market reaches its peak, the investors would be, in general, selling their shares. However, the odd-lotters would be buying proportionately more shares than selling and hence the odd-lot index will increase. Thus, a significant increase in the odd-lot index points to the decline in the market prices of shares that will commence shortly. Similarly, when the odd-lot index decreases noticeably, it points to the upswing in the market prices of shares that will commence shortly. Thus, changes in the odd-lot index helps to prejudge the commencement of the trend of price-rise and price fall.

Mutual Fund Activity

Mutual funds consistently hold a certain portion of their portfolio in the form of cash. Mutual funds keep cash for two reasons viz., for taking advantage of favourable investment opportunities in the market and to provide for redemption by unit holders.

$$\text{Mutual fund cash ratio} = \frac{\text{Cash}}{\text{(Net asset value)}} \times 100$$

The cash ratio moves in a direction opposite to the stock market price movement.

Low cash ratio indicates that the mutual fund has invested its funds nearly fully and has negligible buying power at their hands. Low cash ratios point to market highs and hence once a low cash ratio is reached, the market is about to start its downward journey. When the cash ratio is high, the mutual funds have potential buying power and the market is at its low. The heavy cash balance might have been built up either on account of purchase of new units by investors or due to previous sale of stocks in the portfolio. Whatever may be the source of funds, technicians believe that the accumulated funds will cause an increase in stock prices. Thus, a high cash ratio signals a rise in the price of shares.

6.12. ELLIOTT WAVE THEORY

Elliott Wave Theory is one of the theories in the realm of Technical analysis that seeks to explain the behaviour of market. Ralph N. Elliott observed that the law of creation has a rhythmic regularity.

Elliott observed that all cycles occurring in nature (whether of the tides, the heavenly bodies, the planets, the days and nights, the change of seasons, etc.) had the capability of repeating their cyclic pattern indefinitely. The natural cycles also exhibit an extraordinary numerical relationship discovered by Fibonacci, a great mathematician of the thirteenth century.

Fibonacci formulated a series of numbers as under.

1, 2, 3, 5, 8, 13, 21, 34, 55, 89, 144, 233, etc. ...

Each number in the series is formed by following the rule given below.

- Start with the number 2.
- The third number in the series is formed by adding the previous number (viz., 1) with the number 2 (i.e., 2 + 1 = 3).
- The fourth number in the series is formed by adding the previous number (viz., 2) with the number 3 (i.e., 3 + 2 = 5).
- The fifth number in the series is formed by adding the previous number (viz., 3) with the number 5 (i.e., 5 + 3 = 8).

And the process is repeated ...

The Fibonacci numbers and the proportions between the numbers of the series are found in many manifestations of nature (for example, the number of branches that emanate from the stem of a tree is found to match the Fibonacci number).

Elliott published a series of articles in the year 1939 in which he brought out his observation that in a period of 80 years, the market had moved forward in a series containing five waves and then declined in a series containing three waves (5, 3 and 8 are numbers in the Fibonacci Series). The five waves that are contained in the 'uptrend' consist of three upward moving waves and two corrective waves that are downward sloping. The uptrend containing five waves is followed by a series of three waves that form the down trend. The down trend contains two downward sloping waves and one upward sloping wave. Elliott thus concluded that a single cycle comprised eight waves (Refer Fig. 6.38).

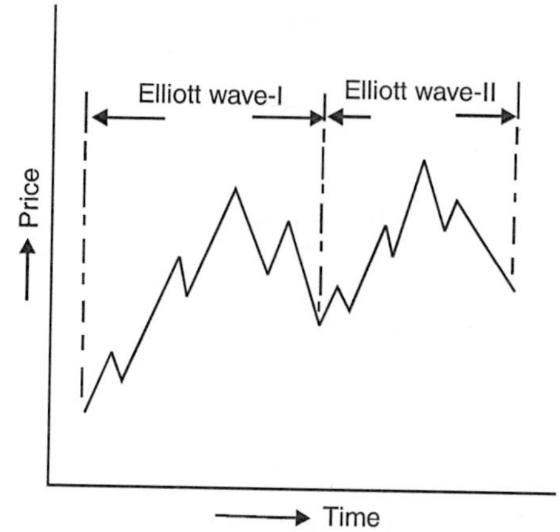

Fig. 6.38 Elliott wave

Elliott believed that the cycle containing eight waves embraces all types of market movements starting with great super cycle to smaller and minute cycles and he hoped that the price behaviour can be predicted following the eight wave pattern. Once the full cycle of eight waves is completed, there will be a fresh cycle starting with similar impulses.

Though interesting, Elliott wave is highly subjective in nature and is of little utility in forecasting the future trend of the market. Irregularity in wavelengths makes it difficult to interpret.

6.13. VOLUME INDICATORS

Volume refers to the number of shares traded in the secondary market during a specified period of time. The time period can be an hour, a day, week, month etc. An analysis of the volume of shares traded will provide strong clues about the likely movements of the share price.

When the volume increases along with increase in share price, it supports the upward price movement. It reflects that market's confidence that the upward price trend is justified and will continue. When the volume increases while the price is in a declining trend, it supports the downward price movement. It reflects the market's consensus that the downward price movement is justified and will further move downwards.

Hence, increasing volume with increasing price indicates bullish trend while increasing volume with decreasing price indicates bearish trend.

Reversal of bullish/bearish trend can also be predicted using volume. When the volume behaves contrary to the price, it indicates likely reversal of the price trend. Accordingly,

- Decreasing volume with increasing price indicates likely change of price trend from bullish to bearish.
- Decreasing volume with decreasing price indicates likely change of price trend from bearish to bullish.

It may be noted that when some investor sells the shares held by him, some other investor purchases the same. When we say that the volume increases it only means that there are many sellers and there are as many buyers. In other words, there is a heavy transaction. Normally, the volume is expected to be high when the price trend is bullish as well as when bearish. When the volume reduces, it shows that the investors are not actively participating in the market and are waiting for a possible reversal in the price trend. A sudden heavy volume indicates that the price has broken a price barrier and has moved out of either a support or a resistance level.

Figures 6.39 to 6.43 indicate charts showing price-volume relationships.

(*a*) Surge in volume at price break-out point

Refer to Fig. 6.39. The price has been fluctuating up and down for about 4½ months starting from the month of April. During these 4½ months the price could not break the price barrier. By the middle of August, the price starts to break the price barrier and surges upwards. The volume remained at low ebb as long as the price lies below the resistance barrier. Once the price barrier is crossed, there is a sudden increase in volume which gives a strong signal that the price is likely to move upwards. Since the price break-out is supported by an increase in volume, it confirms that the price is going to register an upward trend.

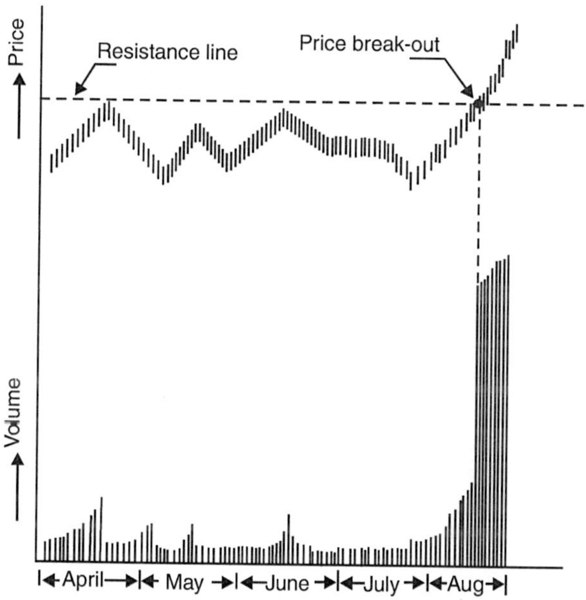

Fig. 6.39 Price volume relationship (Surge in volume at price break-out)

(*b*) Low volume during indecisive period

When the stock price does not either move upwards or downwards distinctly, but fluctuates up and down for some period of time, it indicates that the market is yet to decide on the likely price trend. Such price movements occur typically during consolidation periods after a sufficiently long period of uptrend in price. The trading volume will be at low levels during such indecisive periods.

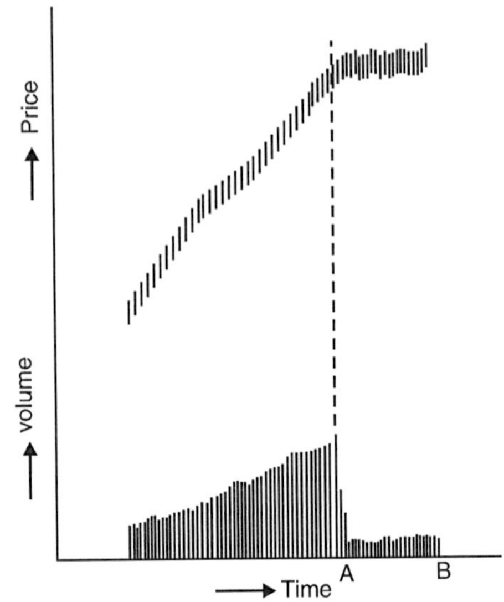

Fig. 6.40 Price-volume relationship (Low volume during indecisive period)

Referring to Fig. 6.40, low volume levels during the period from A to B confirm that the market is in consolidation phase and is yet to decide on the likely price movement.

(*c*) Low volume at market bottom

Refer to Fig. 6.41. The price has been falling from time period A to B and the volume has been gradually increasing during this period evidencing a bearish trend. Between the time period C and D, the volume has been reduced drastically which indicates that the market feels the price has reached a bottom and the market is indecisive as to whether there will be a reversal of trend. During the bearish trend between A and B, the volume has been increasing since there are more and more buyers opting to buy at lower prices in anticipation of a reversal of trend. When the price has reached such a low level that the market becomes skeptical about the reversal of trend, the volume gets drastically reduced.

(*d*) Surge in volume during panic-driven selling

Referring to Fig. 6.41, just before the price has reached its market-bottom (i.e., between time periods B & C), the volume has surged instantly which is caused due to panic-driven selling.

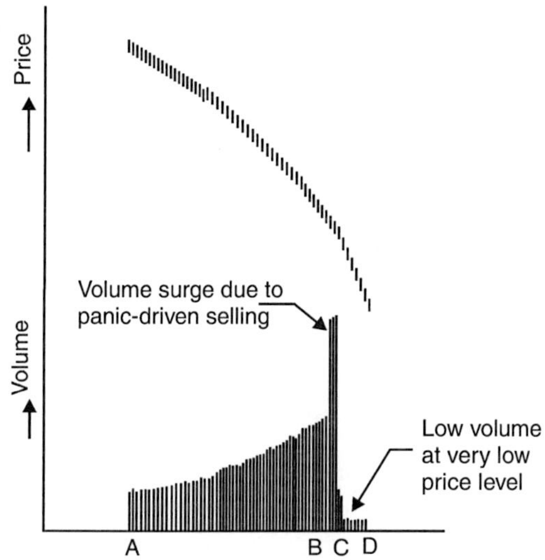

Fig. 6.41 Price-volume relationship (Volume behaviour during downtrend)

(*e*) Healthy upward trend

A general upward trend can be considered healthy, if the volume levels are high during the upward legs of the trend (A-B, C-D, E-F etc.,) and the volume levels are low during the downward legs of the trend (B-C, D-E etc.,). The lower volume during the downward legs is due to the reason that the market is confident of the upward trend in the long run. (Refer Fig. 6.42).

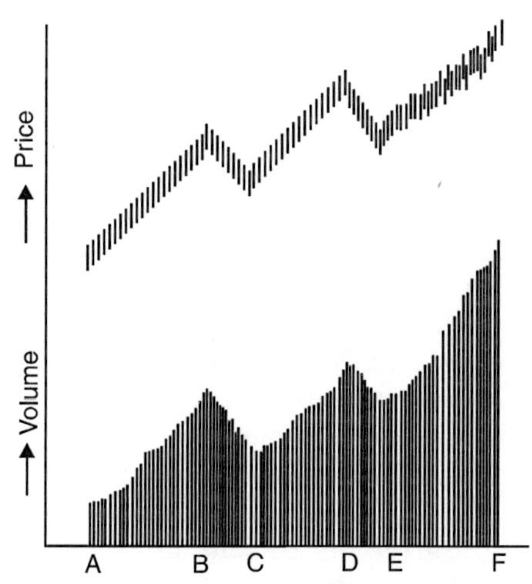

Fig. 6.42 Price-volume relationship (Healthy uptrend)

The downward legs only act as a corrective mechanism to set the price move at the appropriate phase of momentum. When such volume movements are seen, it can be inferred that the upward trend of price is likely to continue in the long run.

(f) Confirmed downward trend

A downward price trend is expected to continue in its downward direction, if the volume levels are higher on the downward legs of the trend and are lower on the upward legs of the trend. The upward legs act as the corrective mechanism (Refer Fig. 6.43).

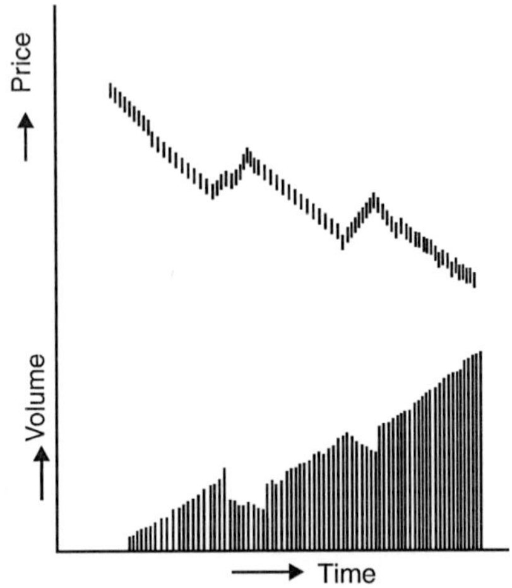

Fig. 6.43 Price-volume relationship (Confirmed downward trend)

6.14. RELATIVE STRENGTH ANALYSIS

It is generally observed that during bull phase of the stock market, the prices of some securities rise more rapidly than the prices of other securities. Similarly, during bear phase, the prices of some securities fall more slowly than the price of other securities. Such securities are said to have greater relative strength and hence they outperform the market. An investor will be interested in identifying such securities that have greater relative strength. Technical analysis is used to identify securities with greater relative strengths by comparing the rates of returns earned by individual securities with the returns earned by the industry as a whole or the market as a whole. Comparison of security return with the industry return will indicate whether the security has performed better or worse as compared to the industry. Similarly, comparison of the security return with the market return will indicate whether the security has performed better or worse as compared to the market. For making these comparisons, the historical returns are made use of. In fact, relative strength disregards the price levels of securities as such, but concentrates on the changes in the price levels of securities as compared to the changes in the price levels of industry/market. Thus, relative strength is nothing but a momentum indicator.

Consider a company in a particular industrial sector. Let company 'A' belongs to Automobile industrial sector and let it manufactures two wheelers catering to a particular segment of customers. The historical share price movements of company 'A', the historical share price movements of the Automobile industry as a whole and the share price movement of the stock market as a whole for the corresponding period can be compared to arrive at meaningful conclusions about the relative strength of company 'A'. The table below gives the historical share price movements.

Year	Average share price of Company 'A' (a)	Average share price of automobile industry (b)	Average price of all listed shares (c)	(a)/(b)	(b)/(c)
2000	Rs. 200	Rs. 180	Rs. 400	1.11	0.45
2001	Rs. 230	Rs. 200	Rs. 440	1.15	0.45
2002	Rs. 250	Rs. 210	Rs. 450	1.19	0.47
2003	Rs. 300	Rs. 240	Rs. 500	1.25	0.48
2004	Rs. 400	Rs. 300	Rs. 520	1.33	0.58

The ratio (a)/(b) compares Company 'A' with the industry. Company 'A' has performed better than the industry (i.e., automobile industry) since the ratio is more than 1.00 and has continuously grown over the years.

The ratio (b)/(c) compares the automobile industry with the market as a whole. This ratio indicates that the automobile industry has almost moved in tandem with the market except in year 2004 where the automobile industry has registered a significant growth.

From the data we can conclude that within automobile industry, the share of company 'A' has performed better and has a relative strength. The automobile industry as a whole has no appreciable relative strength over the market.

Suppose the ratio (b)/(c) is arrived at as below:

Year	(b) / (c)
2000	0.30
2001	0.50
2002	0.70
2003	0.90
2004	1.10

The above data indicates that the automobile industry has grown at a higher phase as compared to the market. Hence, as compared to the market, the automobile industry as a whole has a higher relative strength. Under such conditions if the share of a particular company in the automobile industry shows greater relative strength within the automobile industry, the share of the company will be preferred by investors due to the reasons that the share has a better relative strength within the industry and the industry also has a better relative strength in the stock market.

6.15. LIMITATION OF TECHNICAL ANALYSIS

- While charts used in Technical analysis are fascinating to look at, interpreting them correctly is a very difficult proposition and requires a lot of exposure.
- Technical analysis presumes that the future will resemble the past. There is no guarantee that the past patterns would be repeated in the future. Hence, a technique that gave good results once may not prove good later.
- The changes in the market behaviour observed and studied by technical analysts may not be always reliable. For example, unhealthy practices like cornering and rigging of shares by some stock market operators may give a picture that in far from reality.
- The tools available in technical analysis are less precise and highly subjective in nature. Hence, accurate predictions may not be possible. For example, two technical analysts who observe the same price pattern may arrive at two different interpretations.

6.16. TECHNICAL ANALYSIS VERSUS FUNDAMENTAL ANALYSIS

Technical analysis alone is not adequate to reap benefits from the stock market. While fundamental analysis require large volumes of data and intricate calculations to assess the intrinsic worth of securities, technical analysis need only minimum data, viz., the past data on price and volume of transaction. Thus, technical analysis is comparatively simple and less time consuming. However, technical analysis can only hint at the ideal time for a investment/disinvestment. Technical analysis cannot identify undervalued/overvalued securities which can be done only by fundamental analysis. Hence, the ideal strategy would be to use fundamental analysis for identifying the undervalued/overvalued securities and to use technical analysis to choose the best time for buying/selling of securities. In this way, technical analysis can be made to supplement the effort of fundamental analysis.

Hence, a consensus can be arrived at as to the superiority or otherwise of fundamental and technical analysis as below:

(*a*) Fundamental analysis should be used to arrive at the intrinsic worth of shares.

(*b*) Technical analysis should be used to identify the timing of buying/selling of shares.

6.17. EXERCISES ON INVESTMENT DECISIONS USING CHARTS

Arriving at a decision to buy, sell or hold a stock based on the past price trend is the domain of Technical Analysis. The following exercises will familiarize the readers as to how to read and interpret charts to arrive at fairly correct investment decisions.

***Exercise* 6.1**

Refer to Fig. 6.44. Arrive at a decision as to whether the stock can be bought or sold, at time period 'T'.

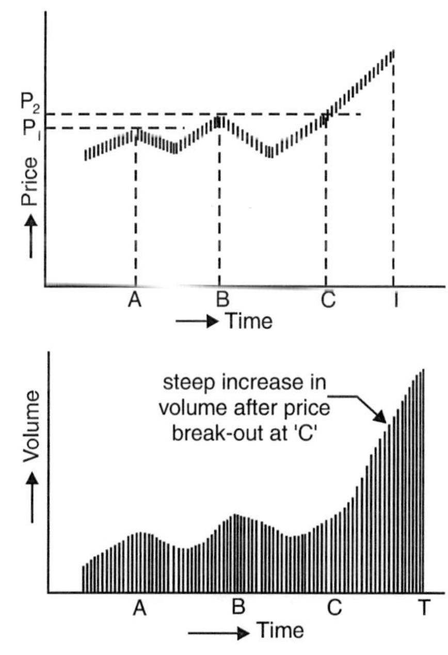

Fig. 6.44

***Exercise* 6.2**

Refer to Fig. 6.45. Arrive at a decision as to whether the stock can be bought or sold, at time period 'T'.

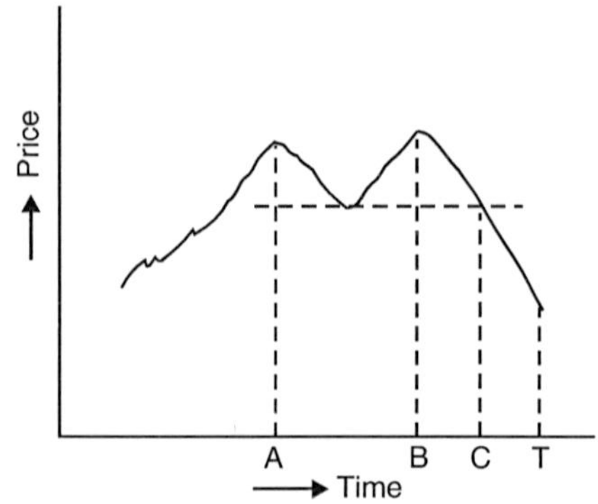

Fig. 6.45

***Exercise* 6.3**

Refer to Fig. 6.46. Arrive at a decision as to whether the stock can be bought or sold, at time period 'T'.

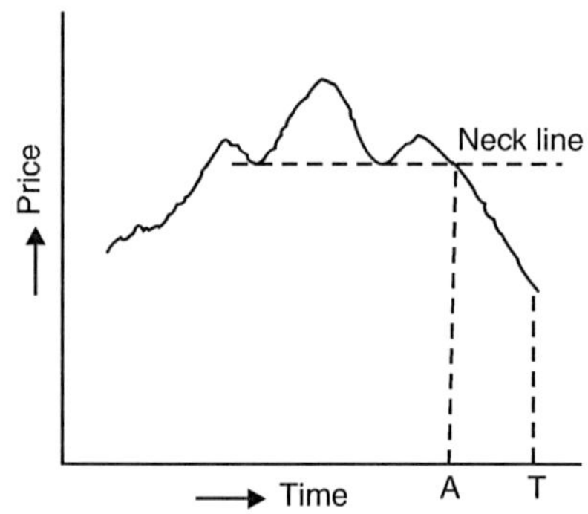

Fig. 6.46

***Exercise* 6.4**

Refer to Fig. 6.47. Arrive at a decision as to whether the stock can be bought or sold, at time period 'T'.

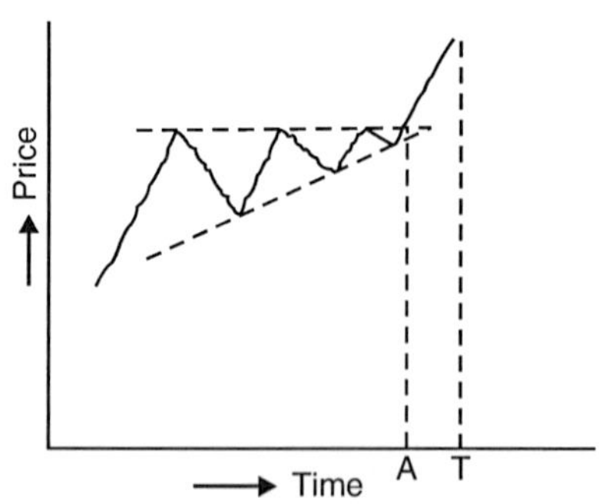

Fig. 6.47

***Exercise* 6.5**

Refer to Fig. 6.48. Arrive at a decision as to whether the stock can be bought or sold, at time period 'T'.

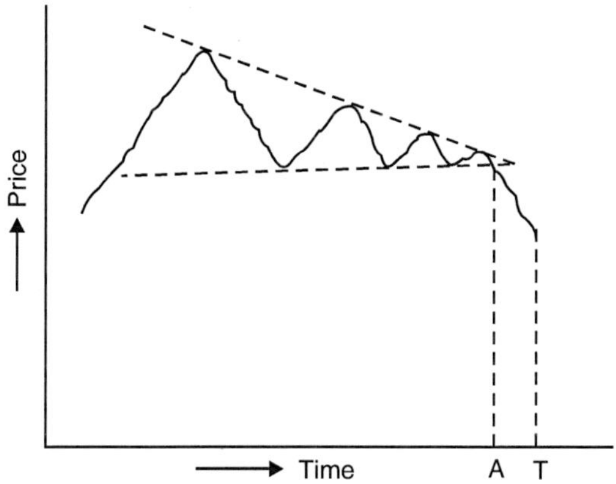

Fig. 6.48

***Exercise* 6.6**

Refer to Fig. 6.49. Arrive at a decision as to whether the stock can be bought or sold, at time period 'T'.

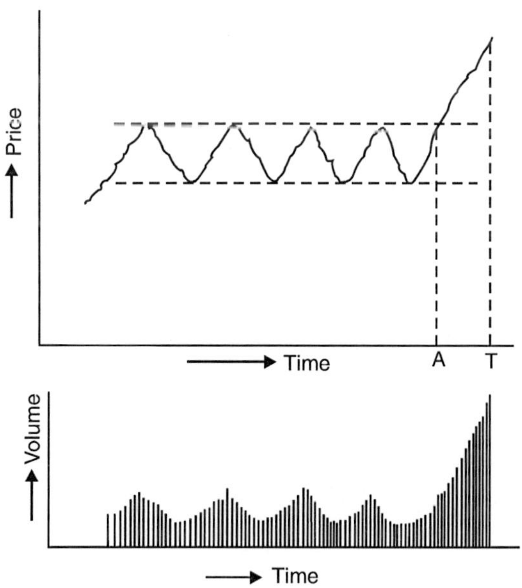

Fig. 6.49

***Exercise* 6.7**

An investor holds two stocks 'X' and 'Y'. The past price trends of the two stocks are given in Fig. 6.50. Arrive at a decision on selling/holding the stocks.

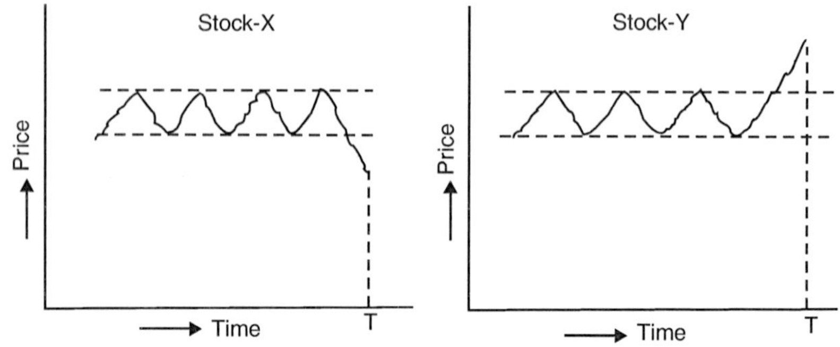

Fig. 6.50

***Exercise* 6.8**

An investor holds two stocks 'X' and 'Y'. The past price trends of the two stocks are given in Fig. 6.51. Arrive at a decision on selling/holding the stocks.

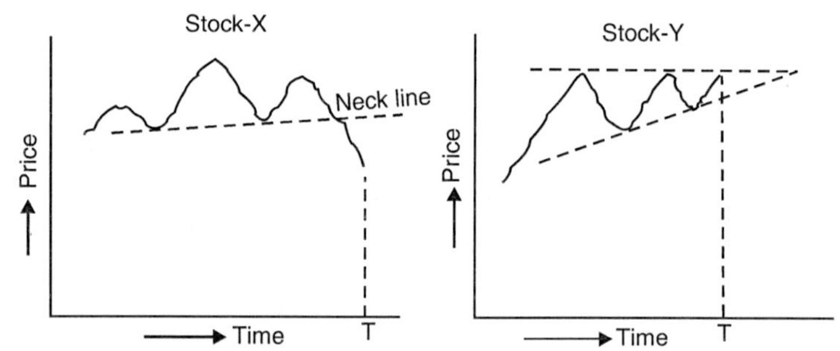

Fig. 6.51

***Exercise* 6.9**

An investor is holding a stock whose price behaviour is shown in Fig. 6.52. Arrive at a decision as to whether the stock can be sold or retained.

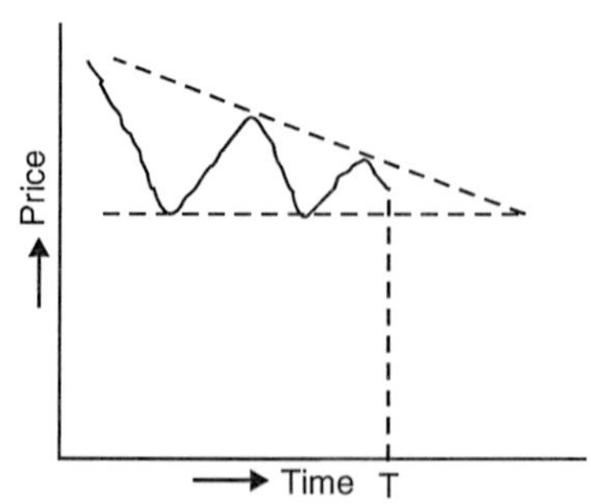

Fig. 6.52

Exercise **6.10**

An investor is holding two stocks 'X' and 'Y'. The past price trends of the two stocks are given in Fig. 6.53. Arrive at a decision as to whether the stocks can be sold or retained.

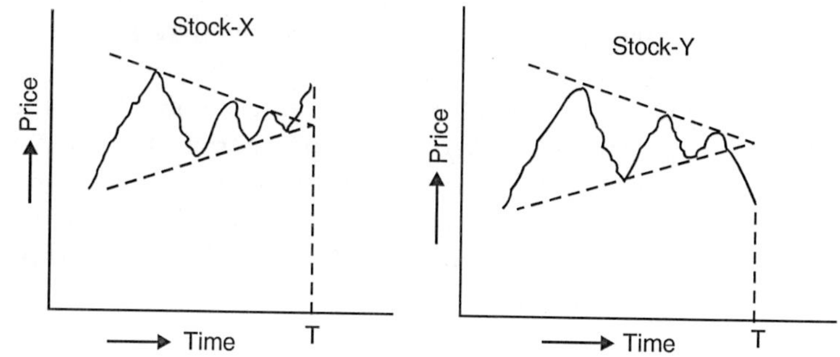

Fig. 6.53

Exercise **6.11**

An investor holds a stock whose price behaviour is shown in Fig. 6.54. Advise whether the stock can be sold or held at time period 'T'.

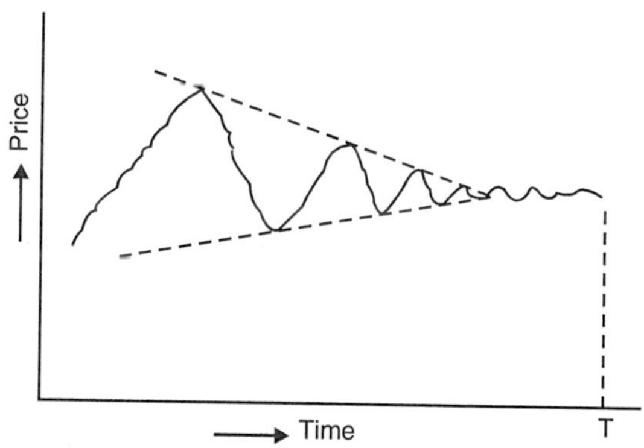

Fig. 6.54

Answers to Exercises:

Exercise **6.1**

At the time period 'A', the price had reached a peak 'P_1' and at time period 'B', the price had reached another peak 'P_2' which is slightly higher than peak 'P_1'. But, the price trend has started falling again after reaching peak 'P_2'. At time period 'C', the price has reached the earlier peak 'P_2' and it has broken the price barrier. Thereafter, the price increase has started progressing continuously upwards. We are now at time period 'T'. The price has all along been rising from time period 'C' till now and the price level has already crossed the barrier. Hence, an investor who does not already own this stock can buy the stock in anticipation of as price increase. An investor who already owns this stock can hold the stock and need not sell at this point of time since the price is expected follow the upward trend.

***Exercise* 6.2**

The price had reached a peak at time period 'A' and another peak at time period 'B'. The price has been falling from the peak at 'B'. This is a Double-Top formation with two price peaks. The price has already started falling below the price corresponding to the valley point (i.e., the price corresponding to time period 'C'). We are at time period 'T'. The price has been falling from time period 'C', till now. Hence, an investor who is already holding this stock can sell the stock since the price is only expected to fall further. For an investor who is not holding this stock, this is not the right time to buy the stock.

***Exercise* 6.3**

It is evidently a Head & Shoulders formation and the price has already penetrated the neck line at time period 'A'. Hence, at the present (i.e., at time period 'T', it is advisable to sell the stock if an investor already owns the stock. In fact, a diligent investor would have sold the stock immediately after the price crossed the neck line. For an investor who does not own the stock, it is not the right time to buy the stock since the price is expected fall further.

***Exercise* 6.4**

The price pattern follows an ascending triangle. The price has broken out (crossing the boundary line of the triangle) at time period 'A'. Hence, at time period 'T', the stock is worth buying since the price is only expected register further growth. An investor who is already owning the stock can hold it.

***Exercise* 6.5**

The price pattern follows a descending triangle. The stock became due for selling when the price level has crossed the support line at the time period 'A'. Hence, at present (i.e., at time period 'T', the stock is worth selling (for an investor who holds this stock) since the price has already started falling further rapidly.

***Exercise* 6.6**

There is an upward breakout from the horizontal channel formation. The price line has broken the price barrier at time period 'A'. Hence, at time period 'T', the stock can be bought. The volume chart shows low levels of volume prior to time period 'A'. After time period 'A', the volume improves suddenly which also supports buying the stock. An investor who is already holding the stock can continue to hold it since there is expected to be further price rise.

***Exercise* 6.7**

At time period 'T', stock 'X' should be sold since the price has been falling down after a channel formation. Regarding stock 'Y', at time period 'T', the price has started rising after a channel formation. Hence, the price is expected to register further growth in future. The investor can hold stock 'Y' as he is expected to get price appreciation.

***Exercise* 6.8**

We are at time period 'T'. Stock 'X' can be obviously sold since the price is under falling trend after a 'Head and shoulders' formation. The price trend of stock 'Y' is in the form of a rising triangle and at present the price is still within the boundary of the ascending triangle. The price is expected to move further within the boundaries of the triangle and is expected to break away from the resistance barrier, moving upwards. As the resistance line remains horizontal and as the support line moves upwards, the price is finally expected to cross the resistance line from below and move upwards. Hence, the investor who already holds stock 'Y' can hold it with himself and look for a quantum leap in price in the near future. This is the time at which the price will cross the price barrier (upper boundary line of the triangle).

***Exercise* 6.9**

The price trend is in the form of a descending triangle. The price movement within the descending triangle will prevail for some more time, showing upward and downward movements until it finally breaks down the lower barrier (price support barrier). This is because of the reason that the support barrier remains horizontal while the resistance barrier moves downwards. Once the price breaks down below the lower barrier of the triangle, the fall in price is expected to be much steeper. Hence, at time period 'T' it is advisable for the investor to sell the stock without waiting any further.

***Exercise* 6.10**

We are presently at time period 'T'. The price line of stock 'X' has crossed the upper price barrier of the triangle formation and has started moving further upwards. Hence, the price of the stock is expected to increase further in the days to come. It is advisable for the investor to hold the stock. As regards stock 'Y', since the price has broken the lower barrier of the triangle and has started falling further, it is advisable to sell the stock.

***Exercise* 6.11**

We are presently at time period 'T'. The price movements were within a pair of boundaries following a symmetrical triangle. The price has neither broken the upper resistance line nor the lower support line but has pierced through the apex of the triangle. Hence, the anticipated future price trend is not known clearly at present. As the future price trend is not distinctly indicated, the investor can hold the stock for some more time till a distinct trend is visible.

REVIEW QUESTIONS

1. What are the principles of Technical Analysis?
2. Explain the logic behind Technical Analysis.
3. Explain the use of the following charts in Technical Analysis:
   - Line Chart
   - Bar Chart
   - Point and Figures Chart
   - Japanese Candle Stick Chart
4. State the postulates of Dow Theory. Explain the use of Dow Theory in Technical Analysis.
5. Explain the interpretation of the following chart patterns with the aid of suitable sketches/figures:
   - Channel pattern
   - Wedge pattern
   - Head and shoulders pattern
   - Triple bottom pattern.
6. Define 'Gap' and explain its use for a Technical Analyst.
7. What are Mathematical Indicators? Explain the use of any two Mathematical indicators in Technical Analysis.
8. What are Market indicators? Explain the use of any two Market indicators in Technical Analysis.
9. Explain the features of Relative strength analysis.
10. What are the limitations of Technical Analysis?

7

CHAPTER

Efficient Market Hypothesis

7.1. RANDOM WALK THEORY

Roberts and Osborne published two articles on the behaviour of share prices, in the year 1959. Both these articles emphasized that change in share prices exhibit a random movement and do not follow any predictable pattern. These two articles suggested that the market is already efficient and hence there is no scope for any prediction. Studies carried out by many others also supported the view that share price movements are at random. Thus, the efficient market theory which gained acceptance during 1960's was then known by the name Random Walk Theory.

Random Walk Theory can be summarized as under:

- Changes in stock prices occur due to changes in the performance of economy, industry or company.
- Changes in the performance of economy, industry or company are known to all investors immediately. As all the investors are aware of the changes in the economy, industry or company at once, there is an instant change in the stock prices based on the changes in the economy, industry or company.
- As all the investors respond to the changes in the economy, industry or company instantly, there is instant adjustment in stock prices, either upwards or downwards.
- As all the information are available to the investors and as the stock prices get instantly adjusted on the basis of the available information, the current stock prices always fully reflect all the available information. Hence, there is no scope for prediction of stock price movements.
- Any further movement in the stock prices from the current prices is effected only on the basis of new pieces of information received.
- As new pieces of information that are received are themselves independent of each other, every change in the stock price is independent of the earlier change.

Thus, Random Walk Theory assumes that stock markets are fully efficient due to which immediate price adjustments take place and as the price changes are based only on new pieces of information which are not predictable, stock price movements resemble a random walk rather than an orderly movement.

The gist of Random walk theory is that new pieces of information arrives randomly due to which the share prices also move randomly in accordance with the type/nature of information arrived. When favourable information about the economy, industry or company arrives, the share prices go up; when unfavourable information arrives, the share prices go down.

Random walk theory supports the view that technical analysis is of no use in predicting share prices since successive price changes are independent of the past price changes. However, Random walk theory does not negate the usefulness of fundamental analysis. The random price movement is due to variations in the intrinsic worth of shares which in turn depends on fundamentals like the P/E ratio, EPS etc. and instances like announcements of financial results dividends, Bonus shares, Rights shares etc.

7.2. EFFICIENT MARKET HYPOTHESIS

The Random walk theory which gained popularity during the 1960s was later known as Efficient market model. Studies done by Elton, Gruber and Eugene Fame supported the Efficient market model.

Efficient market hypothesis states that the capital market is efficient. An efficient market is one in which all the relevant information is reflected in the current stock price. Since any new information that arrives is absorbed instantaneously by the efficient market, the stock prices also get adjusted instantaneously to a new level. Hence, in an efficient market, stock price will always be equal to their intrinsic values at all times. Thus, there can be no scope for bargains in the stock market.

7.2.1. Forms of Efficient Market Hypothesis

The efficient market hypothesis can be divided into three levels, viz., the weak form, the semi strong form and the strong form.

Weak form Efficiency

This is the lowest level of market efficiency. It holds that present stock prices reflect all known information with regard to past stock prices and their movements. Weak form of the efficient market hypothesis says that the current stock prices fully reflect all the information that are contained in the past prices and their movements. Hence, the new price movements are produced only due to new pieces of information and are not dependent on the past price data. Since past price data has no relevance in predicting the future price, there is no scope for technical analysis and the work of chartists is futile. When the market is weak form efficient, the future stock price movements do not depend on the past prices and hence the stock prices movements follows a random walk on the basis of new pieces of information received. The stock price moves at random since new pieces of information are received at random intervals and are immediately reflected in the stock prices.

Semi Strong form Efficiency

Semi strong form of the efficient market hypothesis holds that the current stock prices not only reflect all known information with regard to past stock prices and their movements but also reflect all publicly available information about the company, whose stocks are being studied.

The following are some of the publicly available information:

- Latest corporate annual reports.
- Expectations regarding future annual reports with regard to changes in sales, earnings, dividends, capital structure etc.,
- Company announcements of forthcoming dividends, stock splits etc.,
- Press releases
- Changes in Government policies that will affect/improve the prospects of the company.

If the market is semi-strong efficient, it will also be efficient in the weak sense. The implication of semi-strong form of the efficient market hypothesis is that there is no scope for fundamental analysis and the work of fundamental analysts is futile. This is because stock prices adjust to new pieces of publicly available information as soon as they are received and the fundamental analyst is left with no time gap in which he can trade for achieving superior gains.

Strong form Efficiency

This is the most extreme form of market efficiency. Strong form of the efficient market hypothesis maintains that the current stock prices reflect "all relevant" information. The term 'all relevant information' includes – past price data, all publicly available information and all insider information which are not available to the investing public at large. Strong form efficiency means that no information whether the past price trend, publicly available information or even insider information can be of use to earn superior returns consistently.

7.2.2. Tests for Weak Form Market Efficiency

The following tests are used to test whether a market is really weak form efficient. When the market is weak form efficient, past price data cannot be used to earn superior returns. The tests verify whether past data are useful in earning superior returns and accordingly prove or disprove the weak form efficiency.

Filter Test

Filter test uses a mechanical trading rule. The rule fixes a filter point and directs to buy or sell when the limits for the stock price (upper & lower limits) are exceeded beyond the limits fixed by the filter points due to changes in price movements.

Consider the following price movement of a company's stock:

Date	Price (Rs.)
01.01.2000	154.00
02.01.2000	151.00
03.01.2000	149.00
04.01.2000	148.00
05.01.2000	147.50
06.01.2000	148.00
07.01.2000	153.00
08.01.2000	153.60
09.01.2000	154.00

The stock price shows a falling trend starting from 01.01.2000. The trend starts reversing on 06.01.2000. Suppose 3% is the filter point fixed.

A 'buy' signal is indicated when the stock price increases beyond 3% from the lower level.

Lower level of stock price	:	Rs. 147.50
Add: 3% increase	:	Rs. 4.43
	:	Rs. 151.93

When the stock price touches Rs. 151.93, a 'buy' signal is indicated. Thus, the 'buy' signal is indicated on 07.01.2000.

Let the price movements subsequent to 09.01.2000 are as below:

Date	Price (Rs.)
10.01.2000	154.70
11.01.2000	155.20
12.01.2000	156.00
13.01.2000	158.00
14.01.2000	162.00

15.01.2000	161.50
16.01.2000	161.20
17.01.2000	161.00
18.01.2000	161.20
19.01.2000	161.00
20.01.2000	159.50
21.01.2000	158.00
22.01.2000	157.00

Referring to the above stock price movements, the stock price moves up gradually and reaches a high on 14.01.2000. On 15.01.2000, there is a symptom of fall in stock price since the price has fallen down to Rs. 161.5. Hence according to the filter rule the investor should now get ready to sell his stock. To arrive at the point at which the stock is to be sold, the filter rule is again applied.

Higher level of stock price	:	Rs. 162.00
Less: 3% fall	:	Rs. 4.86
	:	Rs. 157.14

When the stock price touches Rs. 157.14, a 'sell' signal is indicated. Thus the 'sell' signal is indicated on 22.01.2000. The filters may be fixed in the range of 1% to 50%.

The strategy of investment based on filter rule is an active investment strategy where by the investor attempts to gain superior returns based on the trend of stock price movements. Since weak form market efficiency hypothesis states that stock prices move at random, an investor who relies on this hypothesis will follow only a passive investment strategy. In other words, he will prefer 'buy and hold' strategy. He won't plan for trading based on past stock price movements. Thus, 'buy and hold' strategy is opposite to the investment strategy based on filter rules. The strategy following filter rule is to buy a stock when its price rises by a certain percentage and to sell the stock when the price falls by the same percentage from the subsequent high. This strategy is called an active strategy since the investor will be actively involved in buying/selling of stocks following the rule. As against this, a passive investor will buy a stock and hold it for ever. The 'buy and hold' strategy is a passive strategy since the investor is indifferent to the stock price movements and will continue to hold the stock once it is bought.

The returns generated by following filter rule are compared with the returns generated by following 'buy and hold' strategy. If 'buy and hold' strategy offers a superior return than the returns offered by the investment strategy following filter rule, it supports the weak form efficient market hypothesis. If following filter rule offers a superior return, weak form efficient market hypothesis is negated.

Serial Correlation Test

Weak form efficient market hypothesis says that successive price changes are independent. Such independence in stock price movements can be tested by serial correlation test. In this test, a time interval is chosen and the changes in stock price during successive time intervals are noted by observing the stock prices at the beginning and at the end of each time interval. The correlation between the price changes in the successive time intervals are arrived at and studied. The correlation is measured by correlation coefficient which can take values between –1.00 to +1.00. A positive value of correlation coefficient between two successive price changes indicates that there is a direct relationship between them and a negative correlation coefficient indicates absence of direct relationship. If the correlation coefficients between successive price changes are positive, it indicates that the price change during one period is dependent on the price change that has occurred during the preceding period. Such a situation negates weak form efficiency. If the correlation coefficients between successive price changes are negative, it indicates that the price change during one period is independent of the price change during the proceeding period and such a situation supports weak form efficiency. This is because weak form efficiency means that the price movements of stocks are independent of the past price movements/trends.

In 1964, Moore studied the correlation between price changes of stocks during one week with the price changes of the same stocks during the following week. The results of the study showed that there was no correlation between the price changes of successive weeks. There was no tendency to follow a price rise/fall in a particular week, in the succeeding week. In other words, the price changes in a particular week did not show any significant dependence on the price changes in the previous week. Thus, the results supported the weak form efficiency of stock market which says that future price trends cannot be predicted by analyzing the past price data.

Run Test

Randomness in stock price movements can be tested by run test. Run test ignores the absolute values of price changes, but considers only the direction of price change. An increase in the price, is represented by a '+' sign, while a decrease in the price is represented by a '–' sign. When the price does not change, it is represented by '0'. A 'run' is a set of consecutive prices of the same sign.

Let the following are the prices of a particular stock at different points of time (say, the daily price changes).

100, 102, 104, 100, 99, 80, 103, 106, 101, 100, 95, 97, 104, 104, 102, 105

If we assign +, – and 0 signs starting from the price of Rs. 100, the following will be the pattern of price movement

+ + – – – + + – – – + + **0** – +

(The first + represents the price of Rs. 102. (+) sign is given since the price has increased from the starting price of Rs. 100)

Thus, a (+) sign indicates that the stock price under consideration has increased compared to its preceding price and a (–) sign indicates that the price under consideration has decreased compared to its preceding price.

The second + sign indicate that the price has increased from 102 to 104. Since, the price has fallen from 104 to 100, it is indicated by a (–) sign and so on.

In the above example, the price changes in 15 days are recorded. The price changes during the 15 days represented by +, – and 0 signs has 8 "runs".

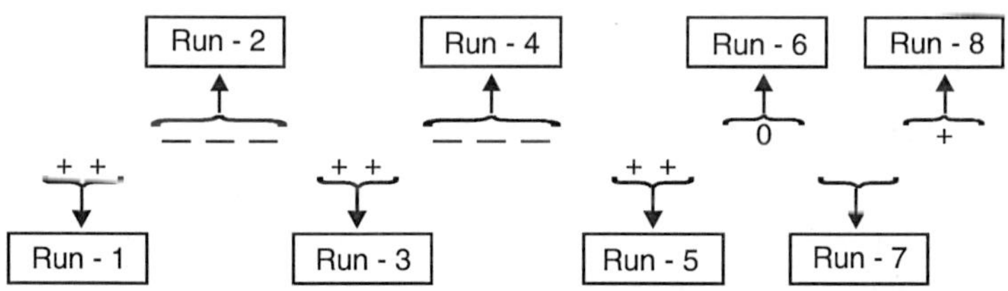

Having obtained the 'runs' contained in a price series, the number of runs contained in a randomly generated number series is compared with the number of runs contained in the price series. In the example given above, random number is to be selected between 80 (the least value) and 105 (the highest value). A set of 16 random numbers are selected between 80 and 105 (both inclusive). Let the following are the random numbers selected.

93, 97, 102, 100, 101, 105, 98, 93, 101, 104, 100, 96, 95, 98, 100, 99.

The number of runs contained in the random number series is 8.

+ + – + + – – + + – – – + + –

(The first + sign represents the number 97. (+) sign is given since there is an increase in value from 93)

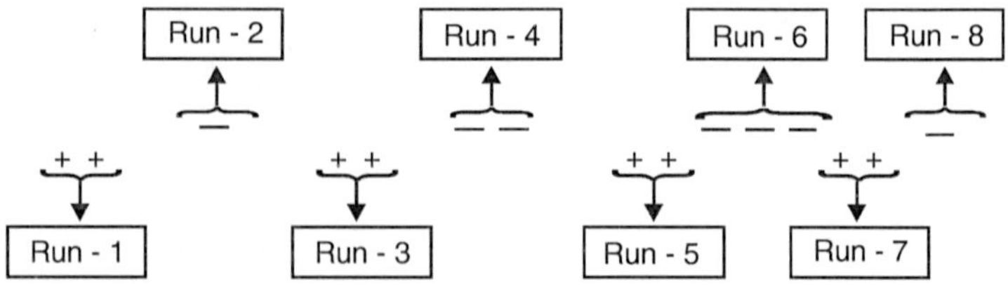

The random number series also has 8 runs. If this is so, it can be concluded that the changes in security prices are random and has no dependence on the previous prices/price changes. As against 8 runs contained in the random number series, if the series of price changes has only, say 3 runs, it indicates dependence of price change on the past prices and randomness of price changes is negated which rejects weak form efficient market hypothesis. As long as no significant difference is noted between the 'run' contained in the price series and in the random number series, it can be taken that the weak form efficient market hypothesis is valid. [For ascertaining the relationship between the number of runs contained in the stock price movements and the number of runs contained in the random number series and to find out if there is significant difference between the two, the number of 'runs' contained in the two series are statistically tested. Please refer to a book on statistical methods to know how to ascertain 'significant difference' in run test].

7.2.3. Test for Semi Strong Form Market Efficiency

Semi strong efficient market hypothesis holds that the market prices of securities adjust "quickly" to new publicly available information and hence it is not possible to earn superior returns based on such information.

According to semi strong form of efficient market hypothesis, the current prices of stocks represent the past price record of the stocks as well as all publicly available information about the company whose stocks are being studied.

To test whether a capital market is semi strong efficient, any publicly available information is chosen and its impact over the share price is measured. The expected share price due to the impact of an event [i.e., a public information like future changes in earnings, capital structure, dividends, etc.] is calculated. If the actual share prices immediately after the public information is made available and the expected share price calculated are the same it indicates that the market is efficient in semi strong form. When the market is semi strong efficient, an investor cannot earn superior returns on the basis of any publicly available information as the share prices adjust to the new publicly available information quickly and efficiently. On the other hand, if for example the actual share price after the availability of a public information is below the expected share price, it gives scope for an investor to earn superior returns and the semi strong form of market efficiency will get negated.

The results of many tests conducted by pioneers in the field of stock market analysis have gone to prove strong empirical support for the semi strong efficient market hypothesis.

7.2.4. Test for Strong Form Market Efficiency

The strong form market efficiency is concerned with whether or not certain individuals who have access to inside information can use such information to earn above average profits.

Studies conducted by expects reveal that strong form efficient market hypothesis is not strictly true. A few investment analysts or firms of advisers have been found to gain above-average returns on the basis of inside information about companies. This result also supports the logical reasoning that as long as information is not wholly free, those who have access to such information can earn excess returns by virtue of their exposure to such information.

Contradictory results are also available with regard to strong form market efficiency. If a market is not efficient in the strong form, mutual funds are expected to earn a better return than an individual investor since they are likely to have excess inside information than individuals. However, results of studies on the performance of mutual funds show that mutual funds have not performed better than randomly constructed portfolios of similar risk. This supports the argument that the market is efficient in the strong form also.

Though such contradictory results are available about strong form efficiency, the following can be inferred.

(*a*) Mutual funds have not been able to earn superior returns by using the additional information available to them. This means that these so called 'additional' information is also available to the market as a whole and hence mutual funds could not earn superior returns. This support the strong form efficiency of market.

(*b*) Despite the failure of mutual funds to earn excess returns, few analysts/advisers have been found to earn excess returns. This might be due to the availability of really 'inside' information to them that are not available either to the public or to the mutual funds. This negates the strong form efficiency of market.

Hence, it can be concluded that the market cannot be efficient in strong form and there always remains scope for earning excess returns on the basis of inside information.

7.2.5. Efficient Market Hypothesis—An Overview

Different views prevail as to whether capital market is efficient or not. Controversy still prevails over market efficiency. There are supporter's infavour of efficient market and also there are critics against efficient market. That is why both the terminologies 'Efficient Market Theory' and 'Efficient Market Hypothesis' are found in the literature of stock market analysis. Those who believe that the market is fully efficient even in its strong form, argue that the efficient market hypothesis has been proved and has become a theory. Those who negate the efficient market (in one form or the other) argue that the hypothesis remains yet to be proved and hence continues to remain only as a hypothesis. The weak form of efficient market hypothesis contradicts technical analysis. The semi strong form of efficient market hypothesis contradicts fundamental analysis. The strong form of efficient market hypothesis holds that 'no body' can earn excess return by virtue of information or by the aid of analysis of any type.

While fundamental and technical analysis appears to have relevance on their own strength and capacity, the efficient market hypothesis repudiates both. The paradox of efficient market hypothesis can be solved if it is understood that the market is efficient only because of the efforts of fundamental analysts and technical analysts in their pursuit to earn superior returns. But for their influence over the stock market, the market cannot remain efficient.

REVIEW QUESTIONS

1. List down the postulates of Random Walk theory.
2. What is Efficient Market Hypothesis?
3. What are the three forms of market efficiency? Explain them in brief.
4. What are the tests used for testing the weak form efficiency of market? Explain any one test in detail.
5. 'Stock Market cannot be efficient in strong form and there always remains hope for earning excess returns on the basis of insider information'. Offer your comments on this statement.

8

CHAPTER

Portfolio Analysis and Construction

8.1. INTRODUCTION

The term portfolio refers to a collection of securities. Investors rarely invest their money in a single security. They invest in few selected securities. The objective of investing in more than one security is to ensure that the loss that might be incurred in a few securities would be compensated by the gain earned in the other securities. The performance of a portfolio of securities will depend upon the performance of the individual securities that constitute the portfolio. What is the reason for investing in a number of different securities instead of in one particular security? Yes, you have guessed the reason. It is to minimize risk. In other words, it is meant to spread the risk by not putting all eggs in one basket.

The risk bearing capacity of investors differ. One may prefer to take a higher risk in anticipation of a higher return. Another investor who is very much risk averse may settle for a lower risk and will be contended with a lower return. Thus, the range of securities (i.e., portfolio) in which an investor invests his money varies according to the risk bearing capacity of the investor.

Hence, in order to achieve the objectives of investing in a portfolio of securities rather than in a single security, the securities contained in the portfolio should be carefully selected. Thus, a portfolio is not merely a collection of securities chosen for investment, but a collection carefully chosen securities of different kinds, that matches the risk bearing capacity of the investor.

8.2. PORTFOLIO ANALYSIS

A number of portfolios can be constructed by choosing different securities from among the securities available for investment. Each such portfolio will have its own risk-return characteristic depending upon the nature of securities contained in the portfolio and the proportion of investment made in each of the securities. Thus, we must know as to how to analyse a portfolio critically with regard to its risk-return characteristic. This step is called portfolio analysis.

Portfolio analysis consists of two phases. The first phase is the construction of an optional portfolio and the second phase is the periodical evaluation of the portfolio to ensure that the portfolio continues to remain as an optimal portfolio.

After an analysis of the securities is done, the risk-return characteristics of the securities are known. Then, the investor selects a range of desirable securities (according to his risk-bearing capacity) and constructs a portfolio of securities. This, however is not an easy task as it may appear to be. After the investor has identified a few desirable securities from among the available securities, the next thing to be done is to decide upon the proportions of investments to be made in the identified securities. A portfolio so selected will have its own risk-return characteristic. Another portfolio if constructed by varying the proportion of investments in the identified securities will have a different risk-return characteristic. Thus, the task of constructing an optimal portfolio involves an analysis of all possible portfolios that can be constructed by varying the proportions of investments in the different identified securities. Thus, the risk-return characteristic of a portfolio varies based on two factors, viz.

(*a*) The risk-return characteristics of the individual securities in the portfolio.

(*b*) The proportions of investments in the different securities contained in the portfolio.

We have seen that a prudent investor constructs an optimal portfolio of securities for his investment. We also know that the risk-bearing capacity of investors differ.

How to construct an optimal portfolio? Portfolio management theory gives answer to this question.

An investor can combine the different securities available in different proportions to suit his tastes and preferences. This itself will result in a large number of portfolios. If all the securities available in the market are combined in various groups and in varying proportions, we will get a very large number of portfolios. All such portfolios put together is called the *feasible set* of portfolios. It means that theoretically these are the portfolios that can be constructed by combining the available securities. The feasible set will contain both efficient and inefficient portfolios.

What is an efficient portfolio? Between two or more portfolios, the portfolio that offers a higher return for the same level of risk or the portfolio that has a lower level of risk for the same level of return is called an *efficient portfolio*. When we consider all the portfolios in the feasible set (also called portfolio opportunity set) as a whole, efficient portfolios are those

(*a*) that offer *the maximum return* for a given level of risk (or)

(*b*) that have *the minimum level of risk* for a given return.

Thus, there will be many efficient portfolios, i.e., those portfolios that provide the maximum return for a given level of risk or the minimum risk for a given return. From among the efficient portfolios the investor has to choose an optimal portfolio for his investment that suits his risk bearing capacity. Modern portfolio theory gives a conceptual framework and analytical tools for the identification of efficient portfolios and for the identification of the optimal portfolio.

8.3. COMPONENTS OF PORTFOLIO MANAGEMENT

As we have already discussed, portfolio management consists of analysis of individual securities that constitute the portfolio and also analysis of the portfolio itself. Thus, portfolio management consists of the following components:

(*a*) Security Analysis

(*b*) Portfolio Analysis

Portfolio analysis consists of the following three stages:

(*i*) Construction of an optimal portfolio of securities.

(*ii*) Periodical evaluation of the portfolio.

(*iii*) Revision of the portfolio as and when warranted.

8.4. TRADITIONAL PORTFOLIO THEORY

In the early days, portfolio analysis was done on the basis of the traditional portfolio theory. The traditional theory was based on the assumption that investment can be made by analyzing the securities individually. This theory believed that the market was not fully efficient and hence fundamental analysis could help in identifying the securities suitable for investment. No doubt the traditional theory supported combination of securities as a measure to diversify risk. However, the interrelationship between the different securities in the portfolio was not given the required attention. There was only a broad, ill defined, vague study of the interrelationship among the securities. For example, growth in agriculture is reflected in the growth of fertiliser industry as well as pesticides industry. Thus, fertiliser stocks were recognized as risk-related with pesticide stocks. Similarly, cement stocks were recognised as risk-related with stocks of construction industry. Though the traditional analysts only relied upon such broad parameters, it does not mean that the traditional analysts were totally unsuccessful in their analysis. They did achieve good results but much of their analysis was based on intuition and they could not explain their mode of analysis/interpretation objectively.

8.5. MODERN PORTFOLIO THEORY

The basic concept behind Modern Portfolio Theory (MPT) is that the assets (or securities) in a portfolio of investments cannot be selected individually based on the merits if the individual securities alone. According to MPT, what is important is to see how the price of each security in the portfolio changes relative to the change in the price of other securities in the portfolio.

Modern portfolio theory is based on a few basic concepts on the behaviour of investors. Harry Markowitz was the first who studied critically the effect of combining securities in his article "Portfolio selection" in the Journal of finance (1952), Markowitz developed a basic portfolio model and derived the expected rate of return for a portfolio of assets with an expected risk measure. In his book "Portfolio selection: Efficient diversification of investments" (John Willey Sons, New York, 1959) he explained the utility of diversification of investments in building up a portfolio. The portfolio selection based on the method proposed by Markowitz is known as Markowitz model. Markowitz model marks the beginning of Modern Portfolio Theory. Markowitz theory aims to build the most efficient portfolio by combining securities of different risk-return characteristics. The most efficient portfolio is one that offers the highest return for the given level of risk or the one that has the smallest risk for the given level of return.

8.5.1. Markowitz Portfolio Theory

The following are the assumptions behind the Markowitz portfolio theory:

(*a*) Investors are risk averse. (This means that given a choice between two securities that offer equal return, an investor will only choose the security with lower level of risk; given a choice between two securities of equal risk, an investor will only choose the one that offers higher return).

(*b*) Investors have full facts about all the securities in the market. (This means that the market is efficient).

(*c*) Investors estimate risk on the basis of variability of expected returns. (This means that either the standard deviation or the variance of the returns offer an estimate of the risk involved in securities).

(*d*) Investors take decisions to invest in securities only based on two factors, viz., the expected risk and the expected return.

(*e*) Investors have homogeneous expectations of risk and return. (This means that all investors estimate the risk-return characteristics of securities identically).

(*f*) Investors have identical time horizon. (This means that all investors have a single common terminal date; they hold their securities till such time and their dispose them off).

Based on the above assumptions, a single security or a portfolio of securities is considered to be an efficient one if no other security/portfolio of securities offers higher expected return with same (or lower) level of risk or lower risk with the same (or higher) level of expected return.

8.5.2. The Effect of Combining Securities

It was Markowitz who first made an analytical study of the effect of combining securities. (He emphasized that the portfolio should be analysed in its entirety and that analysis of individual securities contained in the portfolio, in isolation will not be of help). Markowitz pointed out that the covariance of the returns from securities would help in knowing the risk due to combining securities. When the covariance of returns between two securities is positive, it means that the interactive risk is positive i.e., the rates of return of the two securities will move together either upwards or downwards. Similarily, when the covariance of returns between two securities is negative, it means that the interactive risk is negative, i.e., the rates of return of the two securities will move in the opposite directions. If the rates of return from the two securities are independent, the covariance will be zero. While covariance is an absolute measure of the relationship between the returns of two securities, correlation coefficient is a relative measure and is more amenable for analysis and interpretation. The correlation coefficient can take values from + 1.00 to – 1.00. When there is perfect positive correlation between the returns from two securities, the correlation coefficient is + 1.00. When there is perfect negative correlation between the returns from two securities, the correlation coefficient is – 1.00. A correlation coefficient of 0.00 indicates that there is no correlation between the returns from the two securities.

8.5.3. Portfolio Return

The expected rate of return from a portfolio of securities is simply equal to the weighted average of the expected rates of returns from the individual securities contained in the portfolio, weight being the proportion of the funds invested in a security to the total funds invested in the portfolio.

***Illustration* 8.1:**

A portfolio has four securities and the expected returns from the four securities are as under:

$$r_1 = 15\%$$

$$r_2 = 12\%$$

$$r_3 = 14\%$$

$$r_4 = 20\%$$

The funds invested in the four securities are Rs. 2,00,000, Rs. 2,80,000, Rs. 3,20,000 and Rs. 4,00,000 respectively. Find the expected return from the portfolio.

Solution:

Security	Expected return %	Funds invested (Rs.)	Weight	(Expected return) × (Weight)
1	15	2,00,000	2 ÷ 12 = 0.167	2.505%
2	12	2,80,000	2.80 ÷ 12 = 0.233	2.796%
3	14	3,20,000	3.20 ÷ 12 = 0.267	3.738%
4	20	4,00,000	4 ÷ 12 = 0.333	6.660%
		Σ = 12,00,000	1.00	15.699% (or) 15.70%

Therefore expected return from the portfolio = 15.70%

8.5.4. Covariance and Correlation Coefficient of Returns between Two Stocks

The following two illustrations will help to have a better understanding of the concepts of covariance and correlation coefficient of returns between two stocks, (refer Chapter-2 for explanation of the concepts of covariance and correlation coefficient).

***Illustration* 8.2:**

The monthly returns offered by two stocks A & B over a period of 12 months are as given below.

Month	Rate of return offered by stock – A (%)	Rate of return offered by stock – B (%)
January 2001	4.00	5.00
February 2001	5.00	8.00
March 2001	7.00	7.00
April 2001	6.00	9.00
May 2001	6.00	8.00
June 2001	4.00	7.00
July 2001	6.00	7.00
August 2001	7.00	8.00
September 2001	8.00	9.00
October 2001	8.00	12.00
November 2001	6.00	10.00
December 2001	5.00	9.00

Calculate the covariance of the returns and offer your comments.

Solution:

Let x = return from stock–A

y = return from stock–B

Arithmetic average of
return from stock–A(x) = (4 + 5 + 7 + ... 5) ÷ 12

= 6.00%

Arithmetic average of
return from stock–B(y) = (5 + 8 + 7 + ... 9) ÷ 12

= 8.25%

$$\text{Covariance } (\text{Cov}_{x,y}) = \frac{\Sigma(x-\overline{x})(y-\overline{y})}{N}$$

Month	x	y	$(x-\overline{x})$	$(y-\overline{y})$	$(x-\overline{x})^2$	$(y-\overline{y})^2$	$(x-\overline{x})\cdot(y-\overline{y})$
1	4.00	5.00	–2.00	–3.25	4.00	10.5625	6.50
2	5.00	8.00	–1.00	–0.25	1.00	0.0625	0.25
3	7.00	7.00	1.00	–1.25	1.00	1.5625	–1.25
4	6.00	9.00	0.00	0.75	0.00	0.5625	0.00
5	6.00	8.00	0.00	–0.25	0.00	0.0625	0.00
6	4.00	7.00	–2.00	–1.25	4.00	1.5625	2.50
7	6.00	7.00	0.00	–1.25	0.00	1.5625	0.00
8	7.00	8.00	1.00	–0.25	1.00	0.0625	–0.25
9	8.00	9.00	2.00	0.75	4.00	0.5625	1.50
10	8.00	12.00	2.00	3.75	4.00	14.0625	7.50
11	6.00	10.00	0.00	1.75	0.00	3.0625	0.00
12	5.00	9.00	–1.00	0.75	1.00	0.5625	–0.75
				Σ =	20.00	34.250	16.00

Note: *The values of* $(x - \overline{x})^2$ *and* $(y - \overline{y})^2$ *are not required for solving this problem. But, they are required for arriving at "Standard Deviation" and these values are made use of in illustration 8.3.*

$$\text{Covariance} = \frac{16.00}{12}$$

$$= 1.33$$

The movement of returns from stock–A and stock–B are plotted in Fig. 8.1.

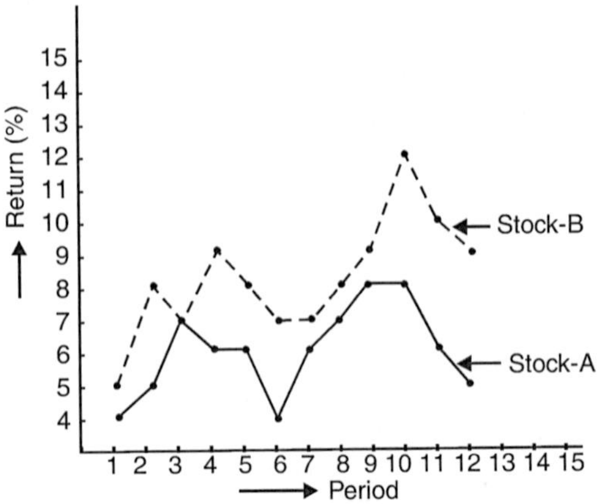

Fig. 8.1 Movements of returns from two stocks over time

Figure 8.1 indicates that there is a positive correlation between the returns of stock–A and that of stock–B. However, interpretation of the value of covariance is a difficult thing since covariance is an absolute value. It cannot be said whether the covariance value of 1.33 is small or big in magnitude.

***Illustration* 8.2:**

Arrive at the covariance of returns from stocks *A* and *B* and offer your comments.

Month	Rate of return offered by stock–A (%)	Rate of return offered by stock–B (%)
1	4.00	5.00
2	5.00	8.00
3	7.00	7.00
4	6.25	9.00
5	6.25	8.00
6	4.00	7.00
7	6.25	7.00
8	7.00	8.00
9	8.00	9.00
10	8.00	12.00
11	6.25	10.00
12	5.00	9.00

Solution:

Arithmetic average of return from stock–A($\bar{x}$) $= (4 + 5 + 7 \; + \ldots 5) \div 12$
$= 6.083\%$

Arithmetic average of return from stock–B($\bar{y}$) $= (5 + 8 + 7 + \ldots 9) \div 12$
$= 10.00\%$

$$\text{Covariance } (\text{Cov}_{x,y}) = \frac{\Sigma(x - \bar{x})(y - \bar{y})}{N}$$

Month	x	y	$(x-\bar{x})$	$(y-\bar{y})$	$(x-\bar{x})^2$	$(y-\bar{y})^2$	$(x-\bar{x})(y-\bar{y})$
1	4.00	5.00	– 2.083	– 5.00	4.3389	25.00	10.415
2	5.00	8.00	– 1.083	– 2.00	1.1729	4.00	2.166
3	7.00	15.00	0.917	5.00	0.8409	25.00	4.585
4	6.25	9.00	0.167	– 1.00	0.0279	1.00	– 0.167
5	6.25	14.00	0.167	4.00	0.0279	16.00	0.668
6	4.00	7.00	– 2.083	– 3.00	4.3389	9.00	6.249
7	6.25	7.00	0.167	– 3.00	0.0279	9.00	– 0.501
8	7.00	8.00	0.917	– 2.00	0.8409	4.00	– 1.834
9	8.00	12.00	1.917	2.00	3.6749	4.00	3.834
10	8.00	14.00	1.917	4.00	3.6749	16.00	7.668
11	6.25	12.00	0.167	2.00	0.0279	4.00	0.334
12	5.00	9.00	– 1.083	1.00	1.729	1.00	1.083
				Σ –	20.7229	118.00	34.50

Note: *The values of* $(x - x)^2$ *&* $(y - y)^2$ *are not required for solving this problem. But, they are required for arriving at "Standard Deviation" and these values are made use of in illustration 8.3.*

$$\text{Covariance} = \frac{34.50}{12}$$
$$= 2.875$$

The movement of returns from stock–A & stock–B are plotted in Fig. 8.2.

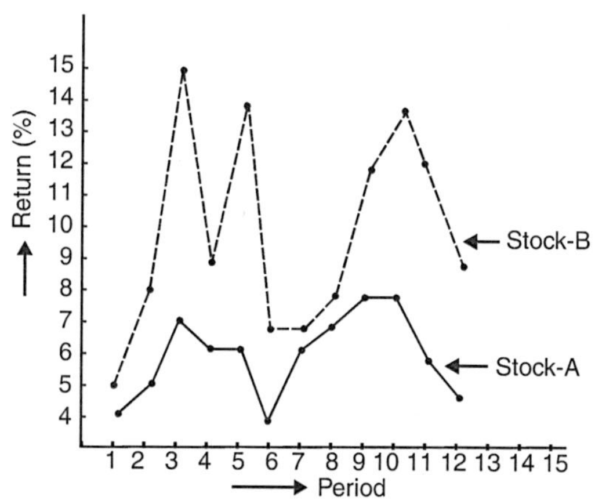

Fig. 8.2 Movements of returns from two stocks over time

The value of covariance of 2.875 between the returns of stocks 'A' and 'B' does not indicate whether the correlation is small or big. In illustration 8.1 we have arrived at a covariance of 1.33. The value of covariance arrived at in the present illustration is 2.875. Can it be said that the correlation between the returns of stock-A & stock-B as given in illustration 8.2 is almost twice as better as that of illustration 8.1? No, it can't be said so since the covariance is only an absolute figure. The only thing that can be inferred is that since covariance is a positive number, the correlation between the two variables is positive. For comparing the degree of correlation, correlation coefficient will be of use.

***Illustration* 8.3:**

Compare the correlation coefficients between the returns of stocks 'A and 'B' given in illustrations 8.1 and 8.2 and offer your comments.

Solution:

For the data given in illustration 8.1 the coefficient of correlation is arrived at as under.

$$\text{Standard deviation of return from stock–A}(\sigma_x) = \sqrt{\frac{\Sigma(x-\overline{x})^2}{N}}$$

$$= \sqrt{\frac{20}{12}}$$

$$= 1.291$$

$$\text{Standard deviation of return from stock –B}(\sigma_y) = \sqrt{\frac{\Sigma(y-\overline{y})^2}{N}}$$

$$= \sqrt{\frac{34.25}{12}}$$

$$= 1.689$$

Covariance ($Cov_{x,y}$) = 1.33 (as already arrived at illustration 8.1)

$$\text{Correlation coefficient } (\gamma_{x,y}) = \frac{(Cov_{x,y})}{\sigma_x \times \sigma_y}$$

$$= \frac{1.33}{(1.291)\times(1.689)}$$

$$= 0.61$$

For the data given in illustration 8.2, the coefficient of correlation is arrived at as under.

$$\text{Standard deviation of return from stock–A}(\sigma_x) = \sqrt{\frac{\Sigma(x-\overline{x})^2}{N}}$$

$$= \sqrt{\frac{20.7229}{12}}$$

$$= 1.314$$

Standard deviation of return from stock–B(σ_y) $= \sqrt{\frac{\Sigma(y-\overline{y})^2}{N}}$

$$= \sqrt{\frac{118}{12}}$$

$$= 3.136$$

Covariance ($Cov_{x,y}$) = 2.875 (as already arrived at in illustration 8.2)

Correlation coefficient ($\gamma_{x,y}$) $= \frac{(Cov_{x,y})}{\sigma_x \times \sigma_y}$

$$= \frac{2.875}{(1.314 \times 3.136)}$$

$$= 0.698$$

Comment

While the covariance of the returns from stock–A & stock–B for the data given in illustrations 8.1 & 8.2 are 1.33 & 2.875 respectively, the respective correlation coefficients are 0.61 & 0.698. The values of the coefficient of correlation indicate that the correlation is positive for both the cases. The returns from stock–A & stock–B as given in the data in illustration 8.2 are more positively correlated than for the data given in illustration 8.1. Since coefficient of correlation is a relative measure, we can say that the positive correlation for the data in illustration 8.2 is about 9% higher than the positive correlation for the data in illustration 8.1. Thus, the extent of correlation between two sets of data can be measured using correlation coefficient.

8.5.5. Standard Deviation of Portfolio Return

The standard deviation of portfolio return can not be arrived at by simply taking the weighted average of the standard deviation of the returns of the securities contained in the portfolio.

Let there are 'n' securities contained in a portfolio.

Let $w_1, w_2, w_3, ..., w_n$ are the weights of the 'n' securities

Let $\sigma_1, \sigma_2, \sigma_3, ..., \sigma_n$ are the standard deviation of returns of the 'n' securities.

Let $Cov_{i,j}$ is the covariance between the returns of securities 'i' and 'j'.

Markowitz derived a general formula for the standard deviation of the portfolio return as under.

$$\sigma_{(port)}^{*} = \sqrt{\sum_{i=1}^{n}\sum_{j=1}^{n} w_i w_j \text{Cov}_{i,j}}$$

The above formula indicates that the standard deviation of portfolio return is a function of the weighted average of the variances of the individual securities contained in the portfolio and two times the weighted covariances between all the securities in the portfolio.

Variance of portfolio return is given by,

$$\sigma^2_{(port)} = \sum_{i=1}^{n}\sum_{j=1}^{n} w_i w_j \text{Cov}_{i,j}$$

For a two asset portfolio, the portfolio variance is given by

$$\sigma^2_{(port)} = w_1^{\,2}\,\sigma_1^{\,2} + w_2^{\,2}\,\sigma_2^{\,2} + 2w_1\,w_2\,\text{Cov}_{1,2}$$

Note: $Cov_{1,2} = \sigma_1\,\sigma_2\,\gamma_{1,2}$

Where $Cov_{1,2}$ = *Covariance between returns from the two assets (or Securities)*

(i.e., assets '1' and '2')

$\gamma_{1,2}$ = *Coefficient of correlation between the returns from the two assets*

8.5.6. Two Asset Portfolio

The portfolio variance** for a two asset portfolio can be written in a box form for easy understanding as under.

	1	2
1	$w_1^2\,\sigma_1^2$	$w_1\,w_2\,\text{Cov}_{1,2}$
2	$w_1\,w_2\,\text{Cov}_{1,2}$	$w_2^2\,\sigma_2^2$

The sum of the expressions contained in the box gives the variance of the portfolio.

$$\sigma^2_{(port)} = w_1^{\,2}\,\sigma_1^{\,2} + w_2^{\,2}\,\sigma_2^{\,2} + 2w_1\,w_2\,\text{Cov}_{1,2}$$

8.5.7. *n*-Asset Portfolio

Similarly, for a n-asset portfolio, the portfolio variance can be obtained by summing up the expressions in all the ($n \times n$) boxes given below.

* *Markowitz, "portfolio selection", Journal of finance No.7, Vol.1, March 1952.*

(** by portfolio variance we mean the variance of the portfolio return)

	1	2	3	—	n
1	$w_1^2 \sigma_1^2$	$w_1\, w_2\, Cov_{1,2}$	$w_1\, w_3\, Cov_{1,3}$	—	$w_1\, w_n\, Cov_{1,n}$
2	$w_2\, w_1\, Cov_{2,1}$	$w_2\, \sigma_2^2$	$w_2\, w_3\, Cov_{2,3}$	—	$w_2\, w_n\, Cov_{2,n}$
3	$w_3\, w_1\, Cov_{3,1}$	$w_3\, w_2\, Cov_{3,2}$	$w_3^2\, \sigma_3^2$	—	$w_3\, w_n\, Cov_{3,n}$
—	—	—	—	—	—
N	$w_n\, w_1\, Cov_{n,1}$	$w_n\, w_2\, Cov_{n,2}$	$w_n\, w_3\, Cov_{n,3}$	—	$w_n^2\, \sigma_n^2$

For a n-asset portfolio, $\sigma^2_{(port)}$

$$= \sum_{i=1}^{n} \sum_{j=1}^{n} w_i\, w_j\, \mathrm{Cov}_{i,j}$$

$$= \sum_{i=1}^{n} \sum_{j=1}^{n} w_i\, w_j\, \gamma_{i,j}\, \sigma_i \sigma_j$$

8.6. EXPECTED RETURN FOR AN INDIVIDUAL RISKY SECURITY

The past trends of returns offered by a security may indicate that the security is a risky one. If we take the arithmetic mean of the past returns, it will only indicate how the security has performed in the past. To know the return that the security is expected to offer in future, probability estimate of the returns likely to be offered is made. For arriving at the probability estimate, the past data will be of use. A sample probability estimate is given below.

Probability	Potential return
0.10	8%
0.25	10%
0.25	12%
0.25	14%
0.15	16%

The above probability estimate gives five probable rates of return with different probabilities. The expected return from the security is arrived at by multiplying the potential returns with their respective probabilities and adding them all.

Probability	Potential return	Expected return	
0.10	8%	0.10 × 8 =	0.80
0.25	10%	0.25 × 10 =	2.50
0.25	12%	0.25 × 12 =	3.00
0.25	14%	0.25 × 14 =	3.50
0.15	16%	0.15 × 16 =	2.40
		Expected return	**12.20%**

8.7. VARIANCE OF RETURN FOR AN INDIVIDUAL RISKY SECURITY

We have arrived at an expected return of 12.20% for a risky security on the basis of the given probability estimate of potential returns.

Consider the following example:

Probability	Potential return	Expected return
0.80	12%	0.80 × 12 = 9.60
0.20	13%	0.20 × 13 = 2.60
	Expected return	**12.20%**

The security given above also offers an expected return of 12.20% but its probability estimates are different and comparatively this is a less risky security as seen from the probability estimates of returns. Thus, though the expected returns of two securities may be the same, their riskiness may differ. The risk contained in an individual security can be measured at in terms of its variance or standard deviation.

Let us arrive at the variance and standard deviation of the two securities shown above.

Potential return (r_i)	Expected return (r_e)	($r_i - r_e$)	$(r_i - r_e)^2$	Probability (p_i)	$(r_i - r_e)^2(p_i)$
0.08	0.122	–0.042	0.001764	0.10	0.0001764
0.10	0.122	–0.022	0.000484	0.25	0.0001210
0.12	0.122	–0.002	0.000004	0.25	0.0000010
0.14	0.122	0.018	0.000324	0.25	0.0000810
0.16	0.122	0.038	0.001444	0.15	0.0002166
					0.000596
Variance (σ^2) = 0.000596 Standard deviation (σ) = 0.024413					

Potential return (r_i)	Expected return (r_e)	($r_i - r_e$)	($r_i - r_e)^2$	Probability (p_i)	($r_i - r_e)^2$ (p_i)
0.12	0.122	0.002	0.000004	0.80	0.0000032
0.13	0.122	0.008	0.000064	0.20	0.0000128
					0.0000160
Variance (σ^2) = 0.0000160 Standard deviation (σ) = 0.004					

As seen from the above two tables, the security that shows higher fluctuation in potential returns exhibit higher risk and this is revealed by the higher values of variance/standard deviation. Though the expected returns of the two securities discussed above are the same (viz., 12.20%), their variances and standard deviations differ. The security that exhibits a higher variance (or standard deviation) has comparatively higher level of risk associated with it.

8.8. TWO ASSET PORTFOLIO WITH THE ASSETS HAVING THE SAME EXPECTED RETURNS THE SAME STANDARD DEVIATION

Let there are two securities, security–A & security–B that offer expected returns of 15% p.a. Let the standard deviation of return of these two securities are 0.20 each. Hence, the two securities have the same level of risk and offer the same level of return. However, when these two securities are combined, the combination will have a different risk pattern based on the correlation of returns between the two securities.

Let us construct a portfolio with these two securities having equal weights. The correlation coefficient between the two securities may take any value from –1.00 to +1.00. Let us assume the following five values for the correlation coefficient and study the risk level of the portfolio.

(*a*) Correlation coefficient $(\gamma_{A,B})$ = 1.00

(*b*) Correlation coefficient $(\gamma_{A,B})$ = 0.50

(*c*) Correlation coefficient $(\gamma_{A,B})$ = 0.00

(*d*) Correlation coefficient $(\gamma_{A,B})$ = – 0.50

(*e*) Correlation coefficient $(\gamma_{A,B})$ = – 1.00

(*a*) **Portfolio of securities A & B each having equal weight in the portfolio and $\gamma_{A,B}$ = 1.00**

Weight of security–A in the portfolio = 0.50

Weight of security–B in the portfolio = 0.50

Standard deviation of security–A = 0.20

Standard deviation of security–B = 0.20

Coefficient of correlation between security–A & security–B = 1.00

Variance of the portfolio (σ^2_{port}) $= w_1{}^2\sigma_1{}^2 + w_2{}^2\sigma_2{}^2 + 2w_1w_2\,\text{Cov}_{1,\,2}$

If one of the securities is referred as 'A' and the other as 'B',

$$\sigma^2_{(port)} = w_A{}^2\,\sigma_A{}^2 + w_B{}^2\,\sigma_B{}^2 + 2w_A\,w_B\,\text{Cov}_{A,B}$$

We know that,

$$\gamma_{AB} = \frac{\text{Cov}_{A,B}}{\sigma_A \cdot \sigma_B}$$

Therefore $Cov_{A,B} = \gamma_{A,B} (\sigma_A.\sigma_B)$

$= 1.00(0.20 \times 0.20)$

$= 0.04$

$$\sigma^2_{(port)} = w_A{}^2 \, \sigma_A{}^2 + w_B{}^2 \, \sigma_B{}^2 + 2w_A \, w_B \, Cov_{A,B}$$

Substituting the values:

$$\sigma^2_{(port)} = (0.5^2 \times 0.2^2) + (0.5^2 \times 0.2^2) + (2 \times 0.5 \times 0.5 \times 0.04)$$

$$= 0.01 + 0.01 + 0.02$$

$$= 0.04$$

Standard deviation of the portfolio $\sigma_{(port)} = \sqrt{0.04}$

$= 0.20$

Result

The standard deviation of the portfolio is equal to the standard deviation of the individual securities (i.e., 0.20). This means that the portfolio of two securities has the same level of risk as the two individual securities. This leads to the conclusion that when the coefficient of correlation between the return from two securities is equal to +1.00, there is no real benefit in combining the two securities since the risk level of the portfolio does not get reduced. In other words, when the coefficient of correlation is +1.00, the standard deviation of the portfolio of two assets is simply equal to the weighted average of the individual standard deviation of the assets.

Instead of assuming equal weights to the two securities, let us assume a proportion of, say 80% to security 'A' and 20% to security 'B' (i.e., a weight of 0.80 to security 'A' and a weight of 0.20 for security 'B'). The portfolio variance will be given by,

$$\sigma^2_{(port)} = (0.8^2 \times 0.2^2) + (0.2^2 \times 0.2^2) + (2 \times 0.8 \times 0.2 \times 0.04)$$

$$= 0.0256 + 0.0016 + 0.0128$$

$$= 0.04$$

Standard Deviation of the portfolio is given by,

$$\sigma_{(port)} = \sqrt{0.04}$$

$$= 0.20$$

Thus, even after changing the weights, the portfolio Standard Deviation remains unchanged. *This proves that the portfolio standard deviation is simply the weighted average of the Standard Deviations of the securities contained in the portfolio.*

(*b*) Portfolio of securities A & B, each having equal weight in the portfolio and $\gamma_{A,B}$ = 0.50:

Weight of security–A in the portfolio = 0.50

Weight of security–B in the portfolio = 0.50

Standard deviation of security–A* = 0.20

Standard deviation of security–B = 0.20

Coefficient of correlation between returns of security–A and security–B = 0.50

$$\gamma_{A,B} = \frac{\text{Cov}_{A,B}}{\sigma_A \cdot \sigma_B}$$

Therefore $\text{Cov}_{A,B} = \gamma_{A,B} (\sigma_A \sigma_B)$

$= 0.50 (0.20 \times 0.20)$

$= 0.02$

$$\sigma^2_{(\text{port})} = w_A^{\ 2} \sigma_A^{\ 2} + w_B^{\ 2} \sigma_B^{\ 2} + 2w_A w_B \text{Cov}_{A,B}$$

Substituting the values,

$$\sigma^2_{(\text{port})} = (0.5^2 \times 0.2^2) + (0.5^2 \times 0.2^2) + (2 \times 0.5 \times 0.5 \times 0.02)$$

$= 0.01 + 0.01 + 0.01$

$= 0.03$

Standard deviation of the portfolio $\sigma_{(\text{port})} = \sqrt{0.03}$

$= 0.1732$

Result

The standard deviation of the portfolio is less than the standard deviation of the individual securities. As the coefficient of correlation has come down from 1.00 to 0.50, the standard deviation of the portfolio has come down from 0.20 to 0.1732.

(c) Portfolio of securities A & B, each having equal weight in the portfolio and $\gamma_{A,B} = 0.00$:

Weight of security–A in the portfolio = 0.50

Weight of security–B in the portfolio = 0.50

Standard deviation of security–A = 0.20

Standard deviation of security–B = 0.20

Coefficient of correlation between security–A & security–B = 0.00

$$\gamma_{A,B} = \frac{\text{Cov}_{A,B}}{\sigma_A \cdot \sigma_B}$$

Since $\gamma_{A,B} = 0$, $\text{Cov}_{A,B} = 0$

$$\sigma^2_{(\text{port})} = w_A^{\ 2} \sigma_A^{\ 2} + w_B^{\ 2} \sigma_B^{\ 2} + 2w_A w_B \text{Cov}_{A,B}$$

$= (0.5^2 \times 0.2^2) + (0.5^2 \times 0.2^2) + 0$

$= 0.01 + 0.01 = 0.02$

* By standard deviation of security–A, we mean standard deviation of returns from security–A

Standard deviation of the portfolio $\sigma_{(port)} = \sqrt{0.02}$

$= 0.1414$

Result

The standard deviation of the portfolio is less than the standard deviation of the individual securities. As the coefficient of correlation has come down from 0.50 to 0.00, the standard deviation of the portfolio has come down from 0.1732 to 0.1414.

(*d*) Portfolio of securities A & B, each having equal weight in the portfolio and $\gamma_{A,B} = -0.50$:

Weight of security–A in the portfolio = 0.50

Weight of security–B in the portfolio = 0.50

Standard deviation of security–A = 0.20

Standard deviation of security–B = 0.20

Coefficient of correlation between security–A & security–B = – 0.50.

$$\gamma_{A,B} = \frac{Cov_{A,B}}{\sigma_A \cdot \sigma_B}$$

$$\text{Therefore } Cov_{A,B} = (-0.50) \times [0.20 \times 0.20]$$

$$= -0.02$$

$$\sigma^2_{(port)} = w_A^{\ 2}\,\sigma_A^{\ 2} + w_B^{\ 2}\,\sigma_B^{\ 2} + 2w_A\,w_B\,Cov_{A,B}$$

$$= (0.5^2 \times 0.2^2) + (0.5^2 \times 0.2^2) + (2 \times 0.5 \times 0.5 \times -0.02)$$

$$= 0.01 + 0.01 + (-0.01)$$

$$= 0.01$$

Standard deviation of the portfolio $\sigma_{(port)} = \sqrt{0.01}$

$= 0.10$

Result

The standard deviation of the portfolio is less than the standard deviation of the individual securities. As the coefficient of correlation has come down from 0.00 to – 0.50, the standard deviation of the portfolio has come down from 0.1414 to 0.10.

(*e*) Portfolio of securities A & B, each having equal weight in the portfolio and $\gamma_{A,B} = -1.00$:

Weight of security–A in the portfolio = 0.50

Weight of security–B in the portfolio = 0.50

Standard deviation of security–A = 0.20

Standard deviation of security–B = 0.20

Coefficient of correlation between security–A & security–B = – 1.00

$$\gamma_{A,B} = \frac{Cov_{A,B}}{\sigma_A \cdot \sigma_B}$$

$$\text{Therefore } Cov_{A,B} = (-1.00) \times [0.20 \times 0.20]$$
$$= -0.04$$
$$\sigma^2_{(port)} = w_A^{\ 2}\, \sigma_A^{\ 2} + w_B^{\ 2}\, \sigma_B^{\ 2} + 2w_A\, w_B\, Cov_{A,\,B}$$
$$= (0.5^2 \times 0.2^2) + (0.5^2 \times 0.2^2) + (2 \times 0.5 \times 0.5 \times (-0.04))$$
$$= 0.01 + 0.01 + (-0.02)$$
$$= 0.00$$

Hence, Standard Deviation of the portfolio $[\sigma_{(port)}] = 0.00$

Result

The standard deviation of the portfolio has been reduced to zero i.e., the portfolio is risk-free. The maximum benefit of diversification has been obtained when the coefficient of correlation is – 1.00. The result of workings in (*a*) to (*e*) have been plotted in the graph shown below (Refer Fig. 8.3).

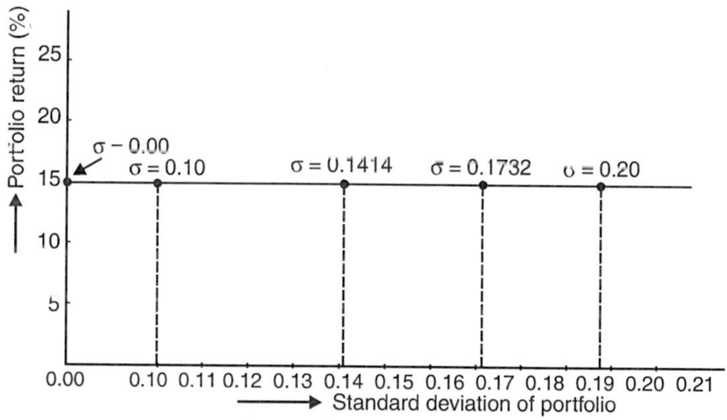

Fig. 8.3 Risk–return relationship of a two security portfolio with different correlations between the two securities

Interpretation of Results

(*i*) The expected return from the portfolio remains the same at 15%. This is because the individual securities have expected returns of 15% each and the securities have equal weight in the portfolio. Since the expected return from the portfolio is the weighted average of the expected returns from the securities, the expected return remains the same at 15% for all the five portfolios.

i.e., Expected portfolio return* $= w_A\gamma_A + w_B\gamma_B$
$= 0.5\ (15\%) + 0.5\ (15\%)$
$= 15\%$

(* the portfolio contains two securities 'A' and 'B' in equal proportion) (*ii*) When the coefficient of correlation is equal to + 1.00, there is no benefit due to diversification. Under such conditions (i.e., has $\gamma_{A,B}$ = 1.00), the standard deviation of the portfolio is equal to the weighted average of the standard deviation of the individual securities in the portfolio.

(*iii*) As the coefficient of correlation comes down from +1.00, there is reduction in portfolio standard deviation and when the value of coefficient of correlation reaches –1.00, the portfolio standard deviation is reduced to zero and the portfolio becomes a 'risk-free' one. This is because, when the correlation coefficient between two security returns is (–) 1.00, the fluctuations of returns above and below the mean for one security are completely offset by the fluctuations of returns below and above the mean of the other security (Ref. Fig. 8.4).

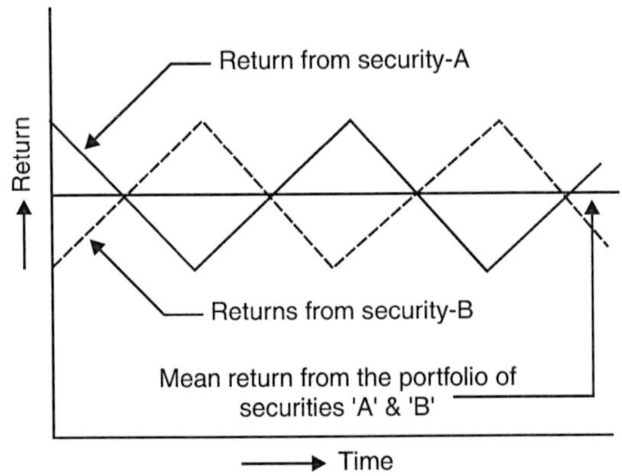

Fig. 8.4 Risk offset mechanism in a two security portfolio with coefficient of correlation equal to – 1.00

8.9. TWO ASSET PORTFOLIO WITH THE ASSETS HAVING DIFFERENT EXPECTED RETURNS, DIFFERENT STANDARD DEVIATIONS, BUT THE SAME WEIGHT

Let the two securities have the equal weight (0.50 each) in the portfolio.

Let expected return from security–A (r_A) = 12%

Let expected return from security–B (r_B) = 16%

Let standard deviation of returns of security–A (σ_A) = 0.08

Let standard deviation of returns of security–B (σ_B) = 0.10

Let us calculate the standard deviation of the portfolio for different values of correlation coefficient.

(*a*) Coefficient of correlation ($\gamma_{A,B}$) = 1.00

$$\sigma^2_{(port)} = w_A{}^2\,\sigma_A{}^2 + w_B{}^2\,\sigma_B{}^2 + 2w_A\,w_B\,\text{Cov}_{AB}$$

$$\gamma_{A,B} = \frac{\text{Cov}_{A,B}}{\sigma_A.\sigma_B}$$

$$\begin{aligned}
\text{Cov}_{A,B} &= \gamma_{AB}\,(\sigma_A.\,\sigma_B) \\
&= 1.00\,(0.08 \times 0.10) \\
&= 0.008 \\
\sigma^2_{(\text{port})} &= (0.5^2 \times 0.08^2) + (0.5^2 \times 0.10^2) + (2 \times 0.5 \times 0.5 \times 0.008) \\
&= 0.0016 + 0.0025 + 0.004 \\
&= 0.0081
\end{aligned}$$

Standard deviation of the portfolio $\sigma_{(\text{port})} = \sqrt{0.0081}$

$= 0.09$

Weighted average of standard deviations is given by (0.50 × 0.08) + (0.50 × 0.10) i.e., = (0.04 + 0.05) = 0.09. Hence, the standard deviation of a two-asset portfolio having equal weight is the weighted average of the standard deviations of the individual securities, when the coefficient of correlation between the returns of the two securities is +1.00, i.e., when the returns from the two securities are in perfect positive correlation.

Let us see how the Standard Deviation of the portfolio changes when the weights of the securities are not equal.

Let

Weight of security – A (w_A) = 0.80

Weight of security – B (w_B) = 0.20

$$\begin{aligned}
\sigma^2_{(\text{port})} &= w_A{}^2\,\sigma_A{}^2 + w_B{}^2\,\sigma_B{}^2 + 2w_A\,w_B\,\text{Cov}_{A,\,B} \\
&= (0.8^2 \times 0.08^2) + (0.2^2 \times 0.1^2) + (2 \times 0.8 \times 0.2 \times 0.008) \\
&= 0.004096 + 0.0004 + 0.00256 = 0.007056 \\
\sigma_{(\text{port})} &= \sqrt{0.007056} \\
&= 0.084
\end{aligned}$$

The weighted average of Standard Deviations is given by,

$$\begin{aligned}
&= (0.8 \times 0.08) + (0.2 \times 0.10) \\
&= 0.084
\end{aligned}$$

(Hence, even if the weights of the securities are not equal, the portfolio Standard Deviation is given by the weighted average of the standard deviations of the securities contained in the portfolio, when the correlation coefficient between the returns of the two securities contained in the portfolio is +1.00).

(*b*) Coefficient of correlation ($\gamma_{A,B}$) = 0.50

$$\begin{aligned} Cov_{A,B} &= \gamma_{A,B}\,(\sigma_A.\sigma_B) \\ &= 0.50\,(0.08 \times 0.10) \\ &= 0.004 \\ \sigma^2_{(port)} &= (0.5^2 \times 0.08^2) + (0.5^2 \times 0.10^2) + (2 \times 0.5 \times 0.5 \times 0.004) \\ &= 0.0016 + 0.0025 + 0.002 \\ &= 0.0061 \end{aligned}$$

Standard deviation of the portfolio ($\sigma_{(port)}$) $= \sqrt{0.0061}$

$= 0.0781$

(*c*) Coefficient of correlation ($\gamma_{A,B}$) = 0.00

$Cov_{A,B}$ will be zero since $\gamma_{A,B}$ is zero.

$$\begin{aligned} \sigma^2_{(port)} &= (0.5^2 \times 0.08^2) + (0.5^2 \times 0.10^2) + 0 \\ &= 0.0016 + 0.0025 \\ &= 0.0041 \end{aligned}$$

Standard deviation of the portfolio ($\sigma_{(port)}$) $= \sqrt{0.0041}$

$= 0.0640$

(*d*) Coefficient of correlation ($\gamma_{A,B}$) = – 0.50

$$\begin{aligned} Cov_{A,B} &= \gamma_{A,B}\,(\sigma_A.\sigma_B) \\ &= -\,0.50\,(0.08 \times 0.10) \\ &= -\,0.004 \\ \sigma^2_{(port)} &= (0.5^2 \times 0.08^2) + (0.5^2 \times 0.10^2) + (2 \times 0.5 \times 0.5 \times -\,0.004) \\ &= 0.0016 + 0.0025 - 0.002 \\ &= 0.0021 \end{aligned}$$

(*e*) Coefficient of correlation ($\gamma_{A,B}$) = – 1.00

$$\begin{aligned} Cov_{A,B} &= \gamma_{A,B}\,(\sigma_A.\sigma_B) \\ &= -\,1.00\,(0.08 \times 0.10) \\ &= -\,0.008 \\ \sigma^2_{(port)} &= (0.5^2 \times 0.008^2) + (0.5^2 \times 0.10^2) + (2 \times 0.5 \times 0.5 \times -\,0.008) \\ &= 0.0016 + 0.0025 - 0.004 \\ &= 0.0001 \\ \sigma_{(port)} &= \sqrt{0.0001} \\ &= 0.01 \end{aligned}$$

Observation

When there is perfect negative correlation (i.e., when $\gamma_{A,B} = -1.00$) the portfolio Standard Deviation has not become zero. This is because of the reason that though $\gamma_{A,B} = -1.00$ and the weight of the securities A & B are the same, their Standard Deviations are different. We have seen earlier that $\sigma_{(port)} = 0$ when the securities A & B had the same Standard Deviations and the same weights. As the Standard Deviations of the returns from securities A & B are now different (viz., 0.08 & 0.10 respectively), the weight of the securities are to be different in order to ensure that the Standard Deviation of the portfolio return is zero).

8.10. WEIGHTS OF THE SECURITIES REQUIRED IN A 'TWO ASSET' PORTFOLIO FOR MAKING THE PORTFOLIO 'RISK-FREE' [i.e., $\sigma_{(port)}$ = 0.00] WHEN THE STANDARD DEVIATIONS OF THE INDIVIDUAL SECURITIES ARE DIFFERENT AND WHEN THE TWO SECURITIES HAVE PERFECT NEGATIVE CORRELATION

$$\begin{aligned}\sigma^2_{(port)} &= w_A^2\,\sigma_A^2 + w_B^2\,\sigma_B^2 + 2w_A\,w_B\,\text{Cov}_{A,B}\\ &= w_A^2\,\sigma_A^2 + (1-w_A)^2\,\sigma_B^2 + 2w_A(1-w_A)\,\gamma_{A,B}\,\sigma_A\,\sigma_B\end{aligned}$$

Substituting $\gamma_{AB} = -1.00$

$$\begin{aligned}\sigma^2_{(port)} &= w_A^2\,\sigma_A^2 + (1 + w_A^2 - 2w_A)\sigma_B^2 + (2w_A - 2w_A^2)\,(-\sigma_A\,\sigma_B)\\ &= w_A^2\,\sigma_A^2 + \sigma_B^2 + w_A^2\,\sigma_B^2 - 2w_A\,\sigma_B^2 - 2w_A\,\sigma_A\,\sigma_B + 2w_A^2\,\sigma_A\,\sigma_B\\ &= w_A^2\,[\,\sigma_A^2 + \sigma_B^2 + 2\,\sigma_A\,\sigma_B] + \sigma_B^2 - 2w_A\,\sigma_B^2 - 2w_A\,\sigma_A\,\sigma_B\\ &= w_A^2\,(\sigma_A + \sigma_B)^2 - 2w_A\,\sigma_B\,(\,\sigma_B + \sigma_A) + \sigma_B^2\\ &= [w_A^2\,(\sigma_A + \sigma_B)^2] - 2w_A\,\sigma_B\,(\,\sigma_B + \sigma_A\,) + \sigma_B^2\\ &= [w_A\,(\sigma_A + \sigma_B) - \sigma_B]^2\end{aligned}$$

Since we want to achieve a risk-free portfolio, $\sigma^2_{(port)} = 0$. Equating the above expression to zero.

$$[w_A\,(\sigma_A + \sigma_B)\;-\sigma_B]^2 = 0$$

i.e., $$w_A\,(\sigma_A + \sigma_B) - \sigma_B = 0$$

i.e., $$w_A = \frac{\sigma_B}{\sigma_A + \sigma_B}$$

since $$\begin{aligned}w_B &= 1 - w_A\\ &= 1 - \frac{\sigma_B}{\sigma_A + \sigma_B}\\ &= \frac{\sigma_A + \sigma_B - \sigma_B}{\sigma_A + \sigma_B}\end{aligned}$$

$$w_B = \frac{\sigma_A}{\sigma_A + \sigma_B}$$

Thus, in order to get a risk-free two-asset portfolio, when the individual securities in the portfolio are perfectly negatively correlated, the weights required of the individual securities in the portfolio are given by the following relationships:

$$w_A = \frac{\sigma_B}{\sigma_A + \sigma_B} \quad ; \quad w_B = \frac{\sigma_A}{\sigma_A + \sigma_B}$$

where,

σ_A = expected standard deviation of returns from security–A

and σ_B = expected standard deviation of returns from security–B

Thus, in a two-asset portfolio, when the standard deviations of returns from the two securities are the same and if there is perfect negative correlation between the returns (i.e., if $\gamma_{A,B} = -1.00$), the portfolio standard deviation will be zero, provided the weights of the two securities in the portfolio are equal. When the standard deviation of returns from the two securities are not the same and if there is perfect negative correlation between the returns (i.e., if $\gamma_{A,B} = -1.00$), still the portfolio standard deviation can be made zero by assigning proper weights to the securities in the portfolio.

8.11. STANDARD DEVIATION OF A TWO-ASSET PORTFOLIO WITH THE RETURNS FROM THE TWO SECURITIES HAVING PERFECT POSITIVE CORRELATION

We have seen that the standard deviation of the return from a two-asset portfolio is equal to the weighted average of the standard deviations of the returns from the two individual securities under the following two conditions.

(*a*) The securities have equal weight in the portfolio, the standard deviations of returns of the two securities are the same and there is perfect positive correlation between the returns of the two securities.

(*b*) The securities have unequal weight in the portfolio, the standard deviations of returns of the two securities are different and there is perfect positive correlation between the returns of the two securities.

Thus, even when the weight of the two securities in the portfolio are not equal, the weighted average of the standard deviations of the individual security's return will yield the standard deviation of the portfolio when the returns from the securities are under perfect positive correlation.

8.12. GAIN TO INVESTOR DUE TO DIVERSIFICATION

We have seen that the return from a portfolio of securities is the weighted average of returns from the individual securities contained in the portfolio. We have also seen that so long as the coefficient of correlation is less than 1.00, the investor stands to gain by combining the securities into a portfolio.

The following simple illustration will further strengthen our understanding.

***Illustration* 8.4:**

Stock	Expected return	Standard deviation
A	10%	0.07
B	15%	0.09
C	20%	0.10

An investor wants to choose any one of the following three options:

(*a*) investing entirely in security–A

(*b*) investing entirely in security–B

(*c*) investing 50% of the amount in security–A & 50% in security–C

Correlation coefficient between the returns of security A & C ($\gamma_{A,B}$ = 1.00). The investor does not want to bear a higher risk than standard deviation of 0.09.

***Solution*:**

(*a*) Investing entirely in security–A:

Return = 10%

Risk (in terms of standard deviation) = 0.07

(*b*) Investing entirely in security–B:

Return = 15%

Risk (in terms of standard deviation) = 0.09

(*c*) Investing 50% in security–A & 50% in security – C.

Return = Weighted average of returns

= (0.50 × 10%) + (0.50 × 20%)

= 5% + 10%

= 15%

The Standard Deviation of the portfolio is equal to the weighted average of the Standard Deviations of the returns of securities A & C since the two securities have perfect positive correlation and also have equal weight in the portfolio.

$$\sigma_{(port)} = (0.50 \times 0.07) + (0.50 \times 0.10)$$
$$= 0.035 + 0.05$$
$$= 0.085$$

Result

Of the three options, the investor is better placed if he invests 50% in security–A and 50% in security–C since he gets a return of 15% at a comparatively lesser risk of 0.085. For getting the return of 15%, if he opts to invest entirely in security–B he will be bearing a higher risk of 0.09. This risk reduction has become possible only because of diversification.

***Illustration* 8.5:**

Consider the following two securities:

***Security*–A**

Expected return (r_A) : 12%

Standard deviation (σ_A) : 0.10

***Security*–B**

Expected return (r_B) : 18%

Standard deviation (σ_B) : 0.15

For coefficient of correlations of + 1.00, + 0.50, 0.00, – 0.50 & – 1.00 between the returns of securities A & B and for different proportions of amount invested in securities A & B, arrive at the expected returns from the portfolio and the corresponding standard deviations of the portfolio.

Solution:

Expected return from the portfolio = $w_A\, r_A + w_B\, r_B$

Where w_A = Weight of security–A in the portfolio

w_B = Weight of security–B in the portfolio (which is equal to $(1 - w_A)$)

r_A = Expected return from security–A

r_B = Expected return from security–B

For different proportions of weights of the two securities A & B, staring from 100% weight for 'A' & 0% weight for 'B' to 0% weight for 'A' and 100% weight for 'B', the risk-return relationship in terms of standard deviation of the portfolio & expected return of the portfolio respectively have been worked out for coefficient of correlation ($\gamma_{A,B}$) of + 1.00 & – 1.00 and the values are given in table.

Proportion invested		Expected return from the portfolio	Standard deviation of the portfolio for different coefficients of correlation	
In security–A	In security–B	%	$\gamma_{A,B}$ = 1.00	$\gamma_{A,B}$ = –1.00
1.00	0.00	12.00	0.1000	0.1000
0.95	0.05	12.30	0.1025	0.0875
0.90	0.10	12.60	0.1050	0.0750
0.85	0.15	12.90	0.1075	0.0625
0.80	0.20	13.20	0.1100	0.0500
0.75	0.25	13.50	0.1125	0.0375
0.70	0.30	13.80	0.1150	0.0250
0.65	0.35	14.10	0.1175	0.0125

0.60	0.40	14.40	0.1200	0.0000
0.55	0.45	14.70	0.1225	0.0125
0.50	0.50	15.00	0.1250	0.0250
0.45	0.55	15.30	0.1275	0.0375
0.40	0.60	15.60	0.1300	0.0500
0.35	0.65	15.90	0.1325	0.0625
0.30	0.70	16.20	0.1350	0.0750
0.25	0.75	16.50	0.1375	0.0875
0.20	0.80	16.80	0.1400	0.0100
0.15	0.85	17.10	0.1425	0.01125
0.10	0.90	17.40	0.1450	0.1250
0.05	0.95	17.70	0.1475	0.1375
0.00	1.00	18.00	0.1500	0.1500

If we plot the risk-return relationship for $\gamma_{A,B}$ = + 1.00 and $\gamma_{A,B}$ = – 1.00 for various proportions of weights of securities, we get three straight lines as in Fig. 8.5. The line 'AB' represents the risk-return relationship for $\gamma_{A,B}$ = + 1.00 and the line 'AC' and 'BC' represent the risk-return relationship for $\gamma_{A,B}$ = – 1.00.

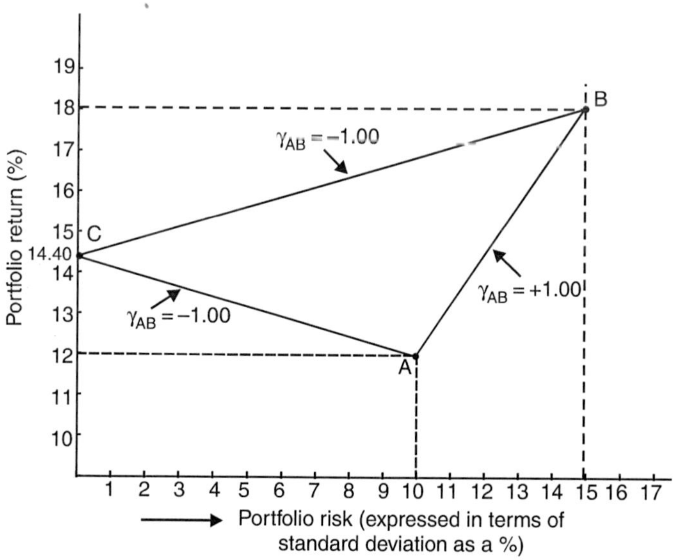

Fig. 8.5 Risk-return relationship of a 'two securities' portfolio for correlation coefficient of correlation values for +1.00 and –1.00

Let us calculate the risk-return relationship for different proportions of weights of the two securities, for values of $\gamma_{A,B}$ in between +1.00 and

–1.00, say for γ_{AB} = +0.50, 0.00 and – 0.50. Refer the following table below for details:

Proportion invested		Expected return from the portfolio %	Standard deviation of the portfolio for different coefficients of correlation		
In security–A	In security–B		$\gamma_{A,B}$ = +0.50	$\gamma_{A,B}$ = 0.00	$\gamma_{A,B}$ = –0.50
1.00	0.00	12.00	0.1000	0.1000	0.1000
0.95	0.05	12.30	0.0990	0.0953	0.0915
0.90	0.10	12.60	0.0984	0.0912	0.0835
0.85	0.15	12.90	0.0982	0.0879	0.0763
0.80	0.20	13.20	0.0985	0.0854	0.0700
0.75	0.25	13.50	0.0992	0.0839	0.0650
0.70	0.30	13.80	0.1004	0.0832	0.0614
0.65	0.35	14.10	0.1019	0.0836	0.0597
0.60	0.40	14.40	0.1039	0.0849	0.0600
0.55	0.45	14.70	0.1063	0.0871	0.0622
0.50	0.50	15.00	0.1090	0.0901	0.0661
0.45	0.55	15.30	0.1120	0.0940	0.0715
0.40	0.60	15.60	0.1153	0.0985	0.0781
0.35	0.65	15.90	0.1189	0.1036	0.0855
0.30	0.70	16.20	0.1228	0.1092	0.0934
0.25	0.75	16.50	0.1269	0.1152	0.1023
0.20	0.80	16.80	0.1311	0.1217	0.1114
0.15	0.85	17.10	0.1356	0.1284	0.1207
0.10	0.90	17.40	0.1403	0.1354	0.1303
0.05	0.95	17.70	0.1451	0.1426	0.1401
0.00	1.00	18.00	0.1500	0.1500	0.1500

The risk-return relationship of the portfolio of two securities A & B for different correlation coefficients between the two securities are plotted in Fig. 8.6. While the risk-return relationship is in the form of a straight line for $\gamma_{A,B}$ = +1.00 and in the form of two straight lines for $\gamma_{A,B}$ = –1.00, the relationship takes the form of a curve for values of $\gamma_{A,B}$ in between +1.00 and –1.00. (Refer Fig. 8.6). The curvature of the curve depends upon the correlation coefficient between the two securities. As the value of $\gamma_{A,B}$ increases, the curvature of the curve becomes greater and greater and the curve shifts to the left of line 'AB'. When there is perfect positive correlation between returns from the two securities (i.e., when $\gamma_{A,B}$ = +1.00), the portfolio return is simply the weighted average of returns from the two securities. This is represented by the straight line 'AB'. This means that there is no risk reduction due to diversification. However, when the returns from the two securities are imperfectly correlated (i.e., when $\gamma_{A,B}$ < +1.00) the portfolio return moves along a curve which lie above the straight line 'AB'. These curves lie to the left of the straight line 'AB' and above the straight line 'AB'. This means that for the same level of risk, the return from the portfolio containing securities with imperfect correlation is more than the return from the portfolio containing securities with perfect correlation. *This makes it clear that whenever the security returns are less than perfectly correlated, the investor gains through diversification.*

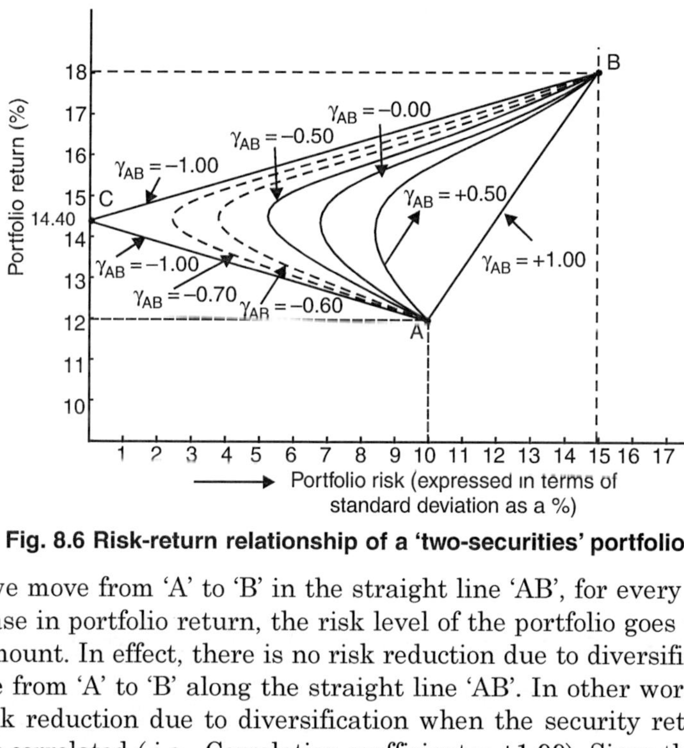

Fig. 8.6 Risk-return relationship of a 'two-securities' portfolio

As we move from 'A' to 'B' in the straight line 'AB', for every one unit of increase in portfolio return, the risk level of the portfolio goes up by an equal amount. In effect, there is no risk reduction due to diversification as we move from 'A' to 'B' along the straight line 'AB'. In other words, there is no risk reduction due to diversification when the security returns are perfectly correlated (i.e., Correlation coefficient = +1.00). Since there is no risk reduction, the variability of the portfolio return (as measured by the Standard Deviation of the portfolio) is simply equal to the weighted average of the Standard Deviations of the returns of the individual securities.

When the security returns are imperfectly correlated (i.e., when γ is less than +1.00 and more than –1.00), the portfolio returns move along a curve. As the value of γ moves towards –1.00, the curve becomes more and steeper and moves towards the point 'C'. Along the curves, the risk level of the portfolio for a particular return is below the weighted average risk of the securities contained in the portfolio. Since all the curves in Fig. 8.6 lie to the left of line 'AB', for a given return, the risk levels on the curves will all be less than the risk levels indicated by the straight line 'AB'.

When there is perfect negative correlation between the security returns (i.e., when $\gamma = -1.00$) as seen in Fig. 8.6 (or in Fig. 8.5), there are different risk levels as represented by the two straight lines 'AC' and 'BC'. We also observe that even for the same level of risk there are two possible returns based on the proportion of the two securities in the portfolio. The interesting point to note is that when $\gamma_{A,B} = -1.00$, for a particular combination of securities 'A' and 'B' in the portfolio, the risk gets totally nullified at this proportion of combination of securities. But, this 'Nil' risk portfolio can be possible only when the two securities are combined in a particular proportion. (This is represented by point 'C' in Fig. 8.6).

Note: *We have already seen that when the standard deviations of two securities 'A' and 'B' are equal, the weight of security 'A' and the weight of security 'B' shall be in equal proportion and the coefficient of correlation between the returns of the two securities shall be equal to* ***–1.00*** *for the standard deviation of the portfolio returns to become zero. If the standard deviations of the two securities differ, though there is perfect negative correlation between them, the standard deviation of the portfolio return can be made zero, provided the weights of the two securities in the portfolio follow the following relationship:*

$$w_A = \frac{\sigma_B}{\sigma_A + \sigma_B} \; ; \quad w_B = \frac{\sigma_A}{\sigma_A + \sigma_B}$$

where w_A *= weight of security 'A' in the portfolio and* w_B *= weight of security 'B' in the portfolio.*

8.13. RISK REDUCTION DUE TO DIVERSIFICATION

We have seen that portfolio risk gets reduced by combining securities. We have seen the method of arriving at the portfolio variance by forming a portfolio containing two securities. In practice, an investor may have a few securities of his/her choice in the portfolio. Let us assume that the portfolio of an investor contains three securities. To arrive at the portfolio variance (or standard deviation) of a three securities portfolio, first the variance of the combination of two securities can be arrived at and then considering the combination of two securities as a single security, the third security can be added and the variance of the combination can be arrived at. Similarly, any number of securities can be combined and the variance of the combination can be arrived at.

The immediate question that may prop up in the mind of a curious investor is as to whether it is possible to reduce the portfolio risk to zero, by combining more and more securities in the portfolio. Can the portfolio variance [$\sigma^2_{(port)}$] be reduced to zero, by including more number of securities in the portfolio? The answer is an obvious 'No'. Why? The reason is as under:

Adding securities to form a portfolio of securities reduces risk because securities are not perfectly positively correlated. If each security has a perfect positive correlation with every other security, then combining these securities will not reduce the risk and the portfolio risk will only be the weighted average of the risk of the securities contained in the portfolio. But this never happens since securities are not perfectly positively correlated. Hence, there is always some risk reduction while combining securities into a portfolio. Just as we have said that securities are not perfectly positively correlated, they are also not perfectly negatively correlated. Portfolio risk will get reduced to zero only if each security is perfectly negatively correlated with every other security. In reality this also never happens. Even it will be very rare to come across zero correlation. Hence, it is obvious that total risk reduction is not possible by combining more and more securities in a portfolio. Hence, it can be said that diversification of a portfolio (i.e., adding more securities to a portfolio) will lead to some reduction in the portfolio risk, but will not result in total elimination of portfolio risk. It is also found that the maximum reduction of portfolio risk takes place when about 25 to 30 securities are added to the portfolio. Further increase in the number of securities in the portfolio reduces the portfolio risk only marginally and very gradually (Refer Fig. 8.7).

We know that the total risk of an individual security consists of two components, viz., the systematic risk that is market-related and the unsystematic risk that is security-related. By combining securities, the unsystematic risk of securities cancels out one another. When the portfolio size increases beyond a limit, the unsystematic risk will be almost eliminated and the portfolio will contain only the systematic risk of the securities included in the portfolio. When all the available securities are included in a portfolio (though it is possible only theoretically), the portfolio is called the Market Portfolio and such a portfolio will be left with no unsystematic risk, but will have systematic risk that is market related.

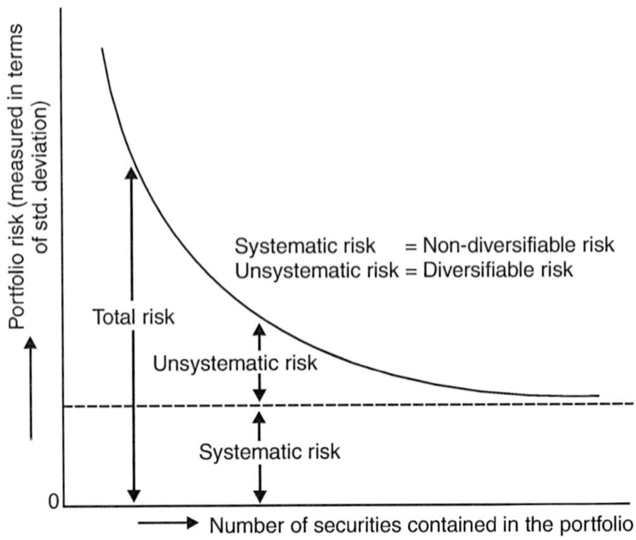

Fig. 8.7 Diversification of risk

8.13.1. Two Securities Portfolio with Minimum Risk

The variance of a portfolio containing two securities 'A' and 'B' is given by,

$$\begin{aligned}\sigma^2_{(port)} &= w_A^2\,\sigma_A^2 + w_B^2\,\sigma_B^2 + 2w_A\,w_B\,\text{Cov}_{A,B}\\ &= w_A^2\,\sigma_A^2 + w_B^2\,\sigma_B^2 + 2w_A\,w_B\,\gamma_{A,B}\,\sigma_A\,\sigma_B\end{aligned}$$

Where,

w_A = Proportion (or weight) of security–A in the portfolio

w_B = Proportion (or weight) of security–B in the portfolio

Since there are only two securities in the portfolio, $w_B = (1 - w_A)$

$$\begin{aligned}\sigma^2_{(port)} &= w_A^2\,\sigma_A^2 + (1 - w_A)^2\sigma_B^2 + 2w_A\,(1 - w_A)\,\gamma_{A,B}\,\sigma_A\,\sigma_B\\ &= w_A^2\,\sigma_A^2 + \sigma_B^2 + w_A^2\,\sigma_B^2 - 2\,w_A\,\sigma_B^2 + 2w_A\,\gamma_{A,B}\,\sigma_A\,\sigma_B\\ &\quad - 2w_A^2\,\gamma_{A,B}\,\sigma_A\,\sigma_B\end{aligned}$$

Risk of the portfolio is minimum when $\sigma^2_{(port)}$ is minimum, i.e., when the first derivative of the equation is equated to zero.

Hence,

$$\frac{d\sigma^2_{(port)}}{dw_A} = 0$$

i.e., $2w_A\,\sigma_A^2 + 0 + 2w_A\,\sigma_B^2 - 2\sigma_B^2 + 2\gamma_{A,B}\,\sigma_A\,\sigma_B - 4w_A\,\gamma_{A,B}\,\sigma_A\,\sigma_B = 0$

$$w_A\,\sigma_A^2 + w_A\,\sigma_B^2 - \sigma_B^2 + \gamma_{A,B}\,\sigma_A\,\sigma_B - 2w_A\,\gamma_{A,B}\,\sigma_A\,\sigma_B = 0$$

$$w_A(\sigma_A^2 + \sigma_B^2 - 2\,\gamma_{A,B}\,\sigma_A\,\sigma_B) - \sigma_B^2 + \gamma_{A,B}\,\sigma_A\,\sigma_B = 0$$

$$w_A(\sigma_A^2 + \sigma_B^2 - 2\,\gamma_{A,B}\,\sigma_A\,\sigma_B) = \sigma_B^2 - \gamma_{A,B}\,\sigma_A\,\sigma_B$$

$$w_A = \frac{\sigma_B^2 - \gamma_{A,B}\,\sigma_A\,\sigma_B}{\sigma_A^2 + \sigma_B^2 - 2\,\gamma_{A,B}\,\sigma_A\,\sigma_B}$$

And, $\quad w_B = (1 - w_A)$

Risk reduction will be maximum when the correlation coefficient between the returns of the two securities, i.e., $\gamma_{A,B}$ *is equal to (–) **1.00**. Accordingly, the proportion of two securities (that have perfect negative correlation between them) that will make the portfolio risk minimum is given by,*

$$w_A = \frac{\sigma_B^2 + \sigma_A\sigma_B}{(\sigma_A^2 + \sigma_B^2 + 2\sigma_A\sigma_B)}$$

$$= \frac{\sigma_B(\sigma_A + \sigma_B)}{(\sigma_A + \sigma_B)^2}$$

$$= \frac{\sigma_B}{(\sigma_A + \sigma_B)}$$

And, $\quad w_B = (1 - w_A)$

When $\gamma_{A,B} = 0.00$, the proportion of securities that will make the portfolio risk the minimum is given by,

$$w_A = \frac{\sigma_B^2}{\sigma_A^2 + \sigma_B^2}$$

And, $\quad w_B = (1 - w_A)$

8.13.2. Portfolio with more than Two Securities

Portfolios are normally constructed by including a number of securities. When more than two securities are contained in a portfolio, the expected return from the portfolio is the weighted average of the individual securities contained in the portfolio. The weights taken for arriving at the weighted average will be the proportion of investment made in each security.

Hence, the expected return from the portfolio is given by,

$$r_p = \sum_{i=1}^{n} w_1 r_1$$

where,

r_p = portfolio return

$w_1, w_2, w_3, w_4 \ldots w_n$ = weights of individual securities contained in the portfolio

$r_1, r_2, r_3, r_4 \ldots r_n$ = expected returns from the individual securities

The variance of the portfolio return is given by,

$$\sigma^2_{(port)} = \sum_{i=1}^{n}\sum_{j=1}^{n} w_i\, w_j\, \gamma_{i,j}\, \sigma_i\, \sigma_j$$

8.14. EFFICIENT FRONTIER

Let us choose two securities A & B for which $\gamma_{A,B} = +0.50$. The risk-return relationship of the portfolio of two securities A & B with $\gamma_{A,B} = +0.50$ is reproduced in Fig. 8.8.

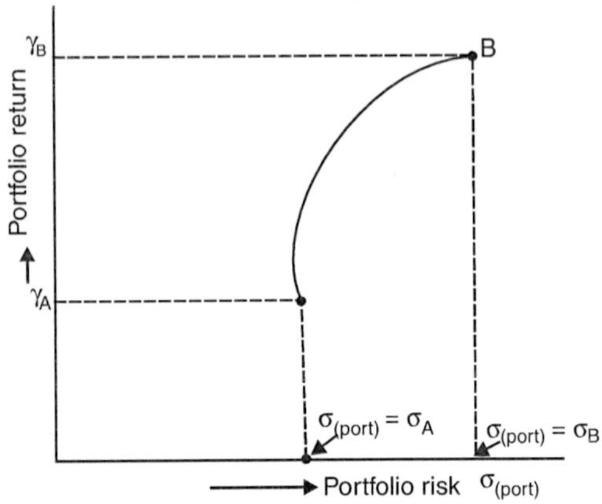

Fig. 8.8 Risk-return relationship of a 'two securities' portfolio with correlation between the security returns at +0.50

Point–A corresponds to a portfolio with all its investments in security–A and point–B corresponds to a portfolio with all its investments in security–B. The points on the curve between A and B corresponds to portfolios of securities A and B with different combination of weights for the two securities.

Let there are two other securities C and D having a different risk-return relationship. If these two securities are combined and a portfolio is formed, we will have another curve (curve – CD) representing the risk-return relationship of this portfolio for different combinations of weights for the two securities C and D (Refer Fig. 8.9).

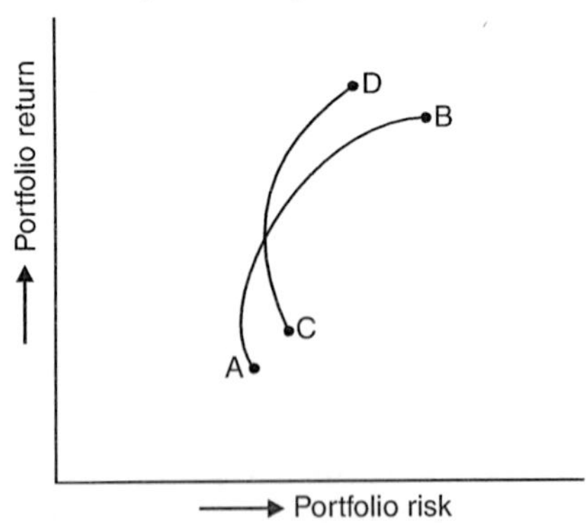

Fig. 8.9 Risk-return relationship of two portfolios each containing two securities

Curve–AB : represents risk-return relationship of portfolio containing securities 'A' and 'B'.

Curve–CD : represents risk-return relationship of portfolio containing securities 'C' and 'D'.

If we examine a number of such securities (remember, there are many securities available for investment and the investor can choose any combination of them that suits his risk bearing capacity) and consider the risk-return relationship of different possible 'two securities' portfolios, we will have a graph as shown in Fig. 8.10. Each individual curve in the figure represents the risk-return relationship of a particular portfolio containing two securities and as there can be many combinations of two securities, there are many curves.

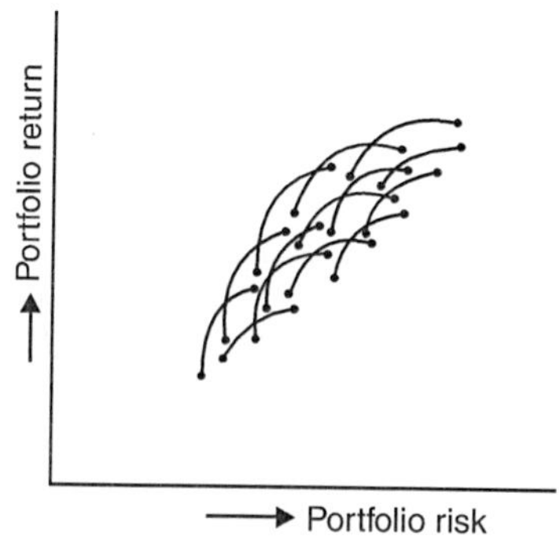

Fig. 8.10 Risk-return relationship of 'two securities' portfolios

An envelope curve can be drawn that contains the best of all the possible combinations. Such a curve that contains all the best possible combinations of securities is referred to as the efficient frontier. Efficient frontier is that set of portfolios that has the maximum return for every given level of risk or the minimum risk for every given level of return. An efficient frontier for two security portfolios is shown in Fig. 8.11.

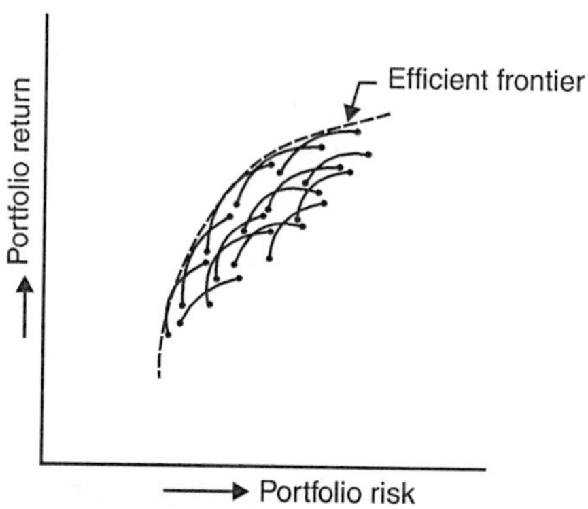

Fig. 8.11 Efficient frontier of 'two securities' portfolios

As can be seen, every portfolio on the efficient frontier has either higher return for equal risk or lower risk for equal return than the portfolios that lie beneath the efficient frontier. We have drawn an efficient frontier for a set of portfolios containing two securities. An investor can include as many securities in the portfolio as he considers right. The concept of building portfolios by combining securities and drawing an envelope curve that contains all the best possible combinations can be extended to portfolios with more than two securities. A portfolio containing a combination of three securities is shown in Fig. 8.12.

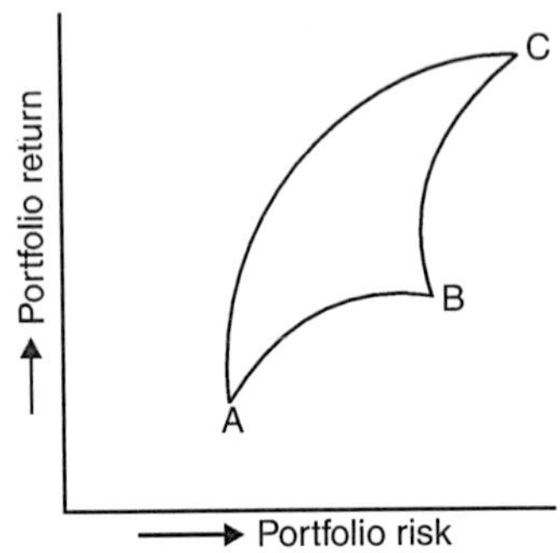

Fig. 8.12 Risk-return relationship of three portfolios containing two securities each out of three securities available

Points A, B and C in Fig. 8.12 represent 100% investment in each of the stocks A, B and C. The curve 'AB' represents all portfolios consisting of securities A and B in different proportions. The curve 'BC' represents all portfolios consisting of securities B and C in different proportions and the curve 'AC' represents all portfolios consisting of securities A and C in different proportions.

Point–D on the curve 'AB' represents a portfolio with securities A and B in some proportion. If security–C is included into this portfolio in different proportions, we will obtain the curve 'DC' representing a portfolio with the three securities A, B and C (Refer Fig. 8.13).

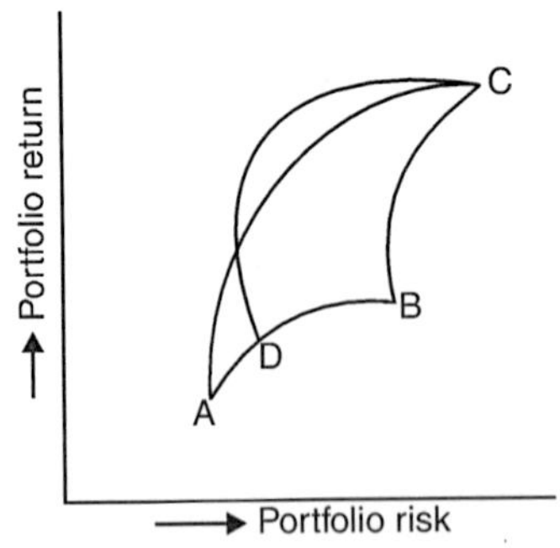

Fig. 8.13 Risk-return relationship of three portfolios containing two securities each out of three securities available and one portfolio with three securities

Curve 'DC' (in Fig. 8.13) represents a portfolio with constant investments in securities A and B and varying investments in security – C. A different point on the curve 'AB' other than D will indicate different proportions of investments in securities A and B. So, if we plot the locus of all possible combinations of securities A, B and C we will get a number of curves (refer Fig. 8.14).

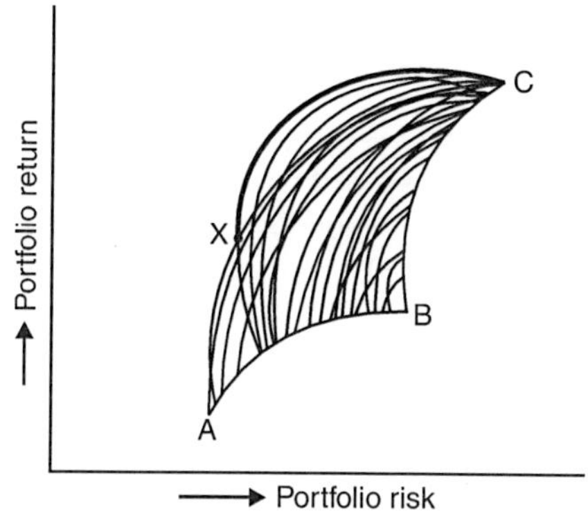

Fig. 8.14 Risk-return relationship of a 'three securities' portfolio

The curve 'CX' represents the efficient frontier for the three security portfolio containing securities A, B and C. Just as we have drawn curves for different possible combinations of three securities A, B & C and identified the efficient frontier which is an envelope curve that offers the best possible risk-return relationship, we can draw the efficient frontier curve for a portfolio containing any number of securities.

8.14.1. Dominance of Efficient Frontier

If we draw the loci of all possible combinations of a portfolio starting from two securities to '*n*' securities, the number of curves will be too many with the result we will get an entire region as a feasible region for investment (Refer Fig. 8.15).

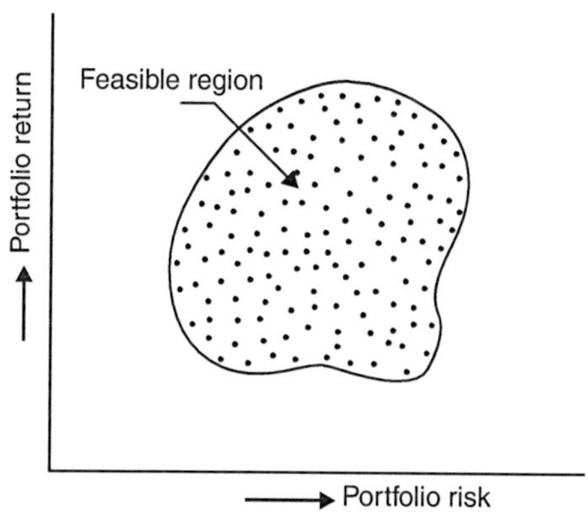

Fig. 8.15 Feasible region for investment

The many points in the feasible region represent the feasible set of portfolios in which an investor can possibly invest. This set of feasible portfolios is called *the portfolio opportunity set.*

It may be noted that if there are '*n*' securities available in the market for investment, it is not necessary (and not practical) for an investor to invest in all the '*n*' securities. He may choose a handful of securities that are acceptable to him and construct a portfolio. However, the extreme situation of choosing all the '*n*' securities can also be not ruled out, since this is also a feasible portfolio theoretically. Thus, the portfolio opportunity set will consist of all feasible combinations of the available securities. Figure 8.15 gives the feasible region for investment. Every point in the feasible region corresponds to a particular portfolio (containing a few securities) that has its own risk-return characteristics. Looking at the feasible region we find that the locus EF (which is called the Efficient Frontier) dominates all other portfolios in the region (Refer Fig. 8.16).

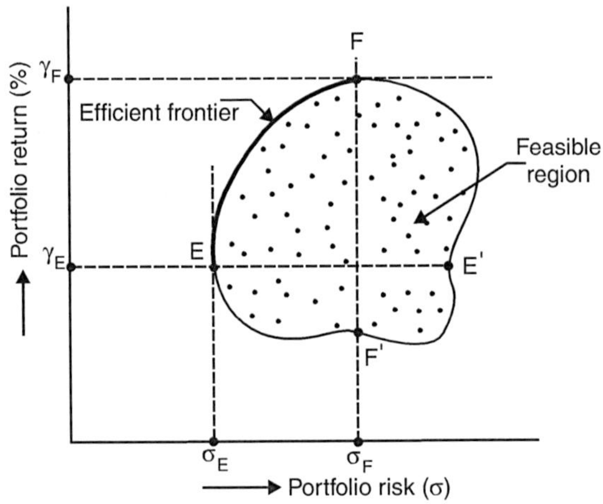

Fig. 8.16 Efficient frontier

The portfolio represented by the point–E offers the minimum risk (represented by minimum standard deviation). This portfolio is called the "global minimum variance portfolio". No other portfolio in the feasible region offers a lesser risk than the global minimum variance portfolio.

The portfolio represented by the point–F offers the maximum returns. Portfolios that lie to the right of point 'F' offer lesser returns for undertaking greater risks. Any investor is guided by the following two criteria:

(*a*) Given two portfolios with the same expected return choose the one with the lower risk.

(*b*) Given two portfolios with the same expected risk, choose the one with the higher return.

If we observe the feasible portfolios in the line EE^{I}, portfolio 'E' gives the minimum risk of σ_E for the same return 'r_E'. If we observe the feasible portfolios lying on the line FF^{I}, portfolio F offers the maximum return 'r_F' for the given risk level of σ_F.

The portfolios lying on the curve 'EF' are more efficient than all other portfolios in the feasible region and the curve 'EF' is called the "Efficient frontier" (Refer Fig. 8.16).

Thus, efficient frontier is that set of portfolios that offers the maximum return for every given level of risk or that has the minimum risk for every level of return.

If we want to define Efficient Frontier in terms of the diagram representing the portfolio opportunity set, it is a concave curve lying on the north west boundary of the feasible region of the risk-return space that extends from the minimum variance portfolio to the maximum return portfolio.

8.15. OPTIMAL PORTFOLIO

All the portfolios that lie on the efficient frontier are efficient portfolios and rational investors opt to invest only in such efficient portfolios. The particular portfolio that an investor will select from among the efficient portfolios depends upon the degree of risk that the investor prefers to bear. An investor who is highly averse to risk may prefer the global minimum variance portfolio (which is the portfolio represented by the lowest point in the Efficient Frontier curve i.e., point–E). An investor who is prepared to take the maximum risk will prefer to choose the portfolio represented by the top most point in the Efficient Frontier curve (i.e., point F in the Efficient Frontier–EF). Investors who opt for moderate risk will choose any portfolio that lie on the Efficient Frontier between the starting and end point of the efficient frontier, depending on their risk bearing capacity.

8.15.1. Investor Indifference Curve

Though the risk bearing attitude of investors differ, each investor does not prefer only one portfolio with a particular risk. Each investor has a range of acceptable portfolios. The locus of these acceptable portfolios is called indifference curve of the investor. Refer Fig. 8.17 for further explanation.

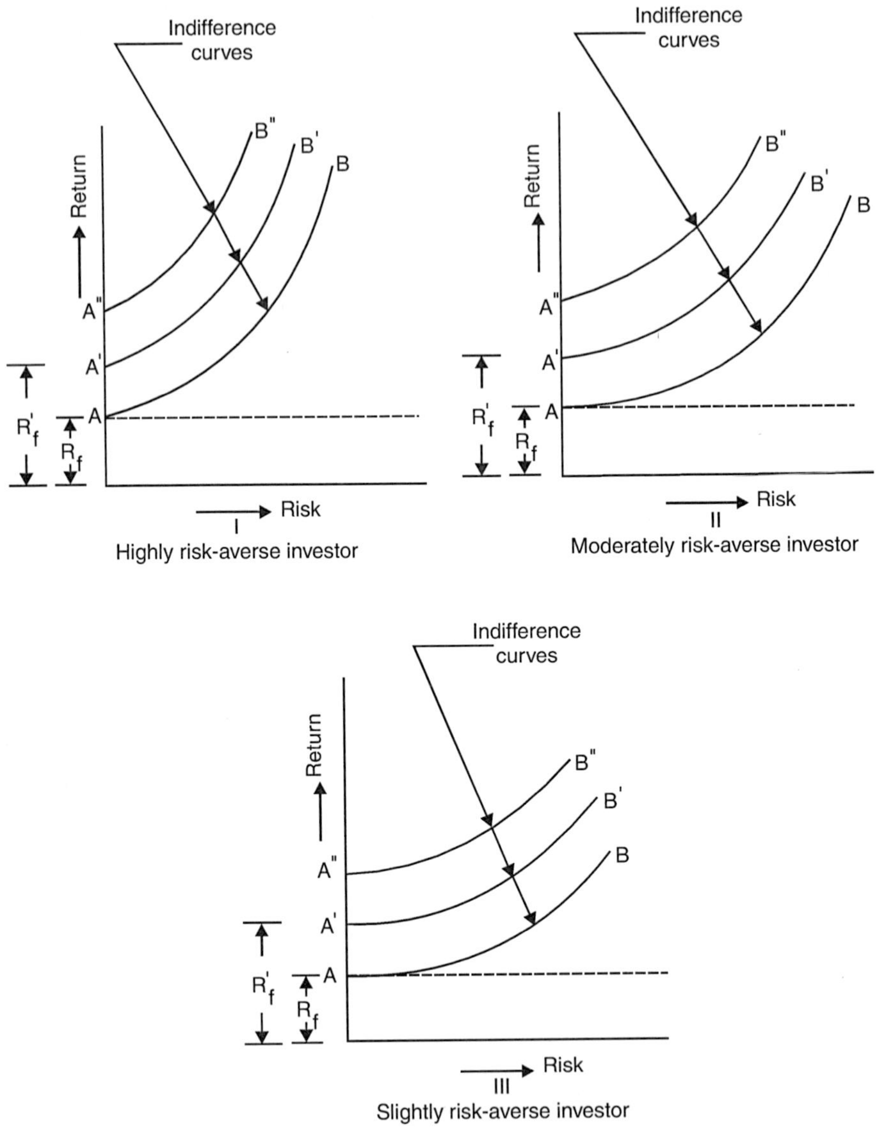

Fig. 8.17 Indifference curves

The indifference curves have the following characteristics.

(*a*) The indifference curves have positive slopes,

(*b*) Irrespective of whether an investor is highly risk-averse, moderately risk-averse or slightly risk-averse, the slopes of the curves increase when moving from left to the right along the curve. This means that investors anticipate more than proportionately higher returns as the risk level increases.

(c) The indifference curves of highly risk-averse investors have steeper slopes than the indifference curves of moderately risk-averse investors. Also, the indifference curves of moderately risk-averse investors will have comparatively steeper slopes than the indifference curves of slightly risk-averse investors. With greater risk aversion, an investor will expect more return for each marginal increase in risk. This makes the indifference curves of highly risk averse investors to slope steeply.

Every category of investor (be he highly risk-averse, moderately risk-averse or slightly risk-averse) has a set of indifference curves since the risk-free return, at a portfolio risk of 'zero' will vary based on market conditions. Refer Fig. 8.17 – I. When the risk free return is 'R_f' a highly risk-averse investor's indifference curve may be AB. This means that the different combinations of risk and return along the curve AB are equally satisfactory to the highly risk-averse investor and he will invest in any of the portfolio that lies on the curve AB. All the portfolios that lie on the curve 'AB' are equally acceptable to the investor. The investor will be indifferent in choosing one or the other portfolio that lies on the curve 'AB'.

When the risk-free return increases to say, R^I_f, the same investor's indifference curve will lie above the curve 'AB' the curve A^IB^I represents the revised indifference curve for a risk free return of R^I_f. Similarly, based on different values of risk-free returns, there will be set of indifference curves.

Figures 8.17 – II & 8.17 – III depict the set of indifference curves for moderately risk-averse and slightly risk-averse investors

8.15.2. Selection of Optional Portfolio

The indifference curves are parallel to one another. The higher the indifference curve (i.e., the farther from *x*-axis), the more desirable it is to the investor. For example, referring to Fig. 8.17 – I, the highly risk-averse investor will prefer curve A^{II} B^{II} to curve A^IB^I or AB. As the position of the indifference curve moves upwards, the satisfaction level of the investor increases. As the goal of an investor is to maximise his satisfaction level, he will prefer investments on the indifference curve that lies as far away as possible from the *x*-axis. However, there may not be portfolios available to satisfy his expectations. The investor has to choose only from among the available portfolios. Since Efficient Frontier is the set of efficient portfolios and as Efficient Frontier forms the North-East boundary of the feasible region, the optional portfolio for an investor would be the portfolio that corresponds to the point of tangency between the Efficient Frontier and the indifference curve of the investor (Refer Fig. 8.18).

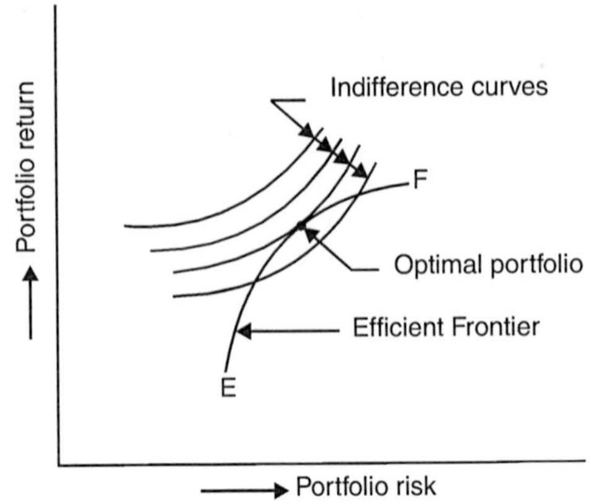

Fig. 8.18 Optimal portfolio

8.15.3. Limitations of Markowitz Model

Major contributions to the Modern Portfolio Theory were done by Markowitz. He was the one who first introduced the 'portfolio approach' to investment management. His great contributions to the portfolio theory started with his simple observation that prudent investors do not invest their money only in one security, but spread out their investment on a few securities. Markowitz provided justification for diversification of investments and for the first time defined 'variability of return' as the appropriate measure of risk of a security/portfolio of securities. Markowitz was awarded Nobel prize in economics in the year 1990 for his pioneering approach to portfolio analysis. At that time, he was a Professor in Finance at Baruch College of the City University, Newyork. Markowitz's model provided the way to plot the efficient frontier and to locate an optimal portfolio for an investor by overlapping the indifference curve of the investor with the efficient frontier.

In this chapter, we have so far seen Markowitz theory and its explanation. Markowitz's model provided the way to plot the efficient frontier and to locate the optimal portfolio for an investor by overlapping the indifference curve of the investor with the efficient frontier. The theory is no doubt formed on sound premises. The concepts of efficient portfolio and efficient frontier are theoretically sound and appealing. However, the computations involved are many that are beyond the comprehension of an average investor.

Markowitz used quadratic programming technique to locate the efficient portfolios. Using the expected risk-return relationship of each available security and the covariance estimates of each pair of securities, Markowitz arrived at the risk-return relationship of any portfolio containing some or all the available securities in different proportions. For a given value of expected return, Markowitz performed calculations to determine the least risk portfolio. He repeated the process for different values of expected return. The locus of the points that connects the points of least risk for every expected return forms the efficient frontier.

The analysis as done by Markowitz require a large number of data inputs and involve lengthily/complex computations. The complexity increases as the number of available securities increases. If there are 'N' securities available for investment, the data inputs required for analysing the risk-return relationship of the portfolio containing the 'N' securities are as under.

No. of return estimates from securities $= N$

No. of variance estimates from securities $= N$

No. of covariance estimates from securities * $= \dfrac{N(N-1)}{2}$

Hence,

Total no. of data inputs $= \left\{2N + \dfrac{N(N-1)}{2}\right\}$

Suppose 50 securities are available for investment. The number of data inputs required are 122500. Thus, the identification of efficient portfolios on the basis of Markowitz's model has found little use in practical applications, though it is theoretically sound. The model suggested by Markowitz can have practical applications only if the data inputs required are considerably reduced and the process of calculation is simplified. In this regard, William Sharpe developed a simplified variant of the Markowitz model.

8.16. SHARPE SINGLE INDEX MODEL

William Sharpe developed a simplified variant of the Markowitz model. This model reduces the data inputs and the computational requirements considerably and thus overcomes the practical difficulties encountered by average investors in the application of Markowitz model.

Sharpe single index model has its name because it relies on a single index that represents the security market. Instead of comparing each security with every other available security, each security is compared only with the market index. In other words, the return from each security is compared only with the market return. The market index may be any widely accepted index like the BSE index in India. Sharpe suggested that the relationship of each security with the market index gives reasonably accurate information about that security and that it is needless to study the relationship of each security with every other security.

(*) [If there are say four securities A, B, C and D available for investment, the covariance estimates of the six pairs, viz., AB, AC, AD, BC, BD and CD are required. This gives the relationship N(N – 1)/2 for the number of covariance estimates of securities required]

Sharpe gave the following relationship for arriving at the expected return from a security.

$$R_i = \alpha_i + \beta_i R_m + e_i$$

Where

R_i = expected return of security 'i'

α_i = component of return from security 'i' that is independent of the performance of the market (Alpha coefficient of security)

β_i = a constant that measures the expected change in R_i for a given change in R_m (Beta coefficient of security)

R_m = rate of return on the market index

e_i = error term representing the residual return*

According to Sharpe, fluctuations in the value of a stock relative to the value of another stock depend on the correlation between each security return with a security market index.

The error term 'e_i' is the unexpected return resulting from influences not identified by the model. Sharpe observed that in the long run (i.e., when more and more number of securities are analysed), the value of 'e_i' turns out to be zero. In other words, + e_i and – e_i cancel out and hence the formula can be simplified as,

$$R_i = \alpha_i + \beta_i R_m$$

i.e.,

Return from a security = 'α' of the security +['β' of the security × Market return]

It may be noted that 'α' is the return that is independent of the market return and (β × Market return) is a component of the return that depends on the market. 'β' measures the sensitivity of the stock's return to the return on the market index. For example, if the 'β' of a security is, say 2.50, the return from the security is expected to increase by 25% when the market return increases by 10%. Similarly, when 'β' is 2.50, the return from the security is expected to fall by 25% when the market return falls by 10%. A 'β' value of more than 1.00 indicates that the security will show greater responsiveness in relation to the market. In other words, the percentage increase/decrease in security price will be more than the percentage increase/decrease in the market index. The 'α' of a security indicates the return that the security is expected to earn when the market return is zero. For example, when 'α' of a security is say, 3.75%, the security will earn a return of 3.75% even when the market return is zero. On the other hand, a negative value of 'α' of , say, (–) 4.00% will mean that the security will give a negative return of 4.00% when the market return is zero. Obviously, a negative value

(* Residual return is the firm-specific return that is not explained by the market index)

for 'α' is not a desired aspect of a security since the security will lose its value even when the market return is zero.

Sharpe's single index model for arriving at a security return in turn indicates that the risk (i.e., variability of return) is the sum of security-specific risk and market related risk.

Total risk = Security-specific risk + Market related risk

$$\sigma_i^2 = \sigma_{ei}^2 + \beta_i^2 \sigma_m^2$$

where,

σ_i^2 = variance of the security '*i*'

σ_{ei}^2 = variance of the 'residual return' of security '*i*'

β_i = beta coefficient of security '*i*'

σ_m^2 = variance of the market index return

The specific risk of a security is that component of risk which is unique to the particular security and is called 'unsystematic risk' while the market related risk is the component of risk that is related to the market as a whole and is called 'systematic risk'. While unsystematic risk can be reduced through diversification, systematic risk can not be reduced through diversification. Unsystematic risk is also called 'diversifiable risk'.

Coming back to Sharpe's formula for security return [i.e., $R_i = \alpha_i + \beta_i R_m$], the values of α and β of a security can be obtained through regression analysis using the historical data of returns from the security and the corresponding historical market returns.

***Illustration* 8.6:**

The historical data on the percentage change in a stock's return and the percentage change in the market return for the corresponding period are given in the table below. Arrive at the 'α' and 'β' values of the security.

Month	% change in stock's return	% change in market return
1	2.00	5.00
2	3.00	2.00
3	4.50	1.50
4	1.00	(–) 1.50
5	7.50	5.00
6	3.00	(–) 2.00
7	(–) 7.00	(–) 10.50
8	16.50	(–) 2.50
9	(–) 7.00	(–) 5.00
10	(–) 11.50	(–) 9.50
11	(–) 5.00	(–) 5.00
12	(–) 4.50	(–) 0.50

Solution:

$$R_i = \alpha_i + \beta_i R_m$$

The historical data on R_i and R_m are available. The formula for R_i is of the form ($y = a + bx$) where 'y' is a dependent variable, 'x' is an independent variable and 'a' and 'b' are constants. The equation can be solved through regression. Solving through regression, we get the following equation

$$R_i = 0.4179 + 1.09 R_m$$

Hence,

'α' of the security = 0.4179

and 'β' of the security = 1.09

*Line 'AB' in Fig. 8.19 shows the relationship between the stock's return and the market return as indicated by the historic data.

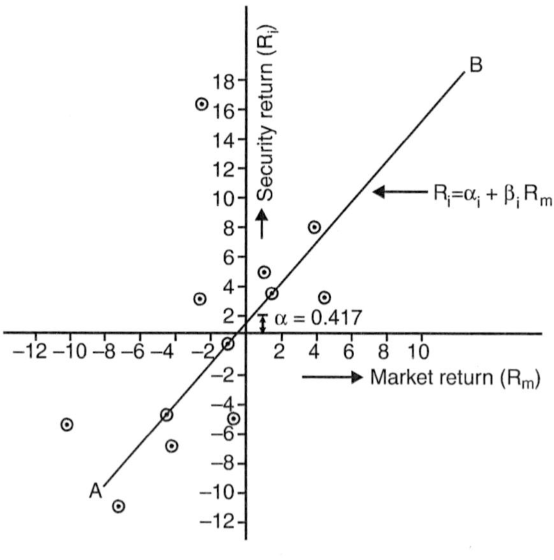

Fig. 8.19 Relationship between security return and market return

***Illustration* 8.7:**

The 'α' and 'β' of a security are 3.00% and 1.80 respectively. The expected Market return is 20.00%. What is the return expected of the security?

Solution:

$$\alpha = 3\%$$

$$\beta = 1.80$$

$$R_m = 20\%$$

$$\text{Expected return from the security } (R_i) = \alpha + \beta R_m$$

$$= 3\% + (1.80 \times 20\%)$$

$= 3\% + 36\%$

$= 39\%$

Illustration **8.8:**

The estimated values of α and β of a security (Security–A) are 2.50% and 1.45 respectively. The variance of residual return is 280. The market index is expected to provide a return of 24%. The variance of the market index is 120. Calculate the expected return from the security and its variance.

Solution:

Return from Security–A = α of Security–A + β (Expected Market return)

$= 2.50\% + 1.45 \times (24.00\%)$

$= 37.30\%$

Variance of Security–A = β^2 (Variance of the Market) + Variance of the residual return

$= \beta^2 . \sigma_m^2 + \sigma_e^2$

$= 1.45^2 \times (120) + 280$

$= 252.30 + 280 = 532.30$

8.16.1. Calculation of Portfolio Return and Portfolio Risk using Sharpe's Single Index Model

Under para 8.16 we have seen the method of arriving at the expected return from an individual security and the variance of the individual security. The expected portfolio return is given by the following relationship.

Portfolio return = $\alpha_p + \beta_p \times$ (Market return)

where

α_p = Portfolio 'Alpha' which is the weighted average of 'Alphas' of individual securities

and β_p = Portfolio 'Beta', which is the weighted average of 'Betas' of Individual securities.

i.e., $\alpha_p = \sum_{i=1}^{n} w_i . \alpha_i$ and $\beta_p = \sum_{i=1}^{n} w_i . \beta_i$

Portfolio Risk = {Weighted average of the Market related risks of individual securities + Weighted average of the Security specific risk of individual securities}

$$\text{Portfolio variance} = \beta_p^2 . \sigma_m^2 + \sum_{i=1}^{n} w_i^2 . \sigma_{ei}^2$$

Where, σ_m^2 = variance of the market return

and σ_{ei}^2 = variance of the residual return of security 'i'

Note: *The first term $\beta_p^2 . \sigma_m^2$ which is the product of the variance of the market return and the square of the portfolio 'Beta' constitutes the systematic risk of the portfolio. The second term $\sum_{i=1}^{n} w_i^2 \cdot \sigma_{ei}^2$ is the weighted average of the variances of residual return of individual securities and this represent the specific risk of the portfolio (or the unsystematic risk of the portfolio).*

When more and more securities are added to the portfolio, the unsystematic risk will get reduced and will become a smaller fraction of the total portfolio risk. When the size of the portfolio becomes large (i.e., when a large number of securities are included in the portfolio), the unsystematic risk will approach zero and the portfolio risk will be equal to $(\beta_p^2 . \sigma_m^2)$ (if the unsystematic risk that will be very minimum is ignored). Hence, for a well diversified portfolio (i.e., a portfolio with a large number of securities), the portfolio Beta (β_p) will be the effective measure of the portfolio risk.

***Illustration* 8.9:**

A portfolio has six securities. The table below shows the weight of the securities in the portfolio. The Alpha and Beta coefficients of the securities and the residual variance (i.e., variance of the residual returns) of the securities are given below. If the market return is 20% and if the variance of the market return is 280, calculate the expected portfolio return and the portfolio variance using Sharpe's Single Index Model.

Security	Weight (w_i)	Alpha (α_i)	Beta (β_i)	Residual variance (σ_{ei}^2)
A	0.30	3.00	1.90	260
B	0.15	2.00	1.10	320
C	0.05	1.00	0.90	340
D	0.20	1.25	1.20	420
E	0.10	0.50	0.80	290
F	0.20	1.10	1.30	210
	1.00			

Solution:

$$\text{Portfolio Alpha } (\alpha_p) = \sum_{i=1}^{n} w_i . \alpha_i$$

$$= (0.30 \times 3.00) + (0.15 \times 2.00) + (0.05 \times 1.00) + (0.20 \times 1.25) + (0.10 \times 0.50) + (0.20 \times 1.10)$$

$$= 1.77$$

$$\text{Portfolio Beta } (\beta_p) = \sum_{i=1}^{n} w_i \cdot \beta_i$$

$$= (0.30 \times 1.90) + (0.15 \times 1.10) + (0.05 \times 0.90) + (0.20 \times 1.20) + (0.20 \times 1.20) + (0.10 \times 0.80) + (0.20 \times 1.30)$$

$$= 1.36$$

$$\text{Expected portfolio return} = \alpha_p + [\beta_p \times (\text{Market return})]$$

$$= 1.77 + [1.36 \times (20.00)]$$

$$= 28.97\%$$

$$\text{Portfolio variance } (\sigma_p^2) = \beta_p^2 \cdot \sigma_m^2 + \sum_{i=1}^{n} w_i^2 \cdot \sigma_{ei}^2$$

$$= (1.36^2 \times 280) + \{ (0.30^2 \times 260) + (0.15^2 \times 320) + (0.05^2 \times 340) + (0.20^2 \times 420) + (0.10^2 \times 290) + (0.20^2 \times 210)\}$$

$$= 517.89 + 59.55$$

$$= 577.44$$

Note: *This portfolio has only six securities. When the portfolio contains a large number of securities, the weight of individual security (w_i) will be very less and hence the second term in the formula for portfolio variance $\sum_{i=1}^{n} w_i^2 \cdot \sigma_{ei}^2$ will become very negligible.*

8.16.2. Advantages of Sharpe's Single Index Model

If there are 'N' securities in a portfolio, for finding out the portfolio return and portfolio risk, Markowitz model requires $2N + \frac{N(N+1)}{2}$ data inputs. As against this, Sharpe's single index model requires only ($3N$ +2) data inputs (viz., α_i, β_i, σ_{ei}^2 for each of the 'N' securities and R_m & σ_m^2). Thus, for a portfolio containing say, 50 securities, Sharpe's single index model requires 152 data inputs while Markowitz model requires 1225 data inputs.

After arriving at the estimated portfolio returns and portfolio variances using the Sharpe's single index model, the set of efficient portfolios can be generated using the quadratic programming routine as in the Markowitz model.

8.17. CAPITAL ASSET PRICING MODEL (CAPM)

While Markowitz advocated the method of reducing risk by diversifying the portfolio, he did not develop a practical solution to aid the investors locate their optimal portfolio. William Sharpe developed a sophisticated reasoning that connected risk and reward and this became known as the Capital Asset Pricing model (CAPM).

According to CAPM, every investment carries two distinct risks. One is the risk of being in the market (which is called as 'Systematic risk') and the other is the 'Unsystematic' risk that is specific to the fortunes of the company. Since the company specific risks (that are called as Unsystematic risk) can be mitigated by appropriate diversification, William Sharpe concluded that the expected return from a portfolio hinges on its 'Beta' – i.e., its relationship with the overall market.

Investment analysts of the pre-Markowitz era were very simplistic in their approach. They advised investors not to put all eggs in one basket. They advocated spreading out the investments in different assets (so to say, putting the eggs in different baskets) and watching them carefully. It was only a qualitative advice. There was little quantification. It was Markowitz who for the first time quantified portfolio risk. He provided a method of locating the efficient frontier that contains all the efficient portfolios of risky assets.

Suppose every investor is fully aware of the portfolio optimization technique advocated by Markowitz. What would happen if every investor started optimizing his/her portfolio? Let some investors, in their process of building an optimum portfolio, opts to hold more of security 'X'. If there are not enough of shares of security 'X' available, it would bring a demand for the shares of security 'X' and this would push the price of the share up. At a point of time the investors would have to change their estimates of risk and return since by now, they would be paying a higher price for the shares of security 'X'. The process of upward and downward pressure on the share prices would continue until the prices reach equilibrium and every investor collectively wants to hold what is available. When the price equilibrium has set in, what would be the risk-return relationship of a security? Sharpe gave the answer to this question stating that the expected return of a security would be proportional to its Beta (β) relative to the market portfolio. (Similarly, the expected return of a portfolio would be proportionate to the 'Beta' of the portfolio relative to the market portfolio).

Sharpe published his paper 'Capital Asset Prices: A theory of Market equilibrium under conditions of risk' in 1964. Eugene Fama called it the Capital Asset Pricing Model (CAPM). The key insight of CAPM is that a security that performs very badly at bad times is the one that will perform much better at good times. The investor who is holding such a security will be losing heavily at bad times, but will be compensated adequately at good times and the investor is said to hold a security with high 'Beta' value. 'Beta' is thus a measure of fluctuations in price as compared to market fluctuations. Securities with high 'Betas' tend to do worse at bad times than those with low 'Betas'. CAPM gives the relationship between the expected return and the systematic risk of a security (or a portfolio of securities). *Thus, CAPM is a model for pricing an individual security or a portfolio.*

8.17.1. Assumptions of CAPM

CAPM makes certain assumptions about investor behaviour. They are as below:

1. Investors are rational and risk-averse. Investors make decisions to invest in a portfolio of assets by assessing the expected returns from the portfolios and the associated risks (measured in terms of Standard Deviations) of the portfolios.
2. When given a choice between two otherwise identical portfolios, investors will choose the portfolio with higher expected return.
3. When given a choice between two otherwise identical portfolios, investors will choose the portfolio with lower risk (i.e., lower standard deviation of returns).
4. Securities are infinitely divisible, meaning that an investor can buy or sell even a fraction of a share if he/she so desires.
5. All the investors search for the ways to maximize the expected return of their portfolios with a single planning period.
6. A single investor cannot affect the prices of securities in the market. There is perfect competition in the market and all the investors in total determine prices by their actions. Thus, an individual investor is only a price taker.
7. There are no transaction costs and taxes.
8. The risk-free return is the same for all investors.
9. Information is available to all investors freely and instantly. No investor can have an edge over others due to possessing extra information.
10. All investors can borrow and lend unlimited amounts at the risk-free rate of return.
11. Investors have homogeneous expectations about returns from assets and the risks associated with them. In other words, their expectations of returns from securities are the same. Also, they have identical expectations of variances of returns from securities and the covariances of all pairs of securities.

Though some of the above assumptions are unrealistic, they do not very much affect the results of CAPM. The model is found to describe the risk-return relationship and pricing of securities and portfolios fairly well.

8.17.2. Efficient Frontier with Lending at Risk-free Rate

Markowitz's portfolio theory deals with portfolio of risky assets. Markowitz devised a method for locating the efficient frontier that contains efficient portfolios of risky assets, with different risk-return combinations. Every efficient portfolio will have a particular combination of risk and return. Since the efficient frontier dominates all other portfolios of risky assets, every portfolio on the efficient frontier will dominate every other portfolio of risky securities in the feasible region. In other words, for a given level of risk, portfolios on the efficient frontier will offer higher returns than the rest of the portfolios in the feasible region.

In the real world, apart from risky assets, risk-free assets are also available for investment and investors also invest in such risk-free assets. Though a totally risk averse investor might invest all his money in such risk-free assets, a normal investor who is prepared to take some risk may also have some risk-free assets in his portfolio, apart from different risky assets. A risk-free asset (or a riskless asset) is one similar to a Government security where the return is assured. The expected return from such asset will not vary and will remain unaltered in spite of fluctuations in the returns offered by other risky securities. Since the return from a risk free security is not expected to vary, the variance of such asset's return is zero.

When an investor invests a portion of his funds in risk-free investments, this would amount to lending a portion of his funds at the risk-free rate of return (R_f). Thus, his investments would have a combination of risky assets and risk-free assets.

The efficient frontier which contains portfolios of risky securities is concave in shape. Let curve 'AC' is the efficient frontier. (Refer Fig. 8.20). Consider an efficient portfolio on the efficient frontier that gives a portfolio return of say, 17%. Let this portfolio is represented by point 'B' on the efficient frontier 'AC'. Let the risk of this portfolio, as measured by its standard deviation (σ_p) is say, 9%.

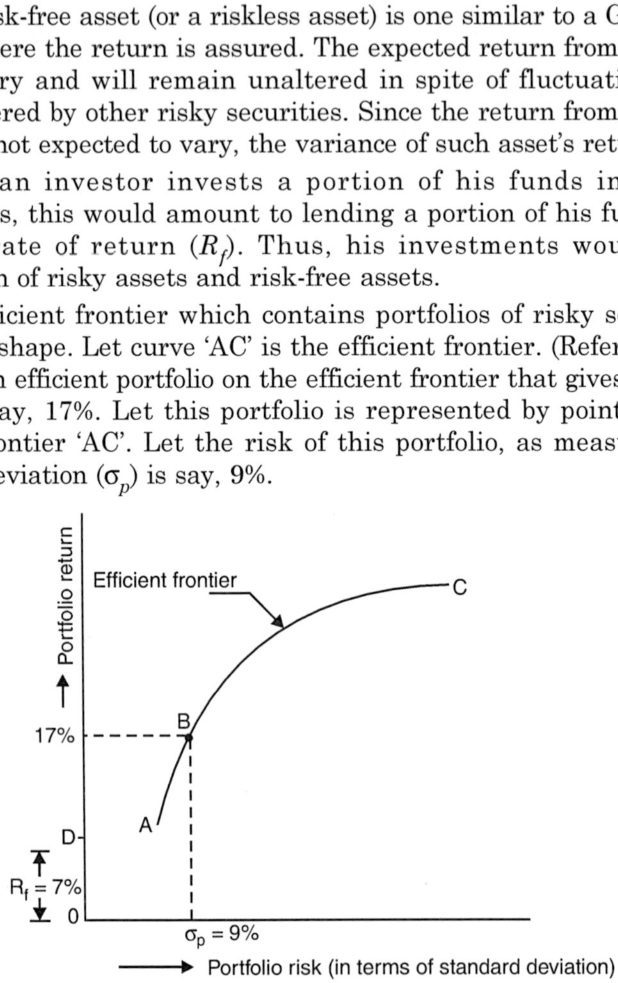

Fig. 8.20 Efficient frontier

Let the rate of return available from risk-free asset is 7%. The risk-free return will not have any variance and it will remain the same despite fluctuations in the returns offered by other risky securities. Hence, the risk-free asset can be represented by a point on the Y-axis (where $\sigma_p = 0$). Let point 'D' represents the risk-free asset.

An investor can have risk-free assets in his portfolio. The proportion of risk-free assets to risky assets in the portfolio can vary. The line 'BD' (Refer Fig. 8.21) represents the risk-return of the portfolios that comprise of efficient portfolio 'B' and risk-free asset in different proportions.

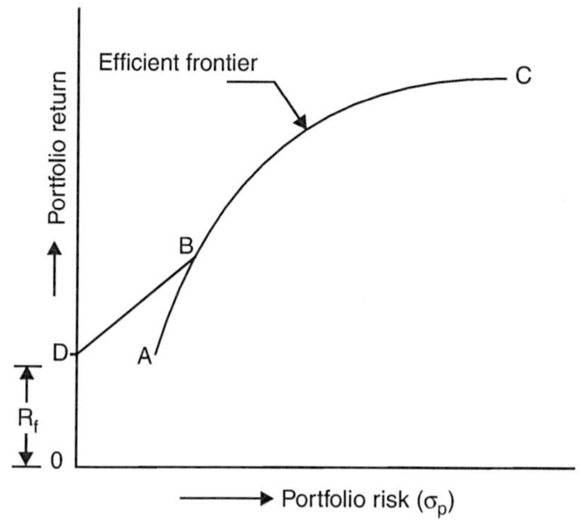

Fig. 8.21 Risk-return relationships of portfolios

Each point on the line 'BD' represents a portfolio that is a combination of risk-free asset and efficient portfolio 'B' in different proportions. When 100% of the amount is invested in risk-free asset, the portfolio is represented by point 'D'. To be precise, it is not a portfolio but an investment in only one asset, viz., risk-free asset. When 100% of the amount is invested in risky assets, the portfolio is represented by point 'B' (Point 'B' represents one of the efficient portfolios on the efficient frontier). When a portion of investment is made in risk-free asset and the remaining amount is invested in efficient portfolio 'B', the portfolio will on the line 'BD'. When the portion of investment in risk-free asset is more, the portfolio will lie close to the point 'D' on the line 'BD'; when the portion of investment in the efficient portfolio 'B' is more, the portfolio will lie close to point 'B' on the line 'BD'.

Consider line 'BD' and the portion of efficient frontier 'AB'. All portfolios that lie on the line 'BD' offer higher returns (for the same level of risk) than the portfolios that lie on the efficient curve 'AB'. Thus, portfolios that lie on the line 'BD' dominate the portfolios that lie on the portion of efficient frontier 'AB'. Since there are many efficient portfolios that lie on the efficient frontier, it is possible to draw a number of straight lines connecting point 'D' (representing risk-free asset) and an efficient portfolio on the efficient frontier. (Refer Fig. 8.22).

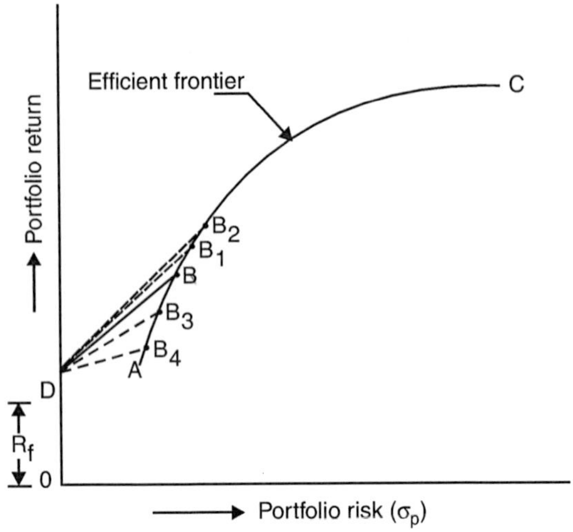

Fig. 8.22 Risk-return relationships of portfolios

DB_1, DB_2, DB_3, DB_4 ...... etc., are such lines that connect different efficient portfolios with the risk-free asset. An observation of the lines DB_1, DB_2, DB_3, DB_4 ...... etc., will show that as we move away from the X-axis, the portfolio return is higher for the same level of risk. The line that will be farther away from X-axis is the line drawn from point 'D', tangential to the efficient frontier curve 'AC'. Let point 'M' is the point of tangency. (Refer Fig. 8.23).

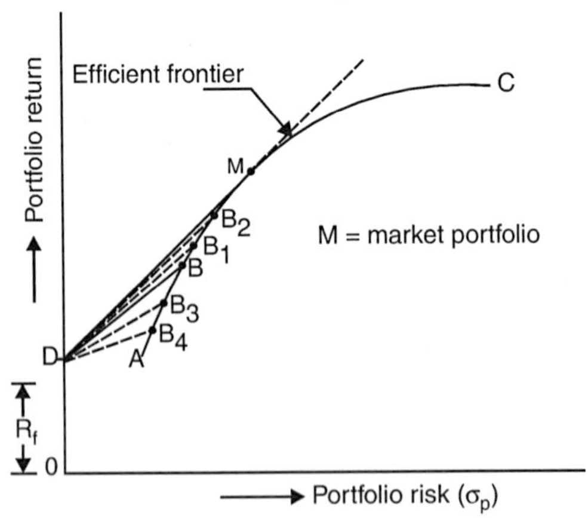

Fig. 8.23 Risk-return relationships of portfolios

All the portfolios that lie on the line 'DM' dominate the portfolios that lie on the efficient frontier for the same level of risk. So, among the efficient portfolio of risky assets that lie on the efficient frontier, we can say that portfolio corresponding to point 'M' represents optimal combination of 'all risky assets'. This being so, 'all investors' will opt to hold the risky portfolio 'M' which means that this optimal portfolio should include 'all' risky securities available in the market. This is nothing but the 'Market portfolio' which contains all the risky securities in the market. Each risky security in the portfolio 'M' will be held in proportion which the market value of the security bears to the total market value of all risky securities in the market. *Thus, all investors (who are rational, risk-averse and who have identical expectations) will hold a combination of only two assets, viz., the market portfolio and a risk-free security.*

8.17.3. Capital Market Line

As discussed in the previous paragraph, in a capital market where all the investors behave rationally and are risk-averse (i.e., all the investors would like to earn maximum return for a given level of risk or would like to bear minimum risk for a given level of return), the investors will hold only two classes of assets, viz., the market portfolio and a risk-free security. Though all the investors are rational and risk-averse, their risk bearing capacity will vary. Hence, the proportion of market portfolio and the risk-free security will vary depending upon the risk that an investor is prepared to bear.

There will be as many levels of risk as the number of investors. All these portfolios will lie along the straight line that is drawn from the point representing the risk-free security (point 'D'), tangential to the efficient frontier (Refer Fig. 8.24). This line on which all the portfolios of rational investors lie (i.e, portfolios consisting different combinations of the market portfolio and risk-free security) is known as Capital Market Line (CML).

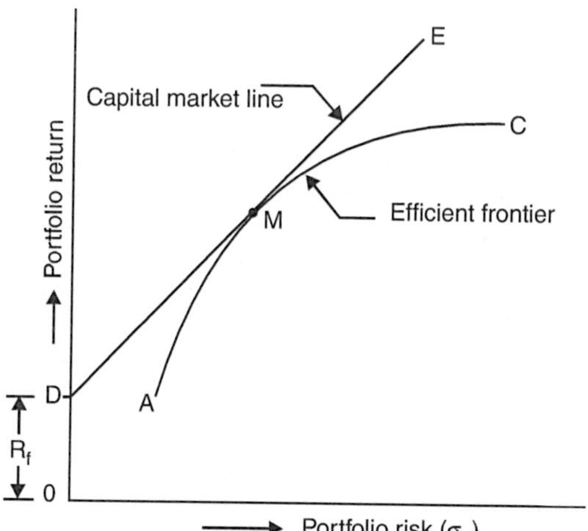

Fig. 8.24 Capital market line

Referring to Fig. 8.24, line 'DME' is the Capital Market Line. All efficient portfolios will lie along the CML. The efficient frontier (represented by curve 'AMC') consists of efficient portfolios of risky securities. The CML contains efficient portfolios that are a combination of market portfolio and a risk-free security. For any given level of risk, the portfolios that lie on the CML offer higher returns than the portfolios that lie on the efficient frontier, for the same level of risk. (Only at one point, the portfolio that lies on the CML and on the efficient frontier will have identical risk-return relationship and that is the point that corresponds to the market portfolio 'M'). Thus, the portfolios that lie on the CML are more efficient than the portfolios that lie of the efficient frontier. *CML, in effect has become the new efficient frontier.*

8.17.4. Efficient Frontier with Borrowing at Risk-free Rate

The lower part of CML (the line segment 'DM' in Fig. 8.24), consists of portfolios that are a combination of market portfolio and a risk-free security. When an investor, whose portfolio lies on the line 'DM', invests a portion of his funds in a risk-free security, this amounts to the investor lending at risk-free interest rate. When the proportion of investment in the risk-free asset gets reduced, the investor's portfolio will move along the line 'DM', towards the point 'M'. Exactly at the point 'M', we reach a situation where the investor would have invested all his money in the market portfolio and none in the risk-free security. For portfolios beyond point 'M', an investor would require additional funds since he would have already invested all his funds in the market portfolio. The segment 'ME' of the CML offers higher return than the efficient frontier for the same level of risk. The investor gets funds for additional investment in the market portfolio, by borrowing at risk-free interest rate. Thus, for all portfolios that lie in the CML beyond the point 'M' (representing the market portfolio),the investors would have borrowed at risk-free rate and invested the borrowed amount in the market portfolio, apart from having invested their owned funds entirely in the market portfolio.

The portfolios that lie beyond the point 'M' are called levered portfolios (or leveraged portfolios) since the investors who invest in these portfolios make use of the leverage of borrowing at risk-free interest rate and investing in the market portfolio, wherein the risk-free interest rate will be lesser as compared to the return available from out of investments in the market portfolio.

Thus, the Capital Market Line contains efficient portfolios of all investors who invest in a combination of market portfolio and risk-free security, either by investing a portion of their funds in risk-free security and the balance in the market portfolio or by borrowing at risk-free rate and investing the borrowed funds and their entire own funds in the market portfolio.

8.17.5. Return from Portfolios that Lie on the CML

(a) *When the investor invests a portion of his funds in risk-free security and the balance in market portfolio (i.e., when the portfolio lies on the lower part of the CML, – between points 'D' and 'M' as read in Fig. 8.24).*

Expected return from the portfolio is given by,

$$R_p = w \cdot R_m + (1 - w) \cdot R_f$$

Where,

R_p = Expected return from the portfolio

w = Weight (or proportion) of funds invested in risky portfolio (i.e., in market portfolio)

R_m = Return from market portfolio

R_f = Return from risk-free security (or risk-free asset)

$(1 - w)$ = Weight (or proportion) of funds invested in risk-free security

Risk of the portfolio is given by,

$$\sigma_p = w \cdot \sigma_m + (1 - w) \cdot \sigma_f$$

where,

σ_p = Standard deviation of portfolio return

w = Weight (or proportion) of funds invested in risky portfolio (i.e., in market portfolio)

σ_m = Standard deviation of the returns from the market portfolio

σ_f = Standard deviation of returns from the risk-free security

$(1 - w)$ = Weight (or proportion) of funds invested in the risk-free security

Since $\sigma_f = 0$, the formula will get reduced to,

$$\sigma_p = w \cdot \sigma_m$$

(b) *When the investor borrows some amount at risk-free interest rate and invests the same in the market portfolio, apart from investing his entire owned funds in the market portfolio. (This is a levered portfolio.)*

Expected return from the portfolio is given by,

$$R_p = w \cdot R_m - (w - 1) \cdot R_f$$

Where,

R_p = Expected return from the portfolio

w = Weight (or proportion) of funds invested in risky portfolio (i.e., in market portfolio)

R_m = Return from market portfolio

R_f = Return from risk-free security (or risk-free asset)

$(w - 1)$ = Weight (or proportion) of funds invested in risk-free security

In a levered portfolio, since the investor borrows at risk-free rate and invests in the market portfolio, 'w' will be greater than 1.00. This is because, when $w = 1$, it means that the investor invests his entire owned funds in the market portfolio. Since, the investor borrows extra money at risk-free rate,, the proportion of borrowed funds will be $(w - 1)$. *(For example, if the owned funds is say, Rs. 100 and if the investor borrows Rs. 25 and invests Rs. 125 in the market portfolio, 'w' will be 1.25).* As the interest that the investor pays on the borrowing is an outflow of funds, $(w - 1)\cdot R_f$ is to be deducted from the term $w\cdot R_m$ to arrive at the portfolio return.

The risk of the levered portfolio is given by,

$$\sigma_p = w\cdot \sigma_m - (w - 1)\cdot \sigma_f$$

Since σ_f is zero,

$$\sigma_p = w\cdot \sigma_m \quad \text{('}w\text{' will be more than 1.00)}$$

8.17.6. Relationship Between Risk and Return of Portfolios that Lie on the Capital Market Line

Refer Fig. 8.25. Consider a portfolio that lie on the lower portion of the CML, i.e., a portfolio that lies between points 'D' and 'M'. (The point 'D' represents the risk-free security and the point 'M' represents the market portfolio.) Let this portfolio is represented by point 'a' on the CML.

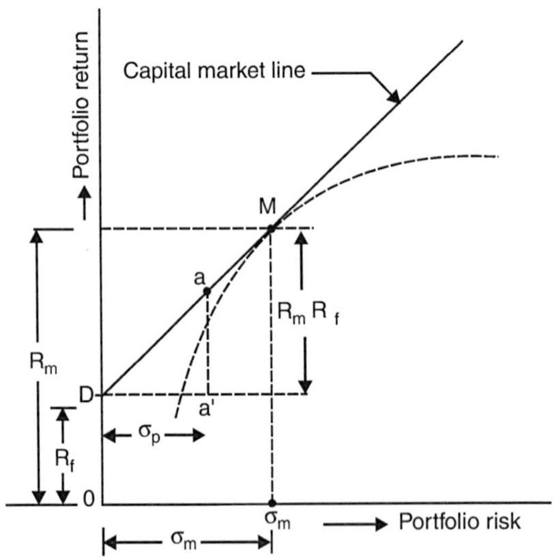

Fig. 8.25 Risk-return relationship of portfolios on the CML

Portfolio return is given by,

$$R_p = R_f + (aa^l)$$

$$= R_f + (R_m - R_f) \times \frac{\sigma_p}{\sigma_m}$$

Similarly, consider a portfolio that lie on the upper portion of the CML, i.e., a portfolio that lies between points 'M' and 'E'. Let this portfolio be represented by point 'b' on the CML (Refer Fig. 8.26).

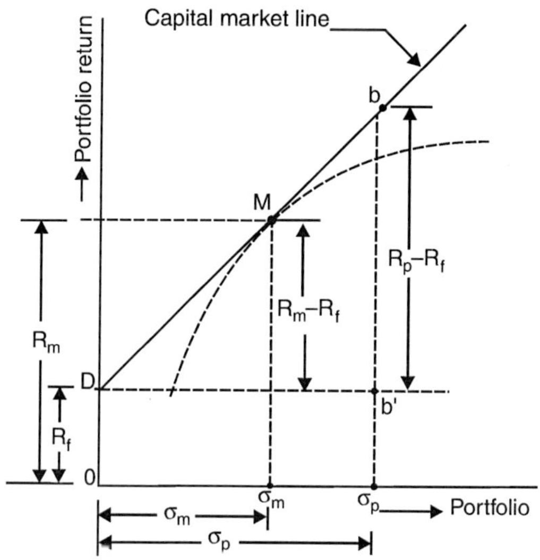

Fig. 8.26 Risk-return relationship of portfolios on the CML

Portfolio return is given by,

$$R_p = R_f + (bb^I)$$

$$= R_f + (R_m - R_f) \times \frac{\sigma_p}{\sigma_m}$$

So, the return from an efficient portfolio on the CML comprises of two components, viz., R_f and $(R_m - R_f) \times (\sigma_p/\sigma_m)$. Out of these two components, the term R_f is the risk-free return and it is a reward for waiting. The other component $(R_m - R_f) \times (\sigma_p/\sigma_m)$ is the risk premium or the price that the investors get for bearing risk. When the risk of the portfolio chosen by an investor is high, (i.e, when σ_p is high), the risk premium will be high, since in the second term $(R_m - R_f) \times (\sigma_p/\sigma_m)$, except σ_p, all other components are constants at a given point of time. Only σ_p is a variable and it will vary depending upon the risk of the portfolio.

Thus, CML provides linear relationship between the risk and return of all efficient portfolios when the risk is measured in terms of Standard Deviation.

The portfolios that lie on the CML are efficient portfolios. They are more efficient than the portfolios that lie on the efficient frontier of portfolios containing only risky securities that is in the shape of a concave curve. This is because, for any given level of risk, the portfolios on the CML offer a higher return than the portfolios that lie on the efficient frontier. But, the portfolios on the CML contain risk-free securities also. The assumption is that investors are able to invest in risk-free securities as well as borrow any amount at risk-free rate and invest in the market portfolio. *The validity of CML rests on the ability of the investors to borrow any amount at risk-free interest rate.*

***Illustration* 8.10:**

An investor invests 30% of his funds in risk-free asset and the remaining 70% of funds in an index fund that represents the market. The risk free return is 8.00%. The index fund is expected to give a return of 21.00%.

(*a*) What is the expected return from the portfolio of the investor? The Standard Deviation of returns from the Index fund is 9.80. What is the Standard Deviation of the portfolio return?

(*b*) If the investor withdraws his investment in the risk-free security and invests the same also in the index fund, what is the expected return? What is the portfolio risk?

(*c*) If apart from investing his entire funds in the index fund, the investor borrows a sum equal to 20% of his available funds at risk-free rate of interest and invests the same also in the index fund, what is the expected return? What is the portfolio risk?

Solution:

An index fund is a fund that invests its corpus in a basket of securities that are contained in a Stock Market Index (such as SENSEX, NIFTY etc.,). The weight of each stock in the fund will be equal to the weight of the respective stock in the Stock Market Index chosen.

It is given that the index fund represents the market. Hence, the portfolio of investments can be taken to fall on the CML.

(*a*) Expected return from the portfolio is given by,

$$
\begin{aligned}
R_p &= w \cdot R_m + (1 - w) \cdot R_f \\
&= (0.30 \times 21\%) + (1 - 0.30) \times 8\% \\
&= 6.30\% + 5.60\% \\
&= 11.90\%
\end{aligned}
$$

Standard Deviation of the portfolio is given by,

$$
\begin{aligned}
\sigma_p &= w \cdot \sigma_m \\
&= 0.30 \times 9.80 \\
&= 2.94\%
\end{aligned}
$$

(*b*) The investor invests his entire funds in the portfolio of index fund and no investment is made in risk-free asset.

Return from the portfolio (R_p) = 21.00%

Standard Deviation of the portfolio (σ_p) = 9.80% (*This is equal to σ_m)

(*c*) The investor invests his entire funds in the portfolio of index fund and also borrows at risk-free rate and invests the borrowings in the index fund.

Let the amount of owned funds = X

Risk-free borrowings (@20%) = $0.2X$

Total investment in the index fund = $X + 0.2X$

= $1.2X$

Hence, the weight of funds invested in the risky portfolio (i.e., index fund) is 1.20.

Expected return from the portfolio is given by,

$$R_p = w \cdot R_m - (w - 1) \cdot R_f$$
$$= (1.20 \times 21\%) - [(1.20 - 1.00) \times 8.00\%]$$
$$= 25.20\% - 1.60\%$$
$$= 23.60\%$$

Standard Deviation of the portfolio is given by,

$$\sigma_p = w \cdot \sigma_m$$
$$= 1.20 \times 9.80$$
$$= 11.76\%$$

Note: *Leveraging a portfolio introduces more risk. This is because the swings in the portfolio returns will now occur on a larger amount of capital. Levered portfolios offer higher return than the market return, but with a higher risk.*

8.17.7. Security Market Line

The CML is a great simplification that has been arrived at with simple and rational assumptions. Though some of the assumptions may not be tenable, still CML gives investors and analysts a simple mechanism to identify efficient portfolios that suits their risk bearing capacity. The CML gives the risk-return relationship of all efficient portfolios. The CML dominates all other available portfolios. All portfolios, other than the efficient portfolios lie below the CML in the risk-return graph.

The CML, however, does not describe the risk-return relationship of inefficient portfolios. Also, the CML does not describe the risk-return relationship of individual securities. Hence, there must be a model that describes the risk-return relationship of all portfolios (efficient or otherwise) and all individual securities. Such a model will be much more useful to investors. CAPM does exactly that.

The risk of a security (as measured by the Standard deviation of its return) consists of two components, viz., systematic risk (or market risk) and unsystematic risk (or diversifiable risk). As more and more risky securities are added to the portfolio, the unsystematic risk gets gradually reduced. When the portfolio becomes well diversified, the unsystematic risk tends to become zero and only the systematic risk will be present. Hence, for a well diversified portfolio, it is only the systematic risk that is relevant. Systematic risk is measured by 'Beta' coefficient (β). Hence, it can be construed that it is 'Beta' that is the correct measure of a security's risk as well the risk of a portfolio.

Thus, we are led to a logical conclusion that the expected return from a security or a portfolio should be related to its 'Beta' ('Beta' of security or portfolio as the case may be). A 'Beta' value of 1.00 indicates that the security (or portfolio) behaves similar to the market and its value moves in the same direction and at the same rate as the market portfolio. When the 'Beta' of a security or portfolio is greater than 1.00, it indicates higher sensitivity to market changes. Obviously, when the value of 'Beta' is less than 1.00, it indicates lower sensitivity to market changes.

The relationship between expected return and Beta (β) of a security or a portfolio can be determined using a linear relationship between the two. Consider Fig. 8.27.

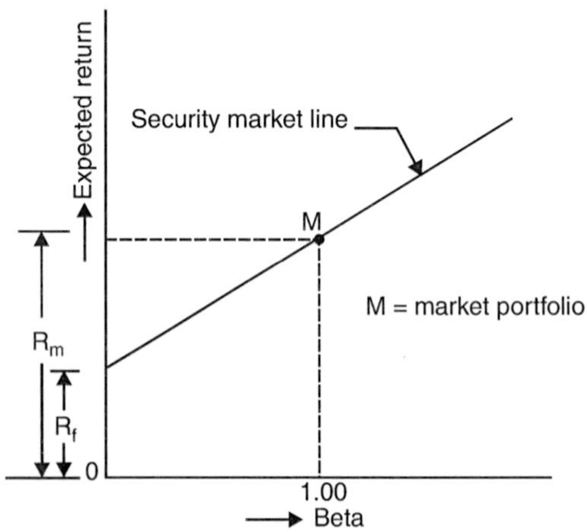

Fig. 8.27 Security market line

Let the Y-axis represents the expected return and the X-axis represents the 'Beta' coefficient. A risk-free return has a 'Beta' of zero since it is not sensitive to changes in market return. If the return from the risk-free security is 'R_f', its position can be located on the Y-axis. 'Beta' value of 1.00 indicates Market Portfolio (or a security whose risk-return characteristic is identical to the Market Portfolio), whose return is 'R_m'. Thus, the point

'M' can be marked at the intersection of 'R_m' and $\beta = 1.00$. If a line is drawn joining the location of risk-free security on the Y-axis and point 'M' representing the market portfolio and extending the line beyond point 'M', this line gives the risk-return relationship of all securities and portfolios. This line is known as 'Security Market Line'. *The relationship between the risk and return established by the Security Market Line (SML) is known as CAPM. The Security Market Line (SML) provides the relationship between 'Beta' and the expected return of a security or a portfolio.* This relationship is expressed as below:

$$R_i = R_f + (R_m - R_f) \cdot \beta_i$$

Where,

R_i = return from the 'i' th security or portfolio

R_f = risk-free return

β_i = 'Beta' of security 'i' or portfolio 'i'

The risk-free return (R_f) is the reward for waiting. The term $(R_m - R_f) \cdot \beta_i$ is the reward for taking risk. It is also called risk premium. $(R_m - R_f)$ is the risk premium of the market which is the excess return offered by the market over the risk-free return.

Thus, CAPM is defined by the following relationship:

Expected return of a security or portfolio = Risk free return + {Beta × (Risk premium of the market)}

8.17.8. CML versus SML

Both CML and SML offer linear relationship between risk and return. The CML offers risk-return relationship of efficient portfolios. In CML, the risk is defined as the total risk and is measured by Standard Deviation of returns. The SML offers risk-return relationship of all portfolios (efficient and inefficient) and all securities. In SML, the risk is defined as the systematic risk and is measured by 'Beta'.

8.17.9. Pricing of Securities with CAPM

CAPM leads to the formation of SML which shows the relationship between risk and expected return of individual securities and portfolio of securities. Hence, SML gives the expected return for a given risk. SML provides the basis for assessing whether a security is correctly priced, over-priced or under-priced. The expected price of a security can be read from the SML, by reading the Y-axis value that corresponds to the 'Beta' value of the security. This is the theoretical value of expected return from the security.

The return that a security is expected to offer can be found out by taking into account the current market price of the security, the estimated market price after one year and the expected devidend for the year. The expected return based on these factors can be arrived at as below:

$$\text{Expected return} = \frac{(\text{Market price after one year} - \text{Current market price}) + \text{Dividend}}{\text{Current market price}}$$

The return so arrived at may lie either above or below the SML. If the return lies above the SML, the security is considered under-priced. This is because the security offers a higher return than what is expected. If the return lies below the SML, the security is considered over-priced. This is because the security offers a lower return than what is expected.

***Illustration* 8.11:**

The risk-free rate of return is 9% and the expected market return is 21%. The estimated rates of return of eight securities 'A' to 'H' and their respective 'Beta' coefficients are as under:

Security	Estimated rate of return*	'Beta' coefficient
A	15.00%	1.15
B	17.00%	1.19
C	23.00%	1.22
D	30.00%	1.75
E	20.00%	1.14
F	18.00%	1.13
G	25.00%	1.21

Using CAPM, identify the securities that are correctly priced, over-priced and under-priced.

Solution:

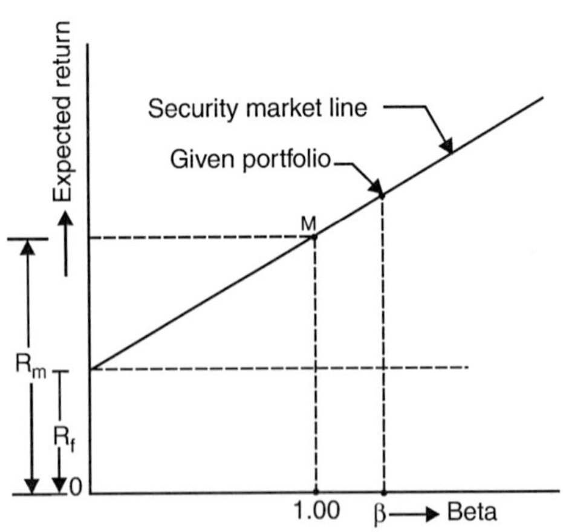

Fig. 8.28 Security market line

(* This would have been arrived at based on the current stock price, anticipated stock price the next year and the anticipated dividend.)

Expected return according to the CAPM is given by,

$$\text{Expected return} = \text{Risk-free return} + \text{Risk Premium}$$
$$= R_f + \beta \times (R_m - R_f)$$

Since $R_f = 9\%$ and $R_m = 21\%$, the expected return from securities is given by,

$$\text{Expected return} = 9.00 + \beta \times (21 - 9)$$
$$= 9 + 12\beta$$

For the given securities 'A' to 'H' the expected returns can be arrived at by substituting their respective 'Beta' values. The results are as under:

Security	**Beta (β)**	**Expected return as per CAPM**
A	1.15	22.80%
B	1.19	23.28%
C	1.22	23.64%
D	1.75	30.00%
E	1.14	22.68%
F	1.13	22.56%
G	1.21	23.52%

The expected return according to CAPM and the estimated return of each security are given below:

Security	**Expected return as per CAPM**	**Estimated return**
A	22.80%	15.00%
B	23.28%	17.00%
C	23.64%	23.00%
D	30.00%	30.00%
E	22.68%	20.00%
F	22.56%	18.00%
G	23.52%	25.00%

The expected returns as per CAPM and the estimated returns of the securities are plotted in a graph (Refer Fig. 8.29).

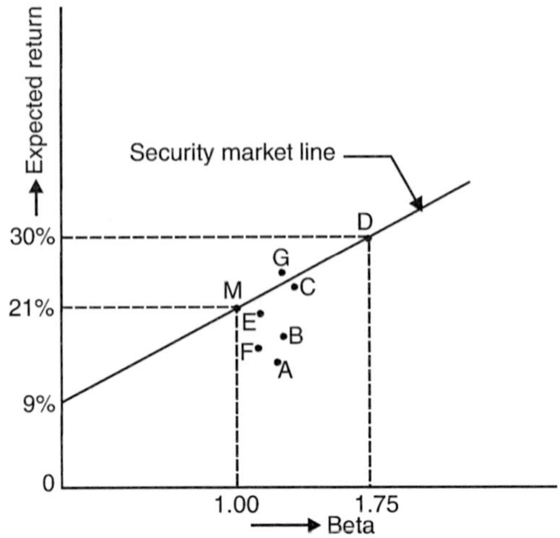

Fig. 8.29 CAPM and security valuation

Observation

Security 'D' is correctly priced.
Securities 'G' is under-priced
Securities 'A', 'B', 'C', 'E' and 'F' are over-priced.

8.18. ARBITRAGE PRICING THEORY

CAPM is a single factor model. It relates the return from an asset or portfolio to its 'Beta'. Hence, CAPM uses a single 'Beta' value. CAPM is not always able to account for the difference in return from assets that have the same 'Beta' value. This led to the development of an alternative approach to asset pricing called the Arbitrage Pricing Theory (APT), that was developed by Stephon A. Ross.

In economics and finance, the term 'Arbitrage' refers to the practice of taking advantage of price differential between two or more markets. It is the simultaneous buying and selling of assets (stocks, bonds, foreign exchange and other commodities) at two different prices in two different markets. By buying at one market where the price is lower and simultaneously selling at the other market where the price is higher, the investor earns a profit without bearing any risk.

Assumptions

APT makes the following assumptions:

1. The investors are risk averse.
2. The investors choose to maximize their returns for a given level of risk.
3. Perfect competition prevails in the market.
4. The investors have homogeneous expectations.

As against a single 'Beta' used in CAPM, APT used many 'Beta' coefficients. The 'Beta' used in CAPM is the coefficient that captures the systematic risk of an asset (or portfolio). According to APT, there are a number of company-specific factors and a number of macro economic factors that affect the security return.

APT states that the expected return from a security depends on how the security reacts to the individual factors and the risk premium associated with each of the factors. APT assumes that the return from an asset (or security) has two components, viz., the expected (or predictable) return and the unexpected (or unpredictable) return.

$$E(R_i) = R_f + UR$$

Where,

$E(R_i)$ = Expected return from asset 'i'

R_f = Predictable return (i.e., risk-free return on a zero 'Beta' asset)

UR = Unpredictable part of the security return

The unpredictable part of the return (UR) again has two components, viz., unpredictable return due to company-specific factors and due to market-related macro level factors that affect all firms.

$$UR = UR_{\text{specific}} + UR_{\text{market related}}$$

Thus,

$$E(R_i) = R_f + UR_{\text{market-related}} + UR_{\text{specific}}$$

The unpredictable return due to market-related factors ($UR_{\text{market-related}}$) may be under the influence of many factors like GDP, inflation, interest rate etc., Again, each of these factors will affect every security differently. The return from one security may be more affected by, say, inflation than another security. Hence, the sensitivity of each asset's return to each of the factors needs to be estimated. Thus, there will be as many 'Betas' as the number of market-related macro level factors.

Thus,

$$E(R_i) = R_f + (\beta_1 \cdot UR_{F1} + \beta_2 \cdot UR_{F2} + \beta_3 \cdot UR_{F3} + \beta_4 \cdot UR_{F4} + \ldots\ldots\ldots) + \text{UR}_{\text{specific}}$$

Where,

β_1 = Beta of factor -1 (i.e., sensitivity of the asset's return to changes in factor values) – also called 'factor-Beta'.

β_2 = Beta of factor -2...........etc.,

UR_{F1} = unexpected component of return due to factor -1

UR_{F2} = unexpected component of return due to factor -2........etc.,

The above equation can be written as,

$$E(R_i) = R_f + \beta_1 \cdot (RF_1 - R_f) + \beta_2 \cdot (RF_2 - R_f) + \beta_3 \cdot (RF_3 - R_f) + \ldots$$
$$\beta_n \cdot (RF_n - R_f) + UR_{specific}$$

Where,

RF_1 = Expected return due to factor-1

RF_2 = Expected return due to factor-2 ... etc.,

$(RF_1 - R_f)$ = Risk premium of factor-1

$(RF_2 - R_f)$ = Risk premium of factor-2 ... etc.,

(Risk premium is the compensation over and above the risk-free return that investors require for the risk contributed by a factor).

So, the steps in calculating the expected return as per APT are as below:

1. Search for the factors that affect the asset's return.*
2. Estimate the risk premium for each factor
3. Estimate the factor Beta for each factor
4. Arrive at the expected return

Risk premium can be estimated using the past data on actual values of return and forecasted values. Factor Beta can be estimated using regression approach.

According to APT, an asset is not correctly priced if the current price is different from the price predicted by the model. The arbitrageur sells the asset that is over-priced and using the sale proceeds, buys the asset that is under-priced.

***Illustration* 8.12:**

The risk-free return is 7% and the expected return from market portfolio is 17%. The following are the 'Beta' coefficients of a security-X.

β_1 = Beta coefficient in relation to market portfolio = 1.45

β_2 = Beta coefficient in relation to GDP growth rate = 0.40

β_3 = Beta coefficient in relation to inflation = 0.30

Expected return due to GDP growth rate is 9% and due to inflation is 3%. Find the expected return from the security according to APT.

---

* Identifying and quantifying all the factors will be a very complex task. However, keeping the complexity in mind, Stephon A. Ross identified the following four macro economic factors which have greater influence on stock prices.

1. Inflation
2. GNP
3. Spread between long term and short term interest rates
4. Spread between low grade bonds and high grade bonds.)

Solution:

Expected return from the security is given by,

$$E(R_i) = R_f + \beta_1 \cdot (RF_1 - R_f) + \beta_2 \cdot (RF_2 - R_f) + \beta_3 \cdot (RF_3 - R_f) + \ldots \beta_n \cdot (RF_n - R_f) + UR_{\text{specific}}$$

$$= 7\% + [0.40 \times (9 - 7) + 0.3 \times (3 - 7)] + [1.45 \times (17 - 7)]$$

$$= 21.10\%$$

[Note: $[1.45 \times (17–7)]$ is UR_{specific}]

Note: *Though APT is theoretically appealing, it is very difficult to be applied in practice since APT requires many subjective estimates that are difficult to arrive at. Hence, APT has not established its superiority over CAPM.*

Portfolio Optimization using APT

According to APT, an investor tries to find out the possibility of increasing the portfolio return, without increasing the total investment in the portfolio. The investor would also like to keep the portfolio risk at the same level, despite aiming for a higher return. Let us see how the investor could do this.

Let the portfolio consists of three securities, *A*, *B* and *C*. The total investment in the portfolio is going to remain unchanged. The investor can only change the proportion of investments made in the securities *A*, *B* and *C*, without any additional financial commitment. Let X_A, X_B and X_C are the proportions of securities *A*, *B* and *C* respectively, in the portfolio. Let ΔX_A, ΔX_B and ΔX_C are the changes in proportions of securities. Since, the total investment made in the portfolio is not going to be altered, the changes in proportions of securities will have to add up to zero.

i.e., $\Delta X_A + \Delta X_B + \Delta X_C = 0.00$

(For example, if ΔX_A and ΔX_B are positive, ΔX_C has to be negative to the same extent, in order to make the total zero. Under such conditions, the investor will buy securities '*A*' and '*B*' and will sell security '*C*' in such a way that the return from the portfolio increases for the same level of risk, the original investment in the portfolio remaining unchanged.)

REVIEW QUESTIONS

1. What are the steps involved in analysis and construction of a portfolio of securities?
2. What is an efficient portfolio?
3. Explain Markowitz portfolio theory.
4. How does risk reduction takes place when securities are combined into a portfolio? Explain with an illustration.

5. Describe Markowitz efficient frontier and explain how it dominates the portfolios that lie below it.
6. What are investor indifference curves and how are they helpful in locating the optimal portfolio for an investor?
7. What are the limitations of Markowitz portfolio model? How does Sharpe's Single index model overcome the limitation of Markowitz model?
8. What is Capital market Line? Explain the use of Capital market Line in calculating portfolio returns.
9. Define Capital Asset Pricing Model(CAPM). Explain the method of pricing securities using CAPM.
10. Explain 'Arbitrage Pricing Theory'.

9 CHAPTER

Portfolio Evaluation and Revision

9.1. INTRODUCTION

Portfolio once constructed, needs to be continuously evaluated and revised. Evaluation of portfolio is done to find out the extent up to which the objective of portfolio management has been achieved. Portfolio evaluation refers to the evaluation of the performance of the portfolio. There is subtle difference between performance assessment and performance evaluation. While performance assessment (or performance measurement) is the process of measuring the return earned by a portfolio during the holding period, performance evaluation is a process that goes one step further and verifies whether the return earned by a portfolio is superior to or inferior to a benchmark portfolio, whether the superior/inferior performance is due to skillful management/bad luck etc.

9.2. PORTFOLIO EVALUATION

Portfolio evaluation refers to the performance evaluation of the portfolio. It is the process of judging whether the performance of a portfolio has been good, bad or satisfactory. The investor designs his portfolio after a detailed analysis and constructs an optimal portfolio.

The need for portfolio evaluation at periodic intervals arises to check up whether the portfolio continues to remain an optimal portfolio. Portfolio evaluation is the process of assessing the performance of the portfolio in terms of risk versus return over a period of time.

Portfolio evaluation consists of two stage, viz.,

(*a*) Measurement of performance of the portfolio i.e., calculating the return earned by the portfolio in the context of the risk associated with the portfolio. The time-weighted rate of return has been accepted as a reasonably good measure of performance.

(*b*) Comparing the performance of the portfolio with other portfolios in the light of risks associated or with a benchmark portfolio and assessing as to whether the performance of the portfolio is superior, reasonable or inferior. Before comparing the performance of a given portfolio, a set of feasible portfolios (taken from the opportunity set of portfolios) with similar risk and other characteristics is to be constructed. The performance of the given portfolio is then compared with the set of feasible portfolios to arrive at a conclusion as to whether the given portfolio has performed well or not.

9.3. NEED FOR PORTFOLIO EVALUATION

The objective of managing a portfolio is to build an optimum portfolio and to ensure that the portfolio continues to remain an optimum one. An optimum portfolio once constructed will not remain an optimum portfolio for ever. Changes in market conditions, changes in the risk-return characteristics of the individual securities that constitute the portfolio, changes in interest rates etc., will have their effect on the portfolio and hence a performance evaluation of the portfolio is required to be done at periodic intervals to check up whether the objectives of the portfolio are being met and to revise the portfolio if required, in order to ensure that the portfolio continues to serve its objectives.

9.4. RATIOS FOR PORTFOLIO EVALUATION

While evaluating the performance of a portfolio, the return from the portfolio is first arrived at. Then, the return earned per unit of risk is arrived at and this "return per unit of risk" is the measure that is used to evaluate the portfolio performance. Two ratios are popularly used for portfolio evaluation. They are,

Sharpe Ratio

and Treynor Ratio

Sharpe Ratio

This ratio was suggested by William Sharpe

$$\text{Sharpe ratio} = \frac{r_p - r_f}{\sigma_p}$$

where

r_p = return realized from the portfolio

r_f = risk free rate of return

σ_p = standard deviation of the portfolio return

Since, standard deviation of the portfolio return is in the denominator of the formula, Sharpe Ratio measures the return over and above the risk-free return per unit of 'Total risk' of the portfolio, as measured by standard deviation of the portfolio.

Treynor Ratio

This ratio was suggested by Jack Treynor.

$$\text{Treynor ratio} = \frac{r_p - r_f}{\beta_p}$$

where

r_p = return realized from the portfolio

r_f = risk free rate of return

β_p = 'β' of the portfolio return

β is the index of the systematic risk. Since β of the portfolio (β_p) is in the denominator of the formula, Treynor Ratio measures the return over and above the risk free return per unit of systematic risk, as measured by 'β' of the portfolio.

9.5. COMPARISON BETWEEN SHARPE RATIO AND TREYNOR RATIO

Both these ratios measure the portfolio return per unit of risk. While Sharpe ratio uses the total risk (represented by standard deviation of the portfolio), Treynor Ratio uses only the systematic risk (represented by 'β' of the portfolio). When the performances of two portfolios are compared on the basis of either Sharpe Ratio or Treynor Ratio, the portfolio that shows a higher value ratio is considered to have performed better. While William Sharpe put forth that the appropriate measure of risk is only the total risk and not the systematic risk alone, Jack Treynor was of the view that it is the systematic risk that is relevant. Rather than going into the merits of these two versions, it would be better if we know where to use Sharpe Ratio and where to use Treynor Ratio.

When a portfolio is a fully diversified one, there won't be any unsystematic risk and the total risk will be represented by systematic risk. In such a case, Treynor Ratio will be a better measure for comparison of portfolios.

When a portfolio is not a well diversified one, it will have both systematic risk as well as unsystematic risk. In such a case, Sharpe Ratio will be a better measure for comparison of portfolios. For sector specific funds, Sharpe's ratio will be an appropriate measure since such funds will have the presence of unsystematic risk.

Let there are a few portfolios and that we want to ascertain if the portfolios are well diversified. We can make use of Sharpe's ratio and Treynor's ratio to find out if the portfolios are well diversified. When the portfolios are ranked on the basis of Sharpe's ratio and also on the basis of Treynor's ratio, both the ranking will be identical, if the portfolios are well diversified.

***Illustration* 9.1:**

Compare the following two portfolios on the basis of Sharpe Ratio and Treynor Ratio and offer your comments:

Portfolio	Return from the portfolio	Standard deviation (%)	Beta (β)
A	10%	13	0.75
B	20%	26	1.45
Market portfolio	14%	18	1.00

Interest free rate of return = 8%.

***Solution*:**

Sharpe Ratio

(*i*) for portfolio–A $= \dfrac{10-8}{13}$

$= 0.154$

(*ii*) for portfolio–B $= \dfrac{20-8}{26}$

$= 0.462$

(*iii*) for market portfolio $= \dfrac{14-8}{18}$

$= 0.333$

Inference

Portfolio–B has performed better than the market portfolio while Portfolio–A has performed below the market portfolio.

Treynor Ratio

(*i*) for portfolio–A $= \dfrac{10-8}{0.75}$

$= 2.67$

(*ii*) for portfolio–B $= \dfrac{20-8}{1.45}$

$= 8.28$

(*iii*) for market portfolio $= \dfrac{14-8}{1.00}$

$= 6.00$

Inference

Portfolio–B has performed better than the market portfolio while portfolio–A has performed below the market portfolio.

Thus, both Sharpe ratio and Treynor ratio have given the same results. However, this need not be the case always.

*Both the portfolios A & B can be assumed to be nearly well diversified portfolios since their Beta values are nearer to **1.00**. Hence of the two ratios, Treynor ratio is the appropriate ratio for measuring the performance of the portfolios.*

***Illustration* 9.2:**

Compare the following two portfolios on the basis of Sharpe ratio and Treynor ratio and offer your comments:

Portfolio	Return from the portfolio	Standard deviation (%)	Beta (β)
A	10%	13	0.40
B	20%	26	3.00
Market portfolio	14%	18	1.00

Interest free rate of return = 8%.

Solution:

Sharpe Ratio

(*i*) for portfolio–A $= \dfrac{10-8}{13}$

$= 0.154$

(*ii*) for portfolio–B $= \dfrac{20-8}{26}$

$= 0.462$

(*iii*) for market portfolio $= \dfrac{14-8}{18}$

$= 0.333$

Treynor Ratio

(*i*) for portfolio–A $= \dfrac{10-8}{0.40}$

$= 5.00$

(*ii*) for portfolio–B $= \dfrac{20-8}{3.00}$

$= 4.00$

$$(iii) \text{ for market portfolio } = \frac{14-8}{1.00}$$

$$= 6.00$$

Inference

Sharpe and Treynor ratios give opposite results. While Sharpe ratio indicates that portfolio–B has performed better than portfolio–A, Treynor ratio indicates that portfolio–A has performed better than portfolio–B.

Since the Beta values of the portfolios are very much away from ***1.00,*** *it indicates that both the portfolios A & B are not well diversified portfolios. Hence, Sharpe ratio is the appropriate ratio to measure the relative performance of the portfolios.*

Accordingly, the result as revealed by Sharpe ratio is to be relied upon. Thus, it can be inferred that Portfolio–B has performed better than the market portfolio while portfolio–A has performed below the market portfolio.

***Illustration* 9.3:**

From the following data, find out the portfolios that are well diversified:

Portfolio	Return (%)	Standard deviation (%)	Beta
A	16.60	24.70	1.24
B	15.15	20.25	0.96
C	9.40	15.70	0.82
D	21.25	16.40	1.13
E	18.30	18.20	1.02

The risk-free return is 7.00%.

Solution:

From the given data, Sharpe's ratio and Treynor's ratio are calculated and given in the table below.

Risk-free return = 7.00%

$$\text{Sharpe's ratio} = \frac{r_p - r_f}{\sigma_p}$$

$$\text{Treynor's ratio} = \frac{r_p - r_f}{\beta_p}$$

Portfolio	Portfolio return (r_p) %	Portfolio std.dev. (σ_p) %	Portfolio Beta (β_p)	Sharpe's ratio	Treynor's ratio	Ranking as per Sharpe's ratio	Ranking as per Treynor's ratio
A	16.60	24.70	1.24	0.389	7.742	**4**	**4**
B	15.15	20.25	0.96	0.402	8.489	**3**	**3**
C	9.40	15.70	0.82	0.153	2.927	**5**	**5**
D	21.25	16.40	1.13	0.869	12.611	**1**	**1**
E	18.30	18.20	1.02	0.621	11.078	**2**	**2**

The ranking of portfolios is the same irrespective of whether Sharpe's ratio or Treynor's ratio is used for ranking. This gives an inference that all the five portfolios are fairly well diversified. This is because, when a portfolio is well diversified, the total risk will be nearly equal to the systematic risk.

***Illustration* 9.4:**

The ranking of five portfolios 'A' to 'E' as per Sharpe's measure and Treynor's measure are given below. Offer your inference about portfolios 'B' and 'E'.

Portfolio	Ranking as per Sharpe's measure	Ranking as per Treynor' measure
A	4	4
B	5	2
C	1	1
D	3	3
E	2	5

Solution:

***Portfolio* 'B'**

The ranking by the two measures differ. The Sharpe's ratio is higher as compared to Treynor's ratio. A higher Sharpe's Measure indicates higher component of unsystematic risk. This gives the inference that the portfolio is poorly diversified.

***Portfolio* 'E'**

The ranking by the two measures differ. The Treynor's ratio is higher as compared to Sharpe's ratio. A lower Sharpe's Measure indicates that the component of unsystematic risk is lower. This means better diversification. A higher value of Treynor's ratio indicates that the 'Beta' of the portfolio is higher. The portfolio will consist of high 'Beta' securities.

9.6. JENSEN'S MEASURE

Michael Jensen developed a method for measuring portfolio performance using CAPM. Jensen's measure calculates the difference between the actual return earned by a portfolio and the expected return from the portfolio as predicted by the CAPM. The CAPM is used to calculate the return expected from the given portfolio for its given level of risk. While the Sharpe's and Treynor's ratios measure the relative performance of the portfolios, Jensen's measure evaluates the absolute performance of portfolios.

The difference between the actual return earned by the portfolio and the expected return from the portfolio as arrived at using the CAPM is called the 'differential return'. Differential return is the return earned by a portfolio over and above the return expected to be earned by the portfolio for its level of systematic risk.

The expected return from a portfolio as given by the CAPM is given by,

$$E(R_p) = R_f + \beta_p (R_m - R_f)$$

where,

$E(R_p)$ = Expected portfolio return

R_m = Market return

R_f = Risk-free return

β_p = Beta coefficient of the portfolio (a measure of the systematic risk)

The differential return of the portfolio (α_p)* is known as the Jensen's measure and is calculated as below:

$$\alpha_p = R_p - E(R_p)$$

where,

R_p = Actual return earned by the portfolio

$E(R_p)$ = Expected return from the portfolio as arrived at by the CAPM

If α_p is positive, it is inferred that the portfolio has earned superior returns due to superior management skills. When α_p is zero, the actual and the expected returns are the same and it is inferred that the portfolio performance is normal. If α_p is negative, it is inferred that the portfolio performance is inferior as compared to the performance of the market and the reason for poor performance is attributed to weaker management skills.

***Illustration* 9.4:**

There are two equity funds A and B, the details of which are as below:

		Fund–A	Fund–B
Actual return from the fund	:	17%	19%
Beta coefficient	:	1.60	0.70

* also called 'Jensen's Alpha

The market return is 18% and the risk-free interest rate is 6%. Evaluate the portfolios on the basis of Jensen's measure.

Solution:

Expected return from portfolio–A as per CAPM $= R_f + \beta_p (R_m - R_f)$

$$= 6\% + 1.60 \times (18\% - 6\%)$$
$$= 6\% + 1.60 \times (12\%)$$
$$= 25.20\%$$

Jensen's measure for portfolio–A is given by,

$$(\alpha_P)_A = R_p - E(R_p)$$
$$= 17\% - 25.20\%$$
$$= (-)\ 8.20\%$$

Expected return from portfolio–B as per CAPM $= R_f + \beta_p (R_m - R_f)$

$$= 6\% + 0.70 \times (18\% - 6\%)$$
$$= 6\% + 0.70 \times (12\%)$$
$$= 14.40\%$$

Jensen's measure for portfolio–B is given by,

$$(\alpha_P)_B = R_p - E(R_p)$$
$$= 19\% - 14.40\%$$
$$= 4.60\%$$

Inference

The negative value of Jensen's measure for portfolio–A indicates that the performance of portfolio–A is poor. The portfolio–B has performed better in view of the positive value of Jensen's measure.

9.7. FAMA'S DECOMPOSITION OF TOTAL RETURN FROM A PORTFOLIO

The performance measures discussed earlier attempt to make an overall assessment of the portfolio performance. Portfolio performance will have a few components. An interested portfolio analyzer will be interested to know the components of portfolio performance. Following the works of Sharpe, Treynor and Jensen, Eugene Fama proposed a method to segregate portfolio performance into its components. Fama advocated a method to assess the returns offered by managed portfolios by comparing the given portfolio with naively selected portfolios having the same level of risk.

Consider a Security Market Line (SML). The SML is a straight line drawn connecting the points representing the risk-free asset and the market portfolio in a graph where the X-axis represents 'Beta' and the Y-axis represents the return. When a portfolio manager desires to have a portfolio with a certain risk level, he can build his portfolio as a combination of a risk-free asset and market portfolio and can identify the required proportion between the two with the help of the SML. Let portfolio 'A' is the chosen portfolio that has a risk (systematic risk) of β_A and offers a return of R_A. (Refer Fig. 9.1). Let there is another portfolio–B that has the same systematic risk of portfolio 'A', but offers a higher return. This portfolio will lie vertically above the portfolio 'A' and let its return is R_B.

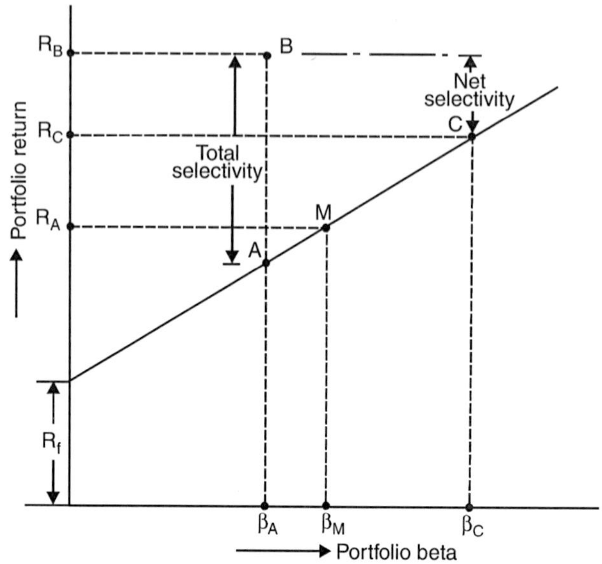

Fig. 9.1 Fama's decomposition of portfolio return

Portfolio 'A' is a combination of risk-free asset and market portfolio. Hence, portfolio 'A' will not have any unsystematic (or diversifiable) risk. Portfolio 'B' is not a market portfolio. Hence, portfolio 'B' will have some diversifiable risk. It is obvious that portfolio 'B' could offer higher return than portfolio 'A', for the reason that it bears some diversifiable risk. Though the systematic risks of both the portfolios are the same, the total risk of portfolio 'B' will be more than the total risk of portfolio 'A'. The total risk borne by portfolio 'A' is completely non-diversifiable. Hence, the total risk borne by portfolio 'A' can be attributed only to the fluctuations in return of the market portfolio. The total risk of portfolio 'A' will be equal to β_A while the total risk of portfolio 'B' will be β_A plus some diversifiable risk. Portfolio 'B' has earned extra return of $(R_B - R_A)$ since portfolio 'B' has assumed some diversifiable risk.

The investor who has chosen portfolio 'B' earns extra return by bearing some diversifiable risk. The question that will become relevant here to know whether the extra return earned is worth the extra risk borne by the portfolio 'B'.

The following discussion gives an answer to the above question. Consider another portfolio 'C' on the Security Market Line, beyond point 'M'. The portfolio 'C' is so chosen that its systematic risk is equal to the total risk of portfolio 'B'. Portfolio 'C' being on the SML has no diversifiable risk (since this portfolio consists of only a combination of risk-free asset and market portfolio) and hence we can say that its total risk and the systematic risk are one and the same, represented by β_C. Thus, portfolios B and C are comparable in terms of total risk.

Let variance of portfolio 'B' $= \sigma_B^2$

We can write the variance of portfolio 'C' in terms of the variance of the market portfolio.

Since the risk of the naive portfolio 'C' is totally non-diversifiable, its total risk is equal to its systematic risk.

Variance of portfolio 'C' $= \beta_C^2 . \sigma_M^2$

Equating the variance of the two portfolios (i.e., Portfolios 'B' & 'C'), we get,

$$\beta_C^2 . \sigma_M^2 = \sigma_B^2$$

$$\beta_C = \sqrt{(\sigma_B^2 / \sigma_M^2)}$$

Using β_C we can locate the comparable portfolio 'C' on the SML.

Let $\sigma_B^2 = 250$ and let $\sigma_M^2 = 120$. Substituting the values we get $\beta_C = 1.443$. We can locate the portfolio 'C' on the SML, corresponding to Beta value of 1.443. Let the return from portfolio 'C' is R_C. If the value of β_C is such that the return R_B is above the return R_C, it indicates that portfolio manager is justified in taking extra risk to earn extra return. But for his extra efforts, he would have only earned a return equal to R_C which is the return that can be earned without taking any special efforts and by combining a risk-free asset and the market portfolio.

Portfolio 'B' and portfolio 'C' have the same total risk. However, portfolio 'B' has earned extra return of $(R_B - R_C)$. This extra return earned is due to superior stock selection skills of the portfolio manager and is called **'Net Selectivity'**.

Portfolio 'A' and portfolio 'B' have the same systematic risk. The difference between the returns of these two portfolios $(R_B - R_A)$ is called **'Total Selectivity'**.

The 'Total selectivity' is the sum of 'Net selectivity' and something else. This 'something else' is $(R_C - R_A)$ which is the extra return earned by the portfolio 'B' due to inadequate diversification.

Hence,

[Return from Total Selectivity] = [Return from Net Selectivity] + [Return for diversifiable risk]

***Illustration* 9.6:**

There are four funds whose details are given in the table below. Using Jensen's Measure identify the funds that have earned excess returns.

Name of the fund	Return earned (%)	Portfolio Beta	Portfolio standard deviation
Super Star	25	1.13	22.70
True Balance	17	0.95	17.20
Sure Return	20	0.98	20.90
Safety Net	15.30	1.00	15.60

Risk-free return is 8.50%

Solution:

The fund 'Safety Net' has a Beta value of 1.00. Hence, it resembles the market. The return of 15.30% earned by this fund can be considered to be the market return for calculation purposes.

Super Star

Expected return from the fund as per CAPM $= R_f + \beta_p\ (R_m - R_f)$

$= 8.50\% + 1.13 \times (15.30\% - 8.50\%)$

$= 8.50\% + 1.13 \times (6.80\%)$

$= 16.184\%$

Jensen's measure for the fund is given by,

$(\alpha_P)_{\text{Super star}} = R_p - E(R_p)$

$= 25.00\% - 16.184\%$

$= 8.816\%$

True Balance

Expected return from the fund as per CAPM $= R_f + \beta_p\ (R_m - R_f)$

$= 8.50\% + 0.95 \times (15.30\% - 8.50\%)$

$= 8.50\% + 0.95 \times (6.80\%)$

$= 14.96\%$

Jensen's measure for the fund is given by,

$(\alpha_P)_{\text{True balance}} = R_p - E(R_p)$

$= 17.00\% - 14.96\%$

$= 2.04\%$

Sure Return

Expected return from the fund as per CAPM $= R_f + \beta_p\ (R_m - R_f)$

$= 8.50\% + 0.98 \times (15.30\% - 8.50\%)$

$= 8.50\% + 0.98 \times (6.80\%)$

$= 15.164\%$

Jensen's measure for the fund is given by,

$(\alpha_P)_{\text{Sure return}} = R_p - E(R_p)$

$= 20.00\% - 15.164\%$

$= 4.836\%$

Safety Net

Expected return from the fund as per CAPM = $R_f + \beta_p\ (R_m - R_f)$

$= 8.50\% + 1.00 \times (15.30\% - 8.50\%)$

$= 8.50\% + 1.00 \times (6.80\%)$

$= 15.30\%$

Since the actual return from the fund and the expected return are the same, Jensen's measure will be equal to zero.

Result

The fund 'Safety Net' has a Beta of 1.00 and it resembles the market portfolio. The other three funds have a positive Jensen's measure and hence all the three funds have generated excess returns than mandated by the CAPM.

***Illustration* 9.7:**

For the funds given in illustration 9.6, find out if the excess returns earned by the funds are due to superior stock selection or due to inadequate diversification or both.

Solution:

Name of the fund	Return earned (%)	Return expected as per CAPM (%)	Jensen's measure (or) Jensen's Alpha*
Super Star	25.00	16.184	8.816
True Balance	17.00	14.960	2.040
Sure Return	20.00	15.164	5.736
Safety Net	15.30	15.300	0.00

Name of the fund	Return earned (%)	Return expected as per CAPM (%)	Jensen's measure (or) Jensen's Alpha*	Total selectivity(%)
Super Star	25.00	16.184	8.816	8.816
True Balance	17.00	14.960	2.040	2.040
Sure Return	15.00	15.164	5.736	5.736
Safety Net	15.30	15.300	0.00	0.00

The next step is to calculate the 'Net selectivity'.

Take the fund 'Super Star' and let it be referred to as portfolio 'B'. Now, refer to Fig. 9.1.

* The Jensen's measure (Jensen's Alpha, as it is normally called) is the differential return earned by a fund in excess of the return mandated by the CAPM. This is nothing but the 'Total Selectivity'

Net selectivity $= R_B - R_C$

$R_{C,}$ is the return as per CAPM, for a comparable portfolio – C on the SML. The value of R_C can be arrived at using the following relationship.

$$R_C = R_f + [(R_m - R_f) \times (\sigma_C/\sigma_M)]$$

For the fund 'Super Star',

$$R_C = 8.50 + [(15.30 - 8.50) \times (22.70/15.30^*)]$$

$$R_C = 18.589$$

Net selectivity of the fund 'Super Star' is given by,

$$(\text{Net selectivity})_{\text{Super Star}} = R_B - R_C$$
$$= 25.00 - 18.589$$
$$= 6.411$$

Return for inadequate diversification = Total selectivity – Net selectivity
= 8.816 – 6.411
= 2.405

Inference

Fund 'Super Star' has earned an excess return of 8.816%, out of which 6.411% was generated due to Net selectivity (i.e., due to superior stock selection) and 2.405% was generated due to inadequate diversification.

Similar calculations are done for the other funds and tabulated below:

Name of the fund	Return earned (%)	Total selectivity(%)	Net selectivity (%)	Return for inadequate diversification(%)
Super Star	25.00	8.816	6.411	4.405
True Balance	17.00	2.040	0.856	1.184
Sure Return	20.00	5.736	2.211	3.525
Safety Net	15.30	0.00	0.00	0.00

Inference

Fund 'Super Star' has done better since the return due to 'Net selectivity' is more than the return for inadequate diversification. Funds 'True Balance' and 'Sure return' have not comparatively performed better since their 'Net selectivity' is lower than the return for inadequate diversification.

* σ_M is the Std. Deviation of the Market which can be taken to be equal to the Std. Deviation of the fund 'Safety Net' that resembles the market.

Note: *The return for inadequate diversification will always be positive. It can not become negative. At the most, it can be equal to zero where a portfolio is 'fully' diversified. It is possible for the 'Net selectivity' to become negative. 'Net selectivity' will become negative, when the stock selection is very poor. When the 'Net selectivity' is negative, it will take away a portion of the excess return earned due to inadequate diversification.*

9.8. PORTFOLIO REVISION

An optional portfolio once constructed will not and cannot remain optional for ever. Due to changes in the economy and due to changes in the financial markets, the risk-return characteristics of securities keep changing. A security that looked very attractive once may lose its attractiveness and vice versa. Moreover, during the course of time, new securities with attractive return and lower risk may enter the financial market. Thus, the changes in the risk-return characteristics of the securities in the portfolio and the emergence of new securities in the securities market necessitate a revision of the portfolio in order to ensure that the portfolio continues to remain an optional one.

Portfolio of securities once built up cannot be allowed to remain unchanged. The very objective of portfolio management is to aim at maximum return for a given level of risk. Hence, when changes take place in the financial market, such changes are required to be incorporated in the portfolio also in order to ensure that the performance of the portfolio does not get affected due to changes in the financial market.

At times, revision of the portfolio may also have to be done due to the following reasons:

- The risk-bearing characteristic of the investor may charge during the course of time. For example, an investor who was once aggressive and ready to take high risk in anticipation of a higher return may change his attitude (probably because of the lessons he has learnt!) and may prefer to take a lower risk and settle for a lower return.
- The investor may be in need of funds for some alternative use and hence may be under compulsion to dispose off some of the securities in the portfolio in the near/distant future.
- Additional funds may be available to the investor and he may prefer to infuse additional funds into the portfolio of securities.

Portfolio construction, portfolio evaluation and portfolio revision are continuous processes and are carried out as long as an investor has his portfolio of investments.

9.9. STRATEGIES FOR PORTFOLIO REVISION

In simple terms, portfolio revision involves changing the mix of existing securities in the portfolio. Either the securities in the portfolio may be changed or the proportion of funds invested in the different securities may be changed (retaining the securities as they are) or a combination of both these techniques can be attempted.

Portfolio revision strategies broadly fall into two categories, viz.,

(*a*) Active revision strategy.

(*b*) Passive revision strategy.

9.9.1. Active Portfolio Revision Strategy

Active portfolio revision strategy is attempted by investors who believe that they can beat the market. They believe that by using their skill, estimates and analysis, they can generate excess returns. Hence, such investors constantly carry out analysis of various factors affecting risk-return relationship of different securities and are always in search of under-priced securities. Obviously, they carry out revision of their portfolio quite frequently and continuously. They spend more time, skill and resources in revising their portfolio.

9.9.2. Passive Portfolio Revision Strategy

The investors who believe that basically they can't beat the market follow passive portfolio revision strategy. They believe that the market is efficient. Passive revision involves only minor and infrequent adjustments in the portfolio over time.

Passive portfolio revision is carried at using a set of predetermined plans. Such plans are called as 'formula plans'. Formula plans help the investors to decide upon the timing of portfolio revision. There is a general tendency among investors not to buy stocks when their prices are falling on the apprehension that the prices might come down still further. Similarly, there is also a tendency not to sell stocks when their prices are rising, on the hope that the prices might rise still further. Thus, they tend to become indecisive as to when to buy/sell. Formula plans help to ease out their problem of timing of investment decisions, i.e., timing of buying and selling stocks.

Formula Plans

Formula plans give certain basic rules for buying/selling of stocks. These plans are meant to overcome the psychological barriers present among the investors and to offer a system for timing of investment decisions. In general, the formula plans aim at minimizing the loss rather than maximizing the return on investments.

The following are some of the formula plans and the investor who follows passive investment strategy can choose any one formula plan that suits his investment goals.

(*a*) Constant rupee value plan

(*b*) Constant ratio plan

(*c*) Variable ratio plan and

(*d*) Rupee cost average plan

(*a*) Constant rupee value plan

As per this plan, the investor constructs two portfolios. One of the portfolios is an aggressive portfolio consisting of equity shares. The other portfolio is a defensive portfolio consisting of bonds/debentures. As the name indicates, this plan keeps the rupee value of aggressive portfolio constant, by buying/ selling of equity shares.

When the share prices increase, the rupee value of the aggressive portfolio will also increase. In order to maintain constant rupee value for the aggressive portfolio, some of the shares from the aggressive portfolio are to be sold so that the total rupee value of the aggressive portfolio will come down to the level of original investment in it. The sale proceeds obtained by selling the shares are invested in bonds/debentures and thus the component of defensive portfolio will increase. Similarly, when the share prices decrease, the rupee value of the aggressive portfolio will also decrease. In order to maintain constant rupee value for the aggressive portfolio, the investor has to buy some more shares from the market and include them into his aggressive portfolio. The money required for buying shares is obtained by selling some of the bonds/debentures from the defensive portfolio, and hence the component of defensive portfolio will get reduced.

This formula plan automatically ensures that the investor buys shares when their prices are falling and sell shares when their prices are increasing.

In order to decide as to when to buy/sell shares, revision points are fixed. Suppose when a revision point is predetermined and fixed at, say, 10%. When the rupee value of the aggressive portfolio fluctuate within the range of 10% (either above or below the original rupee value) no revision of the portfolio is done. When the share prices fluctuate more and the rupee value of the aggressive portfolio deviates more than 10% from the original rupee value, revision of the portfolio is attempted.

The important element in constant rupee value formula is the fixation of revision point. If the revision point is too narrow, (say 5%) revision of the portfolio will be required to be done at frequent intervals. On the contrary, when the revision point is fixed at a higher level (say 25%) portfolio revisions required will be too few. While frequent revisions will help to realize more profit out of price fluctuations, transactions costs will be higher if the revision is done too frequently. On the other hand, when the revision point is fixed at a higher level and the portfolio revisions are done at less frequent intervals, though transaction costs will be minimum, the investor may not reap better profit out of price fluctuations. Thus, an optimum revision point is to be predetermined in order to get better results from constant rupee value plan.

***Illustration* 9.8:**

Two portfolios were constructed, one consisting of equity shares and the other consisting of debentures. The rupee value of equity shares, at the time of constructing the portfolio was Rs. 60,000/- (at the rate of Rs. 100/- per share) and that of the debentures was Rs. 40,000/-. The investor opts to use constant rupee value plan and fixes a revision point of 10%. The share prices show fluctuations at periodical intervals as under.

Period	Share price (Rs.)
1	100 (at the start i.e., at the time of constructing the portfolio)
2	90
3	85
4	75
5	80
6	95

Explain the portfolio revision pattern of the investor.

Solution:

The portfolio of equity shares is the aggressive portfolio and the portfolio of debentures is the defensive portfolio.

Period – 1

Aggressive portfolio: 600 shares of Rs.100 each	Rs. 60,000.00
Defensive portfolio	Rs. 40,000.00
	Rs. 1,00,000.00

Period – 2 (before revision)

Aggressive portfolio: 600 shares of Rs.90 each	Rs. 54,000.00
Defensive portfolio	Rs. 40,000.00
	Rs. 94,000.00

Rupee value of aggressive portfolio at Period – 1	Rs. 60,000.00
Rupee value of aggressive portfolio at Period – 2 (before revision)	Rs. 54,000.00
Reduction in rupee value	Rs. 6,000.00

$$\text{Percentage reduction in rupee value of aggressive portfolio} = \frac{6,000 \times 100}{60,000} = 10\%$$

Since the reduction in the rupee value of the aggressive portfolio is 10% revision of portfolio has become due.

Period – 2 (after revision)

$$\text{Additional shares required to be purchased} : \frac{6,000}{90}$$

$$= 66.67 \text{ say } 67 \text{ shares}$$

Aggressive portfolio: 667 shares of Rs.90 each	Rs. 60,030.00
Defensive portfolio [40,000 – (67 x 90)]	Rs. 33,970.00
	Rs. 94,000.00

Period – 3 (before revision)

Aggressive portfolio: 667 shares of Rs.85 each	Rs. 56,695.00
Defensive portfolio	Rs. 33,970.00
	Rs. 90,665.00

Reduction in rupee value of aggressive portfolio (60,000 – 56,695)		Rs. 3,305.00
% reduction in rupee value of aggressive portfolio	$= \frac{3305 \times 100}{60000}$	5.50%

Since the reduction in rupee value of the aggressive portfolio is below 10%, revision is not warranted at period – 3.

Period – 4 (before revision)

Aggressive portfolio: 667 shares of Rs.75 each	Rs. 50,025.00
Defensive portfolio	Rs. 33,970.00
	Rs. 83,995.00

Reduction in rupee value of aggressive portfolio (60,000 – 50,025)		Rs. 9,975.00
% reduction in rupee value of aggressive portfolio =	$\frac{9,975 \times 100}{60,000}$	16.63%

Since the reduction in rupee value of the aggressive portfolio is more than 10% revision is warranted at period – 4.

Period – 4 (after revision)

Additional shares required to be purchased =	$\frac{9975}{75}$	133
Aggressive portfolio 800 shares [667 + 133] of Rs. 75 each		Rs. 60,000.00
Defensive portfolio [33,970 – (133 x 75)]		Rs. 23,995.00
		Rs. 83,995.00

Period – 5 (before revision)

Aggressive portfolio: 800 shares of Rs.80 each	Rs. 64,000.00
Defensive portfolio	Rs. 23,995.00
	Rs. 87,995.00

Increase in rupee value of aggressive portfolio (64,000 – 60,000)		Rs. 4,000.00
% increase in rupee value of aggressive portfolio =	$\frac{4,000 \times 100}{60,000}$	6.67%

Since the increase in rupee value of the aggressive portfolio is below 10% revision is not warranted.

Period – 6 (before revision)

Aggressive portfolio: 800 shares of Rs. 95 each	Rs. 76,000.00
Defensive portfolio	Rs. 23,995.00
	Rs. 99,995.00

Increase in rupee value of aggressive portfolio (76,000 – 60,000)		Rs. 16,000.00
% increase in rupee value of aggressive portfolio =	$\frac{16,000 \times 100}{60,000}$	26.67%

Since the increase in the rupee value of aggressive portfolio is more than 10% revision is warranted.

Period – 6 (after revision)

$$\text{Number of shares required to be sold} = \frac{16{,}000}{95}$$

$$= 168.42 \text{ say, } 168 \text{ shares}$$

Aggressive portfolio: [No. of shares = (800 – 168) = 632] 632 shares of Rs. 95 each	Rs. 60,040.00
Defensive portfolio [23995 + (168 x 95)]	Rs. 39,995.00
	Rs. 99,995.00

The results are summarized as under.

Period	Aggressive portfolio			Investment in defensive portfolio Rs.	Total portfolio value (Rs.)
	No. of shares	Share price (Rs.)	Rupee value (2) × (3)		
(1)	(2)	(3)	(4)	(5)	(6)
1	600	100	60,000.00	40,000.00	1,00,000.00
2	667	90	60,030.00	33,970.00	94,000.00
3	667	85	56,695.00	33,970.00	90,665.00
4	800	75	60,000.00	23,995.00	83,995.00
5	800	80	64,000.00	23,995.00	87,995.00
6	632	95	60,040.00	39,955.00	99.955.00

Note: *In the illustration shown above it is assumed for the sake of simplicity that the aggressive portfolio consists of only one company's shares. In reality the aggressive portfolio will have a combination of shares of different companies in different proportions and decision on selling/ buying of shares will be done judiciously. It may be also noted that the figures in the column "Investment in Defensive portfolio" represent only the investment made and does not represent the rupee value since market price of bonds/debentures might have also changed.*

(*b*) Constant ratio plan

Just as in constant rupee value plan, constant ratio plan will also have two portfolios, viz., an aggressive portfolio of equity shares and a defensive portfolio of debentures/bonds. In this plan, the ratio of aggressive investment to defensive investment is predetermined and this ratio is maintained within an acceptable range of variations.

For example, the ratio of aggressive to defensive investment may be fixed at, say 1.50 : 1.00. The revision points may also be predetermined, at say 10% i.e., at + 0.10. Wherever the ratio of aggressive investment to defensive investment moves above or below the predetermined ratio by 0.10, i.e., whenever the ratio moves to 1.60 : 1.00 or goes beyond 1.60 : 1.00 and also whenever the ratio moves to 1.40 : 1.00 or falls below 1.40 : 1.00, a revision of the portfolio is warranted. The revision is effected in such a way to bring back the ratio to the predetermined value of 1.50 : 1.00.

When the share prices are falling, the rupee value of aggressive investment will fall and hence the ratio of aggressive investment to defensive investment will also fall below the original value. This necessitates increasing the rupee value of aggressive investment. In other words, this necessitates buying of additional shares by disposing off some of the defensive investments. Similarly, when the share price rises, shares are required to be sold in order to maintain the ratio within the acceptable limits.

***Illustration* 9.9:**

Two portfolios were constructed, one consisting of equity shares and the other consisting of debentures. The rupee value of equity shares, at the time of constructing the portfolio was Rs. 40,000. The investor opts to use constant ratio plan with a ratio of 1.50 : 1.00 [ratio of aggressive investment to defensive investment]. The revision point is fixed at + 0.10. The share price shows fluctuations at periodic intervals as under.

Period	Share price (Rs.)
1	100 (at the start i.e., at the time of constructing the portfolio)
2	90
3	85
4	75
5	80
6	95

Assume that the price of bonds/debentures in the defensive portfolio does not change.

Explain the portfolio revision pattern of the investor.

Solution:

As in illustration 9.8, in this illustration also it is assumed for the sake of simplicity that the aggressive portfolio consists of only one company's shares. This, of course, is far from reality. The purpose of the illustration is to explain the methodology of portfolio revision.

Period – 1

Aggressive portfolio: 600 shares of Rs. 100 each	Rs. 60,000.00
Defensive portfolio	Rs. 40,000.00
	Rs. 1,00,000.00

Ratio of aggressive to defensive investment = 60,000 : 40,000
= 1.50 : 1.00

Period – 2 (before revision)

Aggressive portfolio: 600 shares of Rs. 90 each	Rs. 54,000.00
Defensive portfolio	Rs. 40,000.00
	Rs. 94,000.00

Ratio of aggressive to defensive investment = 54,000 : 40,000
= 1.35 : 1.00

Fall in the ratio (1.50 – 1.35) = 0.15

Since the ratio has changed by more than 0.10 (which is the pre-fixed revision point) the portfolio needs revision.

In order to improve the ratio from 1.35 : 1.00 to 1.50 : 1.00, additional shares are to be purchased.

Rupee value of shares required to bring the ratio to 1.50 : 1.00

$$= \frac{94{,}000 \times 1.50}{2.50}$$

= Rs. 56,400

Amount to be spent towards purchase of additional shares (56,400 – 54,000) = Rs. 2,400

No. of additional shares to be purchased $= \frac{2{,}400}{90}$

= 26.67 say 27 shares

Amount required for the purchase of 27 shares (27 × 90) = Rs. 2,430

Period – 2 (after revision)

Aggressive portfolio: 627 shares of Rs. 90 each	Rs. 56,430.00
Defensive portfolio [40,000 – 2,430]	Rs. 37,570.00
	Rs. 94,000.00

Ratio of aggressive investment to defensive investment = 56,430 : 37,570
= 1.50 : 1.00

Period – 3 (before revision)

Aggressive portfolio: 627 shares of Rs. 85 each	Rs. 53,295.00
Defensive portfolio	Rs. 37,570.00
	Rs. 90,865.00

Ratio of aggressive investment to defensive investment = 53,295 : 37,570
= 1.42 : 1.00

Since the ratio has changed by only 0.08, the change is less than the pre-fixed revision point of 0.10. Hence no revision of the portfolio is warranted.

Period – 4 (before revision)

Aggressive portfolio: 627 shares of Rs. 75 each	Rs. 47,025.00
Defensive portfolio	Rs. 37,570.00
	Rs. 84,595.00

Ratio of aggressive investment to defensive investment = 47,025 : 37,570
= 1.25 : 1.00

Fall in ratio (1.50–1.25) = 0.25

Since the ratio has changed by more than 0.10 (which is the pre-fixed revision point) the portfolio needs revision.

In order to improve the ratio from 1.25 : 1.00 to 1.50 : 1.00, additional shares are to be purchased.

Rupee value of shares required to bring the ratio to 1.50:1.00

$$= \frac{84{,}595 \times 1.50}{2.50}$$

= Rs. 50,757

Amount to be spent towards purchase of additional shares (50,757 – 47,025) = Rs. 3,732

No. of additional shares to be purchased $= \frac{3{,}732}{75}$

$= 49.76$ say 50 shares

Amount required for the purchase of 50 shares (50 × 75) = Rs. 3,750

Period – 4 (after revision)

Aggressive portfolio: 677 shares of Rs. 75 each	Rs. 50,775.00
Defensive portfolio (37,570 – 3,750)	Rs. 33,820.00
	Rs. 84,595.00

Ratio of aggressive investment to defensive investment = 50,775 : 33,820

= 1.50 : 1.00

Period – 5 (before revision)

Aggressive portfolio: 677 shares of Rs.80 each	Rs. 54,160.00
Defensive portfolio	Rs. 33,820.00
	Rs. 87,980.00

Ratio of aggressive investment to defensive investment = 54,160 : 33,820

= 1.60 : 1.00

Increase in ratio (1.60 – 1.50) = 0.10

Since the ratio has changed by 0.10 (which is equal to the prefixed revision point) the portfolio needs revision.

In order to bring down the ratio from 1.60 : 1.00 to 1.50 : 1.00, some shares are to be sold and the sale proceeds should be invested in the defensive portfolio.

Rupee value of shares required to bring the ratio to 1.50 : 1.00

$= \frac{87{,}980 \times 1.50}{2.50}$

= Rs. 52,788

Amount that will be realised out of sale of 17 shares (54,160 – 52,788) = Rs. 1,372

No. of shares to be sold $= \frac{1{,}372}{80}$

$= 17.15$ say 17 shares

Amount required for the purchase
of 17 shares (17 × 80) = Rs. 1,360

Period – 5 (after revision)

Aggressive portfolio: 660 shares of Rs. 80 each	Rs. 52,800.00
Defensive portfolio (33,820 – 1,360)	Rs. 35,180.00
	Rs. 87,980.00

Ratio of aggressive investment to defensive investment = 52,800 : 35,180
= 1.50 : 1.00

Period – 6 (before revision)

Aggressive portfolio: 660 shares of Rs. 95 each	Rs. 62,700.00
Defensive portfolio	Rs. 35,180.00
	Rs. 97,880.00

Ratio of aggressive investment to defensive investment = 62,700 : 35,180
= 1.78 : 1.00

Increase in ratio (1.78 – 1.50) = 0.28

Since the ratio has changed by more than 0.10 (which is the pre-fixed revision point) the portfolio needs revision.

In order to bring down the ratio from 1.78 : 1.00 to 1.50 : 1.00, some shares are to be sold and the sale proceeds should be invested in the defensive portfolio.

Rupee value of shares required to bring the ratio to 1.50 : 1.00

$$= \frac{97{,}880 \times 1.50}{2.50}$$

= Rs. 58,728

Amount to be mobilized out of sale of
shares (62,700 – 58,728) = Rs. 3,972

No. of shares to be sold $= \frac{3{,}972}{95}$

= 41.80 say 42 shares

Amount that will be realised out of
sale of 42 shares (42 × 95) = Rs. 3,990

Period – 6 (after revision)

Aggressive portfolio: 618 shares of Rs. 95 each	Rs. 58,710.00
Defensive portfolio (35180 + 3990)	Rs. 39,170.00
	Rs. 97,340.00

Ratio of aggressive investment to defensive investment = 58,710 : 39,170

= 1.50 : 1.00

The results are summarized as under.

Period	Aggressive portfolio			Investment in defensive portfolio (Rs.)	Total portfolio value (Rs.)	Ratio
	No. of shares	Share price (Rs.)	Rupee value (2) × (3)			
(1)	(2)	(3)	(4)	(5)	(6)	(7)
1	600	100	60,000.00	40,000.00	1,00,000.00	1.50 : 1.00
2	627	90	56,430.00	37,570.00	94,000.00	1.50 : 1.00
3	627	85	53,295.00	37,570.00	90,865.00	1.42 : 1.00
4	677	75	50,775.00	33,820.00	84,595.00	1.50 : 1.00
5	660	80	52,800.00	35,180.00	87,980.00	1.50 : 1.00
6	618	95	58,710.00	39,170.00	97,340.00	1.50 : 1.00

Remarks: Instead of constructing two portfolios, one with equity shares and the other with debentures/bonds, if the investor has a single portfolio consisting of equity shares and debentures/bonds, it can be split into an aggressive portfolio of equity shares and a defensive portfolio of debentures/bonds for the purpose of analysis.

***Illustration* 9.10:**

An investor has constructed a portfolio consisting of shares and debentures in such a way that the ratio between investments in shares (aggressive investment) and investment in debentures (defensive investment) is 1.40 : 1.00. The total amount invested is Rs. 12,00,000/-. After an interval of 3 months the market value of shares in the portfolio has increased to Rs. 10.00 lakhs and that of the debentures has increased to Rs. 6.00 lakhs. After another 3 months the market value of shares has fallen down to Rs. 2.50 lakhs while the market value of debentures increased to Rs. 6.50 lakhs. Suggest the pattern of portfolio revisions required at the two periods if the investor wants to maintain the ratio of 1.40 : 1.00 for aggressive to defensive investment.

Solution:

Period – 1

Total investment made = Rs. 12,00,000

Ratio of aggressive to defensive investment = 1.40 : 1.00

$$\text{Investment in aggressive portfolio (i.e., shares)} = \frac{12,00,000 \times 1.40}{2.40}$$

= Rs. 7,00,000

Investment in defensive portfolio
(i.e., debentures) [12,00,000 – 7,00,000] = Rs. 5,00,000

Period – 2 (before revision)

Market value of shares (aggressive investment) = Rs. 10,00,000
Market value of debentures (defensive investment) = Rs. 6,00,000

Rs. 16,00,000

Ratio of aggressive to defensive investment = 10,00,000 : 6,00,000
= 1.67 : 1.00

Since the ratio is to be retained at 1.40 : 1.00, some of the shares are to be sold and invested in debentures.

Period – 2 (after revision)

Investment required in aggressive portfolio (i.e., shares)

$$= \frac{16,00,000 \times 1.40}{2.40}$$

= Rs. 9,33,333

Investment required in debentures (16,00,000 – 9,33,333)
= Rs. 6,66,667

Ratio = 9,33,333 : 6,66,667 = 1.40 : 1.00

Period – 3 (before revision)

Market value of shares (aggressive investment) = Rs. 2,50,000
Market value of debentures (defensive investment) = Rs. 6,50,000

Rs. 9,00,000

Ratio of aggressive to defensive investment = 2,50,000 : 6,50,000
= 0.38 : 1.00

Since the ratio is to be retained at 1.40 : 1.00, some of the debentures are to be sold and invested in shares.

Period – 2 (after revision)

Investment required in aggressive portfolio $= \frac{9,00,000 \times 1.40}{2.40}$

= Rs. 5,25,000

Investment required in debentures (9,00,000 – 5,25,000)
= Rs. 3,75,000

Ratio = 5,25,000 : 3,75,000 = 1.40 : 1.00

(*c*) Variable ratio plan

In variable ratio plan, the investor, instead of following a fixed ratio between aggressive and defensive investments, follows a variable ratio. The ratio between aggressive and defensive investments is decided based on the changing market conditions. For example, if the prospects for earning higher returns from shares are bright, the investor may prefer to increase the proportion of his investments in shares, i.e., in aggressive investments. On the other hand, if the investments in bonds/debentures are considered to offer attractive returns, the investor may park a larger portion of his funds in defensive investments like bonds and debentures. In a way, variable ratio plan is a better option when compared to fixed ratio plan. But, it requires good forecasting capacity and judgement ability on the part of the investor to reap benefits out of variable formula plan.

(*d*) Rupee cost average plan

This formula plan suggests that a fixed amount may be invested in a specified security or in a portfolio of selected securities at equal intervals of time regularly regardless of the market conditions. The periodical investments are to be made irrespective of rise or fall in the price of the selected securities. This formula plan is based on the assumption that stock prices fluctuate up and down in cycles and the cyclic movement in share prices help to construct a portfolio at a low cost provided the periodic investment is continued over a fairly long period to cover a complete cycle of share price movements. After a portfolio is constructed over a complete cycle of share price movements, further additions to the portfolio can be stopped. This portfolio is found to offer lower average cost per share than the average share price prevailing in the market over the period in which the portfolio was constructed (Illustration 9.11 explains this). Rupee cost average plan gives lower average cost per share than the average price of share prevailing in the market over the period due to the reason that when investments are made as per the plan over the entire cycle of share price movements, more number of shares will be purchased at lower prices than at higher prices. It may be noted that when the periodical investments are continued beyond one complete cycle of share price movements, lower average cost per share may not be ensured.

***Illustration* 9.11:**

An investor prefers to follow rupee cost average plan for building up a portfolio of equity shares. He has decided to invest Rs. 5,000 once in 3 months regularly on a selected share. The movement of the share price in the market at intervals of 3 months is as under.

	Share price
At the start of investment	Rs.100 each
After 3 months	Rs. 90 each
After 6 months	Rs. 70 each
After 9 months	Rs. 65 each
After 12 months	Rs. 60 each
After 15 months	Rs. 70 each
After 18 months	Rs. 75 each
After 21 months	Rs. 90 each
After 24 months	Rs.100 each

The investor has started investing Rs. 5,000 when the share price was Rs. 100 each and continued his investment of Rs. 5,000 once in 3 months till the share price again reaches Rs. 100 each. Estimate the average cost per share of the portfolio built by the investor. Find out if this cost is less than the average market price of share over the period of investment.

Solution:

A comparison of cumulative average cost per share (column-7) and cumulative average market price of share (column-8) reveal that the cumulative average cost per share is always less than the cumulative average market price of share at all points of time which proves the utility of rupee cost average plan.

Period	Market price of share (Rs.)	Periodical (quarterly) investment (Rs.)	No. of shares purchased at every quarter	Cumulative no. of shares at the end of each quarter	Cumulative investment in shares (Rs.)	Cumulative average cost per share (Rs.) (6) ÷ (5)	Cumulative average price of share (Rs.)
(1)	(2)	(3)	(4)	(5)	(6)	(7)	(8)
1	100	5,000	50	50	5,000	100	100 ÷ 1 = 100
2	90	5,000	55.5	105.5	10,000	94.79	(100+90) ÷ 2 = 95
3	70	5,000	71.4	176.9	15,000	84.79	(100+90+70) ÷ 3 = 86.67
4	65	5,000	76.9	253.8	20,000	78.80	(100+90+70+65) ÷ 4 = 81.25
5	60	5,000	83.3	337.1	25,000	74.16	(100+90+70+65+60) ÷ 5= 77.00
6	70	5,000	71.4	408.5	30,000	73.44	(100+90+70+65+60+70) ÷ 6 = 75.83
7	75	5,000	66.7	475.2	35,000	73.65	(100+90+70+65+60+70+75) ÷ 7 = 75.71
8	90	5,000	55.5	530.7	40,000	75.37	(100+90+70+65+60+70+75+90) ÷ 8 = 77.50
9	100	5,000	50	580.7	45,000	77.49	(100+90+70+65+60+70+75+90+100) ÷ 9 = 80.00

REVIEW QUESTIONS

1. What is meant by 'Portfolio evaluation'? What are the two stages in Portfolio evaluation?
2. Define Sharpe Ratio and Treynor Ratio used in portfolio evaluation. Indicate the circumstance under which each of these two ratios will be most suited.
3. What is the use of Jenson's Measure in portfolio evaluation?
4. How did Eugene Fama segregate portfolio returns into its components?
5. Why do portfolios need periodical revisions? What are the two portfolio revision strategies?
6. What is 'Passive portfolio revision strategy'?
7. What do you mean by Formula plan in respect of portfolio revision? What are the four commonly used Formula plans?
8. Distinguish between Constant Ratio plan and Variable Ratio plan.
9. What do investors who follow Active portfolio revision strategy believe in?
10. Explain Rupee Cost Average plan with an example.

Tables Indicating Time Value of Money

Table-A: Present Value of Rupee 1.00

Period (in No. of Years) ↓	1%	2%	3%	4%	5%	6%	7%	8%	9%	10%
1	0.9901	0.9804	0.9709	0.9615	0.9524	0.9434	0.9346	0.9259	0.9174	0.9091
2	0.9803	0.9612	0.9426	0.9246	0.9070	0.8900	0.8734	0.8573	0.8417	0.8264
3	0.9706	0.9423	0.9151	0.8890	0.8638	0.8396	0.8163	0.7938	0.7722	0.7513
4	0.9610	0.9238	0.8885	0.8548	0.8227	0.7921	0.7629	0.7350	0.7084	0.6830
5	0.9515	0.9057	0.8626	0.8219	0.7835	0.7473	0.7130	0.6806	0.6499	0.6209
6	0.9420	0.8880	0.8375	0.7903	0.7462	0.7050	0.6663	0.6302	0.5963	0.5645
7	0.9327	0.8706	0.8131	0.7599	0.7107	0.6651	0.6227	0.5835	0.5470	0.5132
8	0.9235	0.8535	0.7894	0.7307	0.6768	0.6274	0.5820	0.5403	0.5019	0.4665
9	0.9143	0.8368	0.7664	0.7026	0.6446	0.5919	0.5439	0.5002	0.4604	0.4241
10	0.9053	0.8203	0.7441	0.6756	0.6139	0.5584	0.5083	0.4632	0.4224	0.3855
11	0.8963	0.8043	0.7224	0.6496	0.5847	0.5268	0.4751	0.4289	0.3875	0.3505
12	0.8874	0.7885	0.7014	0.6246	0.5568	0.4970	0.4440	0.3971	0.3555	0.3186
13	0.8787	0.7730	0.6810	0.6006	0.5303	0.4688	0.4150	0.3677	0.3262	0.2897
14	0.8700	0.7579	0.6611	0.5775	0.5051	0.4423	0.3878	0.3405	0.2992	0.2633
15	0.8613	0.7430	0.6419	0.5553	0.4810	0.4173	0.3624	0.3152	0.2745	0.2394

Table-A: Present Value of Rupee 1.00

Period (in No. of Years) ↓	11%	12%	13%	14%	15%	16%	17%	18%	19%	20%
1	0.9009	0.8929	0.8850	0.8772	0.8696	0.8621	0.8547	0.8475	0.8403	0.8333
2	0.8116	0.7972	0.7831	0.7695	0.7561	0.7432	0.7305	0.7182	0.7062	0.6944
3	0.7312	0.7118	0.6931	0.6750	0.6575	0.6407	0.6244	0.6086	0.5934	0.5787
4	0.6587	0.6355	0.6133	0.5921	0.5718	0.5523	0.5337	0.5158	0.4987	0.4823
5	0.5935	0.5674	0.5428	0.5194	0.4972	0.4761	0.4561	0.4371	0.4190	0.4019
6	0.5346	0.5066	0.4803	0.4556	0.4323	0.4104	0.3898	0.3704	0.3521	0.3349
7	0.4817	0.4523	0.4251	0.3996	0.3759	0.3538	0.3332	0.3139	0.2959	0.2791
8	0.4339	0.4039	0.3762	0.3506	0.3269	0.3050	0.2848	0.2660	0.2487	0.2326
9	0.3909	0.3606	0.3329	0.3075	0.2843	0.2630	0.2434	0.2255	0.2090	0.1938
10	0.3522	0.3220	0.2946	0.2697	0.2472	0.2267	0.2080	0.1911	0.1756	0.1615
11	0.3173	0.2875	0.2607	0.2366	0.2149	0.1954	0.1778	0.1619	0.1476	0.1346
12	0.2858	0.2567	0.2307	0.2076	0.1869	0.1685	0.1520	0.1372	0.1240	0.1122
13	0.2575	0.2292	0.2042	0.1821	0.1625	0.1452	0.1299	0.1163	0.1042	0.0935
14	0.2320	0.2046	0.1807	0.1597	0.1413	0.1252	0.1110	0.0985	0.0876	0.0779
15	0.2090	0.1827	0.15899	0.1401	0.1229	0.1079	0.0949	0.0835	0.0736	0.0649

Table-A: Present Value of Rupee 1.00

Period (in No. of Years) ↓	21%	22%	23%	24%	25%	26%	27%	28%	29%	30%
1	0.8264	0.8197	0.8130	0.8065	0.8000	0.7937	0.7874	0.7813	0.7752	0.7692
2	0.6830	0.6719	0.6610	0.6504	0.6400	0.6299	0.6200	0.6104	0.6009	0.5917
3	0.5645	0.5507	0.5374	0.5245	0.5120	0.4999	0.4882	0.4768	0.4658	0.4552
4	0.4665	0.4514	0.4369	0.4230	0.4096	0.3968	0.3844	0.3725	0.3611	0.3501
5	0.3855	0.3700	0.3552	0.3411	0.3277	0.3149	0.3027	0.2910	0.2799	0.2693
6	0.3186	0.3033	0.2888	0.2751	0.2621	0.2499	0.2383	0.2274	0.2170	0.2072
7	0.2633	0.2486	0.2348	0.2218	0.2097	0.1983	0.1877	0.1776	0.1682	0.1594
8	0.2176	0.2038	0.1909	0.1789	0.1678	0.1574	0.1478	0.1388	0.1304	0.1226
9	0.1799	0.1670	0.1552	0.1443	0.1342	0.1249	0.1164	0.1084	0.1011	0.0943
10	0.1486	0.1369	0.1262	0.1164	0.1074	0.0992	0.0916	0.0847	0.0784	0.0725
11	0.1228	0.1122	0.1026	0.0938	0.0859	0.0787	0.0721	0.0662	0.0607	0.0558
12	0.1015	0.0920	0.0834	0.0757	0.0687	0.0625	0.0568	0.0517	0.0471	0.0429
13	0.0839	0.0754	0.0678	0.0610	0.0550	0.0496	0.0447	0.0404	0.0365	0.0330
14	0.0693	0.0618	0.0551	0.0492	0.0440	0.0393	0.0352	0.0316	0.0283	0.0254
15	0.0573	0.0507	0.0448	0.0397	0.0352	0.0312	0.0277	0.0247	0.0219	0.0195

Table-A: Present Value of Rupee 1.00

Period (in No. of Years) ↓	1%	2%	3%	4%	5%	6%	7%	8%	9%	10%
16	0.8528	0.7284	0.6232	0.5339	0.4581	0.3936	0.3387	0.2919	0.2519	0.2176
17	0.8444	0.7142	0.6050	0.5134	0.4363	0.3714	0.3166	0.2703	0.2311	0.1978
18	0.8360	0.7002	0.5874	0.4936	0.4155	0.3503	0.2959	0.2502	0.2120	0.1799
19	0.8277	0.6864	0.5703	0.4746	0.3957	0.3305	0.2765	0.2317	0.1945	0.1635
20	0.8195	0.6730	0.5537	0.4564	0.3769	0.3118	0.2584	0.2145	0.1784	0.1486
21	0.8114	0.6598	0.5375	0.4388	0.3589	0.2942	0.2415	0.1987	0.1637	0.1351
22	0.8034	0.6468	0.5219	0.4220	0.3418	0.2775	0.2257	0.1839	0.1502	0.1228
23	0.7954	0.6342	0.5067	0.4057	0.3256	0.2618	0.2109	0.1703	0.1378	0.1117
24	0.7876	0.6217	0.4919	0.3901	0.3101	0.2470	0.1971	0.1577	0.1264	0.1015
25	0.7798	0.6095	0.4776	0.3751	0.2953	0.2330	0.1842	0.1460	0.1160	0.0923
26	0.7720	0.5976	0.4637	0.3607	0.2812	0.2198	0.1722	0.1352	0.1064	0.0839
27	0.7644	0.5859	0.4502	0.3468	0.2678	0.2074	0.1609	0.1252	0.0976	0.0763
28	0.7568	0.5744	0.4371	0.3335	0.2551	0.1956	0.1504	0.1159	0.0895	0.0693
29	0.7493	0.5631	0.4243	0.3207	0.2429	0.1846	0.1406	0.1073	0.0822	0.0630
30	0.7419	0.5521	0.4120	0.3083	0.2314	0.1741	0.1314	0.0994	0.0754	0.0573

Table-A: Present Value of Rupee 1.00

Period (in No. of Years) ↓	11%	12%	13%	14%	15%	16%	17%	18%	19%	20%
16	0.1883	0.1631	0.1415	0.1229	0.1069	0.0930	0.0811	0.0708	0.0618	0.0541
17	0.1696	0.1456	0.1252	0.1078	0.0929	0.0802	0.0693	0.0600	0.0520	0.0451
18	0.1528	0.1300	0.1108	0.0946	0.0808	0.0691	0.0592	0.0508	0.0437	0.0376
19	0.1377	0.1161	0.0981	0.0829	0.0703	0.0596	0.0506	0.0431	0.0367	0.0313
20	0.1240	0.1037	0.0868	0.0728	0.0611	0.0514	0.0433	0.0365	0.0308	0.0261
21	0.1117	0.0926	0.0768	0.0638	0.0531	0.0443	0.0370	0.0309	0.0259	0.0217
22	0.1007	0.0826	0.0680	0.0560	0.0462	0.0382	0.0316	0.0262	0.0218	0.0181
23	0.0907	0.0738	0.0601	0.0491	0.0402	0.0329	0.0270	0.0222	0.0183	0.0151
24	0.0817	0.0659	0.0532	0.0431	0.0349	0.0284	0.0231	0.0188	0.0154	0.0126
25	0.0736	0.0588	0.0471	0.0378	0.0304	0.0245	0.0197	0.0160	0.0129	0.0105
26	0.0663	0.0525	0.0417	0.0331	0.0264	0.0211	0.0169	0.0135	0.0109	0.0087
27	0.0597	0.0469	0.0369	0.0291	0.0230	0.0182	0.0144	0.0115	0.0091	0.0073
28	0.0538	0.0419	0.0326	0.0255	0.0200	0.0157	0.0123	0.0097	0.0077	0.0061
29	0.0485	0.0374	0.0289	0.0224	0.0174	0.0135	0.0105	0.0082	0.0064	0.0051
30	0.0437	0.0334	0.0256	0.0196	0.0151	0.0116	0.0090	0.0070	0.0054	0.0042

Table-A: Present Value of Rupee 1.00

Period (in No. of Years) ↓	21%	22%	23%	24%	25%	26%	27%	28%	29%	30%
16	0.0474	0.0415	0.0364	0.0320	0.0281	0.0248	0.0218	0.0193	0.0170	0.0150
17	0.0391	0.0340	0.0296	0.0258	0.0225	0.0197	0.0172	0.0150	0.0132	0.0116
18	0.0323	0.0279	0.0241	0.0208	0.0180	0.0156	0.0135	0.0118	0.0102	0.0089
19	0.0267	0.0229	0.0196	0.0168	0.0144	0.0124	0.0107	0.0092	0.0079	0.0068
20	0.0221	0.0187	0.0159	0.0135	0.0115	0.0098	0.0084	0.0072	0.0061	0.0053
21	0.0183	0.0154	0.0129	0.0109	0.0092	0.0078	0.0066	0.0056	0.0048	0.0040
22	0.0151	0.0126	0.0105	0.0088	0.0074	0.0062	0.0052	0.0044	0.0037	0.0031
23	0.0125	0.0103	0.0086	0.0071	0.0059	0.0049	0.0041	0.0034	0.0029	0.0024
24	0.0103	0.0085	0.0070	0.0057	0.0047	0.0039	0.0032	0.0027	0.0022	0.0018
25	0.0085	0.0069	0.0057	0.0046	0.0038	0.0031	0.0025	0.0021	0.0017	0.0014
26	0.0070	0.0057	0.0046	0.0037	0.0030	0.0025	0.0020	0.0016	0.0013	0.0011
27	0.0058	0.0047	0.0037	0.0030	0.0024	0.0019	0.0016	0.0013	0.0010	0.0008
28	0.0048	0.0038	0.0030	0.0024	0.0019	0.0015	0.0012	0.0010	0.0008	0.0006
29	0.0040	0.0031	0.0025	0.0020	0.0015	0.0012	0.0010	0.0008	0.0006	0.0005
30	0.0033	0.0026	0.0020	0.0016	0.0012	0.0010	0.0008	0.0006	0.0005	0.0004

Table-A: Present Value of Rupee 1.00

Period (in No. of Years) ↓	1%	2%	3%	4%	5%	6%	7%	8%	9%	10%
40	0.6717	0.4529	0.3066	0.2083	0.1420	0.0972	0.0668	0.0460	0.0318	0.0221
50	0.6080	0.3715	0.2281	0.1407	0.0972	0.0543	0.0339	0.0213	0.0134	0.0085
60	0.5504	0.3048	0.1697	0.0951	0.0535	0.0303	0.0173	0.0099	0.0057	0.0033
70	0.4983	0.2500	0.1263	0.0642	0.0329	0.0169	0.0088	0.0046	0.0024	0.0013
80	0.4511	0.2051	0.0940	0.0434	0.0202	0.0095	0.0045	0.0021	0.0010	0.0005
90	0.4084	0.1683	0.0699	0.0293	0.0124	0.0053	0.0023	0.0010	0.0004	0.0002
100	0.3697	0.1380	0.0520	0.0198	0.0076	0.0029	0.0012	0.0005	0.0002	0.0001

Table-A: Present Value of Rupee 1.00

Period (in No. of Years) ↓	11%	12%	13%	14%	15%	16%	17%	18%	19%	20%
40	0.0154	0.0107	0.0075	0.0053	0.0037	0.0026	0.0019	0.0013	0.0010	0.0007
50	0.0054	0.0035	0.0022	0.0014	0.0009	0.0006	0.0004	0.0003	0.0002	0.0001
60	0.0019	0.0011	0.0007	0.0004	0.0002	0.0001	0.0001	0.0000	0.0000	0.0000
70	0.0007	0.0004	0.0002	0.0001	0.0001	0.0000	0.0000	0.0000	0.0000	0.0000
80	0.0002	0.0001	0.0001	0.0000	0.0000	0.0000	0.0000	0.0000	0.0000	0.0000
90	0.0001	0.0000	0.0000	0.0000	0.0000	0.0000	0.0000	0.0000	0.0000	0.0000
100	0.0000	0.0000	0.0000	0.0000	0.0000	0.0000	0.0000	0.0000	0.0000	0.0000

Table-A: Present Value of Rupee 1.00

Period (in No. of Years) ↓	21%	22%	23%	24%	25%	26%	27%	28%	29%	30%
40	0.0005	0.0004	0.0003	0.0002	0.0001	0.0001	0.0001	0.0001	0.0000	0.0000
50	0.0001	0.0000	0.0000	0.0000	0.0000	0.0000	0.0000	0.0000	0.0000	0.0000
60	0.0000	0.0000	0.0000	0.0000	0.0000	0.0000	0.0000	0.0000	0.0000	0.0000
70	0.0000	0.0000	0.0000	0.0000	0.0000	0.0000	0.0000	0.0000	0.0000	0.0000
80	0.0000	0.0000	0.0000	0.0000	0.0000	0.0000	0.0000	0.0000	0.0000	0.0000
90	0.0000	0.0000	0.0000	0.0000	0.0000	0.0000	0.0000	0.0000	0.0000	0.0000
100	0.0000	0.0000	0.0000	0.0000	0.0000	0.0000	0.0000	0.0000	0.0000	0.0000

Table-B: Present Value of Annuity of Rupee 1.00

Period (in No. of Years) ↓	1%	2%	3%	4%	5%	6%	7%	8%	9%	10%
1	0.9901	0.9804	0.9709	0.9615	0.9524	0.9434	0.9346	0.9259	0.9174	0.9091
2	1.9704	1.9416	1.9135	1.8861	1.8594	1.8434	1.8080	1.7833	1.7591	1.7355
3	2.9410	2.8839	2.8286	2.7751	2.7232	2.6730	2.6243	2.5771	2.5313	2.4869
4	3.9020	3.8077	3.7171	3.6299	3.5460	3.4651	3.3872	3.3121	3.2397	3.1699
5	4.8534	4.7135	4.5797	4.4518	4.3295	4.2124	4.1002	3.9927	3.8897	3.7908
6	5.7955	5.6014	5.4172	5.2421	5.0757	4.9173	4.7665	4.6229	4.4859	4.3553
7	6.7282	6.4720	6.2303	6.0021	5.7864	5.5824	5.3893	5.2064	5.0330	4.8684
8	7.6517	7.3255	7.0197	6.7327	6.4632	6.2098	5.9713	5.7466	5.5348	5.3349
9	8.5660	8.1622	7.7861	7.4353	7.1078	6.8017	6.5152	6.2469	5.9952	5.7590
10	9.4713	8.9826	8.5302	8.1109	7.7217	7.3601	7.0236	6.7101	6.4177	6.1446
11	10.3676	9.7868	9.2526	8.7605	8.3064	7.8869	7.4987	7.1390	6.8052	6.4951
12	11.2551	10.5753	9.9540	9.3851	8.8633	8.3838	7.9427	7.5361	7.1607	6.8137
13	12.1337	11.3484	10.6350	9.9856	9.3936	8.8527	8.3577	7.9038	7.4879	7.1034
14	13.0037	12.1062	11.2961	10.5631	9.8986	9.2950	8.7455	8.2442	7.7862	7.3667
15	13.8651	12.8493	11.9379	11.1184	10.3797	9.7122	9.1079	8.5595	8.0607	7.6061

Table-B: Present Value of Annuity of Rupee 1.00

Period (in No. of Years) ↓	11%	12%	13%	14%	15%	16%	17%	18%	19%	20%
1	0.9009	0.8929	0.8850	0.8772	0.8696	0.8621	0.8547	0.8475	0.8403	0.8333
2	1.7125	1.6901	1.6681	1.6467	1.6257	1.6052	1.5852	1.5656	1.5465	1.5278
3	2.4437	2.4018	2.3612	2.3216	2.2832	2.2459	2.2096	2.1743	2.1399	2.1065
4	3.1024	3.0373	2.9745	2.9137	2.3550	2.7982	2.7432	2.6901	2.6386	2.5887
5	3.6959	3.6048	3.5172	3.4331	3.3522	3.2743	3.1993	3.1272	3.0576	2.9906
6	4.2305	4.1114	3.9975	3.8887	3.7845	3.6847	3.5892	3.4976	3.4098	3.3255
7	4.7122	4.5638	4.4226	4.2883	4.1604	4.0386	3.9224	3.8115	3.7057	3.6046
8	5.1461	4.9676	4.7988	4.6389	4.4873	4.3436	4.2072	4.0776	3.9544	3.8372
9	5.5370	5.3282	5.1317	4.9464	4.7716	4.6065	4.4506	4.3030	4.1633	4.0310
10	5.8892	5.6502	5.4262	5.2161	5.0188	4.8332	4.6586	4.4941	4.3389	4.1925
11	6.2065	5.9377	5.6869	5.4527	5.2337	5.0286	4.8364	4.6560	4.4865	4.3271
12	6.4924	6.1944	5.9176	5.6603	5.4206	5.1971	4.9884	4.7932	4.6105	4.4392
13	6.7499	6.4235	6.1218	5.8424	5.5831	5.3423	5.1183	4.9095	4.7147	4.5327
14	6.9819	6.6282	6.3025	6.0021	5.7245	5.4675	5.2293	5.0081	4.8023	4.6106
15	7.1909	6.8109	6.4624	6.1422	5.8474	5.5755	5.3242	5.0916	4.8759	4.6755

Table-B: Present Value of Annuity of Rupee 1.00

Period (in No. of Years) ↓	21%	22%	23%	24%	25%	26%	27%	28%	29%	30%
1	0.8264	0.8197	0.8130	0.8065	0.8000	0.7937	0.7874	0.7813	0.7752	0.7692
2	1.5095	1.4915	1.4740	1.4568	1.4400	1.4235	1.4074	1.3916	1.3761	1.3609
3	2.0739	2.0422	2.0114	1.9813	1.9520	1.9234	1.8956	1.8684	1.8420	1.8161
4	2.5404	2.4936	2.4483	2.4043	2.3616	2.3202	2.2800	2.2410	2.2031	2.1662
5	2.9260	2.8626	2.8035	2.7454	2.6893	2.6351	2.5827	2.5320	2.4830	2.4356
6	3.2446	3.1669	3.0923	3.0205	2.9514	2.8850	2.8210	2.7594	2.7000	2.6427
7	3.5079	3.4155	3.3270	3.2423	3.1611	3.0833	3.0087	2.9370	2.8682	2.8021
8	3.7256	3.6193	3.5179	3.4212	3.3289	3.2407	3.1564	3.0758	2.9986	2.9247
9	3.9054	3.7863	3.6731	3.5655	3.4631	3.3657	3.2728	3.1842	3.0997	3.0190
10	4.0541	3.9232	3.7993	3.6819	3.5705	3.4648	3.3644	3.2689	3.1781	3.0915
11	4.1769	4.0354	3.9018	3.7757	3.6564	3.5435	3.4365	3.3351	3.2388	3.1473
12	4.2784	4.1274	3.9852	3.8514	3.7251	3.6059	3.4933	3.3868	3.2859	3.1903
13	4.3624	4.2028	4.0530	3.9124	3.7801	3.6555	3.5381	3.4272	3.3224	3.2233
14	4.4317	4.2646	4.1082	3.9616	3.8241	3.6949	3.5733	3.4587	3.3507	3.2487
15	4.4890	4.3152	4.1530	4.0013	3.8593	3.7261	3.6010	3.4834	3.3726	3.2682

Table-B: Present Value of Annuity of Rupee 1.00

Period (in No. of Years) ↓	1%	2%	3%	4%	5%	6%	7%	8%	9%	10%
16	14.7179	13.5777	12.5611	11.6523	10.8378	10.1059	9.4466	8.8514	8.3126	7.8237
17	15.5623	14.2919	13.1661	12.1657	11.2741	10.4773	9.7632	9.1216	8.5436	8.0216
18	16.3983	14.9920	13.7535	12.6593	11.6896	10.8276	10.0591	9.3719	8.7556	8.2014
19	17.2260	15.6785	14.3238	13.1339	12.0853	11.1581	10.3356	9.6036	8.9501	8.3649
20	18.0456	16.3514	14.8775	13.5903	12.4622	11.4699	10.5940	9.8181	9.1285	8.5136
21	18.8570	17.0112	15.4150	14.0292	12.8212	11.7641	10.8355	10.0168	9.2922	8.6487
22	19.6604	17.6580	15.9369	14.4511	13.1630	12.0416	11.0612	10.2007	9.4424	8.7715
23	20.4558	18.2922	16.4436	14.8568	13.4886	12.3034	11.2722	10.3711	9.5802	8.8832
24	21.2434	18.9139	16.9355	15.2470	13.7986	12.5504	11.4693	10.5288	9.7066	8.9847
25	22.0232	19.5235	17.4131	15.6221	14.0939	12.7834	11.6536	10.6748	9.8226	9.0770
26	22.7952	20.1210	17.8768	15.9828	14.3752	13.0032	11.8258	10.8100	9.9290	9.1609
27	23.5596	20.7069	18.3270	16.3296	14.6430	13.2105	11.9867	10.9352	10.0266	9.2372
28	24.3164	21.2813	18.7641	16.6631	14.8981	13.4062	12.1371	11.0511	10.1161	9.3066
29	25.0658	21.8444	19.1885	16.9837	15.1411	13.5907	12.2777	11.1584	10.1983	9.3696
30	25.8077	22.3965	19.6004	17.2920	15.3725	13.7648	12.4090	11.2578	10.2737	9.4269

Table-B: Present Value of Annuity of Rupee 1.00

Period (in No. of Years) ↓	11%	12%	13%	14%	15%	16%	17%	18%	19%	20%
16	7.3792	6.9740	6.6039	6.2651	5.9542	5.6685	5.4053	5.1624	4.9377	4.7296
17	7.5488	7.1196	6.7291	6.3729	6.0472	5.7487	5.4746	5.2223	4.9897	4.7746
18	7.7016	7.2497	6.8399	6.4674	6.1280	5.8178	5.5339	5.2732	5.0333	4.8122
19	7.8393	7.3658	6.9380	6.5504	6.1982	5.8775	5.5845	5.3162	5.0700	4.8435
20	7.9633	7.4694	7.0248	6.6231	6.2593	5.9288	5.6278	5.3527	5.1009	4.8696
21	8.0751	7.5620	7.1016	6.6870	6.3125	5.9731	5.6648	5.3837	5.1268	4.8913
22	8.1757	7.6446	7.1695	6.7429	6.3587	6.0113	5.6964	5.4099	5.1486	4.9094
23	8.2664	7.7184	7.2297	6.7921	6.3988	6.0442	5.7234	5.4321	5.1668	4.9245
24	8.3481	7.7843	7.2829	6.8351	6.4338	6.0726	5.7465	5.4509	5.1822	4.9371
25	8.4217	7.8431	7.3300	6.8729	6.4641	6.0971	5.7662	5.4669	5.1951	4.9476
26	8.4881	7.8957	7.3717	6.9061	6.4906	6.1182	5.7831	5.4804	5.2060	4.9563
27	8.5478	7.9426	7.4086	6.9352	6.5135	6.1364	5.7975	5.4919	5.2151	4.9636
28	8.6016	7.9844	7.4412	6.9607	6.5335	6.1520	5.8099	5.5016	5.2228	4.9697
29	8.6501	8.0218	7.4701	6.9830	6.5509	6.1656	5.8204	5.5098	5.2292	4.9747
30	8.6938	8.0552	7.4957	7.0027	6.5660	6.1772	5.8294	5.5168	5.2347	4.9789

Table-B: Present Value of Annuity of Rupee 1.00

Period (in No. of Years) ↓	21%	22%	23%	24%	25%	26%	27%	28%	29%	30%
16	4.5364	4.3567	4.1894	4.0333	3.8874	3.7509	3.6228	3.5026	3.3896	3.2832
17	4.5755	4.3908	4.2190	4.0591	3.9099	3.7705	3.6400	3.5177	3.4028	3.2948
18	4.6079	4.4187	4.2431	4.0799	3.9279	3.7861	3.6536	3.5294	3.4130	3.3037
19	4.6346	4.4415	4.2627	4.0967	3.9424	3.7985	3.6642	3.5386	3.4210	3.3105
20	4.6567	4.4603	4.2786	4.1103	3.9539	3.8083	3.6726	3.5458	3.4271	3.3158
21	4.6750	4.4756	4.2916	4.1212	3.9631	3.8161	3.6792	3.5514	3.4319	3.3198
22	4.6900	4.4882	4.3021	4.1300	3.9705	3.8223	3.6844	3.5558	3.4356	3.3230
23	4.7025	4.4985	4.3106	4.1371	3.9764	3.8273	3.6885	3.5592	3.4384	3.3254
24	4.7128	4.5070	4.3176	4.1428	3.9811	3.8312	3.6918	3.5619	3.4406	3.3272
25	4.7213	4.5139	4.3232	4.1474	3.9849	3.8342	3.6943	3.5640	3.4423	3.3286
26	4.7284	4.5196	4.3278	4.1511	3.9879	3.8367	3.6963	3.5656	3.4437	3.3297
27	4.7342	4.5243	4.3316	4.1542	3.9903	3.8387	3.6979	3.5669	3.4447	3.3305
28	4.7390	4.5251	4.3346	4.1566	3.9923	3.8402	3.6991	3.5679	3.4455	3.3312
29	4.7430	4.5312	4.3371	4.1585	3.9938	3.8414	3.7001	3.5687	3.4461	3.3317
30	4.7463	4.5338	4.3391	4.1601	3.9950	3.8424	3.7009	3.5693	3.4466	3.3321

Table-B: Present Value of Annuity of Rupee 1.00

Period (in No. of Years) ↓	1%	2%	3%	4%	5%	6%	7%	8%	9%	10%
40	32.8347	27.3555	23.1150	19.7928	17.1591	15.0463	13.3317	11.9250	10.7570	9.7791
50	39.1961	31.4236	25.7300	21.4822	18.2559	15.7919	13.8007	12.2330	10.9620	9.9148
60	44.9550	34.7609	27.6760	22.6235	18.9293	16.1614	14.0392	12.3770	11.0480	9.9672
70	50.1685	37.4986	29.1230	23.3945	19.3427	16.3845	14.1604	12.4430	11.0840	9.9873
80	54.8882	39.7445	30.2010	23.9154	19.5965	16.5091	14.2220	12.4740	11.1000	9.9951
90	59.1609	41.5869	31.0020	24.2673	19.7523	16.5787	14.2533	12.4880	11.1060	9.9981
100	63.0289	43.0984	31.5990	24.5050	19.8479	16.6175	14.2693	12.4940	11.1090	9.9993

Table-B: Present Value of Annuity of Rupee 1.00

Period (in No. of Years) ↓	11%	12%	13%	14%	15%	16%	17%	18%	19%	20%
40	8.9511	8.2438	7.6344	7.1050	6.6418	6.2335	5.8713	5.5482	5.2582	4.9966
50	9.0417	8.3045	7.6752	7.1327	6.6605	6.2463	5.8801	5.5541	5.2623	4.9995
60	9.0736	8.3240	7.6873	7.1401	6.6651	6.2492	5.8819	5.5553	5.2630	4.9999
70	9.0848	8.3303	7.6908	7.1421	6.6663	6.2498	5.8823	5.5555	5.2631	5.0000
80	9.0888	8.3324	7.6919	7.1427	6.6666	6.2500	5.8823	5.5555	5.2632	5.0000
90	9.0902	8.3330	7.6922	7.1428	6.6666	6.2500	5.8823	5.5556	5.2632	5.0000
100	9.0906	8.3332	7.6923	7.1428	6.6667	6.2500	5.8824	5.5556	5.2632	5.0000

Table-B: Present Value of Annuity of Rupee 1.00

Period (in No. of Years) ↓	21%	22%	23%	24%	25%	26%	27%	28%	29%	30%
40	4.7596	4.5439	4.3467	4.1659	3.9995	3.8458	3.7034	3.5712	3.4481	3.3333
50	4.7616	4.5452	4.3477	4.1666	3.9999	3.8461	3.7037	3.5714	3.4483	3.3333
60	4.7619	4.5454	4.3478	4.1667	4.0000	3.8462	3.7037	3.5714	3.4483	3.3333
70	4.7619	4.5455	4.3478	4.1667	4.0000	3.8462	3.7037	3.5714	3.4483	3.3333
80	4.7619	4.5455	4.3478	4.1667	4.0000	3.8462	3.7037	3.5714	3.4483	3.3333
90	4.7619	4.5455	4.3478	4.1667	4.0000	3.8462	3.7037	3.5714	3.4483	3.3333
100	4.7619	4.5455	4.3478	4.1667	4.0000	3.8462	3.7037	3.5714	3.4483	3.3333

Table-C: Future Value of Rupee 1.00

Period (in No. of Years) ↓	1%	2%	3%	4%	5%	6%	7%	8%	9%	10%
1	1.010	1.020	1.030	1.040	1.050	1.060	1.070	1.080	1.090	1.100
2	1.020	1.040	1.061	1.082	1.103	1.124	1.145	1.166	1.188	1.210
3	1.030	1.061	1.093	1.125	1.158	1.191	1.225	1.260	1.295	1.331
4	1.041	1.082	1.126	1.170	1.216	1.262	1.311	1.360	1.412	1.464
5	1.051	1.104	1.159	1.217	1.276	1.338	1.403	1.469	1.539	1.611
6	1.062	1.126	1.194	1.265	1.340	1.419	1.501	1.587	1.677	1.771
7	1.072	1.149	1.230	1.316	1.407	1.504	1.606	1.714	1.828	1.949
8	1.083	1.172	1.267	1.369	1.477	1.594	1.718	1.851	1.993	2.144
9	1.094	1.195	1.305	1.423	1.551	1.689	1.838	1.999	2.172	2.358
10	1.105	1.219	1.344	1.480	1.629	1.791	1.967	2.159	2.367	2.594
11	1.116	1.243	1.384	1.539	1.710	1.898	2.105	2.332	2.580	2.853
12	1.127	1.268	1.426	1.601	1.796	2.012	2.252	2.518	2.813	3.138
13	1.138	1.294	1.469	1.665	1.886	2.133	2.410	2.720	3.066	3.452
14	1.149	1.319	1.513	1.732	1.980	2.261	2.579	2.937	3.342	3.797
15	1.161	1.346	1.558	1.801	2.079	2.397	2.759	3.172	3.642	4.177

Table-C: Future Value of Rupee 1.00

Period (in No. of Years) ↓	11%	12%	13%	14%	15%	16%	17%	18%	19%	20%
1	1.110	1.120	1.130	1.140	1.150	1.160	1.170	1.180	1.190	1.200
2	1.232	1.254	1.277	1.300	1.323	1.346	1.369	1.392	1.416	1.440
3	1.368	1.405	1.443	1.482	1.521	1.561	1.602	1.643	1.685	1.728
4	1.518	1.574	1.630	1.689	1.749	1.811	1.874	1.939	2.005	2.074
5	1.685	1.762	1.842	1.925	2.011	2.100	2.192	2.288	2.386	2.488
6	1.870	1.974	2.082	2.195	2.313	2.436	2.565	2.700	2.840	2.986
7	2.076	2.211	2.353	2.502	2.660	2.826	3.001	3.185	3.379	3.583
8	2.305	2.476	2.658	2.853	3.059	3.278	3.511	3.759	4.021	4.300
9	2.558	2.773	3.004	3.252	3.518	3.803	4.108	4.435	4.785	5.160
10	2.839	3.106	3.395	3.707	4.046	4.411	4.807	5.234	5.695	6.192
11	3.152	3.479	3.836	4.226	4.652	5.117	5.624	6.176	6.777	7.430
12	3.498	3.896	4.335	4.818	5.350	5.936	6.580	7.288	8.064	8.916
13	3.883	4.363	4.898	5.492	6.153	6.886	7.699	8.599	9.596	10.699
14	4.310	4.887	5.535	6.261	7.076	7.988	9.007	10.147	11.420	12.839
15	4.785	5.474	6.254	7.138	8.137	9.266	10.539	11.974	13.590	15.407

Table-C: Future Value of Rupee 1.00

Period (in No. of Years) ↓	21%	22%	23%	24%	25%	26%	27%	28%	29%	30%
1	1.210	1.220	1.230	1.240	1.250	1.260	1.270	1.280	1.290	1.300
2	1.464	1.488	1.513	1.538	1.563	1.588	1.613	1.638	1.664	1.690
3	1.772	1.816	1.861	1.907	1.953	2.000	2.048	2.097	2.147	2.197
4	2.143	2.215	2.239	2.364	2.441	2.520	2.601	2.684	2.769	2.856
5	2.594	2.703	2.815	2.932	3.052	3.176	3.304	3.436	3.572	3.713
6	3.138	3.297	3.463	3.635	3.815	4.000	4.196	4.398	4.608	4.827
7	3.797	4.023	4.259	4.508	4.768	5.042	5.329	5.629	5.945	6.275
8	4.595	4.907	5.239	5.590	5.960	6.353	6.768	7.206	7.669	8.157
9	5.560	5.987	6.444	6.931	7.451	8.005	8.595	9.223	9.893	10.604
10	6.728	7.305	7.926	8.594	9.313	10.086	10.915	11.806	12.761	13.786
11	8.140	8.912	9.749	10.657	11.642	12.708	13.862	15.111	16.462	17.922
12	9.850	10.872	11.991	13.215	14.552	16.012	17.605	19.343	21.236	23.298
13	11.918	13.264	14.749	16.386	18.190	20.175	22.359	24.759	27.395	30.288
14	14.421	16.182	18.141	20.319	22.737	25.421	28.396	31.691	35.339	39.374
15	17.450	19.742	22 314	25.196	28.422	32.030	36.062	40.565	45.587	51.186

Table-C: Future Value of Rupee 1.00

Period (in No. of Years) ↓	1%	2%	3%	4%	5%	6%	7%	8%	9%	10%
16	1.173	1.373	1.605	1.873	2.183	2.540	2.952	3.426	3.970	4.595
17	1.184	1.400	1.653	1.948	2.292	2.693	3.159	3.700	4.328	5.054
18	1.196	1.428	1.702	2.026	2.407	2.854	3.380	3.996	4.717	5.560
19	1.208	1.457	1.754	2.107	2.527	3.026	3.617	4.316	5.142	6.116
20	1.220	1.486	1.806	2.191	2.653	3.207	3.870	4.661	5.604	6.727
21	1.232	1.516	1.860	2.279	2.786	3.400	4.141	5.034	6.109	7.400
22	1.245	1.546	1.916	2.370	2.925	3.604	4.430	5.437	6.659	8.140
23	1.257	1.577	1.974	2.465	3.072	3.820	4.741	5.871	7.258	8.954
24	1.270	1.608	2.033	2.563	3.225	4.049	5.072	6.341	7.911	9.850
25	1.282	1.641	2.094	2.666	3.386	4.292	5.427	6.848	8.623	10.835
26	1.295	1.673	2.157	2.772	3.556	4.549	5.807	7.396	9.399	11.918
27	1.308	1.707	2.221	2.883	3.733	4.822	6.214	7.988	10.245	13.110
28	1.321	1.741	2.288	2.999	3.920	5.112	6.649	8.627	11.167	14.421
29	1.335	1.776	2.357	3.119	4.16	5.418	7.114	9.317	12.172	15.863
30	1.348	1.811	2.427	3.243	4.322	5.743	7.612	10.063	13.268	17.449

Table-C: Future Value of Rupee 1.00

Period (in No. of Years) ↓	11%	12%	13%	14%	15%	16%	17%	18%	19%	20%
16	5.311	6.130	7.067	8.137	9.358	10.748	12.330	14.129	16.172	18.488
17	5.895	6.866	7.986	9.276	10.761	12.468	14.426	16.672	19.244	22.186
18	6.544	7.690	9.024	10.575	12.375	14.463	16.879	19.673	22.901	26.623
19	7.263	8.613	10.197	12.056	14.232	16.777	19.748	23.214	27.252	31.948
20	8.062	9.646	11.523	13.743	16.367	19.461	23.106	27.393	32.429	38.338
21	8.949	10.804	13.201	15.668	18.822	22.574	27.034	32.324	38.591	46.005
22	9.934	12.100	14.714	17.861	21.645	26.186	31.629	38.142	45.923	55.206
23	11.026	13.552	16.627	20.362	24.891	30.376	37.006	45.008	54.649	66.247
24	12.239	15.179	18.788	23.212	28.625	35.236	43.297	53.109	65.032	79.497
25	13.585	17.000	21.231	26.462	32.919	40.874	50.658	62.669	77.388	95.396
26	15.080	19.040	23.991	30.167	37.857	47.414	59.270	73.949	92.092	114.475
27	16.739	21.325	27.109	34.390	43.535	55.000	69.345	87.260	109.589	137.371
28	18.580	23.884	30.633	39.204	50.066	63.800	81.134	102.967	130.411	164.845
29	20.624	26.750	34.616	44.693	57.575	74.009	94.927	121.501	155.189	197.814
30	22.892	29.960	39.116	50.950	66.212	85.850	111.065	143.371	184.675	237.376

Table-C: Future Value of Rupee 1.00

Period (in No. of Years) ↓	21%	22%	23%	24%	25%	26%	27%	28%	29%	30%
16	21.115	24.085	27.446	31.243	35.528	40.358	45.799	51.923	58.808	66.542
17	25.549	29.384	33.759	38.741	44.410	50.851	58.165	66.461	75.862	86.505
18	30.914	35.848	41.523	48.039	55.513	64.072	73.869	85.071	97.862	112.456
19	37.407	43.735	51.073	59.569	69.391	80.731	93.814	108.890	126.242	146.193
20	45.262	53.356	62.820	73.865	86.738	101.721	119.144	139.379	162.853	190.051
21	54.767	65.095	77.269	91.593	108.423	128.169	151.312	178.406	210.080	247.066
22	66.268	79.416	95.041	113.575	135.529	161.493	192.167	228.360	271.003	321.186
23	80.184	96.887	116.900	140.833	169.411	203.481	244.052	292.301	349.594	417.541
24	97.023	118.202	143.787	174.633	211.763	256.386	309.946	374.145	450.977	542.804
25	117.398	144.207	176.858	216.545	264.704	323.046	393.631	478.905	581.760	705.645
26	142.051	175.932	217.536	268.516	330.880	407.038	499.912	612.999	750.470	917.338
27	171.882	214.637	267.568	332.959	413.600	512.868	634.888	784.638	968.107	1192.539
28	207.977	261.857	329.109	412.870	517.000	646.214	806.307	1004.337	1248.858	1550.301
29	251.653	319.466	404.805	511.958	646.251	814.229	1024.010	1285.551	1611.026	2015.392
30	304.500	389.748	497.910	634.828	807.814	1025.929	1300.493	1645.506	2078.224	2620.009

Glossary

1.	**Alpha**	:	It is the component of return from a security that is independent of the performance of the market.
2.	**Bear Market**	:	A market in which share prices are falling.
3.	**Bull Market**	:	A market in which share prices are rising.
4.	**Beta**	:	It is a measure of sensitivity of a security return vis-à-vis the market return. Beta measures the non-diversifiable risk (i.e., systematic risk).
5.	**Capital Asset Pricing Model (CAPM)**	:	It is the relationship between 'Beta' and expected return of a security or a portfolio, represented by the Security Market Line.
6.	**Chartist**	:	A technical Analyst who assesses share prices using charts that depict share price movements.
7.	**Coupon Rate**	:	It is the rate of interest fixed for a bond and printed on the bond certificate.
8.	**Capital Market Line**	:	It is a line on which the portfolios of all investors who have their portfolio as a combination of market portfolio and risk-free asset lie. The Capital Market Line is drawn on a graph representing the Portfolio Standard deviation on its X-axis and Portfolio return on its Y-axis.
9.	**Discount Rate**	:	It is the rate of return required by an investor on his investment.
10.	**Business Risk**	:	See 'Operating Risk'.

11. Deep Discount Bond : See 'Zero Coupon Bond'.

12. Dividend Pay Out (DPO) Ratio : It is the fraction of net income a company pays to its shareholders. It is given by the ratio of dividends to net income. DPO is also obtained by dividing the 'Dividend per share' by 'Earnings per share'.

13. Duration (of a bond) : It is the holding period of a bond for which there will be no interest rate risk.

14. Earnings Per Share (EPS) : It is the earning of a common share in a year. It is arrived at by dividing the income attributable to common share holders by the weighted average of common shares. (If a share is in the market for the entire period of one year, its weight is taken as 1. If a share was issued mid-way during a year and if the share is with the investors only for a fraction of a year, it should be properly weighted. For example, if a share is outstanding only for 5 months in a year, it should be assigned a weight of 5/12).

15. Efficient Frontier : The set of portfolios that offer the maximum return for every given level of risk or that has the minimum risk for every given level of return.

16. Face Value : (or par value). It is the value of an equity share that is originally recorded in the balance sheet of the issuing company as equity capital.

17. Financial Risk : An unsystematic risk that is caused due to the presence of debt capital. The proportion of debt capital to the total capital decides the level of financial risk.

18. Fundamentalist : One who adopts fundamental analysis for taking investment decisions.

19. Index Fund : A mutual fund that seeks to match the performance of a particular market index. It is a passively managed fund since it simply tracks the chosen index and aims to achieve the same return.

20. Indifference Curve	:	It is the locus of acceptable portfolios of an investor. An investor will have equal preference to all the portfolios that lie on the indifference curve.
21. Interest Rate Risk	:	A systematic risk that arises due to fluctuations in interest rate. Fixed interest securities like bonds and debentures are more affected by this.
22. Intrinsic Value	:	(of a security). The value of a security arrived at on the basis the benefits that would accrue to the investors.
23. Leverage	:	It is the degree to which an individual investor or business is utilizing borrowed money. Higher the borrowing, greater the leverage.
24. Operating Risk	:	(Also called Business Risk). It is a risk that arises due to the chances of variability in return caused by a firm's pattern of usage of funds; it is an unsystematic risk.
25. P/E Ratio	:	A ratio obtained by dividing the market price per share by the Earnings per share (EPS).
26. Market Risk	:	A systematic risk that arises due to fluctuations in market price of securities.
27. Purchasing Power Risk	:	A systematic risk caused by inflation.
28. Rights Issue	:	Issue of shares offered to existing share holders as their right. It is opposed to public issue that is open to the public at large.
29. Security Market Line	:	A line that provides the relationship between 'Beta' and the expected return of a security or a portfolio.
30. Spot Interest Rate	:	It is the discount rate that makes the present value of a single cash inflow available to the investor on maturity of the bond equal to the price of the bond.
31. Systematic Risk	:	The risk caused by system-wide factors like changes in economic conditions, changes in political system, changes in social system etc.

32. Unsystematic Risk	:	Risk caused by company-specific factors.
33. Yield To Call (YTC)	:	It is the discount rate that makes the present value of cash inflows till call date (i.e., the annual interests and the specified call price) equal to the cost of the bond.
34. Yield To Maturity (YTM)	:	It is the internal rate of return earned from a bond, holding the bond till its maturity.
35. Zero Coupon Bond	:	(Also called 'Deep Discount Bond'). It is a bond that does not specify any coupon rate. They are issued at a discount from their face value and the difference between the issue price and the face value represents the return offered by the bond.

Bibliography

Clifford Pistolese: *Using Technical Analysis — The Basics,* Vision Books, New Delhi, 2004.

Donald E. Fischer and Ronald J. Jordan: *Security Analysis and Portfolio Management,* Printice-Hall of India Private Limited, New Delhi, 2002.

Gangadhar V.: *Security Analysis and Portfolio Management,* Anmol Publications Private Limited, New Delhi, 2003.

Grewal S.S. and Navjot Grewal: *Profitable Investment in Shares,* Vision Books, New Delhi, 1995.

Kevin S.: *Portfolio Management,* Printice-Hall of India Private Limited, New Delhi, 2001.

Prasanna Chandra: *Investment Analysis and Portfolio Management,* Tata McGraw-Hill Publishing Company Limited, New Delhi, 2003.

Punjithavathy Pandian: *Security Analysis and Portfolio Management,* Vikas Publishing House Private Limited, New Delhi, 2008.

Raghu Palat: *Fundamental Analysis,* Vision Books, New Delhi, 2005.

Robert A. Strong: *Portfolio Management Handbook,* Jaico Publishing House, Mumbai, 2001.

Samir K. Barua, Raghunathan V. and Jayanth R. Varma: *Portfolio Management,* Tata McGraw-Hill Publishing Company Limited, New Delhi, 1996.

Steve Lumby: *Investment Appraisal and Financial Decisions,* Chapman & Hall, London, 1996.

Steven B. Achelis: *Technical Analysis from A-to-Z,* Vision Books, New Delhi, 2005.

Sudhindra Bhat: *Security Analysis and Portfolio Management,* Excel Books, New Delhi, 2007.

Zvi Bodie, Alex Kane and Alan J. Marcus: *Investments,* McGraw-Hill/ Irwin, New York, 2002.

Index